Microsoft® SQL Server™ 2000
Data Transformation Services

Timothy Peterson

SAMS

201 West 103rd St., Indianapolis, Indiana, 46290 USA

Microsoft® SQL Server™ 2000 Data Transformation Services

Copyright © 2001 by Sams Publishing

International Standard Book Number: 0-672-32011-8

Library of Congress Catalog Card Number: 00-103543

Printed in the United States of America

First Printing: December 2000

03 02 01 00   4   3   2   1

Trademarks

Warning and Disclaimer

ACQUISITIONS EDITOR
Sharon Cox

DEVELOPMENT EDITOR
Kevin Howard

EXECUTIVE EDITOR
Rosemarie Graham

MANAGING EDITOR
Charlotte Clapp

PROJECT EDITOR
Elizabeth Finney

COPY EDITOR
Sean Medlock

INDEXER
Tina Trettin

PROOFREADER
Tony Reitz

TECHNICAL EDITORS
Todd Meister
Ivan Oss

TEAM COORDINATOR
Pamalee Nelson

MEDIA DEVELOPER
JG Moore

INTERIOR DESIGNER
Anne Jones

COVER DESIGNER
Anne Jones

Overview

Contents

About the Author

Tim Peterson is one of the owners of SDG Computing, Inc., a company specializing in Microsoft SQL Server data warehousing consulting and development. He has consulted or worked on projects for a number of companies and organizations, including uproar.com, Fisher-Rosemount Systems, the University of Minnesota, Liberty Check, Thrifty Car Rental, and Microsoft. He worked on his first data warehousing project in 1995, using SQL Server 6.0.

Tim is the lead author of *Microsoft OLAP Unleashed*, published by Sams in 1999. He wrote the sections about DTS, data modeling, enterprise data structure, creating cubes, and programming the OLAP server.

Tim is a Microsoft Certified Trainer who teaches courses in the field of SQL Server data warehousing (DTS, Analysis Services, OLAP, Data Mining, and MDX). He currently teaches about one week a month for Mindsharp Learning Centers in Bloomington, Minnesota, and also provides customized on-site instruction.

Tim is also a Microsoft Certified Database Administrator and a Microsoft Certified Systems Engineer. You can visit his company's Web site at `www.sdgcomputing.com`.

Dedication

To our parents, Harold and Alice Melby and Earl and Lorraine Peterson, who taught us about life and love and God, and also how to read and write.

Acknowledgments

I am listed as the author, but this book has really been the combined effort of myself and two other people—my wife and business partner, Donadee, and our son, Nate. I did the writing. Nate did a lot of the programming and code testing. Donadee also did a lot of the programming, was our in-house editor, and kept track of many, many details for the project. Thank you both for your partnership in this huge task!

The Local Cube DTS custom task (see Chapter 31) was created by Nate, who based his work on the Local Cube Creator from last year's book, *Microsoft OLAP Unleashed*, which was programmed by Chris Horgen. Chris also helped us with this book, doing the C++ programming for the custom transformation described in Chapter 32.

I want to thank everyone in my family—Dona, Nate, John, and Elise—for their patience. Writing two books in two years is probably one (or two!) too many. I hope all of you will benefit from the effort.

I would like to thank our extended family and friends for their love and caring. I would also like to thank the people of Arlington Hills Lutheran Church (where I have the privilege of serving as a part-time assistant pastor) for your encouragement.

Thank you to all the readers of my books for your trust and support. Thank you to my teachers, students, co-workers, and clients.

Thank you to the people at Sams Publishing for giving me the opportunity to write this book. Thank you to all who have worked on planning and editing and reviewing at Sams—Sharon Cox, Kevin Howard, Paul Schneider, Elizabeth Finney, and so many others.

Our parents really did teach us how to read and write. My father was my schoolteacher in sixth grade. He gave me more reading and writing assignments than any other teacher I ever had. My mother-in-law was my wife's high school English teacher. All four of our parents enjoy reading a great variety of literature.

We hope that our work, whether in writing, teaching, consulting, or developing, will have some lasting value. We realize that this book will be out of date in a few short years. But we hope that between now and then it can be genuinely useful—to help you be more effective in your work, to assist companies in being more responsive to their customers, to help organizations keep track of the significant factors that are helping them achieve their goals. We thank God for the work He has given us to do, and we pray that He will somehow use our efforts (even our efforts in data transformation!) to make this world a better place.

—*Tim Peterson*
  S.D.G.

Tell Us What You Think!

As the reader of this book, *you* are our most important critic and commentator. We value your opinion and want to know what we're doing right, what we could do better, what areas you'd like to see us publish in, and any other words of wisdom you're willing to pass our way.

As an Executive Editor for Sams Publishing, I welcome your comments. You can fax, email, or write me directly to let me know what you did or didn't like about this book—as well as what we can do to make our books stronger.

Please note that I cannot help you with technical problems related to the topic of this book, and that due to the high volume of mail I receive, I might not be able to reply to every message.

When you write, please be sure to include this book's title and author as well as your name and phone or fax number. I will carefully review your comments and share them with the author and editors who worked on the book.

Fax:	317-581-4770
Email:	Rosemarie.Graham@samspublishing.com
Mail:	Rosemarie Graham
	Executive Editor
	Sams Publishing
	201 West 103rd Street
	Indianapolis, IN 46290 USA

Introduction

Data Transformation Services in Microsoft SQL Server 2000 is a powerful tool for moving data. It's easy to use, especially when you're creating transformation packages with the DTS Wizard. But it's also a flexible tool that you can customize to gain a high degree of control over the transformation of your data.

The size of this book reflects the flexibility and extensibility of DTS. You can begin to use DTS without reading this book—or without even reading a help file. But you have a lot to learn about DTS if you want to take advantage of its full power.

Using DTS in SQL Server 7.0 and SQL Server 2000

I believe DTS in SQL Server 7.0 is a great tool. But DTS in SQL Server 2000 has a number of improvements:

- More tasks.
- More transformations.
- More convenient design environment.
- Better access to object properties.

This book is about DTS in SQL Server 2000. Whenever possible, I have pointed out differences between SQL Server 7.0 and SQL Server 2000 to help you make the transition between the two versions.

Even if you're still using SQL Server 7.0, this book can be helpful to you. Much of the development strategy you will use in building DTS packages is the same in both versions. Most of the ActiveX script examples in this book will also work in SQL Server 7.0. However, most of the Visual Basic examples will not work with SQL Server 7.0 unless they are modified to remove all references to the SQL Server 2000 DTS objects.

The Code Samples

There are a lot of code samples in this book. We realize that you probably won't need to use most of this code, but we hope it will be helpful when you decide to turn to programming. Many times, we ourselves have benefited from programming code that showed us how to do something we couldn't quite figure out.

Please note that you may have to change the connections in the sample DTS packages on the CD so that they will work in your environment. We set all the connections to the local server using integrated security. Hopefully those settings will work for you without the need for adjustments.

Keeping Current with Information on DTS

This book is based on DTS in the initial release of SQL Server 2000. DTS developers will be learning much more about DTS in SQL Server 2000 in the months and years ahead. We would like to help you keep current on DTS strategies, capabilities, and challenges in two ways:

- By adding new information to our Web site at www.sdgcomputing.com.
- By maintaining a mailing list of those who want to receive new DTS tips. You can sign up for this list at www.sdgcomputing.com.

Here are some other places where you can receive current information about DTS:

- The Microsoft DTS newsgroup—microsoft.public.sqlserver.dts on msnews.microsoft.com
- The SQL Server section of Microsoft's Web site—www.microsoft.com
- The SQL Server Magazine Web site—www.sqlmag.com
- SQL Server Professional's Web site—www.pinpub.com
- The Professional Association of SQL Server Users Web site—www.sqlpass.org
- The SQL Server section of www.swynk.com

Getting Started with DTS

PART

I

IN THIS PART

A Quick Look at DTS

1

IN THIS CHAPTER

This chapter provides an introduction to Data Transformation Services. If you have already used DTS in SQL Server 7.0, the first part of this chapter will be familiar to you. But please don't skip the sections on executing a DTS package, using the DTS object model, and using DTS templates. These sections provide information that is needed to understand the material in the rest of the book.

A High-Performance Data Pump—and a Whole Lot More

Data Transformation Services in Microsoft SQL Server 2000 is a high-performance data pump. It is a tool for copying, moving, consolidating, cleansing, and validating data. The data pump loads each row from the data source, manipulates the values in that row, and inserts the row into the data destination.

DTS is also a Rapid Application Development tool for data-oriented programming. It provides a comprehensive set of data manipulation tools organized in a development environment that is both convenient and powerful.

Speed is important when working with data:

- Organizations have to be able to move large amounts of data between different systems within specified processing periods.
- Complex data modifications, including row-by-row processing, are often needed as the data is being moved. If you are manipulating a lot of data, the time required to modify each record must be minimized.
- The design, development, and maintenance of data cleansing applications can be very time-consuming. Tools are needed to speed the development process.

> **NOTE**
>
> If you receive a 1GB file of clickstream data at 8:00 a.m. for the previous day's Web site activity, can you load that data into a SQL Server data mart and process the OLAP cubes so that they're ready for a 10:00 a.m. management meeting?
>
> The need for rapid data transformation is increasing along with the increasing opportunities to gather and analyze data.

There are four basic strategies for developing data manipulation packages with DTS:

- Use the DTS Designer
- Use the DTS Object Model in code

- Use DTS Templates
- Use the DTS Wizards

These four development strategies are discussed in this chapter. I encourage you to become familiar with all of them. Each one is best for a certain type of situation. These strategies are not exclusive—you will often use them with one another to achieve the fastest possible development speed.

Using the DTS Designer to Create Complex Data Transformations

The primary tool for working with Data Transformation Services is the DTS Designer, as shown in Figure 1.1. The Designer is a friendly graphical interface that you can use to create complex data transformations with the tasks of DTS.

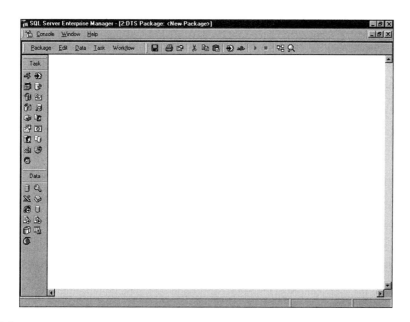

FIGURE 1.1
You can create and edit DTS packages in the DTS Designer.

You access the DTS Designer through SQL Server's Enterprise Manager. Data Transformation Services is in the console tree structure under any of the SQL Servers that have been registered (see Figure 1.2). You can open an existing package that is listed under Local Packages or Meta Data Services Packages. You can right-click on Data Transformation Services and open a DTS package that has been saved as a file. Or, you can open the DTS Designer with a blank Design Sheet to begin the creation of a new package.

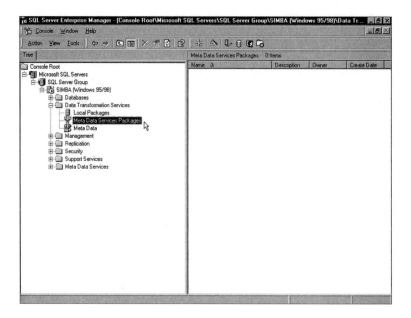

FIGURE 1.2
You can open existing packages in the DTS Designer from the Enterprise Manager.

The Structure of a DTS Package

Whenever you open the DTS Designer, you are working with a DTS Package. Everything that you see in the Designer is part of the package, which is normally executed as a unit.

A DTS package contains one or more complex programmatic units called tasks. These tasks can transform data, execute a SQL statement, copy a database, FTP a file, send a message with the Message Queuing Services, or do any of a number of other things. Each task is represented by an icon, which can be seen on both the task palette and the Design Sheet. All the tasks that Microsoft provides with SQL Server 2000 are shown in Figure 1.3.

DTS Connections are used to specify the source of the data and the destination where it's being moved. You can use DTS with a wide variety of data stores, including relational databases such as Microsoft SQL Server and Oracle, multidimensional databases such as Microsoft OLAP Services, text files, and spreadsheets. DTS Connections use OLE DB providers but can also connect through ODBC drivers and Data Link files. Some of the data sources that are normally installed with SQL Server 2000 are shown in Figure 1.4.

FIGURE 1.3

DTS has a variety of tasks that you can use in a package.

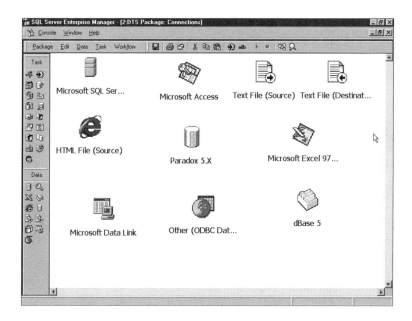

FIGURE 1.4

You can connect to a variety of data sources with DTS.

You can set the order in which the DTS tasks will be executed. This ordering is shown by a variety of colored lines on the DTS Designer's Design Sheet. A variety of connections, tasks, and workflow ordering constraints are shown in Figure 1.5.

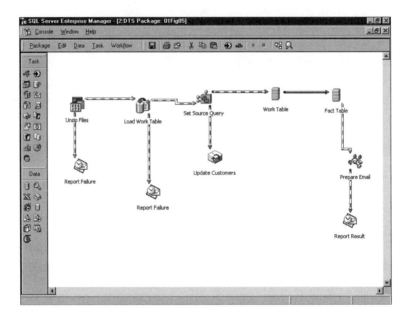

FIGURE 1.5

You draw the workflow in the DTS Designer to determine the order of the tasks.

Creating Connections

You often start designing a DTS process by creating connections. DTS connections are needed for several of the key tasks, such as the Transform Data task and the Execute SQL task.

You can select a connection to a particular type of data source by selecting its icon in the Data Palette and dragging it to the appropriate spot on the Design Sheet. The Connection Properties dialog will automatically open so you can configure the connection.

There are a few basic choices you need to make for every connection. Fundamentally, you have to choose the type of data source. Are you connecting to a SQL Server database, an Oracle database, or a text file? Depending on the type of the data source, you also select the name of the database, the filename, and security information.

To edit the connection in the future, double-click on the connection's icon on the Design Sheet. You can change any of the connection's properties, except for the connection's name. If you want, you can even change the type of data source used for the connection.

Figure 1.6 shows the icon and Connection Properties dialog for a SQL Server connection. Chapter 5, "DTS Connections," has more information about the use of DTS connections.

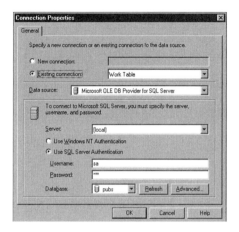

FIGURE 1.6
The Connection Properties dialog gives you the choices you need to connect to each kind of data store.

Creating Tasks

After you have created one or more connections, the next step in creating a package is usually to create some tasks.

For example, if you wanted to copy the information from the Authors table in the pubs sample database into a new table in the Northwind database, you could use these three tasks:

- An Execute SQL task to create the new table in Northwind.
- A Transform Data task to move the data from Pubs to Northwind.
- An ActiveX Script task to display a message box reporting on the result of the transformation.

First you would create the two connections for Pubs and Northwind, and then you would create the three tasks. To create the Execute SQL task and the ActiveX Script task, you could select the appropriate icons on the Task Palette and drag them onto the Design Sheet. To create the Transform Data task, you could click on the black arrow icon in the Task Palette. You would then be instructed to select the source for the transformation (Pubs) and the destination (Northwind). Each of the tasks has a different Task Properties dialog where you set or edit the options that are available for that task. The dialog for the Transform Data task is shown in Figure 1.7.

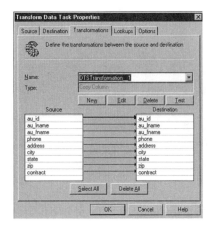

Figure 1.7
The Transform Data Task Properties dialog has five tabs to set the properties for this task.

DTS has three general types of tasks:

- The data transformation tasks allow row-by-row processing of the data. These tasks are discussed in Chapters 6 through 10.
- The data movement and manipulation tasks move or process data but can't process the data in individual rows. These tasks are discussed in Chapters 11 through 15.
- The programmatic control tasks control or coordinate the data transformation process. These tasks are discussed in Chapters 16 through 22.

Setting the Workflow

After creating connections and tasks, you can determine the order of the tasks by setting the appropriate workflow. You can choose from three types:

- A blue line directs the ordering of tasks on completion, regardless of success or failure.
- A green line indicates what will happen if a task succeeds.
- A red line indicates what will happen when a task fails.

NOTE

A black line joining two connections is the icon for a Transform Data task. It is not one of the workflow options.

The three tasks created in the previous section must be executed in the proper order. First the table has to be created, then the data has to be loaded, and finally the message is displayed. Follow these steps:

1. Highlight the Execute SQL task icon.

2. Press the Shift key and highlight the Pubs connection icon.

3. Select On Completion from the Workflow menu.

4. Highlight the Northwind connection icon.

5. Press the Shift key and highlight the ActiveX Script icon.

6. Select On Completion from the Workflow menu.

The completed package, with connections, tasks, and workflow, is shown in Figure 1.8. You can find this package in the file named Chapter1DTSDemo.dts in the Chapter 1 section of this book's CD. You can find more information about workflow in Chapter 24, "Steps and Precedence Constraints."

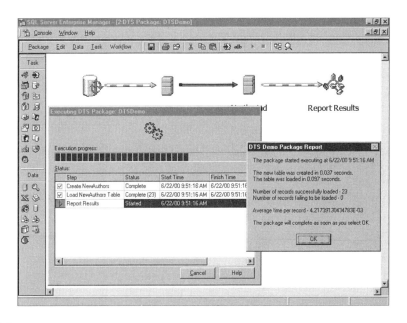

FIGURE 1.8
This demo DTS package creates a table, loads it with data, and produces a report.

Saving and Retrieving DTS Packages

After you have created a package, you will usually want to save it. Choose Package and Save from the DTS Designer menu. The Save DTS Package dialog, shown in Figure 1.9, will open. This dialog gives you a Location box with a list of four possible places to save your package:

- SQL Server
- SQL Server Meta Data Services
- Structured Storage File
- Visual Basic File

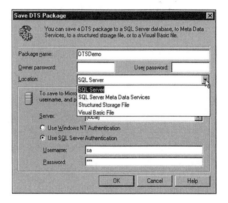

FIGURE 1.9

You have four choices for the storage location of your DTS packages.

These choices are discussed in the following sections. You can find more detailed information about storage of DTS packages in Chapter 23, "The DTS Package and Its Properties."

SQL Server Storage

The first choice of location in the Save DTS Package dialog is SQL Server. When you make this selection, all the information in the DTS package is stored in the msdb system database.

SQL Server storage usually provides the fastest saving and retrieving time. If you use SQL Server storage, you can also back up your DTS packages as a part of a regularly scheduled database backup.

The tables used to store a DTS package are not meant to be accessed directly. You can open a package stored in SQL Server from the Local Packages node under Data Transformation Services in the Enterprise Manager.

SQL Server Meta Data Services Storage

The second choice, SQL Server Meta Data Services, is very similar to the first. The information about the package is physically stored in the msdb database, but in different tables as a part of the Microsoft Repository.

The Microsoft Repository provides a standard interface where different types of databases can share information. It contains a general information model for storing information about data transformations and a specific model for storing information about Microsoft DTS packages.

If you store a package in SQL Server Meta Data Services, the information about the package will be more available to transformation tools created by other companies. You can also retrieve more detailed information about the transformations.

The tables used to store a DTS package in the Repository are not meant to be accessed directly. You can access this information programmatically through the Meta Data Services specification. You can open a package stored in Meta Data Services from the Meta Data Services Packages node under Data Transformation Services in the Enterprise Manager.

The use of the Microsoft Repository is discussed in Chapter 29, "Integrating DTS with Meta Data Services."

Structured Storage File

You can save one or more packages in a single COM-structured storage file. By default, the file is created with a .dts extension. This storage method is convenient for transferring DTS packages from one user to another. For example, each of the DTS packages discussed in this book has been saved as a file and placed on the CD. You can copy those files to your hard drive and use them on your machine. This method of storage is also convenient for keeping a separate archive copy of DTS packages, independent of the SQL Server backup process.

You can retrieve a DTS package stored as a file by right-clicking on the Data Transformation Services node in the Enterprise Manager and selecting Open Package. The Select File dialog will open so that you can choose the .dts file. When you have selected the file, you will be given the opportunity to choose the particular package and version from the file that you want.

Visual Basic File

SQL Server 2000 has added a new choice for DTS package storage—the Visual Basic file. In this type of storage, DTS creates a Visual Basic code module that has all the code needed to re-create the DTS package.

When you save a package to a Visual Basic file, you have the opportunity to use a text editor to globally change names throughout the package. There are some situations where you can control package behavior more precisely through Visual Basic code than you can through designing with the Package Designer. When you save a package to Visual Basic code, you have the opportunity to do that fine-tuning.

You cannot open a DTS package stored as a Visual Basic file. You have to load that package into Visual Basic and execute it.

The storage of DTS packages in Visual Basic files is discussed in Chapter 26, "Managing Packages with Visual Basic and Stored Procedures."

Package Versions

Every time you save a package to SQL Server, SQL Server Meta Data Services, or a structured storage file, you create a new version of the package. You never overwrite a previous version when you use these saving locations.

This is not true when you save a package as a Visual Basic file. Versions are never created for this storage location unless you create separate files with different names.

Whenever you open a package from SQL Server, SQL Server Meta Data Services, or a structured storage file, you have the option of choosing a particular version of that package. If you don't make a specific choice, the most recent version of the package will be loaded.

You can delete particular versions of packages stored in SQL Server. You cannot delete any of the versions stored in SQL Server Meta Data Services or in a structured storage file.

> **NOTE**
>
> Periodically I archive files that are holding packages that I frequently modify, and I start a new file so that the file doesn't reach an unmanageable size.

How to Execute a DTS Package

There are several ways to execute a DTS package, including a new SQL Server 2000 tool called the DTSRun Utility for Windows.

From the DTS Designer

At any time, you can execute a package from the DTS Designer by doing one of the following:

- Selecting the Execute button on the toolbar.
- Selecting Execute from the Package menu.
- Using the F5 key.

One of the new features in SQL Server 2000 is that you can now also execute an individual task by right-clicking on it and selecting Execute Step.

NOTE

It is very useful to test a package during development, checking each new bit of functionality as it is added. It's important to limit the number of rows the package is processing so that each test will go quickly. You can limit the number of rows being processed by all the transformation tasks and bulk insert tasks. Chapter 16, "Writing Scripts for an ActiveX Script Task," shows how to create a simple utility that applies and removes a row limit to all the tasks in a package.

From the Wizards

When you create a DTS package with the Import/Export Wizard or the Copy Database Wizard, you have the opportunity to execute the package immediately. You can't test the package while you are creating it; you can only execute it once as the last step of the process. If you want to make a change and retest, you have to do one of the following:

- Open the wizard and restart the design process from the beginning.
- Open the package in the Package Designer and continue your development with that tool.

From the Enterprise Manager

You can execute DTS packages saved in SQL Server or in Meta Data Services directly from the SQL Server Enterprise Manager by doing the following:

1. Open the Data Transformation Services node under the SQL Server where the package is stored.
2. Highlight Local Package for packages stored in SQL Server or Meta Data Services Packages for packages saved in the Repository.
3. Right-click on the package you want to execute and select Execute Package from the popup menu, or highlight the specific package you want to execute and select Execute Package from the Action menu.

When you execute a package from the Enterprise Manager, you must always execute the most recent version. If you want to execute an earlier version, open that version in the DTS Designer and execute it from there.

From Visual Basic Code

You can execute a DTS package from a Visual Basic application, as well as from any other type of programming language that supports the Component Object Model (COM). You have to do the following:

1. Add a reference to the Microsoft DTSPackage Object Library to the Visual Basic project.
2. Declare a DTS `Package` object variable.
3. Open an existing package or create a new package in code.
4. Use the `Execute` method of the `Package` object.

There are three separate methods for opening an existing package, one each for loading a package from SQL Server storage, from Meta Data Services storage, and from a file. Here's sample code for all three:

```
Dim pkg As New DTS.Package
pkg.LoadFromSQLServer "(local)",,,DTSSQLStgFlag_UseTrustedConnection,,,, _
    "SQLPackage"
'pkg.LoadFromRepository "(local)", "msdb", "sa", "", _
"{3E6D34D4-340F-4636-A514-8A782D36454F}"
'pkg.LoadFromStorageFile "C:\DTS\FilePackage.dts", "", , , "FilePackage"
pkg.Execute
```

A separate option with Visual Basic is to execute a package using the SQLNamespace Object Model. When you use SQLNamespace, you see the same progress information that you see when you execute a DTS package from the Enterprise Manager. This strategy is discussed in Chapter 26.

With the OLE Automation System Stored Procedures

You can execute and manipulate DTS packages using the OLE Automation system stored procedures. These procedures give you access to COM objects, their properties, and their methods. Listing 1.1 has some simple Transact-SQL code that executes a package stored in SQL Server. You can find this code in a file called OAProcedureCode.sql with the material for Chapter 1 on the book's CD. The package that the code references is stored in a file called TestDTS.dts. Load the package in the Package Designer, make sure it runs in your security context, and save it in local SQL Server storage. Each time the package is run, a new record is added to a table called TestDTS that is created in the Pubs sample database.

LISTING 1.1   Executing a DTS Package Using OLE Automation System Stored Procedures

```
declare @hResult int
declare @pkg int
exec @hResult = sp_OACreate 'DTS.Package', @pkg output
exec @hResult = sp_OAMethod @pkg, 'LoadFromSqlServer', null
```

LISTING 1.1   Continued

```
  , @ServerName = '(local)'
  --, @ServerUserName =  --Not needed for integrated security
  --, @ServerPassword = --Not needed for integrated security
  , @Flags= 256 --Integrated security. Use 0 for SQL Server authentication
  --, @PackagePassword = @pkgPwd
  --, @PackageGuid =
  --, @PackageVersionGuid =
  , @PackageName = 'TestDTS'
exec @hResult = sp_OAMethod @pkg, 'Execute'
exec @hResult = sp_OAMethod @pkg, 'UnInitialize'
```

The use of these OLE Automation procedures, including how to handle package errors when using them, is discussed in Chapter 26.

As a Data Provider

You can use the Microsoft OLE DB provider for DTS Packages to return a recordset from a DTS package. The results of a specific Transform Data task are returned to the application that calls the package. You can find an explanation of how to do this in Chapter 23, "The DTS Package and Its Properties."

Using the DTSRun Command Prompt Utility

DTSRun is a command prompt utility that executes a DTS package. You can use DTSRun to execute packages stored in SQL Server, in Meta Data Services, or in a file.

You can encrypt many of the parameters used by DTSRun, such as user ID, password, and server name.

You can pass values to global variables inside a DTS Package by using the /A parameter. You use this parameter once for each global variable you are passing. The syntax for this parameter includes the name and the datatype of the global variable:

```
/A global_variable_name:typeid=value]
```

The typeid is a particular number that has been assigned for each of the global variable datatypes. Some of the values for typeid are

- Integer—3
- Date—7
- String—8
- Boolean—11
- Decimal—14

> **NOTE**
>
> The easiest way to create a DTSRun command line is with the DTSRun Utility for
> Windows, discussed in the following section.

An encrypted parameter is indicated by placing a tilde (~) before the argument.

Here is the syntax for DTSRun:

```
dtsrun
[/?] |
[
    [
        /[~]S server_name[\instance_name]
        { {/[~]U user_name [/[~]P password]} | /E }
    ]
    {
        {/[~]N package_name }
        | {/[~]G package_guid_string}
        | {/[~]V package_version_guid_string}
    }
    [/[~]M package_password]
    [/[~]F filename]
    [/[~]R repository_database_name]
    [/A global_variable_name:typeid=value]
    [/L log_file_name]
    [/W NT_event_log_completion_status]
    [Z] [/!X] [/!D] [/!Y] [/!C]
]
```

The DTSRun utility arguments are as follows:

- /S   The instance of SQL Server where this package is being run. Since there can now
  be more than one instance of SQL Server on the same server, you will need to specify an
  instance name if you don't want to use the default instance. To specify the instance
  name, you must type the "\" character after the server name and then type the instance
  name.

- /U   The login ID used to connect to SQL Server.

- /P   The password for the login ID.

- /E   A trusted connection is being used. A password is not needed when this argument is
  chosen.

- /N   The DTS package name. This argument is not required if the /G argument is
  included.

- /M   The DTS package password. DTS packages can have passwords, but it's not required. If the DTS package has been given a password, this argument is required.
- /G   The DTS package ID. This argument is not required if the /N argument is used.
- /V   The DTS version ID. It uniquely identifies the version. This argument must be used if the /G argument is used. If this argument is not used, the most recent version of the package is used.
- /F   The filename of a DTS package stored as a file. If this argument is used together with /S, the server name, the DTS package stored on the named SQL Server is executed and then added to the named file. A new version is added to the file if the package already exists in the file. If /S is not used, /F specifies the file that contains the package to execute.
- /R   The repository database containing the DTS packages. This argument is required if you are trying to run a package stored in SQL Server Meta Data Services.
- /A   The name, datatype ID, and value of a global variable you want to create for your package. This command may be used multiple times to create multiple global variables.
- /L   The full path and name of the package log file.
- /W   Determines whether or not to write information about the package execution to the application log, which can be found in the Event Viewer in Windows. The default is false.
- /Z   Used before a command encrypted with SQL Server 2000 DTS encryption, which encrypts all the parameters together.
- /!X   The package is not executed when this argument is used.
- /!D   Deletes a DTS package stored in SQL Server. The package is not executed when this argument is used.
- /!Y   Displays an encrypted command. The package is not executed when this argument is used.
- /!C   Copies the DTSRun command being used, together with all its arguments, to the Microsoft Windows clipboard.

Here are a few examples that show you how to use the DTSRun command:

Using DTSRun with a package saved as a file:

```
DTSRun /U "sa" /P Password /N PackageName /M PackagePassword /F
c:\temp\StarImport.dts
```

Using DTSRun with a package saved in the repository:

```
DTSRun /S "(local)" /U "sa" /P Password /N PackageName /R msdb
```

Here's how you can encrypt a command with SQL Server 2000 encryption. The /!Y parameter encrypts the command and the /!C parameter copies the encrypted command to the clipboard so you can retrieve it.

```
DTSRun /S "(local)" /U "sa" /P Password /N PackageName /R msdb /!Y /!C
```

You can execute the SQL Server 2000 encrypted command created with the previous example like this:

```
DTSRun /~Z0xD3CB5FAC0542E5744A2E023DB6BD8438AEBEFC9AA5AE22DC69C0CB100
95477A87D91B343E0F847CA4100168D89B75156D13D1F25546314FEF0D41122ADD20E
A7A9F31303BB0EC127035C3A15ED0775C0F732DE97AE9B80B1637031F2891F525D1B3
0FF25A444913BA1746D
```

In this example, the Package ID and Version ID are used, together with integrated security (/E), with a package saved in SQL Server:

```
DTSRun /S "(local)" /E /G "{DC23785E-C9CD-43B5-B6AE-5E4AE6B99A28}" /V
"{DA85C8E8-574B-4006-8238-142A88601929}"
```

The following example shows how to use parameters with DTSRun. The file containing the ParameterExample DTS package is on the CD under Chapter 1. Copy that package to the C:\Temp directory, run this line of code, and the parameters will be displayed in message boxes generated by the package.

```
DTSRun /N "ParameterExample" /F "C:\Temp\ParameterExample.dts" /A
"StringVariable":"8"="Changed" /A "IntegerVariable":"3"="5"
```

Using the DTSRun Utility for Windows

The DTSRun Utility for Windows is a new tool provided with SQL Server 2000. You can use this utility to execute a DTS package, to schedule a DTS package, or to prepare a DTSRun command line. Figure 1.10 shows the DTSRun Utility for Windows with the Advanced DTS Run dialog opened.

> **NOTE**
>
> You can register the DTSRun Utility for Windows and it will be available on the Tools menu of the Enterprise Manager. To register a new tool:
>
> 1. Select External Tools from the Enterprise Manager Tools menu.
> 2. Click the Add button.
> 3. Type "dtsrunui" in the Command box. There are no parameters. Click OK.
> 4. Type "DTS Run Utility for Windows" for the menu text.

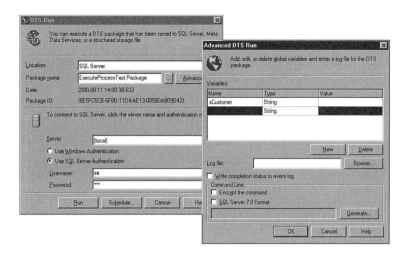

FIGURE 1.10
The new DTSRun Utility for Windows gives a convenient interface for executing a DTS package.

You start the DTSRun Utility by executing the DTSRunUI command without any switches.

You can select any version of any DTS package stored in SQL Server, Meta Data Services, or a file. You can set all the parameters that are available with DTSRun. When you have made all the appropriate selections, you can take one or more of these three actions:

- Execute the package by selecting the Execute button on the DTS Run dialog.
- Schedule the package by selecting the Schedule button on the DTS Run dialog. You will have all the choices available for scheduling, as they are discussed in the following section.
- Generate a dtsrun command line by selecting Generate on the Advanced DTS Run dialog. You can create the command line without being encrypted, with each parameter encrypted separately (SQL Server 7.0 format), or encrypted as one parameter (default SQL Server 2000 format). You can copy this command and use it in a batch file or for scheduling the execution of a DTS package.

From Another DTS Package

There is a new Execute Package task in SQL Server 2000 (see Figure 1.11) that allows you to execute one DTS package from another package. You can pass global variable values between the calling package and the called package.

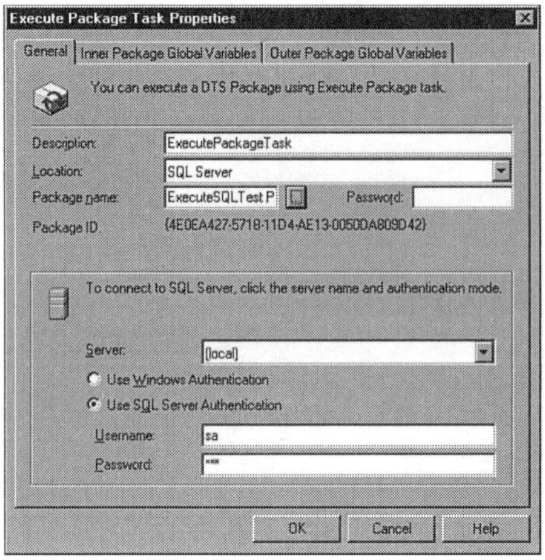

FIGURE 1.11

The Execute Package Task dialog lets you set global variables to the DTS package you are executing.

The Execute Package task is the topic of Chapter 18.

There are several other ways that you can execute one DTS package from another. All these methods are available in both SQL Server 7.0 and SQL Server 2000.

- Use VBScript in an ActiveX Script task. The syntax is very similar to executing a package from VB.
- Use DTSRun in an Execute Process task.
- Use the OLE Automation procedures in an Execute SQL task. This method is especially useful for changing the context in which the package is executed.

Scheduling a DTS Package

Many DTS packages are executed on a regular schedule as a particular set of data needs to be refreshed or reloaded. Here are some of the ways you can schedule a DTS package:

- Right-click on a package in the Enterprise Manager and select Schedule.
- Select schedule on the last tab of the Import/Export Wizard and the Copy Database Wizard.
- Select the Schedule button in the DTSRun Utility for Windows.

Figure 1.12 shows the Edit Recurring Job Schedule dialog that is used to schedule a DTS package. You can schedule the package to occur once or periodically. You can use a particular time frame or choose to let the task execute indefinitely. There are choices for daily, weekly, and monthly scheduling.

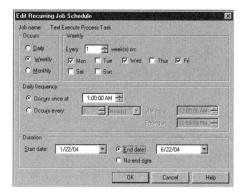

FIGURE 1.12
The Edit Recurring Job Schedule dialog gives you an interface for scheduling your DTS packages.

Whenever you schedule a DTS package, SQL Server creates a job for the SQL Server Agent. This job uses the DTSRun utility with the appropriate parameters. The scheduler always uses encrypted parameters. If you want to create a job that executes DTS packages without using encryption, you can create the DTSRun command line using the DTSRun Utility for Windows and manually schedule the job in the Enterprise Manager.

The Execution Context for a DTS Package

When you execute a DTS package, it is normally executed in the context of the local machine and the security context of that machine's current user. When you schedule a package, it is executed on the machine where it is scheduled and in the security context of the SQL Server Agent.

The execution context can cause two problems:

- The security context might not be adequate for accessing database resources or file system resources. The package might not have permission to execute programs or to send emails.

- Performance could be hurt because data is being pulled across the network to the location where the DTS package is executing.

> **NOTE**
>
> Many DTS developers have run into the security problem when they schedule their DTS packages. You can log on to your computer with the same user ID as the SQL Agent is using. This will allow you to test your DTS packages in the security context that will be used when the package is executed by the SQL Agent.

The performance issue can be confusing because some of the DTS tasks are executed locally where the package is executing, while others are executed remotely on the database server.

Here are some of the tasks that are executed in the local context:

- All the transformation tasks—The Transform Data, Data Driven Query, and Parallel Data Pump tasks. The performance of these tasks can be significantly degraded when they are executed on one machine and the data they are processing is on another.
- The Execute Process task.
- The Execute Package task.

The following list contains tasks that are executed on the database server and not on the machine where the package is executed. If you are only using these tasks, you will not have performance problems caused by execution context:

- The Bulk Insert task
- The Copy SQL Server Objects task
- The Transfer Databases task
- The Execute SQL task

Here are some of your options for executing a DTS package on a database server, instead of on your workstation, when you do not have direct access to the server:

- Use remote management software and execute the package using DTSRun.
- Schedule the package on the server. Make sure the SQL Server Agent has all the permissions needed to carry out the package's operation.
- Execute the package on the server using the OLE Automation system stored procedures or by using xp_cmdshell with DTSRun. You could do either of these from an Execute SQL task within another DTS package.

Chapter 26 has more information on the solution using the OLE Automation system stored procedures.

Using the DTS Object Model for Programmatic Control

DTS is implemented with the Component Object Model (COM). You can manipulate DTS packages and their components through the appropriate collections, objects, properties, and methods that are exposed in the DTS object model.

NOTE

If you're a programmer, you'll be interested in this section.

If you're not a programmer (and I know a lot of excellent database developers who aren't), you'll still find this material valuable. You can access the properties of DTS objects through two new features—the Dynamic Properties task and Disconnected Edit. These tools allow you to manipulate object properties directly, without programming.

Throughout the book, I will attempt to connect what you can do in the DTS Designer interface with what you can do with the DTS object model, so that you can use code, the Dynamic Properties task, and Disconnected Edit to extend your control over DTS.

The DTS object model is the theme of Chapter 30. Almost all of the chapters in this book refer to the various structures within the object model.

The DTS Object Model

The Package object is at the top of the DTS object hierarchy. All the objects that do the work of a DTS package stem from this object.

The Package object contains four collections of objects:

- Connections—Defined links to particular sources of data.
- Tasks—The actions that take place in a package.
- Steps—An object associated with a task that controls how the task fits into the workflow of the package as a whole.
- Global Variables—Variables that allow for sharing of information between the various tasks. Values of global variables can also be sent into a package.

Each task has an associated object called a custom task that contains the properties specific to that particular kind of DTS task.

There are several other DTS objects that do not fit under the Package object. These other objects primarily provide information:

- `Application`—System properties and information.
- `TransformationInfo`—DTS transformations that are registered.
- `ScriptingLanguageInfo`—Scripting languages that are registered.
- `SavedPackageInfo`—Packages that are stored as files.

Using the DTS Object Model with the Dynamic Properties Task

You can use the new Dynamic Properties task to change the properties of DTS objects while a package is being executed. You create the workflow for this task so that the values are updated at the correct point in the package execution, as shown in Figure 1.13.

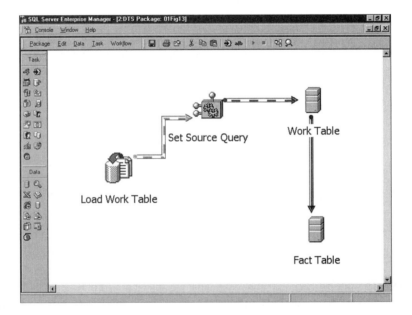

FIGURE 1.13

The Dynamic Properties task allows you to change properties of an object as a package is executing.

When you are selecting a new property for modification, a tree structure is displayed (see Figure 1.14). This tree shows all the objects that have been defined for that particular package. You can select any of them and specify the new value you want assigned to a particular property. Besides setting the value to a constant, you can set the value to a global variable, retrieve a value in a query, load the value from a file, or look up the value in an INI file.

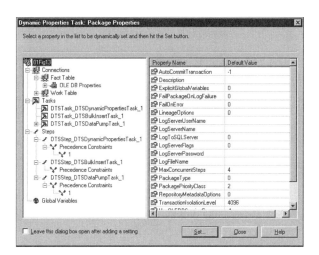

FIGURE 1.14
There are many properties of the DTS objects that can be set with the Dynamic Properties task.

The Dynamic Properties task has one very significant limitation—you cannot add any new objects with this task. If you want to dynamically create a new connection, task, lookup, transformation, or any other object while a package is executing, you have to create it using code.

Using the DTS Object Model with Disconnected Edit

Disconnected Edit is a tool that allows you to directly edit a number of properties of DTS objects. You can get to Disconnected Edit by right-clicking on the Design Sheet and choosing it from the menu, or by selecting Disconnected Edit from the Package menu. When you choose Disconnected Edit, the Edit All Package Properties dialog opens, as shown in Figure 1.15.

The interface for Disconnected Edit looks very similar to the interface for Dynamic Properties Task, but there are three significant differences:

- The Dynamic Properties task is a tool for making property changes while a package is executing, while Disconnected Edit is a tool for modifying properties while designing a package.

- You can modify many more properties with Disconnected Edit than you can with the Dynamic Properties task.

- When you use Disconnected Edit, you always set the properties to a value, whereas the Dynamic Properties task allows you to set property values in a variety of ways.

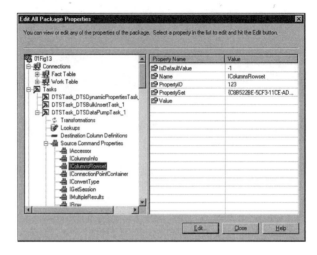

FIGURE 1.15

You can edit the greatest number of properties when you use Disconnected Edit.

CAUTION

Disconnected Edit and, to a lesser extent, the Dynamic Properties task allow you to change properties of DTS objects to invalid or inappropriate values.

When you are setting values of object properties in the Package Designer, the Designer checks the data structure in the connection to see if those values are appropriate. The fundamental purpose of Disconnected Edit is to allow you to set values for data sources in situations where you are not connected to them.

I believe that the usefulness of Disconnected Edit goes far beyond its basic purpose. However, whenever you change something in Disconnected Edit, you are responsible for ensuring that the change is appropriate. The Package Designer does very little checking beyond assuring that you have used the correct datatype for the value.

Using Disconnected Edit is somewhat analogous to using the Windows Registry. When you make a change in the Registry, the system doesn't check if that change is appropriate for the programs that are being affected. You have to know what you're doing.

You can change properties with Disconnected Edit in a way that will confuse your package. If you change the ID of a Connection object, for example, you will break the link between that Connection and all the tasks that use it.

> Another issue in using Disconnected Edit is that you can unintentionally overwrite some of your changes in your ongoing development. In the Transform Data task, for example, there is a property called ExceptionFileOptions that holds a value that is the sum of a number of possible bit flags. Some of the flags can be set in the Transform Data Task Properties dialog. You can add additional flags using Disconnected Edit, but if you then open the tab of the dialog where the value is set, the values you have added in Disconnected Edit will be overwritten.
>
> I encourage you to become familiar with the power of Disconnected Edit, but I also encourage you to be careful in using that power. It's always better to use the Package Designer interface if it will allow you to do what you want to accomplish.

Programming DTS with VBScript

You can use the DTS object model in the ActiveX scripts inside your DTS packages to create new objects and modify their properties. The examples in this book show how to do this with VBScript, but you can also use the other scripting languages. Programming with the DTS object model in ActiveX scripts is useful in at least three ways:

- You can dynamically modify the package as it is executing. You can modify properties, and you can also create new objects such as connections, tasks, and transformations.

- You can run scripts in ActiveX Script tasks as part of the design process to simplify the process of making changes throughout the package.

- You can query the structure of the package for the purpose of reporting or documenting the package design.

The use of the DTS object model in VBScript is discussed in Chapter 16, "Writing Scripts for an ActiveX Script Task," and Chapter 7, "Writing ActiveX Scripts for a Transform Data Task." Chapter 16 explains how to change code from VB to VBScript and back again.

Programming DTS with Visual Basic

DTS in SQL Server 2000 is more integrated with Visual Basic than DTS in SQL Server 7.0. You now have the option of saving a package to VB. You can do the following with Visual Basic in DTS:

- Create new packages.
- Save packages to VB for editing.
- Execute packages and handle errors that are generated from them.

- If you execute a package from VB, you can build an interface that allows a user to modify the package before it is executed.

- Create new DTS custom tasks.

These topics are discussed in Chapter 26 and Chapter 31, "Creating a Custom Task in VB."

Programming DTS with VC++

Almost everything you can do with a DTS package using VB, you can also do with VC++. The major difference, of course, is that you can't save a package to VC++ as you do for VB.

The one additional thing you can do with VC++ that you can't do with Visual Basic is create custom transformations. You can greatly increase the speed of a transformation by moving it from an ActiveX script into a custom transformation.

Programming custom transformations with VC++ is the topic of Chapter 32.

DTS Templates

SQL Server 2000 has added DTS templates to speed the development of DTS packages. If you are creating a number of packages that are similar, you can create the package once as a template and then use that template as the basis for all your individual packages.

Using Templates

A DTS template is always saved as a file with a .dtt extension. You can open a template in one of two ways:

- Right-click on the Data Transformation Services node in the Enterprise Manager and select All Tasks and Open Template from the popup menu.

- Highlight the Data Transformation Services node and select All Tasks and Open Template from the Action menu.

The template has a set of tasks and precedence constraints that have already been created. You use these objects as the starting point for a new DTS package.

You cannot modify a template. The first time you save the new package you will be asked to enter storage information.

Creating Templates

You create a DTS template in the same way you create a DTS package, except for these things:

- Use Disconnected Edit to fill in object properties that will be changed when the template is used. This is especially important for connection properties, because the connections will not be able to be validated at the time the template is created. You can use a phrase that indicates the need to change the value, such as "Enter Source Server Name Here".

- Add annotations to explain to the template users where they have to fill in property values.

- When you have finished your template, save it as a Structure Storage File. As you're saving it, change the extension from .dtt to .dts, so that SQL Server will recognize it as a template file.

If you want to change an existing template you have to open it up, make the changes, and save it with a different file name.

Using Wizards for Rapid Application Development

SQL Server 2000 provides two wizards that automate the process of creating a DTS package. One of these wizards, the Import/Export Wizard, is almost unchanged from SQL Server 7.0. The other one, the Copy Database Wizard, is new.

Both wizards create DTS packages. You can modify these packages with the DTS Designer.

The two DTS Wizards are the topic of Chapter 25.

Copy Database Wizard

The Copy Database Wizard is used for the following tasks:

- Moving a SQL Server database from one server to another.
- Moving meta data that's critical to the operation of a database between servers.
- Upgrading a SQL Server database to SQL Server 2000.

  It's important to be able to transfer the meta data along with the databases. Databases depend on certain types of information that is stored by SQL Server in the master and msdb databases. The kinds of meta data that can be moved with this wizard are

- User-defined error messages.
- Shared stored procedures from the master database.
- Logins.
- Scheduled jobs.

You can open the Copy Database Wizard in the Enterprise Manager by highlighting the SQL Server node and selecting Wizards from the Tools menu. The Copy Database Wizard is listed under the Management node in the Select Wizard dialog. The opening screen of the wizard is shown in Figure 1.16.

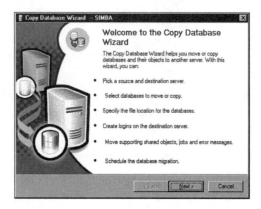

FIGURE 1.16
The new Copy Database Wizard allows you to copy or move one or more SQL Server databases to SQL Server 8.0.

You cannot use one of the sample databases to try the Copy Database Wizard because you are not allowed to copy a database to a server that already has a database with that name. If you want to try using the Wizard, I suggest that you create a new database and choose that database for copying:

1. Create a new database on the SQL Server you are going to use as the source.
2. Open the Copy Database Wizard.
3. Select the source server.
4. Select the destination server.
5. Select Move or Copy for the database you have created.
6. You should not have to change the database file location.
7. You can leave the default choices for the related objects.
8. Select the Run Once option and schedule the package to run a couple of years from now.
9. Open the package in the DTS Designer to see what the wizard has created. Run the package and view the results.

DTS Import/Export Wizard

You can use the DTS Import/Export Wizard to rapidly create a DTS package that moves data. You can use it to do the following:

- Create connections.
- Transfer SQL Server Object tasks.
- Transform data tasks.
- Execute SQL tasks to drop and create tables, if necessary.

You can open the DTS Import/Export Wizard in a number of ways, including opening it in the Enterprise Manager by highlighting the SQL Server node and selecting Wizards from the Tools menu. The DTS Export Wizard and the DTS Import Wizard are listed under the Data Transformation Services node. These two wizards are identical except for the order in which you select the data source and the data destination.

Figure 1.17 shows one of the screens of the Import/Export Wizard.

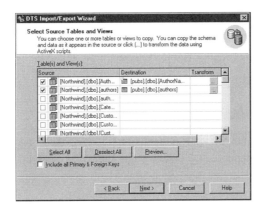

FIGURE 1.17
You can transfer multiple tables with the DTS Import/Export Wizard.

To try the Import/Export Wizard, I suggest copying a couple of tables from the Pubs sample database to the Northwind sample database:

1. Open the wizard.
2. Select Pubs as the data source.
3. Select Northwind as the data destination.
4. Select the Copy tables and views from the source database Option.
5. Select a couple of tables in the list of available tables and views.
6. Uncheck Run immediately. Check Save DTS Package. Choose the SQL Server option.
7. Enter the appropriate package name, server, and security information for saving the package.
8. Select Finish to create the package.
9. Open the package in the DTS Designer to see what the wizard has created. Run the package and view the results.

> **NOTE**
>
> The Import/Export Wizard is a convenient tool if you're new to DTS. As with other wizards, the steps you need to complete are presented in a logical, sequential format.
>
> This wizard is also an excellent tool for speeding up the development of a package that uses Transform Data tasks to move data in many tables. You cannot create a package with multiple Transform Data tasks nearly as quickly using the DTS Designer.
>
> I often start a DTS package using the Import/Export Wizard and then continue development with the DTS Designer, where I have more control over the details of all the objects.

Practical Uses for DTS

The primary focus of this book is on the details of DTS implementation—how to use Data Transformation Services. Chapter 3, "DTS and the Flow of Data Through the Enterprise," and Chapter 4, "Using DTS to Move Data into a Data Mart," give some of the big picture of designing a data transformation strategy for an organization.

This final section of this chapter also discusses some of the opportunities for data transformation provided by DTS.

Upgrading a Database from Microsoft Access to SQL Server

Microsoft has created an upsizing tool for moving a Microsoft Access database to SQL Server. This tool creates the links from the Access application to the SQL database.

However, sometimes people will move a database from Microsoft Access (or some other database) to SQL Server, where it's not important to maintain the user interface that was being used previously. In that case, the DTS Import/Export Wizard is a very convenient tool for creating the new tables in SQL Server and importing the data. For more information about this process, see Chapter 25.

Consolidating Data from Multiple Sources

Companies typically have data in a variety of different OLTP and business analysis systems. DTS is a tool that can connect to a variety of different types of data sources and load that information into one central location. In some cases, companies will use this consolidated data to replace the data stored in diverse places. Other companies will continue to use their data in separate locations, but will use their consolidated information for enterprise-wide business analysis.

Data consolidation often also includes merging data obtained by the company from outside sources. This outside data can present significant processing challenges because it might not be in the same format that is used internally by the company.

The consolidation of data from multiple sources often involves much more than just copying data. There can be

- Homogenization of data that uses different codes.
- Verification of data that is contradictory or incorrect.
- The removal of duplicate data where there is a partial overlap between data sets.
- Aggregation or summarization of data.
- Recalculation of values that are calculated in different ways by different source systems.
- Connecting data that is related, but in which the relationship is missing in the source data.

The DTS transformation tasks, with individual row processing and the ability to look up values, can accomplish all of these tasks.

Initial and Periodic Loading of a Data Mart or a Data Warehouse

For some companies, consolidated data will be used to build a data warehouse and/or one or more data marts for the purpose of business analysis. In addition to all the issues involved in consolidating data, there are these additional data transformation issues:

- Creation and initial loading of fact and dimension tables.
- Periodic loading of additional facts into the fact table.
- Periodic loading of new records into the dimension tables.
- Updating dimension table records.
- Creating and maintaining meta data for the business analysts.
- Moving data from the data warehouse to the data marts.
- Processing data mining models.
- Processing server cubes and local cube files.

DTS has two tasks for processing business analysis information—the Analysis Services Processing task and the Data Mining Prediction task. These two tasks are the topic of Chapter 21. Chapter 4 discusses how to organize data for use by business analysis systems. Chapter 31,

"Creating a Custom Task with VB," shows how to create a custom task that will automate the creation of local cube files.

Reporting on Data from Transaction Processing Systems

Existing On Line Transaction Processing (OLTP) systems usually have some reporting capability, but the flexibility of these reports can be quite limited:

- Some of the significant information might not be available in the reports.
- Some of the information might be aggregated already so that the detailed information is not available.
- The reports might not be tied together very well with information from other parts of the OLTP system or outside the system.
- The reports might not provide information for all significant time periods.

It is often very difficult to modify existing systems to obtain the desired reports. Fortunately, it may be possible to extract the information from the OLTP system and load it into another database, such as SQL Server or Microsoft Access, for reporting purposes. You can use DTS to access the data in one of two ways:

- If there is an OLE DB provider or an ODBC driver to the OLTP database, you can connect using the provider or the driver and use that connection as the source for a Transform Data task.
- You can export the data from the OLTP system to a text file, and use the Bulk Insert task or the Transform Data task to load the data into another database.

Building an Interface to the Web for a Legacy System

Existing OLTP systems may not have the capability to present their data in a way that can be accessed by a Web server. The data can be moved to SQL Server or another database that has a built-in Web interface.

Archiving a Database

DTS can be used for extracting data from a database and building an archive with that data. An archive is needed for two fundamental reasons:

- The store of data in the OLTP system is getting too large for efficient processing. After the older data is copied to an archive, that data can be deleted from the OLTP system.
- The OLTP system may automatically summarize older data and delete the details underlying that data. If the detailed data is not archived periodically, it will be unavailable for business analysis purposes.

Analyzing Internet Clickstream Data

One of the most important uses of data transformation today is the processing of Internet clickstream data. Companies want to analyze the use of their Web sites. They often want to know the following:

- How are people getting to the site?
- What pages are they looking at?
- What ads are they seeing?
- How long are they spending on each page and on the site as a whole?
- What path do people follow when moving through the site?
- How many people are viewing the site?
- Who's viewing the site?
- What is the demographic information for the people viewing the site?

Web servers create a log that records all the requests received for files. These logs contain some or all of the following information:

- The identity of the requesting computer.
- The time the request was made.
- The text of the requesting line.
- The status code returned to the client.
- The number of bytes sent to the client.
- The URL of the referring server.
- The name and version of the browser being used by the client.
- The time taken to service the request.
- The URL or the resource requested.
- The cookie on the client machine.

Web hosting companies sometimes process these logs and give the client company a summary of the significant data. At other times, the raw log is the only format in which the information is available.

A very significant amount of data transformation is needed to extract valuable information out of the clickstream data. You could use the DTS tasks in the following ways:

- The FTP task moves the logs to a local server.
- The Execute Process task starts a process that could do one or more of the following—unzip the files, convert the files from binary to textual format, and/or pre-aggregate the data.

- The Bulk Insert task loads the clickstream data from the text files into SQL Server. The logs are often very large (1GB or larger), and the Bulk Insert task can achieve the fastest speed for loading.

- The Execute SQL task does set-oriented processing of the data.

- The Transform Data task does row-level processing of the data.

- The Analysis Services task processes OLAP cubes that are based on the data.

- The Send Mail task reports on the results of the import when it is completed.

- ActiveX Script tasks, Message Queue tasks, Dynamic Property tasks, and Execute Package tasks manage the data transformation process.

Importing and Exporting with XML

The Extensible Markup Language (XML) is a data-oriented Internet language that will be a key technology for the exchange of data in the future. There are many new features in SQL Server 2000 for working with XML, including the following:

- The Transact-SQL OpenXML function allows you to decompose XML documents. The process of XML decomposition allows you to move XML data into a relational database.

- The FOR XML clause in the SELECT statement allows you to create XML documents from the recordset created by the SELECT statement.

- You can query a SQL Server database from a web page using an XML query. SQL Server will return an XML document with the data.

- You can use XPath queries to map SQL Server tables to XML structures.

There are some new DTS features that support make it easier to work with XML documents:

- The ReadFile and WriteFile transformations give you a way to import and export XML files as a part of your transformations.

- The Parallel Data Pump task, which is the topic of Chapter 10, allows you to process the hierarchical recordsets that are used in XML.

An XML OLE DB provider is not provided with SQL Server 2000. However, they are available from third-party sources. With an OLE DB provider you can use an XML document as the source for a transformation task.

Conclusion

Data Transformation Services is a very powerful, versatile tool for moving and manipulating data. It was a great tool in SQL Server 7.0, and it's greatly improved in SQL Server 2000.

The next chapter focuses on the most significant new DTS features in SQL Server 2000.

DTS Enhancements for SQL Server 2000

IN THIS CHAPTER

Microsoft first released Data Transformation Services (DTS) in SQL Server 7.0. It quickly became popular because of its powerful data transformation capabilities and its integrated application environment for developing transformation packages. As a new product, DTS had some rough edges. Some obvious features were missing, not everything was as convenient as it could have been, and, of course, there were a few bugs. Some of these shortcomings were fixed with the SQL Server 7.0 service packs. Microsoft also provided an additional task for DTS, the OLAP Services Processing task, on their Web site.

Microsoft has now made many improvements to DTS in SQL Server 2000. The new DTS features are significant for one or more of the following reasons:

- They increase your ability to control what happens in your DTS packages.
- They speed the development process, making DTS an even better Rapid Application Development environment for data transformation.
- They extend the ability of DTS to interoperate with other systems.

If you didn't use DTS in SQL Server 7.0, you can skip this chapter. Everything mentioned here is discussed in more detail in other chapters. But if you're already using DTS and you just want to know what has changed, or if you're evaluating whether you should switch from SQL Server 7.0 to SQL Server 2000, this chapter is for you.

Top Ten New DTS Features

Here are the top ten new features that have extended the power of DTS in SQL Server 2000:

10. Package Templates—You can use templates to help create packages more quickly.
9. The FTP Task—You can incorporate FTP processes into your DTS packages.
8. The Execute Package Task—A DTS package can call another package and pass parameters to it.
7. The Message Queue Task—DTS packages can send, wait for, and receive messages.
6. Multiple Phases in the Transform Data Task—You can write code for eight different events inside one Transform Data task.
5. The Package Object Browser—This new browser gives you access to some of the most important objects and constants while you're writing ActiveX scripts.
4. The Dynamic Properties Task—Modify the properties of your package while it's running—without writing code.
3. The New Data Transformations—You have seven new options from which to choose when creating data transformations.

2. Using Parameters in Queries—Parameters can now be used in the Transform Data task's source query, the query of an Execute SQL task, and the output of an Execute SQL task.

1. The Parallel Data Pump Task—Create a data transformation for the multiple tables of a hierarchical rowset.

These top ten new features are discussed in this chapter and are covered in greater detail in other parts of the book.

The New DTS Tasks

All eight of the original DTS tasks included with SQL Server 7.0 have returned with SQL Server 2000. There are also 12 new tasks.

Dynamic Properties Task

In SQL Server 7.0, you could modify the properties of connections, tasks, and steps dynamically by using code in ActiveX scripts. You can still do that with SQL Server 2000, but now you also have a Dynamic Properties task that makes this process more straightforward. This task gives you many options for assigning values to these properties, including database lookups, INI files, system properties, data files, and constants. Figure 2.1 shows some of the properties that can be modified with this task.

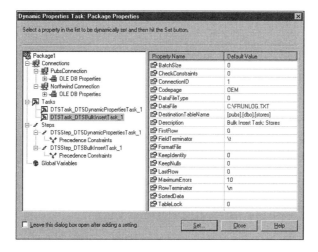

FIGURE 2.1

The Dynamic Properties task makes it easier to modify the properties of DTS package objects as the package is executing.

The Dynamic Properties task is the topic of Chapter 17, "The Dynamic Properties Task."

The File Transfer Protocol (FTP) Task

The movement of data often includes the use of FTP. Now you have an FTP task so that you can include this functionality in your DTS packages. This task is discussed in Chapter 14, "The File Transfer Protocol (FTP) Task."

The Execute Package Task

In SQL Server 7.0, it was possible to call one DTS package from another using the DTS Object Model. Now this call is made easier with a task specifically designed to execute another DTS package. This new functionality makes it possible to place DTS tasks in separate packages and then join those packages together into larger applications to create complex data transformations.

The Execute Package task is discussed in Chapter 18, "The Execute Package Task."

The Message Queue Task

The Message Queue task is another new task that lets you combine DTS packages together into a complex data transformation. You can send and receive messages with the Message Queue task. Also, you can have one package wait for an event to happen in another package.

The Message Queue task is the topic of Chapter 19, "The Message Queue Task."

The Parallel Data Pump Task

I believe that the most important new feature of Data Transformation Services in SQL Server 2000 is the Parallel Data Pump task. You can use this task to process hierarchical rowsets, transforming data in several tables at the same time. The Parallel Data Pump task will make it easier to move data to and from XML.

You won't find the Parallel Data Pump task listed with the available tasks in the DTS Designer. It can be used in SQL Server 2000, but Microsoft has not yet given it a graphical user interface.

The Parallel Data Pump task is the topic of Chapter 10, "The Parallel Data Pump Task."

The Analysis Services Processing Task

Microsoft first distributed the OLAP Services Processing task on its Web site in the Data Transformation Services Task Kit I. This task was renamed the Analysis Services Processing task in SQL Server 2000. It has all the functionality of the OLAP Services Processing task, with the additional capability to process Data Mining Models.

The Analysis Services Processing task is discussed in Chapter 21, "The Analysis Services Tasks."

The Data Mining Prediction Query Task

You can use some of the data mining functionality in SQL Server 2000's Analysis Services with the Data Mining Prediction Query task, shown in Figure 2.2. To use this task, you have to create a data mining model with Analysis Services. Then you can specify a prediction query and an output table for that data mining model.

The Data Mining Prediction Query task is also discussed in Chapter 21.

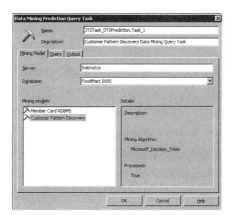

FIGURE 2.2
The user interface for the new Data Mining Prediction Query task.

The Transfer Databases Task

SQL Server 2000 includes a new tool called the Copy Database Wizard. This wizard creates a DTS package with a Transfer Databases task and, optionally, the four other new Transfer tasks discussed below. The package created by this wizard is shown in Figure 2.3.

The Transfer Databases task is discussed in Chapter 15, "The Transfer Database and Other Transfer Tasks." The Copy Database Wizard is discussed in Chapter 25, "Rapid Development with the Copy Database Wizard and the DTS Import/Export Wizard."

The Transfer Master Stored Procedures Task

Databases can use stored procedures from the master database. When a database is transferred from one server to another, these stored procedures also need to be moved. This task moves stored procedures from the master database of one instance of SQL Server 2000 to the master database of another instance of SQL Server 2000.

This task is discussed in Chapter 15.

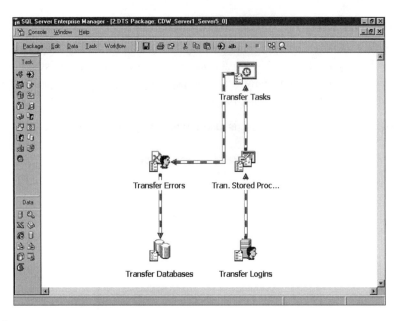

FIGURE 2.3
You can create a package with the Copy Database Wizard that has one of each of the five new DTS transfer tasks.

The Transfer Jobs Task

You can transfer jobs that have been scheduled on one instance of SQL Server 2000 to another instance of SQL Server 2000 by using the Transfer Jobs task.

This task is discussed in Chapter 15.

The Transfer Logins Task

You can transfer logins between instances of SQL Server 2000 with the Transfer Logins task.

This task is discussed in Chapter 15.

The Transfer Error Messages Task

Developers can create user-defined error messages for their database applications. These messages are stored in the sysmessages table of the master database. You can move these error messages to a different instance of SQL Server 2000 by using the Transfer Error Message task.

This task is discussed in Chapter 15.

Transformation Task Enhancements

Many of the most significant changes in SQL Server 2000 have been made in the data transformation tasks. Microsoft has extended the power, enhanced the control, and increased the ease of development for both the Transform Data task and the Data Driven Query task. All the changes in this section apply to both of these tasks.

The Transform Data task is now implemented with the `DataPumpTask2` object, which extends the functionality of the `DataPumpTask` object used in SQL Server 7.0. The `DataPumpTask2` object inherits all the properties, methods, and collections of the `DataPumpTask` object. In the same way, the `DataDrivenQueryTask2` object inherits from and extends the functionality of the `DataDrivenQueryTask` object.

These tasks are discussed in detail in Part II of this book, "DTS Connections and the Data Transformation Tasks."

Multiple Phases in the Data Transformation Tasks

In SQL Server 7.0, you could write programming code at only one point in a transformation task—the point where the data transformation was actually taking place. In SQL Server 2000, you can now write code for several different phases and subphases of the Transform Data task or the Data Driven Query task:

- Pre Source phase
- Row Transform phase—The place where you can write code with SQL Server 7.0
- Transform Failure subphase
- Insert Success subphase
- Insert Failure subphase
- Batch Complete phase
- Post Source phase
- Pump Complete phase

The interface for writing code for all these phases is shown in Figure 2.4.

The use of multiple phases in the transformation tasks is the topic of Chapter 9, "The Multiphase Data Pump."

Package Object Browser When Writing Scripts

Microsoft has added a Package Object Browser so that source columns, destination columns, script constants, global variables, and lookups are readily available when you're writing ActiveX scripts. In SQL Server 7.0, only the lists of source and destination columns were shown in the ActiveX Script Transformation Properties dialog. Figure 2.5 shows the Package Object Browser as it appears when you're writing a transformation script.

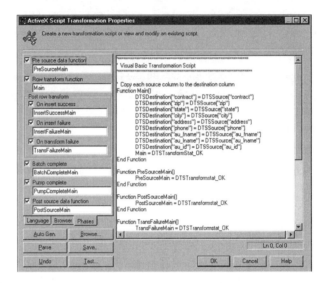

FIGURE 2.4
You can write code for eight different phases and subphases when you enable the Multiple Phase Option.

FIGURE 2.5
The Package Object Browser enhances the interface for writing ActiveX Scripts.

The Package Object Browser is discussed in Chapter 7, "Writing ActiveX Scripts for a Transform Data Task."

The New Data Transformations

SQL Server 7.0 included only two built-in choices for data transformations—Copy and ActiveX Script. SQL Server 2000 now includes nine. You could have created all these transformations with ActiveX Script transformation code in SQL Server 7.0, but these new choices add convenience and shorten development time. The new data transformations are

- DateTime String
- Uppercase String
- Lowercase String
- Middle Of String
- Trim String
- Read File
- Write File

These transformations are discussed in Chapter 6, "The Transform Data Task."

Using Parameters in the Source Query

You can now use parameters in the source queries of the data transformation tasks. The most likely use of these parameters is to specify conditions in a where clause. You supply the values for these parameters through global variables, which can be set to the appropriate values dynamically as the package is executed.

The use of parameters in the source query is discussed in Chapter 6.

New Error File Options

With SQL Server 7.0, you can generate an error file that contains the information about a data transformation and the full text of all the source fields for every record that generates an error.

With SQL Server 2000, you can still generate the SQL Server 7.0 style error file, but you can also choose to generate three files in a more convenient format:

- Error text—A description of the errors that took place in the transformation.
- Source error rows—A text file with the values from the source columns for all the records that generated an error while being transformed.
- Destination error rows—A text file with the values from the destination columns for all the records that generated an error while DTS was attempting to insert them into the data destination.

The new error file format makes it much easier to examine and reprocess the data transformation records that generate errors. The use of the error files is described in Chapter 6 and Chapter 27, "Handling Errors in a Package and Its Transformations."

Lookups Can Now Modify Data

In SQL Server 7.0, lookups could only be used for retrieving data. The Lookup object in the Transform Data task can now be used for data modification queries. This allows you to use the Transform Data task in many situations where the Data Driven Query task would have been needed previously. You can easily insert data into one table, update records in another table, and delete records in a third table.

The use of lookups to modify data is described in Chapter 7.

New Features in Other Tasks

Most of the other DTS tasks in SQL Server 7.0 have similar functionality in SQL Server 2000. This section describes the most important changes in these other tasks.

Three of these tasks have been implemented with new objects that inherit from SQL Server 7.0 and extend its functionality:

- `ExecuteSQLTask` and `ExecuteSQLTask2`
- `TransferObjectsTask` and `TransferObjectsTask2`
- `CreateProcessTask` and `CreateProcessTask2`

The other three tasks are implemented with the same object in SQL Server 7.0 and SQL Server 2000:

- `BulkInsertTask`
- `ActiveScriptTask`
- `SendMailTask`

Using Input Parameters in the Execute SQL Task

In SQL Server 7.0, you were required to hard-code the text of a query in the Execute SQL task. If you wanted to modify any part of the query dynamically, you had to use the DTS Object Model in ActiveX Scripts to change the task's SQL property.

With SQL Server 2000, you can include parameters in Execute SQL task queries. You use global variables to supply the values for these parameters. By using the Dynamic Properties task, you can assign the values for these global variables with an INI file, a text file, or a database lookup. You could also assign the values for these global variables in a Transform Data task or an ActiveX Script task.

The Execute SQL task is the theme of Chapter 12.

Assigning the Result of the Execute SQL Task to Parameters

You can use parameters to capture the output of an Execute SQL task. You choose a set of global variables to be used for the fields from the first row that's returned when the query is executed. The interface used to assign these global variables is shown in Figure 2.6.

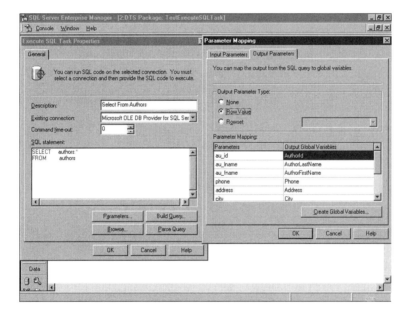

FIGURE 2.6
You can assign the values returned from an Execute SQL task to a set of global variables.

This functionality is discussed in Chapter 12.

Assigning the Result of the Execute SQL Task to Recordset

You can also capture the entire rowset returned by an Execute SQL task and map it to a global variable. This rowset can then be manipulated as a disconnected ADO recordset in ActiveX scripts in other tasks of the package.

This functionality is discussed in Chapter 12. The use of the resulting recordset is discussed in Chapter 16, "Writing Scripts for an ActiveX Script Task."

Package Object Browser for Writing ActiveX Scripts

The ActiveX Script task now has a Package Object Browser to assist with writing the ActiveX scripts. This browser is identical to the one added for the transformation scripts—except, of course, that there are no source columns or destination columns.

The ActiveX Script task is the topic of Chapter 16.

Auto-Generating a Format File in the Bulk Insert Task

By using the Bulk Insert task, you can obtain the highest level of performance in importing text files into SQL Server with DTS. When you have a fixed-length text file, you need to use a format file to specify the length of the fields. In SQL Server 7.0, you had to create this text file manually or by using the bcp command-line utility interactively. With SQL Server 2000, you now have a convenient graphical user interface that lets you create format files for the Bulk Insert task.

Chapter 11, "The Bulk Insert Task," describes how to generate a format file for the Bulk Insert task.

Other New Features in DTS

There are several other new features in DTS with SQL Server 2000 that aren't associated with a particular task.

Copy Database Wizard

SQL Server 7.0 has a DTS Import/Export Wizard, which captures much of the functionality of the Transform Data task and the Copy SQL Server Objects task. This wizard provides a tremendous productivity boost when you're working with many tables at the same time.

SQL Server 2000 adds an additional wizard for copying databases and additional objects that may be needed for the proper functioning of a copied database. One of the pages of this wizard is shown in Figure 2.7.

The Copy Database Wizard is discussed in Chapter 25.

FIGURE 2.7
The new Copy Database Wizard allows you to move one or more databases to a different SQL Server 2000.

Save To Visual Basic File

Microsoft provided a utility on the SQL Server 7.0 CD called `scriptpkg.exe`. This application scripted a DTS package out to Visual Basic code in a text file. This file could then be edited and used to re-create the package.

This utility was so popular that the DTS developers decided to include its functionality in the DTS object model and the user interface for SQL Server 2000. "Save To Visual Basic File" is a new choice for the storage of a DTS package.

See Chapter 26, "Managing Packages with Visual Basic and Stored Procedures," for a description of the structure of the saved Visual Basic file, as well as ideas for using Visual Basic to manage DTS packages.

Setting Values of the Package Global Variables with DTSRun

You can now set the values of global variables when you execute a DTS package with the DTSRun command-line utility. The syntax for doing this is described in Chapter 1, "A Quick Look at DTS."

DTSRunUI—A Windows Interface for DTSRun

The DTSRun command-line utility now has a Windows version called DTSRunUI. This new utility implements all the functionality of DTSRun, including the new feature of setting package global variables. You can execute a package immediately or schedule it for later execution. You can also use DTSRunUI to create a command that can be executed with DTSRun.

DTSRunUI is described in Chapter 1.

Package Templates

You can now use DTS package templates to speed the process of setting up DTS packages. Templates can be created with a set of connections, tasks, and steps to accomplish a particular goal.

The use of DTS Package Templates is discussed in Chapter 1.

Disconnected Edit

Disconnected Edit is a powerful new Package Designer tool for editing the properties of a DTS package and its objects. The Package Designer does not verify any changes made to properties with this tool. This functionality is essential in situations where a package cannot be connected to the data sources it will be using. But it's also very useful for changing other properties that previously could only be changed with code.

The Disconnected Edit interface, shown in Figure 2.8, is very similar to the interface for the Dynamic Properties task.

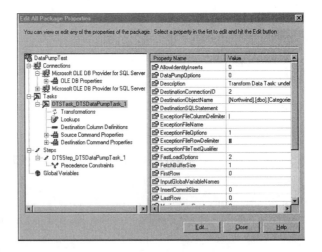

FIGURE 2.8

Disconnected Edit allows you to change almost any property of a DTS object.

The use of Disconnected Edit is discussed toward the end of Chapter 30, "Programming with the DTS Object Model."

Option Explicit for Global Variables

With SQL Server 7.0, you would always create a new global variable in DTS simply by referencing it. The automatic creation of variables without declaration is convenient, but it always carries the risk of introducing difficult bugs through misspelled variable names.

With SQL Server 2000, you have the choice of allowing or disallowing the automatic creation of global variables. By choosing Explicit Global Variables, you force yourself to always declare global variables, as you would by choosing Option Explicit in Visual Basic.

The use of global variables is discussed in Chapter 7.

Just-In-Time Debugging

You can now choose whether or not to open the debugger when an unhandled runtime error occurs in ActiveX Script code, as shown in Figure 2.9. You can set this property by right-clicking on Data Transformation Services in the Enterprise Manager and then selecting Properties.

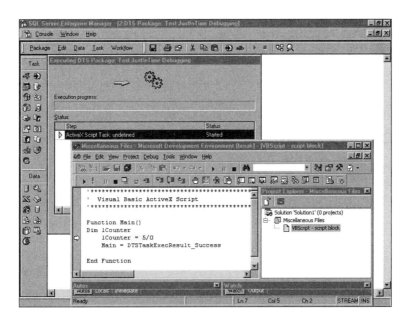

FIGURE 2.9
If you select Just-In-Time Debugging, the debugger will be called when an unhandled error occurs.

Just-In-Time debugging is discussed in Chapter 27, "Handling Errors in a Package and Its Transformations."

Turn On Package Cache

When you select the Turn On Package Cache option, DTS packages will open much more quickly. This option only makes a difference when you're using DTS with SQL Server 2000. You select this option by right-clicking on Data Transformation Services in the Enterprise Manager and then selecting Properties.

Executing Individual Steps in the Package Designer

You can now right-click on any task in the DTS Package Designer and select Execute Step to execute that one step. No other steps will be executed, even if precedence constraints have been set so that they would have executed.

DTS Package Logs

In SQL Server 7.0, you could record what happened in the execution of a DTS package in an error file. With SQL Server 2000, Microsoft has added a DTS Package Log so that package execution results and step execution results can be conveniently viewed in the Enterprise Manager.

The use of DTS package logs is discussed in Chapter 23, "The DTS Package and Its Properties."

Other New Features in SQL Server 2000 That Enhance Data Transformation

The improvements that Microsoft has made to SQL Server 2000 have a positive impact on the use of DTS as a data transformation tool. As SQL Server has become a more powerful, reliable, and scalable database, DTS is becoming a more widely used tool for data transformation.

There are many non-DTS changes in SQL Server 2000 that affect the DTS developer. Three of those enhancements are discussed in this section.

Integration with XML

XML is becoming the medium for data exchange, and SQL Server 2000 has enabled several XML features. There are already many ways that XML can be integrated with DTS, of course. See the discussion of XML in Chapter 3 and the description of the Parallel Data Pump task in Chapter 10.

Indexed Views

One of the ways that Microsoft has improved the performance of SQL Server 2000 is by introducing indexed views. You can create an index on a view that joins two or more tables.

User-Defined Functions

The Transact-SQL language in SQL Server 2000 has been extended with the ability to create user-defined functions. These functions can simplify complex SQL and ActiveX script code.

Conclusion

DTS has many features in SQL Server 7.0, but there's a lot more functionality in SQL Server 2000. Take the time to learn these new features. They will speed your DTS development time and make your transformation packages more powerful.

DTS and the Flow of Data Through the Enterprise

IN THIS CHAPTER

Organizations have both an increasing need and an expanding capability to transform data.

Some of the increasing need for data transformation comes from a desire to improve and extend transaction processing systems:

- Data is being published from the existing transactional systems to the Internet.
- e-Commerce is bringing data from the Internet into the existing systems.
- Clickstream logs (usage reports from web servers) are providing more information about customer behavior than has ever before been available.
- As companies merge, data needs to be moved from multiple-source systems into a unified format.
- Data is extracted and merged from a variety of sources to build new Customer Relationship Management (CRM) systems.
- As a company uses more data, there are increased needs for data archiving.

There are also many companies that are developing Business Intelligence systems. Businesses want to view and analyze data more quickly and effectively. These systems often require a very significant amount of data transformation:

- Moving data into an enterprise-wide data warehouse.
- Moving data into a multidimensional format for OLAP, as discussed in Chapter 4, "Using DTS to Move Data into a Data Mart."
- Homogenizing data that is being extracted from a variety of sources.
- Data cleansing, because poor-quality data cannot be effectively used for Business Intelligence.

One of the most important reasons that companies are transforming more data is that the technology used to manage data works better and costs less than ever before. There have been rapid improvements in both hardware and software:

- Disk drives for storage of large amounts of data.
- Multiprocessor servers with larger amounts of memory, which can transform more data more quickly.
- OLAP and data mining software, such as Microsoft Analysis Services, that make it possible to gain new insights from good-quality data.
- Data transformation software, such as Data Transformation Services in Microsoft SQL Server 2000.

The purpose of this chapter is to examine the flow of data through an organization and show how DTS can be used for a significant portion of that data transformation.

Enterprise Data Structure and Data Flow

It's important to look at data from an enterprise-wide perspective.

Data transformations are often created on an ad hoc basis. A manager wants data in a particular format for a specific report. This data is currently located in several different data stores. A new set of tables and the data transformations to fill those tables have to be created to fulfill this one request.

It's more efficient when an organization can take a comprehensive view. If enterprise data is in different source systems, consider bringing it together into a consolidated database, as is done in data warehousing.

Data is a critical resource for the modern enterprise. The flow of data through an enterprise should be examined so that the use of this resource can be maximized in every possible way.

Here are some things to consider when you're looking at enterprise data flow:

- What data is needed by each of the departments in the enterprise?
- What data is needed for ongoing operations?
- What data is needed for Business Intelligence?
- What data is available in each department?
- How does the data need to be transformed?
- How is data stored?
- How is data archived?
- Who makes the decisions about data transformation, data storage, and enterprise data flow?

No matter how effectively you manage your corporate data assets, you will still receive ad hoc requests for data in a particular format. But if you analyze the needs of your organization, you can design a data structure that will more effectively serve the whole enterprise.

Business Drivers for Enterprise Data Transformation

As you consider the design of your enterprise data structure, you need to continually examine the business drivers that are involved. What is the business purpose for transforming data?

Data transformation is a task for the database administrators and the database developers in the Information Systems department. But deciding on the purpose and goals for data transformation is a top-level management decision. Data transformation can be very expensive, but the availability of high-quality data can be very profitable.

It's possible for an organization to do too much data transformation. Data can be transformed into a variety of contradictory formats, so that business analysts are left wondering which version of the data to trust. Organizations sometimes move their data into data marts or a data warehouse without a clear understanding of the financial gain to be realized from that effort.

But it's also possible for an organization to do too little data transformation. Many businesses are leaving their data in incompatible systems and they can't view their corporate operations as a whole. Many businesses also are not taking advantage of the possibilities of OLAP and data mining. Significant information about customer behavior is being ignored—information that is readily available in existing transaction systems and Internet clickstream logs.

Data transformation has to be driven by business needs. What are the financial benefits that can be achieved by transforming data in a particular way? Is the financial benefit of data transformation greater than the expense?

Here are some of the factors that push organizations to invest in data transformation systems:

- Effective response to customers—Customers are expecting rapid response to their orders, requests, questions, and needs. Data about these customers, their orders, and the products they are ordering has to be available so that an immediate, accurate, intelligent, and appropriate response can be given.

- Efficient use of resources—An organization needs to know what resources it has, where those resources are stored, and when they're needed. If all this information is available for making decisions, resource availability can be improved, movement of resources can be optimized, and excess inventory can be cut.

- Efficient processes—Purchasing, manufacturing, advertising, financial management, and personnel management can all be improved by analyzing the available data. The data generated by each business process can be captured and analyzed to find opportunities for improvement.

- Dealing with complexity and change—Business realities are changing more rapidly than ever before. Whereas in the past businessmen could rely on their experience to make intelligent estimates, there is now a greater need to make decisions with actual data. Last year's commonly accepted reality might not be true this year. Data is needed to understand the rapidly shifting reality of modern business.

- A competitive advantage for you or for someone else—All businesses compete in a global environment. If you can use your data more effectively than your competitors do, you can gain an advantage over them. If other companies are using their data to improve their business processes and you are not, you will start slipping behind. Your customers will know whether or not you are providing them with the highest possible level of service.

Sometimes it may be possible to calculate a specific financial gain that results from transforming data in a particular way. I have seen this done most precisely in situations where data analysis results in inventory reduction.

If the goal of your data transformation is improved customer satisfaction, the calculation of your financial gain probably won't be so precise. However, it might be even more significant for your organization's overall success.

Ways to Use Data

There are three general ways that enterprise data is used:

- To process transactions.
- To discover strategic business information.
- To maintain history.

Much of the same enterprise data is used in all three ways. This data often needs to be moved and transformed as it is being used for different purposes.

Transaction Processing

Companies gather a great deal of data during the ongoing operation of their business. This data includes information about the following:

- Orders
- Purchases
- Production
- Sales
- Shipping
- Inventory
- Employees
- Expense and revenue
- Customers
- Customer contacts

The primary purpose of On Line Transaction Processing (OLTP) data is to keep track of individual transactions so that each one can be handled properly. A company needs to be able to answer these questions:

- What did the customer order?
- Are the ordered products available?

- How much was the customer charged?
- To what address was the product shipped?
- When was the order shipped?
- When was the payment received?

Business Analysis

Data is needed for business analysis. A company needs to know more than the individual details of its business transactions. This information has to be assembled into a meaningful format so that it can be used for business decisions.

The business analyst asks these kinds of questions:

- Which stores had the greatest increase in sales this past month?
- Which types of products are increasing in sales? Which are decreasing?
- Who are our most profitable customers? The least profitable?
- What are our most profitable products? Our least profitable?
- Did we make a profit?
- How can we make a greater profit in the future?

There are three broad categories of business analysis—reporting, OLAP, and data mining.

Reporting

Business analysis has traditionally taken the form of reporting. A report is typically a collection of spreadsheets that provide information about a company's performance from a variety of perspectives.

OLAP

In recent years, a new kind of interactive reporting tool has been developed. On Line Analytical Processing (OLAP) is a software tool that presents millions of different spreadsheet views to an analyst. An OLAP tool allows a user to easily move between these different spreadsheets:

- Drilling down to a level of greater detail.
- Drilling up to see the broader picture.
- Looking at the data from different perspectives or dimensions.
- Slicing (filtering) on a particular factor.
- Combining dimensions to see how different factors interact.

Microsoft included OLAP Services with SQL Server for the first time in version 7.0. In SQL Server 2000, OLAP is part of the functionality of Analysis Services. Figures 3.1 and 3.2 show the process of drilling down to a greater level of detail using the Excel PivotTable.

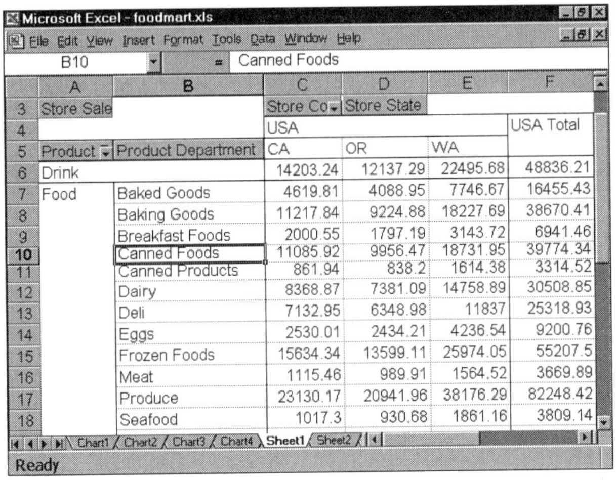

Microsoft Excel - foodmart.xls

B10 = Canned Foods

	A	B	C	D	E	F
3	Store Sale		Store Co	Store State		
4			USA			USA Total
5	Product	Product Department	CA	OR	WA	
6	Drink		14203.24	12137.29	22495.68	48836.21
7	Food	Baked Goods	4619.81	4088.95	7746.67	16455.43
8		Baking Goods	11217.84	9224.88	18227.69	38670.41
9		Breakfast Foods	2000.55	1797.19	3143.72	6941.46
10		Canned Foods	11085.92	9956.47	18731.95	39774.34
11		Canned Products	861.94	838.2	1614.38	3314.52
12		Dairy	8368.87	7381.09	14758.89	30508.85
13		Deli	7132.95	6348.98	11837	25318.93
14		Eggs	2530.01	2434.21	4236.54	9200.76
15		Frozen Foods	15634.34	13599.11	25974.05	55207.5
16		Meat	1115.46	989.91	1564.52	3669.89
17		Produce	23130.17	20941.96	38176.29	82248.42
18		Seafood	1017.3	930.68	1861.16	3809.14

Chart1 / Chart2 / Chart3 / Chart4 / Sheet1 / Sheet2

Ready

FIGURE 3.1
OLAP data viewed in Excel 2000.

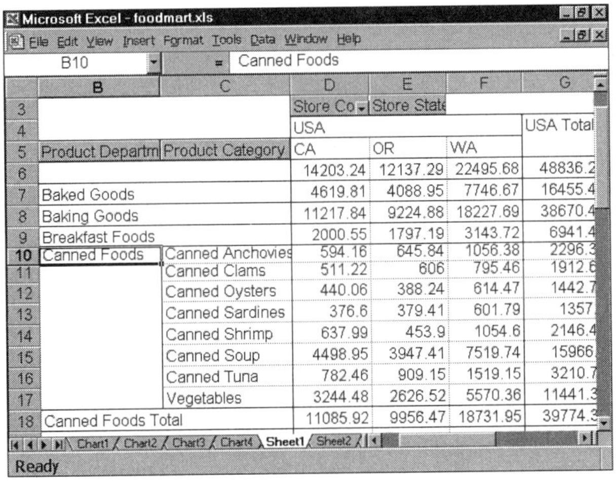

Microsoft Excel - foodmart.xls

B10 = Canned Foods

	B	C	D	E	F	G
3			Store Co	Store Stat		
4			USA			USA Total
5	Product Departm	Product Category	CA	OR	WA	
6			14203.24	12137.29	22495.68	48836.2
7	Baked Goods		4619.81	4088.95	7746.67	16455.4
8	Baking Goods		11217.84	9224.88	18227.69	38670.4
9	Breakfast Foods		2000.55	1797.19	3143.72	6941.4
10	Canned Foods	Canned Anchovies	594.16	645.84	1056.38	2296.3
11		Canned Clams	511.22	606	795.46	1912.6
12		Canned Oysters	440.06	388.24	614.47	1442.7
13		Canned Sardines	376.6	379.41	601.79	1357
14		Canned Shrimp	637.99	453.9	1054.6	2146.4
15		Canned Soup	4498.95	3947.41	7519.74	15966
16		Canned Tuna	782.46	909.15	1519.15	3210.7
17		Vegetables	3244.48	2626.52	5570.36	11441.3
18	Canned Foods Total		11085.92	9956.47	18731.95	39774.3

Chart1 / Chart2 / Chart3 / Chart4 / Sheet1 / Sheet2

Ready

FIGURE 3.2
You can drill down to a greater level of detail.

Figure 3.3 shows the data from a different perspective or dimension—customer income instead of store location.

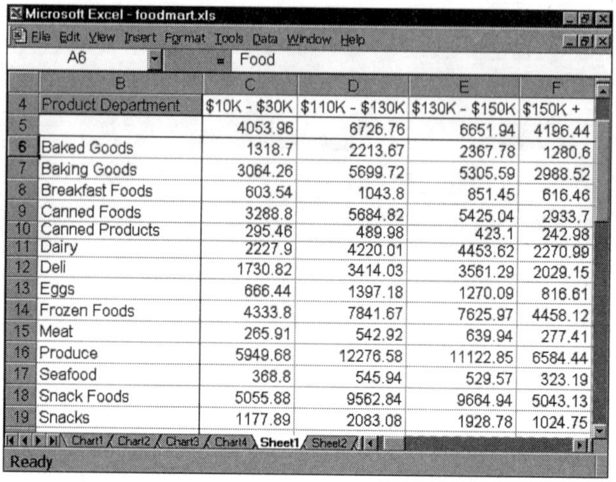

FIGURE 3.3

You can change perspectives (dimensions).

Figure 3.4 shows the Store Location being used to filter, or slice, the results.

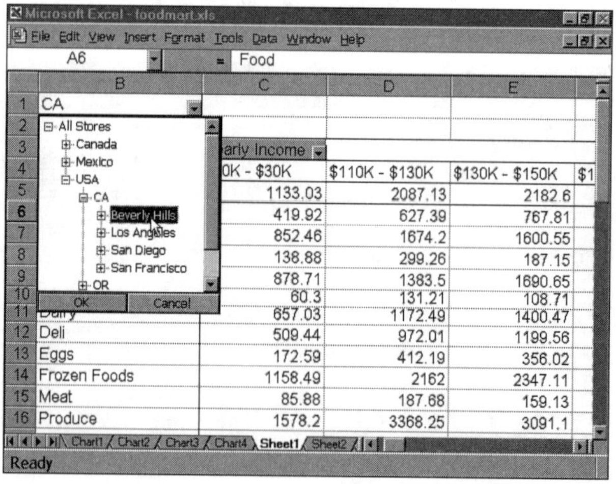

FIGURE 3.4

You can filter (slice) the data from another perspective.

Chapter 21, "The Analysis Services Tasks," describes the use of the Analysis Services Processing task for processing cubes. Chapter 31, "Creating a Custom Task in VB," shows how to create a custom task for generating local cube files.

Data Mining

Data mining is an automated form of business intelligence. A data mining tool is programmed to analyze a set of data to find significant patterns.

Microsoft Analysis Services in SQL Server 2000 includes data mining functionality. There are two data mining algorithms included with Analysis Services:

- Decision Trees—Discovering the most likely patterns for predicting data values.
- Clustering—Finding the natural ways that records can be assembled into groups.

Figure 3.5 shows the Customer Pattern Discovery mining model from the Foodmart 2000 sample database.

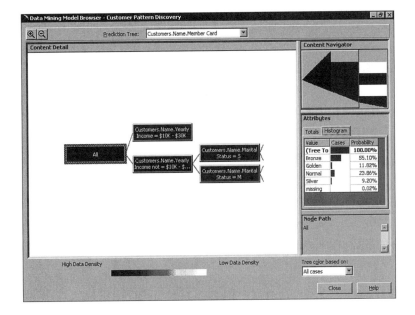

3

DTS AND THE
FLOW OF DATA

FIGURE 3.5

The data mining model browser in Analysis Services.

Chapter 21 explains how to use the Analysis Services Processing task to process cubes and data mining models, and how to use the Data Mining Prediction Query task to use a mining model to predict unknown data values.

> **NOTE**
>
> I think "data mining" is a wonderfully descriptive term for the automated analysis of business data. Tons of ore have to be processed to obtain a few ounces of gold. In the same way, we have a mountain of data—much more than we could ever understand. The data as a whole is worthless, but hidden in that data are nuggets of significant business information. Our data mining tools sift through the massive quantity of data to find the facts that have significance for our business processes.

Maintaining History

The third primary need of an enterprise data structure is to maintain history. A company needs to have an accurate record of what has happened in its past—for historical business analysis and because these transactional records may be needed to resolve business disputes.

Data used for maintaining history usually does not have to be as readily available as the current transaction or business analysis data. It is often archived to a different database so that the volume of data in the current OLTP and OLAP databases can be maintained at a manageable size. Archived data is often kept online in a summarized form for business analysis.

Sources of Data

In designing the way that data flows through your enterprise, one of the first steps is to consider where you are obtaining that data. Traditionally, businesses have only thought of one data source—their on line transaction processing (OLTP) systems. This is still a significant source of data, but it's important to recognize the variety of other data sources from inside and outside the organization.

On Line Transaction Processing (OLTP) Systems

All the detailed transaction information that is generated in OLTP systems can be used to understand what is happening in a company.

Web Clickstream Data

Web clickstream data is the record of Web site activity. It includes information about customers, where they're coming from, what they're looking at, and where they're going.

The use of DTS in transforming clickstream data is discussed in Chapter 1, "A Quick Look
at DTS."

Data from Outside the Organization

More enterprises are using data from outside the organization. Address lists can be purchased
to help cleanse customer data. Census data, market research data, and potential customer lists
can be purchased to assist in the process of making business decisions.

The Data Warehouse

A corporate data warehouse is a destination for data transformation—a place where data is
gathered from multiple OLTP systems and integrated into a single, unified perspective. A data
warehouse is organized into functional areas, and it provides a historical perspective on corporate operations.

The data warehouse is also a data source. Because its data has already been unified, homoge-
nized, and cleansed, it is often the best source of data for business analysis.

Results from Business Analysis Systems

Business analysis has always affected the ongoing operation of a business. Managers look at
the data and make decisions about future operations on the basis of that data.

One of the current emphases in the field of data warehousing is closed-loop business analysis.
In a closed-loop system, the OLTP data is brought into a data warehousing system, it is analyzed, and the results of the data are sent back to the OLTP system to automatically modify the
transaction processes.

Here's an example of closed-loop business analysis. A data mining program analyzes which set
of customers is likely to want to buy a newly published book. This information is automatically transferred to the OLTP system, which sends out information on the book to the selected
customers.

Figure 3.6 shows the flow of data from the various sources to the analysis systems and then
back to the OLTP system.

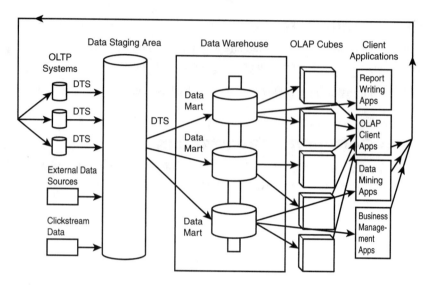

FIGURE 3.6

Closed-loop business analysis brings Business Intelligence back to the OLTP system.

Meta Data

There is one more significant factor in the flow of data through an organization. You have to understand what is happening to the data as all these transformations are taking place.

Meta data is data *about* data—the information that people need to know about the data they are using. Meta data answers the following questions:

- What is the source of this data?
- What is the meaning of this particular piece of data?
- What are the data types used to store this data?
- What data transformations were used on this data?
- When was this data transformed?
- Who is responsible for maintaining this data?
- Who has permission to access this data?
- How reliable is this data?

Meta data is important at every point in the enterprise data structure. It provides information about the sources of data, the data transformation processes, and the current location of the data. It provides information to the data transformation tools and to the users of the data. Figure 3.7 shows the place of meta data in the flow of data through the enterprise.

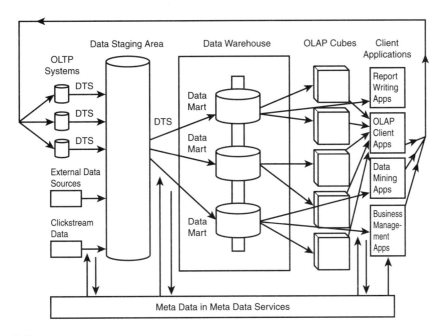

FIGURE 3.7

Meta data is essential throughout the data transformation process.

Microsoft has included a tool called Meta Data Services with SQL Server 2000. This tool is integrated with Data Transformation Services to provide information about the data in the databases and the transformations that are used to modify that data.

The use of meta data is described in Chapter 29, "Integrating DTS with Meta Data Services."

> **NOTE**
>
> Many people use "metadata" as one word, but in SQL Server 2000 Books Online it's two words. What is called Meta Data Services in SQL Server 2000 was referred to as the Repository in SQL Server 7. The term "repository" is still used to describe the place where Meta Data Services stores the meta data.

Types of Data Storage

If you always generated, used, and stored data in a standard format, you wouldn't need to do much data transformation. But as data is used for different purposes, it is stored in different formats. A data transformation tool has to be able to take data in one format and move it to another.

This section outlines the support provided by DTS for transforming data in some of the primary types of storage. More technical information about creating DTS connections for various types of data storage systems can be found in Chapter 5, "DTS Connections."

Text Files

Text files remain one of the primary ways for storing data. They are often used to transfer data from one system to another.

DTS provides access to text files through an OLE DB provider. You can import data from or export data to text files. You can also use the Bulk Insert task with text files, but only to transfer data from a text file into SQL Server.

Listing 3.1 shows a standard text file of clickstream data from a web server.

LISTING 3.1   Clickstream Data in a Text File

```
cacheflow19.isu.net.sa - - [01/Jan/2000:02:04:52 -0600]
    "GET /whatis.htm HTTP/1.0" 200 13589
cacheflow19.isu.net.sa - - [01/Jan/2000:02:04:53 -0600]
    "GET /image4.gif HTTP/1.0" 200 6276
cacheflow19.isu.net.sa - - [01/Jan/2000:02:04:54 -0600]
    "GET /navibar.gif HTTP/1.0" 200 1031
cacheflow19.isu.net.sa - - [01/Jan/2000:02:04:54 -0600]
    "GET /image6.gif HTTP/1.0" 200 991
cacheflow19.isu.net.sa - - [01/Jan/2000:02:04:54 -0600]
    "GET /home.gif HTTP/1.0" 200 1272
cacheflow19.isu.net.sa - - [01/Jan/2000:02:04:54 -0600]
    "GET /image5.gif HTTP/1.0" 200 1552
```

XML

XML is an Internet-ready form of text file data storage. It provides a powerful format for sharing data between different applications.

SQL Server 2000 provides XML support in a number of ways:

- You can export relational data to XML by using the FOR XML clause in a SELECT statement.
- You can import data into a relational database by using the OpenXML rowset provider.
- You can access SQL Server through a URL using XML.
- You can use XML-Data schemas and Xpath queries.
- You can set XML documents as command text and return result sets as a stream.

Listing 3.2 shows the output of the following SELECT query:

```
select top 8
    o.OrderID, o.CustomerID,
    od.ProductID, od.Quantity
from orders o
join [order details] od
    on o.orderid = od.orderid
order by o.OrderID
```

LISTING 3.2   Result Set from Querying the Orders and Order Details Tables

OrderID	CustomerID	ProductID	Quantity
10248	VINET	11	12
10248	VINET	42	10
10248	VINET	72	5
10249	TOMSP	14	9
10249	TOMSP	51	40
10250	HANAR	41	10
10250	HANAR	51	35
10250	HANAR	65	15

Listing 3.3 shows the same query with the FOR XML AUTO clause:

```
select top 8
    o.OrderID, o.CustomerID,
    od.ProductID, od.Quantity
from orders o
join [order details] od
    on o.orderid = od.orderid
order by o.OrderID
for xml auto
```

LISTING 3.3   The Same Result Set Returned with FOR XML AUTO

```
XML_F52E2B61-18A1-11d1-B105-00805F49916B
<o OrderID="10248" CustomerID="VINET">
  <od ProductID="11" Quantity="12"/>
  <od ProductID="42" Quantity="10"/>
  <od ProductID="72" Quantity="5"/>
</o>
<o OrderID="10249" CustomerID="TOMSP">
  <od ProductID="14" Quantity="9"/>
  <od ProductID="51" Quantity="40"/>
</o>
```

LISTING 3.3   Continued

```
<o OrderID="10250" CustomerID="HANAR">
  <od ProductID="41" Quantity="10"/>
  <od ProductID="51" Quantity="35"/>
  <od ProductID="65" Quantity="15"/>
</o>
```

The Parallel Data Pump task (described in Chapter 10) is a useful tool for handling XML data because it provides support for hierarchical recordsets. The Transform Data task (see Chapter 6) has transformations designed to load text into a database, which can be used for loading XML files. There are third-party companies that are offering OLE DB providers that read XML data so that it can be used as the source for a transformation task.

Spreadsheets

Many companies store some of their data, and especially their business analysis data, in spreadsheets. DTS uses the Jet OLE DB provider to connect to Microsoft Excel spreadsheets. DTS can import and export data to Excel.

Relational Database Management Systems

A significant portion of corporate data is stored in Relational Database Management Systems (RDBMSs). These systems provide powerful tools for querying and updating the data, using SQL.

DTS has an OLE DB provider for Microsoft SQL Server, Microsoft Access, and Oracle. The OLE DB provider for ODBC can be used for other database systems that have ODBC drivers available, but not OLE DB providers.

Normalized Database Schema

A normalized database schema is the most efficient format for storing OLTP data. In a normalized database, each piece of information is only stored once, so it can be updated in a single location. It is the more efficient schema for accessing individual records.

Figure 3.8 shows a typical normalized database schema.

Multidimensional (Star) Database Schema

A multidimensional, or star, schema is the most efficient format for storing data used for Business Analysis. In a star schema, the facts being analyzed are stored in a central fact table. This table is surrounded by dimension tables, which contain all the perspectives by which the facts are being analyzed.

Figure 3.9 shows a typical star database schema.

Chapter 4, "Using DTS to Move Data into a Data Mart," discusses the use of the star schema.

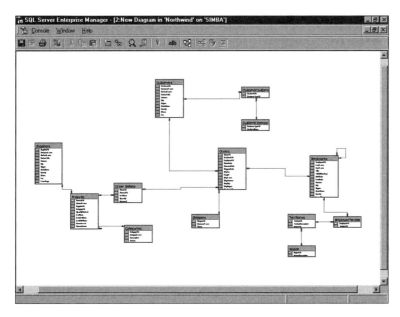

FIGURE 3.8

A diagram of a database with a normalized schema.

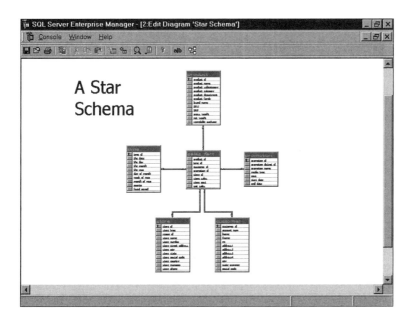

FIGURE 3.9

A diagram of a database with a star schema.

Multidimensional Database Management Systems (OLAP)

You can create a multidimensional database schema in a relational database system. There are also database systems that are specifically designed to hold multidimensional data. These systems are typically called OLAP servers. Microsoft Analysis Server is an example of an OLAP server.

The primary unit of data storage in a relational database system is a two-dimensional table. In an OLAP system, the primary unit of storage is a multidimensional cube. Each cell of a cube holds the data for the intersection of a particular value for each of the cube's dimensions.

The actual data storage for an OLAP system can be in a relational database system. Microsoft Analysis Services gives three data storage options:

- MOLAP—Multidimensional OLAP. Data and calculated aggregations stored in a multidimensional format.
- ROLAP—Relational OLAP. Data and calculated aggregations stored in a relational database.
- HOLAP—Hybrid OLAP. Data stored in a relational database and calculated aggregations stored in multidimensional format.

Conclusion

The importance of data transformation will continue to grow in the coming years as the usefulness of data becomes more apparent. DTS is a powerful and flexible tool for meeting your data transformation needs.

The next chapter, "Using DTS to Move Data into a Data Mart," describes the particular challenge of transforming relational data into a multidimensional structure for business analysis and OLAP. The rest of the book gives you the details of how to use DTS.

Using DTS to Move Data into a Data Mart

CHAPTER

4

IN THIS CHAPTER

With the introduction of OLAP Services in SQL Server 7.0, Microsoft brought OLAP tools to a mass audience. This process continued in SQL Server 2000 with the upgraded OLAP functionality and the new data mining tools in Analysis Services.

One of the most important uses for DTS is to prepare data to be used for OLAP and data mining.

It's easy to open the Analysis Manager and make a cube from FoodMart 2000, the sample database that is installed with Analysis Services. It's easy because FoodMart has a star schema design, the logical structure for OLAP.

It's a lot harder when you have to use the Analysis Manager with data from a typical normalized database. The tables in a relational database present data in a two-dimensional view. These two-dimensional structures must be transformed into multidimensional structures. The star schema is the logical tool to use for this task.

The goal of this chapter is to give you an introduction to multidimensional modeling so that you can use DTS to get your data ready for OLAP and data mining.

> **NOTE**
>
> A full treatment of multidimensional data modeling is beyond the scope of this book. Most of what I wrote about the topic in *Microsoft OLAP Unleashed* (Sams, 1999) is still relevant. I also recommend *The Data Warehouse Lifecycle Toolkit* by Ralph Kimball, Laura Reeves, Margy Ross, and Warren Thornthwaite.

Multidimensional Data Modeling

The star schema receives its name from its appearance. It has several tables radiating out from a central core table, as shown in Figure 4.1.

The fact table is at the core of the star schema. This table stores the actual data that is analyzed in OLAP. Here are the kinds of facts you could put in a fact table:

- The total number of items sold
- The dollar amount of the sale
- The profit on the item sold
- The number of times a user clicked on an Internet ad
- The length of time it took to return a record from the database
- The number of minutes taken for an activity

- The account balance
- The number of days the item was on the shelf
- The number of units produced

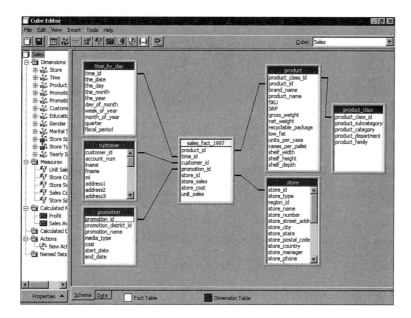

FIGURE 4.1
The star schema of the Sales cube from the Food Mart 2000 sample database, as shown in the Analysis Manager's Cube Editor.

The tables at the points of the star are called *dimension tables*. These tables provide all the different perspectives from which the facts are going to be viewed. Each dimension table will become one or more dimensions in the OLAP cube. Here are some possible dimension tables:

- Time
- Product
- Supplier
- Store Location
- Customer Identity
- Customer Age
- Customer Location
- Customer Demographic

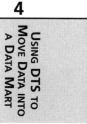

- Household Identity
- Promotion
- Status
- Employee

Differences Between Relational Modeling and Multidimensional Modeling

There are several differences between data modeling as it's normally applied in relational databases and the special multidimensional data modeling that prepares data for OLAP analysis. Figure 4.2 shows a database diagram of the sample Northwind database, which has a typical relational normalized schema.

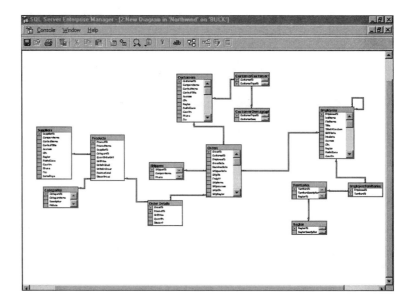

FIGURE 4.2

A typical relational normalized schema—the Northwind sample database.

Figure 4.3 shows a diagram of a database that has a star schema. This star schema database was created by reorganizing the Northwind database. Both databases contain the same information.

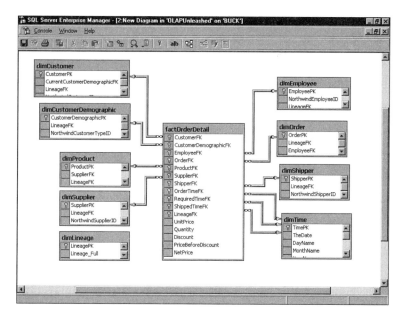

FIGURE 4.3

A typical star schema, created by reorganizing the Northwind database.

Star schema modeling doesn't follow the normal rules of data modeling. Here are some of the differences:

- Relational models can be very complex. The proper application of the rules of normalization can result in a schema with hundreds of tables that have long chains of relationships between them.

  Star schemas are very simple. In the basic star schema design, there are no chains of relationships. Each of the dimension tables has a direct relationship with the fact table (primary key to foreign key).

- The same data can be modeled in many different ways using relational modeling. Normal data modeling is quite flexible.

  The star schema has a rigid structure. It must be rigid because the tables, relationships, and fields in a star schema all have a particular mapping to the multidimensional structure of an OLAP cube.

- One of the goals of relational modeling is to conform to the rules of normalization. In a normalized database, each data value is stored only once.

  Star schemas are radically denormalized. The dimension tables have a high number of repeated values in their fields.

- Standard relational models are optimized for On Line Transaction Processing. OLTP needs the ability to efficiently update data. This is provided in a normalized database that has each value stored only once.

  Star schemas are optimized for reporting, OLAP, and data mining. Efficient data retrieval requires a minimum number of joins. This is provided with the simple structure of relationships in a star schema, where each dimension table is only a single join away from the fact table.

The rules for multidimensional modeling are different because the goals are different.

The goal of standard relational modeling is to provide a database that is optimized for efficient data modification. The goal of multidimensional modeling is to provide a database optimized for data retrieval.

The Fact Table

The fact table is the heart of the star schema. This one table usually contains 90% to 99.9% of the space used by the entire star because it holds the records of the individual events that are stored in the star schema.

New records are added to fact tables daily, weekly, or hourly. You might add a new record to the Sales Fact table for each line item of each sale during the previous day.

Fact table records are never updated unless a mistake is being corrected or a schema change is being made. Fact table records are never deleted except when old records are being archived.

A fact table has the following kinds of fields:

- Measures—The fields containing the facts in the fact table. These fields are nearly always numeric.
- Dimension Keys—Foreign keys to each of the dimension tables.
- Source System Identifier—Field that identifies the source system of the record when the fact table is loaded from multiple sources.
- Source System Key—The key value that identifies the fact table record in the source system.
- Data Lineage Fields—One or more fields that identify how and when this record was transformed and loaded into the fact table.

The fact table usually does not have a separate field for a primary key. The primary key is a composite of all the foreign keys.

> **NOTE**
>
> I believe that the Source System Identifier and the Source System Key should be considered standard elements in a fact table. These fields make it possible for fact table records to be tied back to source system records. It's important to do that for auditing purposes. It also makes it possible to use the new drillthrough feature in SQL Server 2000 Analysis Services.
>
> I also believe that a typical fact table should have data lineage fields so that the transformation history of the record can be positively identified.

Choosing the Measures

Some of the fields you choose as measures in your star schema are obvious. If you want to build a star that examines sales data, you will want to include Sale Price as one of your measures, and this field will probably be evident in your source data.

After you have chosen the obvious measures for your star, you can look for others. Keep the following tips in mind for finding other fields to use as measures:

- Consider other numeric fields in the same table as the measures you have already found.
- Consider numeric fields in related tables.
- Look at combinations of numeric fields that could be used to calculate additional measures.
- Any field can be used to create a counted measure. Use the COUNT aggregate function and a GROUP BY clause in a SQL query.
- Date fields can be used as measures if they are used with MAX or MIN aggregation in your cube. Date fields can also be used to create calculated measures, such as the difference between two dates.
- Consider averages and other calculated values that are non-additive. Include all the values as facts that are needed to calculate these non-additive values.
- Consider including additional values so that semi-additive measures can be turned into calculated measures.

Choosing the Level of Summarization for the Measures

Measures can be used either with the same level of detail as in the source data or with some degree of summarization. Maintaining the greatest possible level of detail is critical in building a flexible OLAP system. Summarizing data is sometimes necessary to save storage space, but consider all the drawbacks:

- The users will not be able to drill down to the lowest level of the data.
- The connection between the star schema data and the source data is weakened. If one record in the star schema summarizes 15 records in the source data, it is almost impossible to make a direct connection back to those source records.
- The potential to browse from particular dimensions can be lost. If sales totals are aggregated in a star schema for a particular product per day, there will be no possibility of browsing along a customer dimension.
- Merging or joint querying of separate star schemas is much easier if the data is kept at the lowest level of detail. Summarized data is much more likely to lead to independent data marts that cannot be analyzed together.
- The possibilities for data mining are reduced.

Summarizing data in a star schema makes the most sense for historical data. After a few years, the detail level of data often becomes much less frequently used. Old unused data can interfere with efficient access to current data. Move the detailed historical data into an offline storage area, where it's available for occasional use. Create a summarized form of the historical data for continued online use.

A cube created with summarized historical data can be joined together with cubes based on current data. You join cubes together by creating a virtual cube. As long as two or more cubes have common dimensions, they can be joined together even if they have a different degree of summarization.

The Dimension Tables

By themselves, the facts in a fact table have little value. The dimension tables provide the variety of perspectives from which the facts become interesting.

Compared to the fact table, the dimension tables are nearly always very small. For example, there could be a Sales data mart with the following numbers of records in the tables:

- Store Dimension—One record for each store in this chain—14 records.
- Promotion Dimension—One record for each different type of promotion—45 records.
- Time Dimension—One record for each day over a two-year period—730 records.
- Employee Dimension—One record for each employee—300 records.
- Product Dimension—One record for each product—31,000 records.
- Customer Dimension—One record for each customer—125,000 records.

- Combined total for all of these dimension records—157,089 records.
- Sales Fact Table—One record for each line item of each sale over a two-year period—60,000,000 records.

While the fact table always has more records being added to it, the dimension tables are relatively stable. Some of them, like the time dimension, are created and then rarely changed. Others, such as the employee and customer dimension, are slowly growing.

One of the most important goals of star schema design is to minimize or eliminate the need for updating dimension tables.

Dimension tables have the following kinds of fields:

- Primary Key—The field that uniquely identifies each record and also joins the dimension table to the fact table.
- Level Members—Fields that hold the members for the levels of each of the hierarchies in the dimension.
- Attributes—Fields that contain business information about a record but are not used as levels in a hierarchy.
- Subordinate Dimension Keys—Foreign key fields to the current related record in subordinate dimension tables.
- Source System Identifier—Field that identifies the source system of the dimension record when the dimension table is loaded from multiple sources.
- Source System Key—The key value that identifies the dimension table record in the source system.
- Data Lineage Fields—One or more fields that identify how and when this record was transformed and loaded into the dimension table.

The Primary Key in a Dimension Table

The primary key of a dimension table should be a single field with an integer data type.

> **TIP**
>
> Smallint (2-byte signed) or tinyint (1-byte unsigned) fields are often adequate for the dimension table primary keys. Generally, you will not be concerned about the size of your dimension tables, but using these smaller values can significantly reduce the size of the fact tables, which can become very large. Smaller key fields also make indexes work more efficiently. But don't use smallint or tinyint unless you are absolutely certain that it will be adequate now and in the future.

Levels of the Dimension Hierarchy

The levels of the dimension hierarchy are modeled in the star schema with individual fields in the dimension tables. The names of these fields can be mapped to the levels of the dimension's hierarchies. The data values in these fields are the members of the levels in the hierarchies of a dimension.

Table 4.1 shows what data looks like in the hierarchy fields of a customer dimension table. This example is taken from the FoodMart 2000 sample database. Country, State Province, City, and Name are levels of the one hierarchy in the Customer dimension. USA, CA, Altadena, and Susan Wilson are all examples of members. Arcadia is one of the members of the City level in the single hierarchy of the Customer dimension. Note all the repeated values in the fields at the higher levels of the hierarchy.

TABLE 4.1 Sample Data in the Product Dimension

Country	State Province	City	Name
USA	CA	Altadena	Susan Wilson
USA	CA	Altadena	Michael Winningham
USA	CA	Altadena	Daniel Wolter
USA	CA	Altadena	Velma Wright
USA	CA	Altadena	Gail Xu
USA	CA	Arcadia	Christine Abernathy
USA	CA	Arcadia	Roberta Amidei
USA	CA	Arcadia	Van Armstrong

One dimension table can have more than one dimension hierarchy stored in it. Dimensions often are viewed from a variety of different perspectives. Rather than choose one hierarchy over another, it is usually best to include multiple hierarchies. The fields containing the levels of multiple hierarchies in a dimension can be distinguished by using compound names such as Sales District, Marketing District, Sales Region, and Marketing Region.

Attributes of the Dimension

Attribute fields give additional information about the members of a dimension. These fields are not part of the hierarchical structure of a dimension.

The attributes in a product dimension could include fields such as Size, Weight, Package Type, Color, Units Per Case, Height, and Width. Attributes most often use one of the string data types, but they can also use numeric, datetime, or Boolean data types.

Attributes usually apply to members at the lowest level of the dimension, but they can be used at higher levels. For example, if there is a geographic dimension where District is one of the levels, District Population could be included as an attribute for that level of the dimension.

Rich, detailed attributes add value to the star schema. Each attribute provides a new perspective from which the cube can be browsed.

Here are some of the attribute fields in the Customer dimension of the FoodMart 2000 sample database:

- Total Children
- Number Children at Home
- Marital Status
- Education
- Yearly Income
- Occupation
- Member Card
- Gender

The Time Dimension

Almost every star schema has a time dimension. By definition, data warehouse information is gathered with respect to particular periods of time. The data reflects the state of reality at various times in history.

A time dimension often has more than one hierarchy built in to it because time can be aggregated in a variety of ways. The lowest level of the time hierarchy varies greatly. It could be the day, the shift, the hour, or even the minute. The lower levels would be included only if there were some valid reason to query at those levels of detail.

Significant attributes for a time dimension could include the following:

- A Special Day field, which could have the names of various holidays and other days of significance for an organization.
- A Selling Season field, which could have a particular company's self-defined annual sales periods.
- Boolean fields indicating special types of days, such as Is Weekend, Is Holiday, Is School Year, Is First Day Of Month, Is Last Day Of Month, and so on.

Subordinate Dimension Keys

Subordinate dimensions are dimensions that have been split off from a primary dimension for the purpose of avoiding dimension table updates. This strategy is described in the last section of this chapter, "Avoiding Updates to Dimension Tables."

If you have a Customer dimension and a subordinate dimension called Customer Demographic, you would include a subordinate dimension key field in the Customer table. This field would hold the foreign key to the Customer Demographic record that currently describes the customer.

Loading the Star Schema

A DTS package built for a nightly data mart load could have the following elements:

1. Tasks that load data from the sources into the staging area.
2. Tasks that load and update the dimension tables.
3. A task that loads the fact table.
4. Tasks that use the data that has just been loaded—to process cubes and mining models, to generate predicted data values, and to feed information back to the operational systems.

A package that loads a data mart is shown in Figure 4.4.

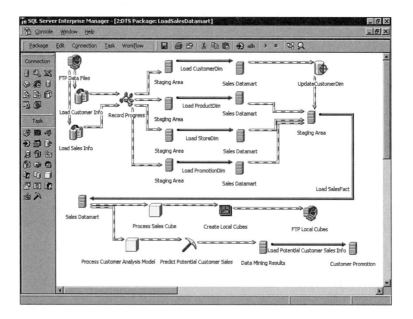

FIGURE 4.4

A DTS package that loads a data mart.

Loading Data into a Staging Area

A staging area is a set of tables that are used to store data temporarily during a data load. Staging areas are especially useful if the source data is spread out over diverse sources. After you have loaded the staging area, it's easier to handle the data because it's all in one place.

Data often needs to be cleansed as it's loaded into a data mart. Data cleansing can involve the following:

- Verifying the accuracy of the data.
- Correcting, flagging, or removing incorrect records.
- Homogenizing data that is in different formats.
- Replacing codes with meaningful data values.
- Filling in missing data from lookup tables.

Developers have different ideas about where data cleansing fits in the load process. It could be done at any of the following times:

- As the data is loaded into the staging area.
- In the staging area, with the data being moved from one table to another, or with queries that directly update the data in a table.
- As the data is moved from the staging area into the data mart.

CAUTION

I prefer not to use the first strategy. I like to copy data directly into the staging area so that it is as similar to the source data as possible. If there is some question about the data values, I can examine the data in the staging area as if it's the same as the source data.

In complex data cleansing situations, I cleanse it in steps in the staging area.

I prefer to do all the data cleansing as the data is moved from the staging area into the data mart. I like to change the data in just one step so that everything that happens to the data can be examined by looking at the one step.

You can use the following DTS tasks to load data into a staging area:

- The FTP task to retrieve remote text files.
- The Bulk Insert task to load text files into SQL Server.
- The Parallel Data Pump task for hierarchical rowsets.

- The Execute SQL task when the data is being moved from one relational database to another.

- The Transform Data task, for situations that require data cleansing or when none of the other tasks are appropriate.

Loading the Dimension Tables

The dimension tables have to be loaded before the fact tables because there might be new dimension records that need to have key values assigned before they can be referenced in the fact table.

> **NOTE**
>
> If possible, dimension tables should be preloaded with records. This is often done with a Time dimension that has one record for each day. It could also be done for a customer demographic dimension that has a limited number of combinations of possible values.

It's easier and more efficient if your source systems can give you the new records for the dimension tables. It's sometimes possible to generate a list of new products or new customers, for example.

In many situations, you have to compare the data currently in your dimension table with the data in the source to determine which of the records are new. You can do this by searching for NULL values on the inner table of an outer join. The outer join gives you all the fields from the source table, with the matching records from the dimension table. You search for NULL values in the dimension table, which will limit the results to the new records that need to be added to the dimension.

I prefer to include a field in all my dimension tables that specifies the source system and one or more fields that contain the key values for the records in the source system. If I have these fields in my dimension table, it's simple to write a query that will retrieve all the new dimension records, using the following pattern:

```
SELECT src.ProductFamily,
       src.ProductName,
       src.ProductID,
       3 As SourceSystemID
FROM Products src
    LEFT OUTER JOIN dimProduct dim
        ON src.ProductID = dim.ProductID
            AND dim.SourceSystemID = 3
WHERE dim.ProductID IS NULL
```

> **TIP**
>
> It's important to include a check for the correct SourceSystemID in the join clause. If the same ProductID is used in different systems for different products, this query will ensure that both of those records will be entered into the dimension table.

The query that retrieves the new records for the dimension table can be used as the source query for a Transform Data task. It could also be used in an Execute SQL task as a part of an `INSERT INTO` command:

```
INSERT INTO dimProductID
        (
        ProductFamily,
        ProductName,
        ProductID,
        SourceystemID
        )
SELECT  src.ProductFamily,
        src.ProductName,
        src.ProductID,
        3 As SourceSystemID
FROM Products src
    LEFT OUTER JOIN dimProduct dim
        ON src.ProductID = dim.ProductID
            AND dim.SourceSystemID = 3
WHERE dim.ProductID IS NULL
```

There can be many more complications. You may also want to do one or more of the following:

- Add joins to lookup tables to fill in missing values or homogenize inconsistent data.
- Cleanse the data by writing transformation scripts.
- Create a natural key field in situations where there is no reliable source key. A natural key is a concatenation of all the fields in a record that are needed to guarantee unique records.
- Determine whether or not a record is new by using a complex algorithm in a transformation script.

There are a couple of possibilities for storing the data lineage:

- You can use the built-in DTS lineage variables. These variables are described in Chapter 29, "Integrating DTS with Meta Data Services."
- You can use a foreign key that references a lineage table, where the table stores all the needed data lineage information. This solution would normally take up less space.

Updating the Subordinate Dimension Keys

My strategy for data mart design avoids the updating of dimension tables except for one type of field—the subordinate dimension keys. You update these keys after all the dimensions have been loaded, but before the fact table is loaded.

For example, if the import contains information about customers who have new addresses, the CurrentAddressKey field in the Customer dimension table would have to be updated to the appropriate value for the new address. The CustomerAddress dimension would have the appropriate source key fields to join to the source record so that the correct key value could be found. The Customer dimension would have the appropriate source key fields to join to the source record so that the proper customer could be identified. A data modification Lookup query or a Data Driven Query task could be used to perform the update.

Loading the Fact Table

After the dimension tables have all been loaded and updated, the fact table is loaded.

The query used in the fact table load usually involves a join between the source data table and all of the primary (but not the subordinate) dimension tables. The values for the measures and the source key fields are filled from fields in the source table. The values for the dimension keys are filled with the Primary Keys and the subordinate dimension keys in the dimension tables.

If you had a star schema with four dimension tables, one of which was a subordinate dimension, the fact table query could look like this:

```
SELECT  dimP.ProductKey,
        dimC.CustomerKey,
        dimC.CurrentAddressKey,
        dimT.TimeKey,
        src.SalesID,
        3 As SourceSystemID
        src.SalesCount,
        src.SalesAmount
FROM Sales src
    INNER JOIN dimProduct dimP
```

```
    ON src.ProductID = dimP.ProductID
        AND dim.SourceSystemID = 3
INNER JOIN dimCustomer dimC
    ON src.CustomerID = dimC.CustomerID
        AND dim.SourceSystemID = 3
INNER JOIN dimTime dimT
    ON dimT.TheDate = src.SalesDate
        AND dim.SourceSystemID = 3
```

As with loading the dimension tables, this query can be used as the source query for a transformation task or with an INSERT INTO statement in an Execute SQL task.

It's often easier to identify the new fact table records than the new dimension table records in the source data. Fact table records often come from data that is handled in batches or can be identified by a particular date.

As with dimension table records, though, sometimes filtering can't help you determine which records are new and which have been already entered into a fact table. In those situations, you can use an outer join with a search for the null values on the inner table. That outer join could significantly hurt performance if your source data tables and your fact table are large.

There is an alternative strategy for loading a fact table when there are too many large tables involved in the load. Even though this alternative involves more steps, it can be quicker when the database server does not have adequate memory:

1. Modify the fact table's primary source table in the data staging area by adding fields for all of the dimension keys that are in the fact table.
2. Create a series of Execute SQL or Transform Data tasks, each of which updates the source table by inserting the proper dimension key value. Each of these tasks will have a query that joins from the source table to one of the dimension tables.
3. After the record has been updated with all the keys, insert the record into the fact table without joining to any of the dimension tables. If you need to do an outer join between the fact table and the source table, you do it in this step.

Using the Data

After the star schema is loaded, the DTS package can continue with tasks that make use of the new data:

- You can use the Analysis Services Processing task to process your cubes and your mining models so that the new data is reflected in these analytical tools.
- You can use the Data Mining Prediction Query task with the new data to predict significant business information, such as which additional product you could most likely sell to the new customers you have just loaded into your data mart.

- Local cube files and reports could be created and emailed or sent by FTP to the appropriate individuals.

- The output of the prediction query could be used to update information in the OLTP system.

Avoiding Updates to Dimension Tables

I believe that one of the most significant design goals in setting up a star schema is avoiding updates to dimension tables.

Many people have described three options for handling changes to records in dimension tables:

1. Change the record.
2. Add a new record with the new values.
3. Add new fields so that a single record can have both the old and new values.

Each of these options is of value in limited situations, but none of them is adequate for normal changes in dimension records.

Consider the simple problem of a customer moving from Minneapolis to St. Paul. Assume that, as with the FoodMart 2000 sample database, you have been using the customer's address information as the single hierarchy of the Customer dimension. Here are the problems with each of the strategies for changing dimensions:

- If you change the Customer dimension record to reflect the new address, you will invalidate historical browsing of the information. If the customer bought something last year, that purchase should be viewed with purchases made by people in Minneapolis, but it will now appear as if a person living in St. Paul made the purchase.

- If you add a new record, you will take care of the first problem, but then you won't be able to easily connect the identities of your customers across a time period. If you query your data mart for your best customers in the past year, the moving customers will not be treated fairly because their purchases will be split between the two separate records. You can work around this problem in Analysis Services by using calculated sets, but in my opinion, the administrative problem in implementing the workaround is too great.

- The worst solution is to add new fields to keep track of new addresses and old addresses. The data structure of the cube would become far too complex—and people are going to keep on moving. The only time it's practical to add new fields to track dimension change is when there is a massive one-time change, such as a realignment of sales regions.

The only effective way to handle changing dimensions is to avoid them. You can avoid the need to change dimensions by splitting off potentially changing fields into subordinate dimensions.

Subordinate dimensions are used for business analysis like any other dimension. Each subordinate dimension has a key value in the fact table, just like a regular dimension.

The difference between subordinate and regular dimensions is in how they are used to load the fact table. The fact table's dimension keys to subordinate dimensions are loaded from the regular dimension that is related to that subordinate dimension.

The customer dimension provides one of the best illustrations of this strategy. A customer dimension could have several subordinate dimensions:

- CustomerLocation—Information about the country, region, state, and city where a customer lives.
- CustomerAge—The customer's age.
- CustomerLongevity—The number of years and months since the customer's first purchase.
- CustomerValue—A classification of the customer based on how valuable that customer is to the company.
- CustomerCategory—The demographic category that describes the customer.

The primary customer dimension could be called CustomerIdentity to distinguish it from all the subordinate dimension tables.

The CustomerIdentity dimension would have the following fields:

- CustomerIdentityKey
- CurrentCustomerLocationKey
- BirthDate
- FirstPurchaseDate
- CurrentCustomerValueKey
- CurrentCustomerCategoryKey
- CustomerSourceID
- SourceSystemID
- LineageKey

The portion of a star schema containing the customer dimension tables is shown in Figure 4.5.

When loading the fact table, the CustomerIdentityKey, CurrentCustomerLocationKey, CurrentCustomerValueKey, and CurrentCustomerCategoryKey fields would be used to fill the dimension key values.

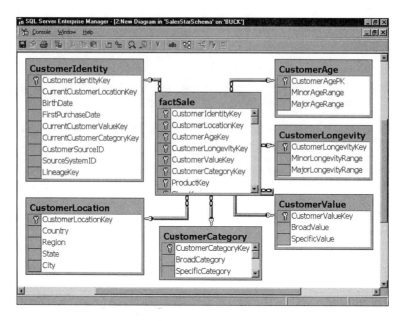

FIGURE 4.5

The customer dimension tables in a star schema.

I recommend using a Primary Key for the CustomerAge and CustomerLongevity tables that represents the actual length of time in years or months. You can then load the fact table by using the DATEDIFF function with the BirthDate and FirstPurchaseDate fields in the CustomerIdentity table.

The data in a CustomerAge table is shown in Table 4.2. The actual age is used for the Primary Key, so the dimension key value to be entered into the fact table is always DATEDIFF('y', PurchaseDate, BirthDate). A tinyint field can be used for this key. The CustomerLongevityKey would probably use the number of months as the primary key value.

TABLE 4.2   Sample Data for a CustomerAge Table

AgePK	MinorAgeRange	MajorAgeRange
0	0-4	0-17
1	0-4	0-17
2	0-4	0-17
3	0-4	0-17
4	0-4	0-17
5	5-9	0-17

TABLE 4.2 Continued

AgePK	MinorAgeRange	MajorAgeRange
6	5-9	0-17
7	5-9	0-17
8	5-9	0-17
9	5-9	0-17
10	10-14	0-17
11	10-14	0-17
12	10-14	0-17
13	10-14	0-17
14	10-14	0-17
15	15-17	0-17
16	15-17	0-17
17	15-17	0-17
18	18-20	18-24

You can find the current description of a customer by joining the CustomerIdentity dimension to its subordinate dimensions. Whenever the customer makes a purchase, the current value of all the customer characteristics is entered into the fact table. If you examine the customer's purchases over a period of time, they will all be properly aggregated together. If you analyze the customers by any of the subordinate dimensions, the value in effect at the time of the purchase will always appear in the data.

NOTE

There is one obvious drawback to the strategy of using subordinate dimensions—there get to be a lot of dimensions!

Analysis Services in SQL Server 2000 can handle up to 128 dimensions in a cube. If you want to do business analysis on a particular dimension, the key business need is to see that the analysis can be done accurately.

The risk in adding more dimensions is that you increase the time required for processing the cubes. You have to judge whether you have adequate time for cube processing based on available hardware, the amount of data in the cubes, the amount of time available for processing, your strategy in designing aggregations, and your strategy in choosing processing options.

Storage space can be conserved by proper use of smallint and tinyint fields.

Here is what you have to do to create subordinate dimensions:

1. Identify all the fields in a dimension that could possibly change.

2. Divide these potentially changing fields into those that are going to be used for business analysis and those that are not.

3. Choose and implement one of the strategies for the fields that are not going to be used for business analysis.

4. Divide the fields being used for business analysis into logical groupings to create subordinate dimensions. Values based on dates, such as birth dates, often work best in their own dimension. Values that are part of a common hierarchy should be placed in the same dimension.

5. It's all right if the original dimension has all of its hierarchy and attribute fields removed. The original dimension still has value in TOP COUNT, BOTTOM COUNT, and DISTINCT COUNT analysis.

6. Add the subordinate key fields in the original dimension to hold the current value for the record in each of the subordinate dimensions.

7. Add dimension keys for all the subordinate dimensions into the fact table.

8. Modify the import process to update the subordinate keys in the dimension tables when necessary and to load all the subordinate keys into the fact table.

You have three options for fields that are not going to be used for business analysis. I prefer the third option if it is practical in that particular information system. All of these options provide full flexibility for business analysis, though:

1. You can leave them in the primary dimension table and change them whenever you want.

2. You can move them into a separate information table that has a one-to-one relationship with the dimension table. This information table is not really a part of the star schema.

3. You can eliminate them from the data mart and retrieve that information by joining on the key value to the source system.

Conclusion

DTS is a great tool for loading a data mart. This chapter has given you some ideas about what you need to do to accomplish that task.

The next chapters discuss the details of setting up DTS connections and the process of creating transformation tasks.

DTS Connections and the Data Transformation Tasks

IN THIS PART

DTS Connections

IN THIS CHAPTER

This chapter discusses data connections. You can use DTS to connect to a variety of different database systems and file-based data storage systems. These connections are used as the source and the destination of transformations. They are needed for five of the built-in DTS tasks:

- Transform Data task
- Data Driven Query task
- Parallel Data Pump task
- Bulk Insert task
- Execute SQL task

A unique ID number identifies each connection within the DTS Package. The connection's ID property is used to tie particular connections together with particular tasks. This ID number is automatically assigned when a connection is created in the DTS Designer. When a connection is selected for use with a task, this number is also automatically associated with that task.

Connections can be made to any data source that has an OLE DB provider available through DTS, including database systems that have ODBC drivers. Although not all OLE DB providers are available through DTS, most important providers are included. You can connect using some OLE DB providers through a Microsoft Data Link connection even when you can't connect to those OLE DB providers directly. The definition of a connection object varies depending on the type of connection that is being made.

OLE DB providers are supplied with SQL Server 2000 for these data sources:

- Microsoft SQL Server
- Microsoft Access 2000
- Microsoft Excel 2000 worksheets
- HTML files
- Text files
- Oracle
- DB2
- Dbase 5
- Paradox
- Other databases that have ODBC drivers available

Creating DTS Connections

Data connections are created in the DTS Designer with the following procedure:

1. Click or drag one of the data source icons on the data connection palette, choose one of the items on the Data menu, or right-click the design sheet and choose Add Data Connection. I have found that clicking and dragging is the best option when you have many connections in a package, because it lets you place the icon where you want it on the design sheet. If you use one of the other options, the icon will be placed in the upper-left corner of the sheet and everything else will be moved down and to the right.

2. Use the option buttons to indicate whether you want to create a new connection or use an existing connection. If you choose an existing connection, you don't have to do anything else. A new icon on the design sheet is created for a connection that already exists. Creating new icons for a connection can make the workflow lines in a package diagram easier to read, as shown in Figure 5.1.

3. Choose the appropriate data source.

4. Provide the additional information that is needed for the particular type of connection being created, as shown in Figure 5.2. For instance, the information needed to access a text file is different from what is needed to access an Oracle database.

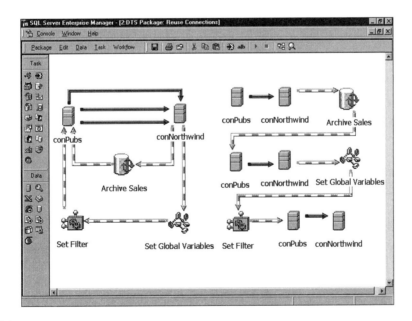

FIGURE 5.1

You can make a package easier to read by making copies of connections that are used for several purposes. The tasks on the right use copies of connections to show the ordering of the tasks.

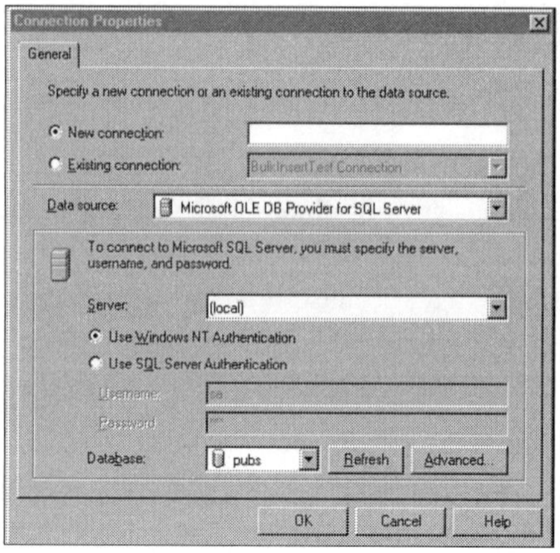

FIGURE 5.2
The Connection Properties dialog displays different information for different OLE DB Providers. This is the dialog for the OLE DB provider for SQL Server.

The DTS Import/Export Wizard creates connections when you use it to transfer data. You usually don't have to modify the connections as they are created by the wizard.

You can create connections with Visual Basic. Connections are created with the `Connection` object for SQL Server 7.0 connections and the `Connection2` object for SQL Server 2000 connections. The following sections will show you how to create connections in code.

DTS Connection Properties

The `Connection` object contains 12 read/write properties, 5 read-only properties, and 1 property that points to a collection of more detailed OLEDB properties, as shown with Disconnected Edit in Figure 5.3. The `Connection2` object used in SQL Server 2000 inherits all the properties of the `Connection` object and adds one new property—`UDLPath`. I will first discuss the properties that identify a DTS connection and then the properties that determine access to the data source.

Properties That Identify a DTS Connection

Connections are associated with the tasks, lookups, and queries that use them through the connection's `ID` property. The `ID` is assigned automatically when you create connections and tasks in the Package Designer. When you create connections and other objects in code, you use the `ID` property to programmatically create the same associations.

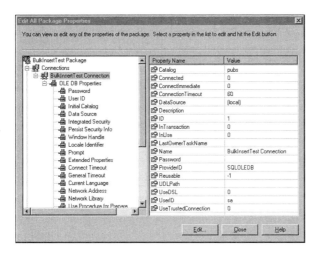

FIGURE 5.3

The Connection2 *object has 18 properties and a collection of OLE DB properties.*

When you want to reference an existing connection, use the connection's Name property. You select the connection from all the members of the Connections collection, as in this VBScript code:

```
Dim pkg, con
Set pkg = DTSGlobalVariables.Parent 'Get an object reference
Set con = pkg.Connections("Sales Connection")
```

You can also reference a connection by its ordinal number, but that reference will be unreliable:

```
Dim pkg, con
Set pkg = DTSGlobalVariables.Parent 'Get an object reference
Set con = pkg.Connections(3) 'Don't do this!
```

The ordinal number of a connection in the Connections collection is not the same as the connection's ID property. Every time a connection is modified using the DTS Designer, the modified connection is moved to the end of the Connections collection and all the other Connections have their ordinal number moved up. The connection's ID property is never reassigned. It always maintains the link between a connection and the objects that use the connection.

ID

The connection's ID property has an integer data type. The ID is assigned to the following properties of other DTS objects to associate the connection with those objects:

- The `SourceConnectionID` of the Transform Data task, Data Driven Query task, and Parallel Data Pump task.
- The `DestinationConnectionID` of the Transform Data task, Data Driven Query task, and Parallel Data Pump task.
- The `ConnectionID` of the Bulk Insert task.
- The `ConnectionID` of the Execute SQL task.
- The `ConnectionID` of the `Lookup` object.
- The `SourceQueryConnectionID` property of the `DynamicPropertiesTaskAssignment` object, used in the Dynamic Properties task.

The `ID` property is assigned automatically when a connection is created with the Package Designer, but it must be manually assigned when you're creating connections in code. You must ensure that a unique value is assigned to it. One way of doing this is to use the following VBScript function, which returns a number that's one greater than the highest ID value currently being used:

```
Function fctNextConnectionID()

dim pkg, con
dim lMaxConnectionID

lMaxConnectionID = 0
set pkg = DTSGlobalVariables.Parent

for each con in pkg.Connections
    if con.ID > lMaxConnectionID  then
      lMaxConnectionID = con.ID
    end if
next

fctNextConnectionID = lMaxConnectionID + 1

End Function
```

Name

When you create a new connection, you have the chance to give it a name in the New Connection box. If you don't specify a name, the name will be the same as the Data Source.

After creating a connection, you cannot change the `Name` property in the Connection Properties dialog. If you type in a new name, the DTS Designer will create a new connection with a different ID. If tasks were using the original connection, they'll still be using it and not the connection that was just made.

The ID property is an example of a property that could not be changed in the DTS Package Designer interface with SQL Server 7.0, but you can now change it in SQL Server 2000 by using Disconnected Edit. I've tried it and it works—as long as I also remember to change the references to the ID in all the objects that are using it. Disconnected Edit even allows me to change the value to an ID that is already being used, which causes very strange behavior.

Don't change values in Disconnected Edit unless you have a clear reason for doing so and you understand all the implications of that action. Changing the ID property is not a good way to use this tool.

You can use Disconnected Edit or code to change the Name property. After you change the Name property, be sure to also change the code where you have referenced the connection by its name.

After you change the connection name with Disconnected Edit, you'll find that the old name still shows up under the connection icon in the DTS Designer. To make the new name appear, open the Connection Properties dialog and choose OK.

ProviderID

The ProviderID refers to the OLE DB Provider that the connection is using. It is a read-only property. In the Connection Properties dialog, you can change the OLE DB Provider from the Data Source list. The DTS Designer will drop the connection and re-create it with the new provider, while keeping the connection's ID and all its other properties the same. You cannot change the ProviderID in Disconnected Edit, with the Dynamic Properties task, or with code.

Some examples of Provider ID's are

- SQLOLEDB—Microsoft OLE DB Provider for SQL Server
- Microsoft.Jet.OLEDB.4.0—Microsoft Jet 4.0 OLE DB Provider
- DTSPackageDSO—Microsoft OLE DB Provider for DTS Packages
- MSOLAP—Microsoft OLE DB Provider for OLAP Services

You can list the objects in the `OLEDBProviderInfos` collection of the DTS `Application` object to generate a list of the providers available to DTS. Here's how to do that with VBScript:

```
Function Main()

dim app, OLEDBProv
set app = createobject("DTS.Application")

for each  OLEDBProv in app.OLEDBProviderInfos
    msgbox OLEDBProv.Name & "    " & OLEDBProv.Description
next

    Main = DTSTaskExecResult_Success
End Function
```

Properties That Determine Access to the Data Source

Here are the properties that determine access to the data source. There are three different ways to set these properties: with the properties of the connection, through the `ConnectionProperties` property, and with a Data Link file.

Properties of the Connection Object

You can determine access to a data source by setting the following properties of the connection:

- `UseTrustedConnection`—If `True`, the `UserID` and `Password` are not needed.
- `UserID`—The name used when making a connection.
- `Password`—The password used when making a connection.
- `Catalog`—The database name.
- `DataSource`—The server name.

> **NOTE**
>
> When you're looking at the Connection Properties dialog, the Data Source is the label of the box that shows the Provider, and the Server box shows the Server. However, when you use the DataSource property in Disconnected Edit, Dynamic Properties, or code, DataSource refers to the server name.

Here's a piece of Visual Basic code that sets these properties:

```
Dim con As New DTS.Connection
con.UseTrustedConnection = True
```

```
'con.UserID = "sa"              'Set UserID and Password When Not
'con.Password = ""              'TrustedConnection
con.Catalog = "Northwind"
con.DataSource = "SQLServer1"
```

The *ConnectionProperties* Property and the *OLEDBProperties* Collection

Each connection contains one collection, OLEDBProperties. This collection contains different values for each specific OLE DB provider. Some of these values can be set in the Connection Properties dialog and the Advanced Connection Properties dialog. You can find the complete list of OLEDBProperties when you're using Disconnected Edit. You can reference the OLEDBProperties values in code through the connection's ConnectionProperties property. The following code is equivalent to the code in the section above:

```
Dim con As New DTS.Connection
con.ConnectionProperties("Integrated Security") = "SSPI"
'con.ConnectionProperties("UserID") = "sa"
'con.ConnectionProperties("Password") = ""
con.ConnectionProperties("Initial Catalog") = "Northwind"
con.ConnectionProperties("Data Source") = "SQLServer1"
```

You can choose either way to set the properties of your connections. The corresponding properties will be automatically set by DTS. For example, if you set the "Integrated Security" OLE DB Property to "SSPI", DTS will automatically set the connection's UseTrustedConnection property to True.

CAUTION

Although you can change other OLE DB properties both on the Advanced tab of the Connection Properties dialog and in Disconnected Edit, it is usually not necessary to do so. Changes to some of these properties can cause unpredictable problems for your connections.

UDLPath and *UseDSL*

The UDLPath and UseDSL properties determine Microsoft Data Link characteristics of the data connection. UseDSL is a Boolean value that determines whether or not the data connection is created as a Microsoft Data Link. The UDLPath property sets a reference to the filename of the Data Link file that is used to set the connection's properties.

A Data Link connection is similar to a regular connection. You have to set all the other properties, including the ProviderID. The format looks different because you're setting the properties within the context of a Data Link. The primary difference in functionality is the ability to store, modify, and read the connection properties in a file.

There are three different ways you can set up a Data Link connection:

- The connection properties are read from a Data Link file every time the connection is opened. If the file is changed, the connection will be changed.

- The connection properties are read from a Data Link file when the connection is created, but the relationship to that file is not maintained. If the file is changed after the connection is created, there is no effect on the connection.

- The connection properties are set without using a Data Link file.

The UseDSL property is set to True whenever you select Microsoft Data Link in the Data Source box on the Connection Properties dialog. You can also change whether or not a connection is a Microsoft Data Link by editing this property in Disconnected Edit.

When you specify a value for the UDLPath property, new with the Connection2 object in SQL Server 2000, a persistent connection is made to the Data Link file. In the Connection Properties dialog for Data Link connections (see Figure 5.4) you set this property by choosing a value for the UDL filename and selecting the checkbox labeled Always read properties from UDL file. If you choose a Data Link file but do not select the checkbox, that Data Link file will be used to set the properties of the Data Link connection, but the connection to the file will not be maintained. The UDLPath property will remain an empty string.

FIGURE 5.4
You can choose a UDLPath and make it persistent in the Connection Properties dialog.

When you use a persistent connection to a Data Link file, you can change server, database, security information, the OLE DB provider, and other OLE DB properties at runtime without modifying the DTS Package at all. Change the Data Link file and the connection will have the changed values the next time it is opened. This new capability in SQL Server 2000 makes it easier to deploy DTS packages into different environments.

UDL Files

You can create a Data Link file in Windows Explorer by doing the following:

1. Create a new text file. Do not type any text into it.

2. Change the extension of the file to .udl.

3. Double-click on the file. The Data Link Properties dialog will open, as shown in Figure 5.5. You can set the properties of the Data Link, choosing an OLE DB provider, setting connection information, and selecting other properties.

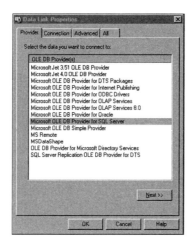

FIGURE 5.5
The Data Link Properties dialog allows you to set the properties of a UDL file.

After you have created a Data Link file, you can reference it in the DTS Connection Properties dialog for a Data Link connection.

Here's an example of the content of a Data Link file:

```
[oledb]
; Everything after this line is an OLE DB initstring
Provider=SQLOLEDB.1;Integrated Security=SSPI;Persist Security Info=False;
Initial Catalog=pubs;Data Source=INSTRUCTOR
```

Other Properties

There are several other properties for the connection object.

Read-Only Properties

These properties can be read while a package is executing to determine the current state of the connection:

- Connected—Whether or not the connection is currently connected. Many properties of a connection cannot be changed while it is connected.

- InUse—Whether or not a task is currently using the connection. A connection can be used by only one task at a time.

- InTransaction—If there's a current transaction, whether or not the connection is included in that transaction.

- LastOwnerTaskName—The name of the last task to use the connection.

- Parent—The Connections collection is always the parent of the connection.

Description

The default value of the Description property is an empty string. You cannot edit the Description in the Connection Properties dialog. You have to use Disconnected Edit, the Dynamic Properties Task, or code.

The value assigned to the connection's Description property is not very persistent. The value is returned to an empty string every time the Connection Properties dialog is closed or when the package is saved.

> **Note**
>
> The Package Designer displays labels for tasks and connections. The label displayed for a task is the value of the Description property. The label displayed for a connection is the Name property. The connection's Description doesn't appear to be used for anything.

ConnectImmediate

If the ConnectImmediate property is set to True, the connection will be opened as soon as the package execution begins. When it's set to False, the connection is first opened when a task that uses the connection runs. This property can be changed with code or in Disconnected Edit.

Books Online states that the default value for ConnectImmediate is False. In my experience, the default value is True for SQL Server connections and False for text file connections. I think it's wise to know for sure what the value is in a particular situation.

ConnectionTimeout

The ConnectionTimeout property sets the number of seconds that the connection will wait while being opened. The default is 60 seconds. After that time, an error will be generated.

Reusable

The Reusable property specifies whether or not multiple steps can use that one connection. It defaults to True.

CAUTION

I have changed the Reusable property to False, both using code and using Disconnected Edit. This property prevents the connection from being reused, but it does not prevent that connection from showing up in the list of connections in the Connection Properties dialog.

Setting and Reading Connection Properties

Here is a piece of VBScript code that displays the read-only properties and sets several of the read/write properties for the Connection object:

```
Option Explicit

Function Main()

Dim pkg, con

set pkg = DTSGlobalVariables.Parent
set con = pkg.Connections("Northwind Connection")

With con

    'Read the read-only properties
    msgbox "LastOwnerTaskName - " & .LastOwnerTaskName
```

```
    msgbox "InUse - " & CStr(.InUse)
    msgbox "InTransaction - " & Cstr(.InTransaction)
    msgbox "Connected - " & CStr(.Connected)
    .ConnectionTimeout = 30
    .UseDSL = 1
    .ConnectImmediate = 1
    .Description ="Changes Made"
End With

    Main = DTSTaskExecResult_Success
End Function
```

Creating Connections for Different OLE DB Providers

When you choose a different provider in the Connection Properties dialog, you are presented with the choices appropriate for that type of connection.

The SQL Server OLE DB Provider

Here is the additional information you need to set in the Connection Properties for SQL Server connections:

- The name of the server, which can be picked from a list.
- Whether to use Windows NT authentication or SQL Server authentication. (If you choose SQL Server authentication, a user name and a password are required.)
- The name of the database, which you can also pick from a list.

Listing 5.1 shows you how to create a new package with a single SQL Server connection in Visual Basic. It saves the package to a file. This code is on the book's CD for this chapter in a file named CreateConnection.bas.

LISTING 5.1 A VB Procedure That Creates a DTS Connection to SQL Server

```
Option Explicit

Private Sub Main()

Dim pkg As New DTS.Package2
Dim con As DTS.Connection2
```

LISTING 5.1   Continued

```
pkg.Name = "Test"
Set con = pkg.Connections.New("SQLOLEDB")

con.Name = "Northwind Connection"
con.ID = 1

'CODE OPTION #1
'Set the connection properties using properties of the Connection object
con.UseTrustedConnection = True
'con.UserID = "sa"              'Set UserID and Password When Not
'con.Password = ""             'TrustedConnection
con.Catalog = "Northwind"
con.DataSource = "SQLServer1"

'CODE OPTION #2
'Set the same properties using OLEDB Properties
con.ConnectionProperties("Integrated Security") = "SSPI"
'con.ConnectionProperties("UserID") = "sa"
'con.ConnectionProperties("Password") = ""
con.ConnectionProperties("Initial Catalog") = "Northwind"
con.ConnectionProperties("Data Source") = "SQLServer1"

pkg.Connections.Add con
Set con = Nothing

pkg.SaveToStorageFile "C:\Temp\ConnectionTest.dts"
pkg.UnInitialize
Set pkg = Nothing

End Sub
```

Text File Connections

When you create a connection for a text file, you have to choose between Text File (Desti-nation) and Text File (Source). All other providers are selected using the same icon for both destination and source. The Connection Properties dialog for a text file is shown in Figure 5.6.

The Properties button brings up the Text File Properties dialog. The dialog's choices differ depending on whether or not the connection is being used for import or for export. Figure 5.7 shows the Text File Properties dialog for a destination connection.

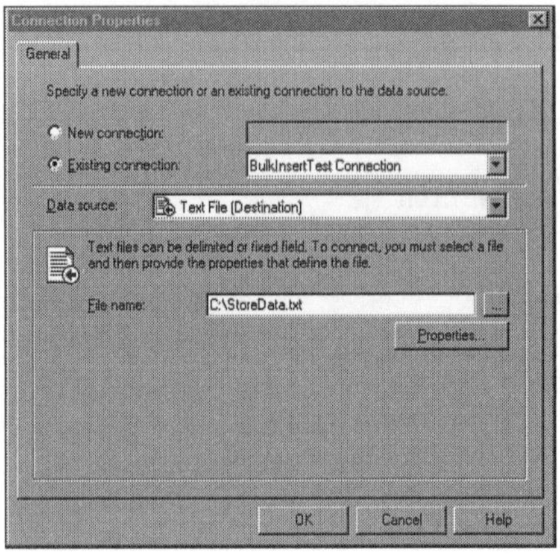

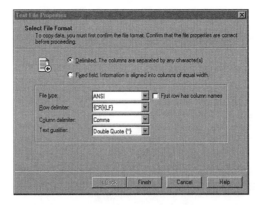

FIGURE 5.6

The Connection Properties dialog for a text file looks the same for Destination and Source text files, but the Properties button leads to different options.

FIGURE 5.7

There is only one screen for the Text File Properties dialog when it is used for a destination connection.

The choices for specifying a file format for a destination include the following:

- Whether the fields are to be separated with a specified delimiter, or if a fixed field width is going to be used.
- Whether to include the column name in the export, using the column names as the fields of the first row.
- The type of text file to be created. The available choices are ANSI, OEM, or Unicode. ANSI is the default choice.

- What character, if any, is to be used for a row delimiter.
- What character is to be used for a column delimiter.
- What character, if any, is to be used for a text qualifier.

For a source connection, there are at least two screens in the Text File Properties dialog, sometimes three. The first screen is shown in Figure 5.8.

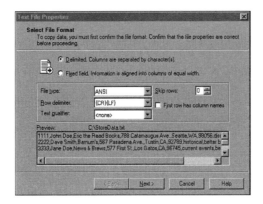

FIGURE 5.8
The first screen of the Text File Properties dialog for a source connection has most of the same options as the one for a destination connection.

Several of the source text file properties selected on this first screen are the same as the choices for the destination text file properties:

- Delimited or fixed fields.
- First row has column names.
- File type.
- Row delimiter. (The column delimiter is chosen on the last screen of the dialog.)
- Text qualifier.

In addition, there is a spin box to enter the number of rows at the top of the file that are to be skipped. A value of 9 for Skip rows means that this connection sees the 10th record in the file as the first.

The text file can be previewed in a box at the bottom of the dialog's first screen.

If this is a fixed-length file and there is no row delimiter, the second screen gives you the opportunity to specify the total length of the record. You see the contents of the file and you move a red line to divide the first and second records, as shown in Figure 5.9. Alternatively, you can specify the total length of fields in a row by entering a value in the spin box.

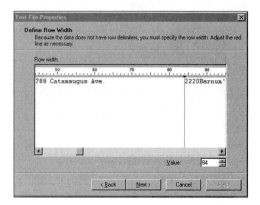

FIGURE 5.9

The second screen of the Text File Properties dialog is only used for a connection source that has fixed-length fields and no row delimiter. The purpose of the screen is to designate the width of each row.

Figure 5.10 shows the last screen of the Text File Properties dialog as it appears when fixed-length fields are used. This screen is used to set the widths of each field. The field dividing lines are created with a click and deleted with a double-click, and they can be dragged to the proper place onscreen.

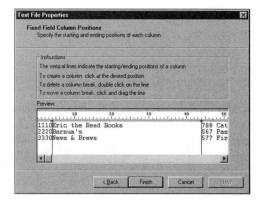

FIGURE 5.10

The last screen of the Text File Properties dialog is used to set the widths of fixed-length fields.

For text files with delimited fields, the last screen of the Text File Properties dialog shows a sample of the file and gives you an opportunity to select the correct field delimiter.

The choices you make in the Text File Properties dialog are all OLE DB Properties for the DTSFlatFile OLE DB Provider. You can view these properties in Disconnected Edit, as shown in Figure 5.11. As with other properties of the OLEDBProperties collection, you can query and modify these properties in code as members of the ConnectionProperties collection:

```
msgbox con.ConnectionProperties("Column Lengths")
con.ConnectionProperties("Column Lengths") = "35,40,4,100"
```

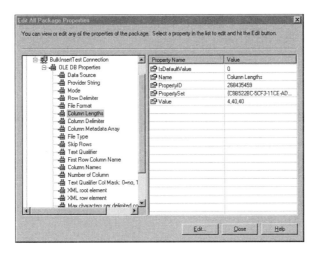

FIGURE 5.11
The OLE DB properties for a text file connection determine how that file is parsed.

The OLE DB Provider for OLAP Services

You can create a connection with an OLAP data source by selecting Microsoft OLE DB Provider for OLAP Services from the Data Source drop-down list on the Connection Properties page. Then click the Properties button, which opens the Data Link Properties page. In the Data Source box, type in the name of the server you want to use. You can then choose an OLAP database from a list.

If you want to connect to a local cube, type the filename of the .cub file into the Data Source box, as shown in Figure 5.12.

Other OLE DB Providers

The Connection Properties dialog for the OLE DB Provider for ODBC is shown in Figure 5.13. You can choose an existing User, System, or File Data Source Name (DSN), or you can create a new User or System DSN. The New button opens up the Create New Data Source Wizard.

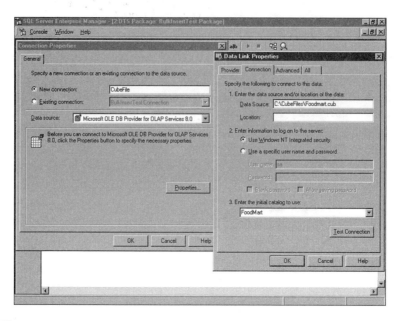

FIGURE 5.12
You can create a connection to an OLAP Services cube or, as shown here, a local cube file.

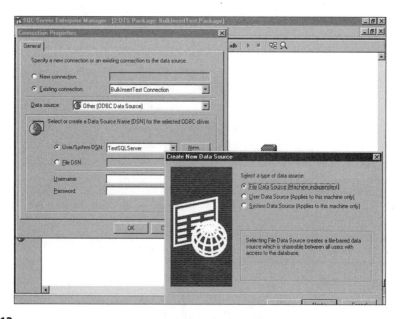

FIGURE 5.13
Choose an existing DSN or create a new one with the Connection Properties dialog for the OLE DB Provider for ODBC.

The dialog for the Oracle DB Provider is very similar to the one for SQL Server.

Microsoft Access, Microsoft Excel, dBase, and Paradox connections require a filename and security information. A Connection Properties dialog for Microsoft Access is shown in Figure 5.14.

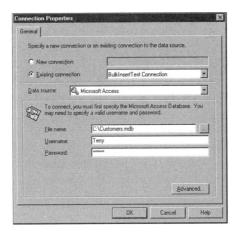

FIGURE 5.14
A Microsoft Access data connection requires a filename and appropriate security information.

Modifying Data Connections Dynamically

You can modify connections in the interface by selecting the connection's icon, modifying any of the properties in the dialog, and saving those changes.

Connections can be modified while a DTS Package is running. This allows you to simplify your code by using the same connection for several different data sources.

The following code changes the DataSource property of a text connection. It can be used within a loop to import multiple text files (discussed in Chapter 16, "Writing Scripts for an ActiveX Script Task"), or with a Workflow ActiveX Script (discussed in Chapter 24, "Steps and Precedence Constraints").

```
Option Explicit
Function Main()

Dim pkg, con

set pkg = DTSGlobalVariables.Parent
set con = pkg.Connections("Northwind Connection")
```

```
If con.Connected = 0 Then 'Must not be connected
    con.DataSource = "C:\Temp\Text1.txt"
End If

    Main = DTSTaskExecResult_Success
End Function
```

> **NOTE**
>
> If the connection is open when you attempt to change the DataSource, you will gen-
> erate an error. To close a connection, open the Workflow Properties dialog for the
> step that previously used the connection. Select Close Connection on Completion on
> the Option tab.
>
> I have occasionally used an Execute SQL task that's specifically designed to close a
> connection. Set the ConnectionID of the task to the connection that you want to
> close. Set the SQLStatement to a query that doesn't do anything, such as Select 1.
> Select the Close Connection on Completion option in the Workflow Properties dialog.
> Set Precedence Constraints so the ActiveX Script task that changes the connection
> runs upon completion of this Execute SQL task.

> **NOTE**
>
> The Connection object has two methods—AcquireConnection and
> ReleaseConnection. These methods are used when building custom tasks, as
> described in Chapter 31, "Creating a Custom Task in VB". They are not intended to be
> used in VB or VBScript code when running a package.

Performance Issues with DTS Connections

You can improve the performance of your DTS package by using connections efficiently.
Connecting to databases is time-consuming and can be a significant drain on resources. You
can optimize the use of connections in the following ways:

- One connection in a DTS package can be used for several different tasks. Or, you can
  create several separate connections to a data source, one for each time it's used for a
  task. Each connection you open will take time, but memory is taken up when a connection is left open. Each connection can be used by only one task at a time. If you want
  several tasks to run concurrently, they must use separate connections.

- You can open each connection when the execution of a package is started, or you can open each connection when it's needed. You can change this option, the `ConnectImmediate` property of the `Connection` object, with code or in Disconnected Edit.

- You can choose whether or not to close a connection when a task is finished. The default is to leave the connection open. This setting is set on the Options tab of the Workflow Properties dialog for the step associated with each task that is using a connection.

> **NOTE**
>
> You can usually achieve better performance for your DTS connections by using native OLE DB providers instead of ODBC drivers.

Chapter 30, "Programming with the DTS Object Model," will show you how to create a procedure that creates a report showing where each connection is being used. This information can help you when you are deciding whether to reuse an existing connection or create a new one.

Conclusion

Microsoft has given you a lot of control over connections. You can connect to a variety of data sources. You can set a lot of properties—more than are really necessary. If you want, you can change connections dynamically.

The rest of the chapters in this section will tell you about using these connections as part of the process of creating data transformation tasks.

The Transform Data Task

IN THIS CHAPTER

As indicated by its name, the Transform Data task is at the heart of Data Transformation Services. This task is a data pump that moves data from a data source to a data destination, giving you the opportunity to modify each record as you move it.

Three chapters of this book are devoted to the Transform Data task:

- This chapter outlines the task's basic functionality and properties.
- Chapter 7, "Writing ActiveX Scripts for a Transform Data Task," describes the use of ActiveX scripts to programmatically control data transformations. This chapter also discusses creating and using lookups.
- Chapter 9, "The Multiphase Data Pump," shows how to use the new SQL Server 2000 capability to write code for eight different events in the operation of the Data Pump.

There are also chapters devoted to the other two data transformation tasks:

- Chapter 8, "The Data Driven Query Task," describes a task that can define several output queries in the process of data transformation.
- Chapter 10, "The Parallel Data Pump Task," describes a new task that lets the data pump use hierarchical recordsets.

Additional key information relating to the Transform Data task can be found in these chapters:

- Chapter 5, "DTS Connections"
- Chapter 27, "Handling Errors in a Package and Its Transformations"
- Chapter 28, "High Performance DTS Packages"
- Chapter 32, "Creating a Custom Transformation with VC++"

> **NOTE**
>
> It's possible to get confused about the naming of the Transform Data task. Some people refer to it as the Data Pump task, reflecting the `DataPumpTask` and `DataPumpTask2` objects that implement this task. It is also called the Data Transformation task.

When to Use the Transform Data Task

I have built DTS packages that don't have any Transform Data tasks, and I have built other packages in which this task did all the movement and manipulation of the data.

The Transform Data task is one of the most versatile of all the DTS tasks. Many of the others have limitations that prevent them from being used in certain circumstances. The Transform Data task can be used with a variety of data sources and destinations, it delivers high performance, and you can manipulate data in a very precise way.

I decide whether or not to use the Transform Data task by going through a process of elimination. If another task will do the job better, I choose it. If I can't use any of the other tasks because of their limitations, I use the Transform Data task.

Consider these specialized situations where other tasks are more effective:

- If you are transferring whole databases from SQL Server 7.0/2000 to SQL Server 2000, use the Transfer Databases task.

- If you are transferring database objects (tables, views, stored procedures, and so on) from a SQL Server 7.0/2000 database to a SQL Server 7.0/2000 database, use a Transfer SQL Server Objects task.

- If you need to choose between several queries when transforming each row of data, consider using the Data Driven Query task. (But the Transform Data task in SQL Server 2000 now allows you to modify data using lookups, which removes some of the Data Driven Query task's advantage in this area.)

- If your data source is a text file, your data destination is SQL Server, you are not transforming the data as it's being imported, and you want the fastest possible speed for your data movement, use the Bulk Insert task.

- If you are moving data between tables in the same type of relational database, consider using an Execute SQL task. It will be faster than the Transform Data task, but you lose the flexibility of row-by-row processing.

- If you are moving hierarchical rowsets, take advantage of the new Parallel Data Pump task.

- If you need to move data files to another location, use the FTP task.

In all other cases, use the Transform Data task to transform your data.

TIP

When I was first learning DTS development, I used the Transform Data task a lot more than I do now.

I've realized that there are many situations where one or more Execute SQL tasks will move my data significantly faster. The Transform Data task is a high-speed data pump, but it still has to process each row of data sequentially, and the high performance of set-oriented SQL queries can often beat it.

I've also started using the Bulk Insert task more often because it delivers much better performance.

If you need the Transform Data task, use it. It gives you Rapid Application Development and excellent performance. But it's also good to be aware of the alternatives.

Creating a New Transform Data Task

You can create Transform Data tasks in the Package Designer, in the DTS Import/Export Wizard, and in code.

Using the Package Designer

You can create a new Transform Data task in the Package Designer in several different ways. I recommend the new way provided in SQL Server 2000:

1. Create two connections, one for the data source and the other for the data destination.

2. Select the Transform Data task from the task palette, the toolbar, the Task menu, or Add Task on the pop-up menu.

3. An icon will appear that contains the words "Select source connection." Move the cursor to the connection you are going to use for the source and select it.

4. The icon will change and will now have the words "Select destination connection," as shown in Figure 6.1. Click on the connection to be used for the destination. You've just created a Transform Data task.

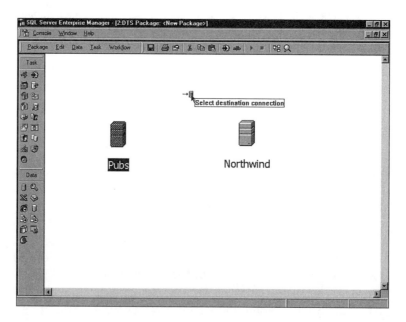

FIGURE 6.1

An icon directs you to choose a source connection and then a destination connection.

You can also create a Transform Data task by doing any of the following:

- Reverse steps 2 and 3. If you select a connection before choosing the Transform Data task, that connection will be used as the source.
- Select a connection for the source. Press and hold the Shift key while selecting the connection for the destination. Then select the Transform Data task.
- Draw a marquee around the two connections to be used for the Transform Data task. Then select the Transform Data task. The first connection included in the marquee will usually be used as the source (but not always).

Using the DTS Import/Export Wizard

If you want to create Transform Data tasks for several tables at the same time, consider using the Import/Export Wizard. If the tables have the same names in the source and the destination, those tables will be connected automatically. If any table does not exist in the destination, the wizard will also make an Execute SQL task with a CREATE TABLE statement for that table. This statement creates a destination table with the same design and structure as the source table. The wizard sets a precedence constraint so that the table is created before the Transform Data task is executed.

Using Code

The Transform Data task is implemented in SQL Server 2000 with a DataPumpTask2 object. This object inherits all the collections, properties, and methods of the SQL Server 7.0 DataPumpTask object and adds some new properties. All these collections and properties are described in this chapter. The last two sections of the chapter have code samples showing how to create a Transform Data task and all the different types of transformations.

The Description and Name of the Task

The Source tab of the Transform Data Task Properties dialog has a place to enter a description of the task. This sets the Description property of the task, which is displayed for each task in the DTS Designer and when the package is executed.

The Description property of a task is more important than the Name property—unless you want to refer to a task in code. The names of many of the tasks, including the Transform Data task, are not shown in the Package Designer interface. If you want to view or set the Name property, you have to use Disconnected Edit or code.

The most convenient way to refer to a task in code is by using its name, as shown in this sample of VBScript:

```
Dim pkg, tsk, cus

set pkg = DTSGlobalVariables.Parent
set tsk = pkg.Tasks("tskLoadSalesFact")
```

> **TIP**
>
> When I create a task using the Package Designer, I often rename it immediately using Disconnected Edit. The name has to be changed in two places—the Name property of the Task object and the TaskName object of the Step object.
>
> The default names created by the Package Designer are not very descriptive:
>
> DTSTask_DTSDataPumpTask_1
>
> DTSTask_DTSDataPumpTask_2
>
> DTSTask_DTSDataPumpTask_3
>
> The names created by the Import/Export Wizard are very descriptive, but they are long and difficult to type in code:
>
> Copy Data from dbEmployee to [SalesDataMart].[dbo].[Employee] Task
>
> Copy Data from dbCustomer to [SalesDataMart].[dbo].[Customer] Task
>
> Copy Data from dbProductInfo to [SalesDataMart].[dbo].[Product] Task
>
> I prefer task names that are short but also descriptive:
>
> tskLoadEmployee
>
> tskLoadCustomer
>
> tskLoadProduct
>
> Make sure you change the TaskName of the Step object at the same time as you change the Name of the Task object. If you don't, the task will not be executed.
>
> I don't believe there are any other risks in changing task names in Disconnected Edit, unless the existing names are referenced in code.
>
> If you aren't planning to refer to a task in code, you don't need to rename it. But if you are referencing your tasks in ActiveX Scripts or exporting your packages to VB for editing, you can make your code clearer by creating better task names.

The Source of a Transform Data Task

The Source tab of the Transform Data Task Properties dialog, shown in Figure 6.2, displays the name of the source connection. You cannot change this connection without using code or Disconnected Edit.

FIGURE 6.2
The first tab of the Transform Data Task Properties dialog displays the data source properties.

In some cases, you have the opportunity to specify which data from the source is to be used. Your choices differ depending on the type of source you are using—a text file, a relational database, or a multidimensional database.

Text File Source

If the data source is a text file, you don't have any more choices to make on this tab. The file, as it is specified in the connection, will be the source for the transformation.

> **NOTE**
>
> You cannot use binary files as the source for the Transform Data task. You have to convert them to text files first, and you cannot use any of the built-in DTS tasks to do this conversion.

SQL Table, View, or Query for a Relational Database Source

If the data source is a relational database, you can choose between using a table, a view, or a query as the source for the transformation. A list shows the names of all the tables and views.

If you elect to use a query as the transformation source, you have three options for creating the query:

- Type the query into the box on the Source tab.
- Choose the Browse button to find a file that has a SQL statement in it.
- Choose the Build Query button and design the query in the Data Transformation Services Query Designer.

There is also a Parse Query button that checks the query syntax and the validity of all the field and table names used.

> **TIP**
>
> Do as much of the data manipulation as possible in the source query of the data transformation. Consider using CASE statements or joins to lookup tables to homogenize data values. You can greatly improve performance, especially if you are able to move from ActiveX Script transformations to the faster Copy Column transformations.

The Data Transformation Services Query Designer

The Data Transformation Services Query Designer is shown in Figure 6.3. It is the same query designer that is available in the Enterprise Manager for looking at table data and for creating a view.

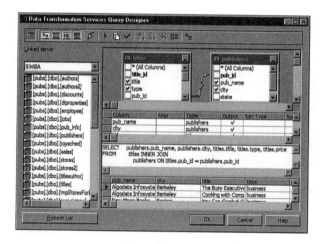

FIGURE 6.3

The Data Transformation Services Query Designer provides an interactive design environment for creating queries.

There are four panes in the Query Designer:

- The Diagram pane is shown at the top of Figure 6.3. Any changes that you make in this box are immediately reflected in the Grid and SQL panes. In the Diagram pane, you can do the following:

  Drag tables into the pane from the table list at the left.

  Join tables by dragging a field from one table to another.

  Right-click the join line to choose a dialog for setting the properties of the join.

  Select fields to include in the query output.

  Right-click a field and choose it for sorting.

  Highlight a field and pick the group by icon on the toolbar.

- The Grid pane provides a more detailed view for specifying how individual columns are used in the query. Changes in this pane are immediately reflected in the Diagram pane and the SQL pane.

- The SQL pane shows the text of the SQL statement that is being generated for this query. Changes here are not made immediately in the Diagram and Grid panes, but they are made as soon as you click any object outside the SQL pane.

- The Results pane shows the results of running the query you are designing. The effects of the changes you make in the query design are not reflected until you rerun the query by clicking the Execute button on the toolbar.

> **TIP**
>
> Right-clicking in any of the panes brings up a menu that includes the Properties dialog for the query. Among other things, you can choose the TOP X or TOP X PERCENT of the records in a resultset.

MDX Query for a Multidimensional Cube Source

You may also want to get data from an OLAP cube. You can connect to Microsoft OLAP Services cubes with the Microsoft OLE DB Provider for OLAP Services.

On the Source tab of the Transform Data Task Properties dialog, select SQL Query and type your MDX Statement in the box. You can also use the browse button to find a file that has the MDX statement in it. Don't try to use the Query Designer. It's not ready to generate MDX queries—yet!

> **NOTE**
>
> You could choose to use a Table/View option, but the choices that show up in the list are entire cubes. You will generate a cellset that returns every cell of the cube. The lowest level of every dimension is returned. It can take a long time to load even a small cube like Warehouse from the Foodmart sample OLAP database.

I've used MDX statements to return a single value to verify the results of a data load and cube process. For example, if I know the number of new orders that are being imported into the cube's fact table, I can query the cube before and after it's processed to verify that number:

```
select {[Measures].[Order Count]} on columns from OrdersCube
```

> **NOTE**
>
> The MDX language allows you to return a cubeset of any number of dimensions from 0 to 64. The Transform Data task can only handle 1- and 2-dimension cubesets.
>
> The task won't handle the following valid MDX query, which returns a 0-dimension cellset:
>
> ```
> select from warehouse
> ```
>
> This query fails because it doesn't supply a column heading, so the resulting value can't be referenced to create a transformation.

Using XML as the Source

You can use an XML document as the data source for a Transform Data query, if you have an OLE DB provider that supports XML. An XML provider was not shipped with the initial release of SQL Server 2000.

> **NOTE**
>
> I have used the DataDirect XML ADO Provider from Merant.

Using Parameters in a Source Query

One of the new features in SQL Server 2000 is the ability to use parameters in a source query of the Transform Data task:

```
SELECT ProductID, Quantity, Price, SalesDate
FROM Sales
WHERE SalesDate = ?
```

You assign a value to the parameter by using a global variable. This reference is resolved at runtime.

You make the assignments by clicking on the Parameters button. Then, on the Parameter Mapping dialog (shown in Figure 6.4), choose a global variable to use as the Input Global Variable for each of your parameters.

FIGURE 6.4

You map the parameters in your source query to global variables using the Parameter Mapping dialog.

If you want to create a new global variable, click the Create Global Variables button. Within the Global Variables dialog, you can create, modify, or delete each global variable in the DTS package. Each global variable must have a unique name and a datatype. You can also assign the variable a default value.

> **NOTE**
>
> It's possible to accomplish this same result without using parameters. You can create an ActiveX Script task that dynamically modifies the SourceSQL property of the Transform Data task. This script can build the string used for the SQL using the same global variable that holds the appropriate SalesDate value.
>
> You had to follow this procedure if you wanted to change the source query dynamically in SQL Server 7.0. It's a lot easier now with the parameters.

The choice of global variables for the parameters is stored in the InputGlobalVariableNames property. The names of the global variables are stored in a semicolon-delimited list. A source query for the Transform Data task with three parameters could be written like this:

```
select * from pubs.dbo.authors
where au_id = ? and au_lname = ? and au_fname = ?
```

If you used global variables with the same names as the fields in the table, the value for InputGlobalVariableNames would be

```
au_id;au_lname;au_fname
```

DataPumpTask Source Properties

The DataPumpTask object has four properties that determine the source for the Transform Data task:

- SourceConnectionID—An integer value that references the ID property of the source Connection object.
- SourceObjectName—The name of the table or the view used for the source.
- SourceSQLStatement—The text of the query used for the source.
- SourceCommandProperties—A reference to the collection of OLE DB Command properties for the source connection. These read-only properties provide information about the properties of a particular provider.

> **NOTE**
>
> You can view all of the OLE DB Command properties in Disconnected Edit. In the ADO object model, each Connection object contains a Recordset and a Command object. The properties referenced through SourceCommandProperties are the ones used by the Recordset and Command objects. The OLE DB properties referenced by a connection's ConnectionProperties are a different set of properties—those properties that are associated with the ADO Connection object itself.

The Destination of a Transform Data Task

The destination for a Transform Data Task is set on the Destination tab of the Transform Data Task Properties dialog. You have two choices in this dialog:

- Select one of the tables in the drop-down list box.
- Create a new table.

Creating a New Destination Table

When you select the Create New button, the Create Destination Table dialog opens, as shown in Figure 6.5. The Create Table SQL statement is generated automatically for you, matching the fields of the source that have been chosen. Edit this SQL statement to create the table the way you want it to be. Click OK in the Create Destination Table and the new table is created immediately in the Destination database.

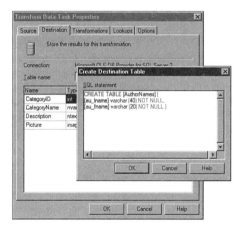

FIGURE 6.5

Create a new table to serve as the destination of a Transform Data task by using the Destination tab of the Data Transformation Properties dialog and the Create Destination Table dialog.

> **NOTE**
>
> When you're creating a new table and your source is an MDX statement, the columns are often named illegally because they have embedded square brackets. Rename the fields before saving the table.

Text File Destination

When you are using a text file as the destination for a transformation, the Destination tab has a button that opens the Define Columns dialog (shown in Figure 6.6). The columns needed to match the columns from the source are selected automatically. Click the Execute button to set these columns as the ones to be used for the data destination.

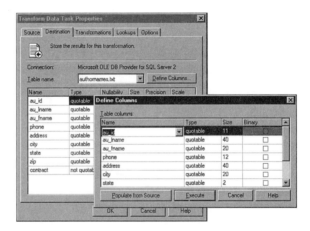

FIGURE 6.6

The Define Columns dialog is used to set the destination columns for a text file in a Transform Data task.

`DataPumpTask` Destination Properties

6

The properties for the destination of a Transform Data task are similar to those for the source:

- `DestinationConnectionID`—An integer value that references the `ID` property of the destination `Connection` object.

- `DestinationObjectName`—The name of the table or the view used for the destination. (See the following note.)

- `DestinationSQLStatement`—The text of the query used for the destination. (See the following note.)

- `DestinationColumnDefinitions`—A reference to the collection of column definitions for the task's destination.

- `DestinationCommandProperties`—A reference to the collection of OLE DB Command properties for the destination connection.

> **NOTE**
>
> By using Disconnected Edit or code, you can set a view or a SQL query as the destination for a Transform Data task.
>
> This is of limited value, though, because you can insert data into only one destination table. If you use a view, you have to base that view on only one table. If you use a query, you can reference multiple tables, but you can only insert data into one of them.
>
> The Parallel Data Pump task allows you to insert data into several destination tables at the same time. In a more limited way, you can also do this by using insert query lookups in the Transform Data task or multiple insert queries in the Data Driven Query task.

Mapping Source Columns to Destination Columns

The next operation in setting up the Transform Data task is to map the source columns to the appropriate destination columns.

The Transformations tab of the Transform Data Task Properties dialog (shown in Figure 6.7) is the place where source columns are mapped to destination columns. The tab displays all the columns of the source table and all the columns of the destination table. The datatypes of the columns and their nullability are displayed as ToolTips.

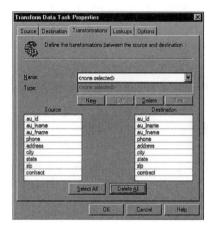

FIGURE 6.7

Create mappings from source to destination on the Transformations tab of the Transform Data Task Properties dialog.

CAUTION

If you create a transformation and later select the Source or Destination tab, you will change the ordering of the columns in the DTSDestination or DTSSource collections. The mapping of columns in Copy Column transformations is changed by this action. If you have referenced columns by their numbers in ActiveX scripts, those references will become invalid.

You map columns to each other by selecting them in the listing for each table. Select more than one column in a table by holding down the Ctrl key while selecting. Select a range of columns by holding down the Shift key while selecting. You can also select all of the columns from both sides by clicking the Select All Button.

You can remove mappings by selecting the mapping line, or by selecting the corresponding columns and clicking the Delete button. You can also use the Delete All button to remove all the transformations. I find it's often convenient to delete all the Default mappings before I start making my own.

After selecting all the columns you want from both lists, click the New button and then select the type of transformation from the Create New Transformation dialog. The types of transformations are discussed in the next section of this chapter.

When you click OK, the Transformation Options dialog will open. You can add or remove source and destination columns for the transformation in this dialog, as shown in Figure 6.8.

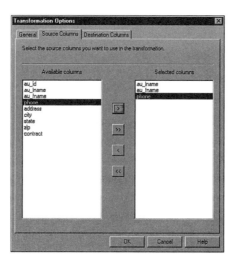

FIGURE 6.8

You can use the Source and Destination tabs in the Transformation Options dialog to change your selected columns.

When you click OK on the Transformation Options dialog, a black mapping line will be created between the source and destination columns. To use this mapping line to get back to the Transformation Properties dialog after a transformation has been created, do one of the following:

- Double-click a mapping line.
- Right-click a mapping line and choose Properties from the pop-up menu.
- Select a mapping line. Use the Ctrl+P keystroke combination.

Figure 6.9 shows a one-to-one mapping for all the columns.

Figure 6.10 shows a many-to-many mapping for all the columns. A many-to-many mapping reduces the overhead of a Transform Data task and can significantly improve performance.

Figure 6.11 shows a combination of mappings.

Figure 6.12 shows how columns in the source table can participate in many transformations. The author ID is being transferred directly to the destination in one transformation. In a second transformation, various coded information in the ID is split into separate columns. In a third transformation, the transformation of the contract information is being handled differently, depending on which author is involved. On the other hand, columns in the destination table normally only participate in one transformation.

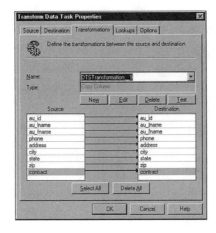

FIGURE 6.9

In a one-to-one mapping, each source column is connected to one destination column.

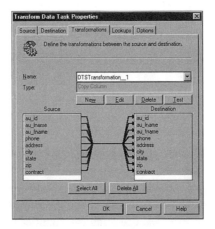

FIGURE 6.10

In a many-to-many mapping, all the selected source columns participate in one transformation with all the selected destination columns.

It is also possible to have mappings that include only source columns or only destination columns (see Figure 6.13). This could happen for a destination column if its value is being set by a global variable or a lookup. This could happen for a source column if it's being used to set a global variable but its value is not being used in the destination table. A transformation script is run for these one-sided cases even though no transformation is actually taking place.

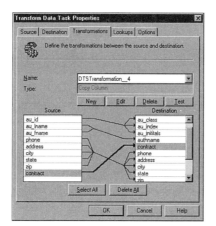

FIGURE 6.11

One Transform Data Task can include one-to-one, one-to-many, many-to-one, and many-to-many mappings.

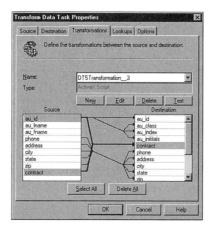

FIGURE 6.12

Many transformations can use the same column from the source table. In this case, three transformations are using au_id.

NOTE

You can even create a transformation that contains no source columns or destination columns. I can't imagine why you would want to do that while transforming rows of data. It does make sense, though, for ActiveX scripts in other phases of the data pump.

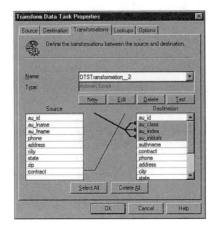

FIGURE 6.13

A transformation that only has a column from the source and another that only has columns from the destination are represented as lines that end somewhere between the two tables.

Transformation Flags

Figure 6.14 shows the Transformation Flags dialog. Choose this dialog by right-clicking a mapping line and selecting the Flags pop-up menu choice. The flags determine how transformations are applied when datatypes do not match between the source and the destination.

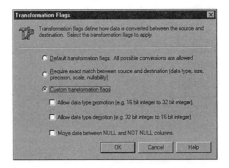

FIGURE 6.14

The Transformation Flags dialog provides datatype transformation choices that can be customized for each mapping.

These choices are implemented by the `TransformFlags` property of the `Transformation` object. Here are the choices in the Transformation Flags dialog, with the `DTSTransformFlags` constant that is used for each choice:

- `DTSTransformFlag_Default`—All possible conversions between varying datatypes are allowed. This is the default choice.

  This default choice is a combination of the flags that allow datatype promotion, demotion, null conversion, string truncation, numeric truncation, and sign change.

  Value: 63

- `DTSTransformFlag_RequireExactType`—An exact match of datatypes is required. This match includes datatype, size, precision, scale, and nullability.

  Value: 64

- Customized conversion flags can be set to the following:

  `DTSTransformFlag_AllowPromotion`—Allow datatype promotion. A 16-bit integer is allowed to be changed into a 32-bit integer.

  Value: 2

  `DTSTransformFlag_AllowDemotion`—Allow datatype demotion. A 32-bit integer is allowed to be changed into a 16-bit integer.

  Value: 1

  `DTSTransformFlag_AllowNullChange`—Allow a `NULL` conversion, where a `NULL` datatype is allowed to receive data from a `NOT NULL` datatype.

  Value: 16

Several additional choices and combinations of choices are available when you set the `TransformFlag` property in code or with Disconnected Edit:

- `DTSTransformFlag_Strict`—No flags are specified.

  Value: 0

- `DTSTransformFlag_AllowStringTruncation`—Strings will be truncated without an error or warning message.

  Value: 4

- `DTSTransformFlag_AllowNumericTruncation`—Numeric truncation (such as stripping off the fraction when converting to an integer) is allowed without an error or warning message.

  Value: 8

- `DTSTransformFlag_AllowSignChange`—Conversions are allowed between numbers in which one has a signed datatype and the other has an unsigned datatype.

  Value: 32

- `DTSTransformFlag_ForceConvert`—Forces conversion in all circumstances, even when datatypes are very dissimilar.

  Value: 128

- `DTSTransformFlag_PreserveDestRows`—The values in the destination rows are not cleared at the end of row processing. When you set this flag, you can reference the destination values from the previous record in your current record processing.

  Value: 256

- `DTSTransformFlag_AllowLosslessConversion`—Allows conversion in all lossless conversion situations.

  Value: 512

Testing a Transformation

You can right-click a mapping line and select Test from the pop-up menu (or click the Test button) to test that particular transformation. Figure 6.15 shows the data generated by a test of one transformation. The results of these tests are written to a text file and do not affect the data in either the source or destination connection.

FIGURE 6.15

Test an individual transformation by right-clicking the mapping line and selecting Test. The progress of the test is shown in the Testing Transformation dialog, and the data produced by the test is shown in the View Data dialog.

The Collections That Implement a Transformation

A Transform Data task has a `Transformations` collection that contains one object for each transformation that has been defined. Each mapping line corresponds to one `Transformation` object.

The `Transformation` object itself has two collections, one containing the source columns and the other containing the destination columns. These collections are referenced in Visual Basic as the `SourceColumns` and `DestinationColumns` of the `Transformation` object:

```
'Assume DTS.Transformation variable tran has already been set
Dim col as DTS.Column
For Each col in tran.SourceColumns
  msgbox col.Name
Next col
For Each col in tran.DestinationColumns
  msgbox col.Name
Next col
```

Inside a transformation ActiveX script, these same collections are referenced as the `DTSSource` and `DTSDestination` collections without explicitly identifying them as collections of the `Transformation` object:

```
Function Main()
    DTSDestination("au_id") = DTSSource("au_id")
    DTSDestination("au_lname") = DTSSource("au_lname")
    Main = DTSTransformStat_OK
End Function
```

Other Properties of a Transformation

The `Transformation` object has four properties that specify the type of transformation being used. These four properties are discussed in the following section.

There is one new property available in the `Transformation2` object—`TransformPhases`. This property is discussed in Chapter 9, "The Multiphase Data Pump."

There are five other properties, none of which can be viewed or changed without using code or Disconnected Edit:

- `Name`—You only need the name of the transformation if you want to reference the transformation in code. You may want to change the name so that it is more descriptive.
- `ForceBlobsInMemory`—Boolean value that forces binary large objects (BLOBs) to be stored in a single memory allocation.
- `ForceSourceBlobsBuffered`—Value that specifies whether or not to buffer BLOBs in a transformation.
- `InMemoryBlobSize`—The amount of memory in bytes allocated per column in a transformation for BLOBs.
- `Parent`—The `CustomTask` object that contains this transformation.

The Transformation Types

In the SQL Server 7.0 version of Data Transformation Services, you could choose between two types of transformations, Copy Column or ActiveX script. There are seven more choices in SQL Server 2000.

The DateTime String

In the previous version of DTS, it was possible to convert dates to new formats, but it took a lot of ActiveX programming. You can get the same results much faster with the new DateTime String transformation. The DateTime String Transformation Properties dialog is shown in Figure 6.16. You simply choose the format of the dates in the source and how you want them to show up in the destination, and they will be transformed. There are preset formats, but you can also create your own by typing them into the Format box and selecting the Preview button.

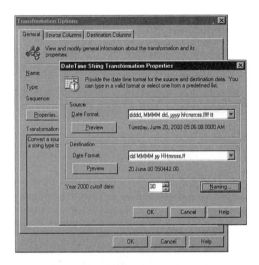

FIGURE 6.16
The DateTime String Transformation Properties dialog lets you choose the format for the source date and the destination date.

NOTE

If you have a date in the source data that does not match the format you specify, an error will be generated. You can send this record to an error file for reprocessing.

There are two more features with the DateTime String Transformation, shown in Figure 6.17. One of them is a spin box for adjusting the Year 2000 Cutoff Date. The second feature allows you to adjust the strings that represent the months, days of the week, and AM/PM to your desired format. To do this, you must click the Naming button.

FIGURE 6.17

The DateTime String Transformation Properties dialog allows you to specify the format of the dates you want to convert.

Uppercase Strings, Lowercase Strings, and Copy Column

Copy Column is the simplest of transformations. It changes the datatype to match the destination column and copies it into the destination.

If you want to transform a string into all uppercase or lowercase letters, you can use one of the case transformations. The source column will be copied into the destination column with the case specification. Of course, these transformations must have a string datatype in both the source and destination columns.

With each of these three types of transformations, the only transformation property you can change is the column order. If there are multiple source and destination columns within the transformation, you may need to adjust the mappings. By clicking on one of the names, you will get a list of all the columns from which to choose, as shown in Figure 6.18.

Middle of String and Trim String

The Trim String transformation, shown in Figure 6.19, allows you to get rid of unwanted spaces in your string as it is transformed to the destination column. You can choose to trim whitespace from the beginning, middle, or end of the string, or all three.

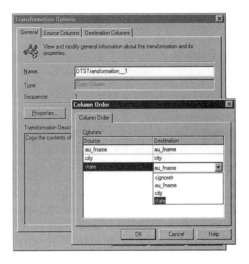

FIGURE 6.18

You can change the mapping of the columns in the Column Order dialog.

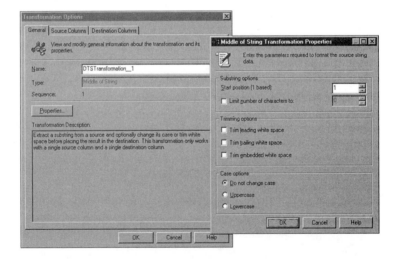

FIGURE 6.19

The Trim String Transformation Properties dialog gives choices for removing whitespace and changing the case.

When you use Trim String, you also have the option of converting the string to uppercase or lowercase, or leaving the case alone.

The Middle of String transformation gives you all of the functionality of Trim String. It also lets you select the start position within the string and how many characters you want to limit the string to.

Read File

The Read File Transformation is used to move the complete contents of files into the destination column, according to the filenames in the source column.

On the Transformation Properties Dialog, shown in Figure 6.20, you must select a directory where the files can be found. You can also choose a file type—either ANSI, OEM, or Unicode. If you select the Error if File Not Found check box, the transformation will fail when a filename specified in the source column is not in the directory you specified.

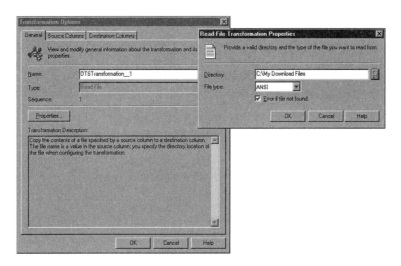

FIGURE 6.20
Choose the file to read from in the Read File Transformation Properties dialog.

Write File

The Write File Transformation is used to create new files, append data to existing files, replace files, or delete files. The contents of one source column (Data column) are copied into a file whose name is found in another source column (File Name column).

On the Transformation Properties Dialog, you must select a directory where the files will be saved, a file type, which source column is the File Name column, and how to handle existing files.

There are three choices for how to handle files that already exist:

- Overwrite if file exists: file is deleted and a new file is created. If the data column is null, the file will be deleted and no new file will be created.
- Append if file exists: The contents of the data column are appended to the file.
- Error if file exists: The transformation fails.

> **NOTE**
>
> Although you must have a source and destination connection when working with a Write File transformation, you are not allowed to specify any destination columns.

ActiveX Script

Writing ActiveX scripts for data transformations gives you much more flexibility than the other types of transformations. Here are some of the most important features of ActiveX scripts:

- You can create and reference global variables.
- You can look up values in other tables by using the Lookup object.
- You can manipulate other COM objects.
- You can create new rows in the destination that are not in the source data.
- You can combine two or more rows in the source into one row in the destination.
- You can skip some of the rows in the source data (not including them in the destination).

The ActiveX Script Transformation Properties dialog is shown in Figure 6.21. The ActiveX Script transformation is covered in detail in Chapter 7.

Custom Transformation

Another possibility for creating transformations is the Custom Transformation. You can create a new type of transformation, or use a Custom Transformation that someone else has made. For more information about Custom Transformations, refer to Chapter 32.

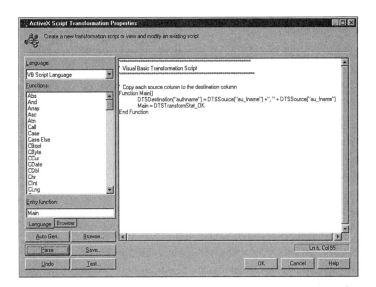

FIGURE 6.21
The ActiveX Script Transformation Properties dialog gives you a place to write code that executes for each row of data.

Other Properties of the Transform Data Task

You can set error handling, data movement, and SQL Server-specific properties on the Options tab of the Transform Data Task Properties dialog, shown in Figure 6.22.

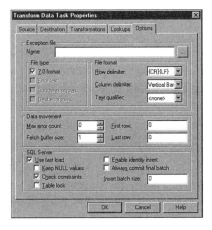

FIGURE 6.22
Error handling and data movement are among the properties set on the Options tab of the Transform Data Task Properties dialog.

Error Handling Properties

In SQL Server 7.0, you could only generate a single file that held all the error information. This error file is very informative, but it is difficult to parse the information in it.

With SQL Server 2000, you can still use the 7.0 error file format, but you also have the option of using three separate files for error information:

- Error Text—Contains a description of the errors.
- Source Error Rows—A text file that has all the columns of all the source rows that contained errors. You can use this file to reprocess the failed records, as discussed in Chapter 27, "Handling Errors in a Package and Its Transformations."
- Destination Error Rows— A text file that has all the destination columns for records that failed to be inserted into the destination table because they would have violated table constraints.

ExceptionFileName

The ExceptionFileName property is used as the full path for all of the error handling files, with the following adjustments:

- For SQL Server 7.0 Format file, used as is.
- For the Error Text file, used as is.
- For the Source Row file, used with .Source appended at the end of the filename.
- For the Destination Row file, used with .Dest appended at the end of the filename.

Choosing Which Files to Use

The 7.0 file format is chosen by default in the Transform Data Task Properties dialog. When you remove the checkmark from the 7.0 Format box, you can choose one or more of the files in the new format.

This selection is implemented with the ExceptionFileOptions property. The DTSExceptionFileOptions constants are used for this property. The first four options can be selected in the interface. The other options have to be set with Disconnected Edit or code. Here are the options:

- 1—DTSExceptionFile_SingleFile70—Create the 7.0 format file.
- 2—DTSExceptionFile_ErrorFile—Create the SQL Server 2000 Error Text file. This cannot be used at the same time as the 7.0 format file because they are assigned the same filename.
- 4—DTSExceptionFile_SourceRowFile—Create the SQL Server 2000 Source Row file.
- 8—DTSExceptionFile_DestRowFile—Create the SQL Server 2000 Destination Row file.

- 256—DTSExceptionFile_Ansi—Create the files in ANSI format.
- 512—DTSExceptionFile_OEM—Create the files in OEM format.
- 1024—DTSExceptionFile_Unicode—Create the files in Unicode format.
- 4096—DTSExceptionFile_Overwrite—Overwrite any existing files. The default is to append the new information to any existing information in the file.
- 8192—DTSExceptionFile_AbortOnRowLogFailure—Abort the transformation task if it is impossible to log the rows.

CAUTION

If you want to change the behavior of the error files so that the old files are always overwritten, you can use Disconnected Edit to add 4096 to the value of the ExceptionFileOptions property for each of your Transform Data tasks.

If you then open the Transform Data Task Properties dialog, select the Options tab, and choose OK, the value of ExceptionFileOptions will return to what it was before you edited it. The value of this property will be determined by which files are selected at the time the dialog is closed.

If you want to persist a particular value for ExceptionFileOptions that is not available in the interface, you have two choices. Either never open the dialog and select the Options tab, or always execute some code before the Transform Data task is run that adds the desired values into ExceptionFileOptions.

Here's a function that you could use in an ActiveX Script task that would add this option for all the Transform Data tasks in your package:

```
Option Explicit
Function Main()

Dim pkg, tsk, cus

Set pkg = DTSGlobalVariables.Parent

For Each tsk in pkg.Tasks

    If tsk.CustomTaskID = "DTSDataPumpTask" Then

        Set cus = tsk.CustomTask

        If  (cus.ExceptionFileOptions And 4096) = 0 Then
            cus.ExceptionFileOptions = cus.ExceptionFileOptions + 4096
        End If

    End If

End If
```

```
Next

    Main = DTSTaskExecResult_Success
End Function
```

Error File Format

You can set the format used by the Source Rows and Destination Rows error files with these three properties:

- ExceptionFileRowDelimiter
- ExceptionFileColumnDelimiter
- ExceptionFileTextQualifier

Data Movement Properties

You can set the following data movement properties on the Options tab:

- MaximumErrorCount—The maximum number of allowed errors before the Transform Data task is terminated. The default is 0, which means that the Transform Data task will fail when the first error is encountered.
- FetchBufferSize—The number of records fetched at one time from the OLE DB provider. The default is 1. Raising this number can improve performance, but it also increases the use of the computer's memory resources.
- FirstRow—The number of the first row that is imported. The default is 0, which means that the copy starts with the first record.
- LastRow—The number of the last row that is imported. The default is 0, which means that all the records are copied. It can be useful to set LastRow to a low value for testing purposes so that only a few records are transformed.

By default, DTS raises an OnProgress event when every 1,000 rows are copied. You can modify the ProgressRowCount property to a higher or lower number if you want to change the frequency with which this event is fired. The ProgressRowCount property can be viewed and modified in Disconnected Edit and with code.

There are two read-only properties that report on the results of a Transform Data task:

- RowsComplete—The number of rows that were successfully transformed.
- RowsInError—The number of rows that failed to be transformed because of an error.

Options for Improving Performance with SQL Server Destinations

There are several performance-related options for data transformations that are only available when the UseFastLoad property is set to TRUE. You can't use fast load unless you are using the Microsoft OLE DB provider for SQL Server for the destination connection.

> **NOTE**
>
> Chapter 28, "High Performance DTS Packages," has charts showing the relative performance of the Transform Data task with different options.
>
> The most important performance choice with the Transform Data task is to use fast load, which is selected by default. A data transformation with fast load executes about 130 times faster than a data transformation without fast load.

The UseFastLoad and FastLoadOptions Properties

The fast load option uses batch processing. Without the fast load option, SQL Server commits each separate record that is inserted into a table. Fast loading saves time by committing a specified number of records at the same time in a batch.

You should set the following database options for the destination whenever you're doing a fast load:

- Select into/bulkcopy should be on:

  sp_dboption Northwind, 'select into/bulkcopy', TRUE

- Truncate log on checkpoint should be on:

  sp_dboption Northwind, 'trunc. log on chkpt.', TRUE

- Auto create statistics should be off:

  sp_dboption Northwind, 'auto create statistics', FALSE

There are several options that are set with the FastLoadOptions property:

- 0—DTSFastLoad_NoOptions—None of the three options are selected.
- 1—DTSFastLoad_KeepNulls—If there are nulls in the source data, they are kept in the destination, even if there are default values supplied in the destination.

- 2—DTSFastLoad_CheckConstraints or DTSFastLoad_Default—Constraints are checked as the data is loaded, and an error is generated when records violate those constraints. If this value is not selected, data that violates constraints will be loaded without generating an error. The default in the DTS Designer is to check constraints. Performance will be improved if this option is unselected.

- 4—DTSFastLoad_TableLock—The entire table is locked during the data transformation. If this option is not selected, individual row locks are used for loading data. You can improve performance by selecting this option.

> **NOTE**
>
> Remember, you can't choose any of these fast load options unless you are using SQL Server as the destination and you use fast load. When you don't use fast load, you can never keep null values, you cannot ignore constraints, and you cannot use a table lock.

AllowIdentityInserts

SQL Server has an Identity property that you can use to create an auto-incrementing integer field in a table. You have to set the identity_insert table option to TRUE if you want to explicitly insert a value into a field that has the Identity property. You can turn on identity_insert during a data transformation by setting the Boolean property AllowIdentityInserts to TRUE. This option only applies to SQL Server data destinations.

Always Commit Final Batch

When you are using fast load, all the records in a batch are normally committed together. If an error occurs in a later batch that terminates the data pump, it does not affect the records in the batches that have been committed already.

The default behavior, though, is for all the records in the final batch to be removed from the destination. After all, batches are committed as a single unit.

This property changes that behavior. All records that have been transformed successfully before the final error takes place are saved in the destination table.

The DataPumpOptions property implements this choice. This property has two possible values:

- 0—The default value. Do not commit any records from the final batch.
- 1—Commit all the records from the final batch that were transformed before the error took place.

InsertCommitSize

The `InsertCommitSize` property sets the number of records that are loaded together. If one of the records fails, the entire batch fails. The default is 0, which loads all the records in a single batch. A large batch size improves performance, but it also takes up more of the computer's memory resources and can cause problems if the destination database's transaction log is filled up. Try an `InsertCommitSize` of 100,000 or 999,999 (the highest possible setting in the user interface) if you're doing a large import.

Column Properties

The `Column` object that is used for both source columns and destination columns has several properties. When you create a transformation with the DTS Package Designer or the Import/Export Wizard, all these properties are set automatically from the meta data available from the connections.

You can use Disconnected Edit or code to view or modify these properties. Normally, there is no need to modify the properties that are set automatically.

You have to at least set the `Name` and `Ordinal` properties when you create a column in code. Here's code that adds the `LastName` column in ordinal position 1 to the collection of source columns for a transaction referenced by the object variable `trn`:

```
Dim col As DTS.Column
Set col = trn.SourceColumns.New("LastName", 1)
trn.SourceColumns.Add col
Set col = Nothing
```

The `Column` object properties are

- `Name`—The name of the column. You can use the `Name` property to refer to a column in an ActiveX script:

  ```
  DTSSource("au_id")
  ```

- `Ordinal`—The position of the column in the collection. You can also use the `Ordinal` property to refer to a column:

  ```
  DTSSource(1)
  ```

- `ColumnID`—This property does not appear to be set by the DTS Designer or to be used for any purpose.

- `DataType`—The datatype of the column. Values are the same as those used in ADO and OLE DB.

- `Nullable`—Boolean value indicating whether or not null values are allowed in the column.

- `Precision`—The number of digits in a number for decimal and numeric datatypes.
- `NumericScale`—The number of digits allowed to the right of the decimal point for decimal and numeric datatypes.
- `Size`—The maximum size of a column.
- `Flags`—The OLE DB DBCOLUMN values that describe a particular column.
- `Parent`—The collection of which the column is a member.

Some of the common values used for the `DataType` property are

- 3—An integer. (4 bytes signed)
- 129—A string.
- 131—Numeric value with fixed precision and scale.
- 135—Date and time value.

Some of the common values used for the `Flags` property are

- 8—The provider cannot determine if the field can be updated.
- 16—The field has a fixed length.
- 96—The field can have null data.

An example of a combination of these flags is 120 (8 + 16 + 96). This indicates a nullable field with fixed-length data.

Creating a Transform Data Task in Visual Basic

I have created a Visual Basic procedure, `fctCreateTransformDataTask`, which creates a connection, a step, a task, and a custom task for a Transform Data task. This procedure allows you to set all of the task's properties, but none of the properties of the transformations. The task that this procedure creates cannot be executed as it is because it does not have any transformations defined. The next section of this chapter has code that explains how to programmatically create transformations.

The `fctCreateTransformDataTask` uses a parameter `sBaseName` for assigning names and descriptions to the DTS objects that are created. For example, if `sBaseName` is TransformDataTest, the following assignments would be made:

- Task `Description`—TransformDataTest
- Step `Description`—TransformDataTest
- Source Connection `Description`—SourceTransformDataTest
- Destination Connection `Description`—DestTransformDataTest
- Task `Name`—tskTransformDataTest

- Step Name—stpTransformDataTest
- Source Connection Name—conSourceTransformDataTest
- Destination Connection Name—conDestTransformDataTest

You can find the code for this procedure in several forms on the book's CD in the directory for Chapter 6:

- In a Visual Basic Project, with files CreateTransformDataTask.vbp, CreateTransformDataTask.frm, CreateTransformDataTask.bas, and AddTransformations.bas.
- Modified for VBScript as CreateTransformDataTask.scr.
- In a DTS package, CreateTransformDataTask.dts, which contains the modified VBScript code. This package also has a freestanding Transform Data task icon with no task assigned to it. Right-click on the ActiveX Script task and select Execute Step. The Transform Data task will be created and associated with the freestanding icon's step. The two connections will be created, but will not be visible in the package. You can make those connections visible by right-clicking on the Design Sheet, selecting Add Connection, and choosing the connections in the list of existing connections.

The code for fctCreateTransformDataTask is shown in Listing 6.1. The procedure needs some utility functions that are included with the code listings on the CD. The project requires references to the Microsoft DTSPackage Object Library and the Microsoft DTSDataPump Scripting Object Library.

LISTING 6.1   The Visual Basic Code to Create a Transform Data Task

```
Option Explicit

Public Function fctCreateTransformDataTask( _
    pkg As DTS.Package2, _
    Optional sBaseName As String = "TransformDataTask", _
    Optional sSourceDataSource As String = "",
    Optional sDestDataSource As String = "", _
    Optional sSourceCatalog As String = "",
    Optional sDestCatalog As String = "", _
    Optional sSourceUserID As String = "",
    Optional sDestUserID As String = "", _
    Optional sSourcePassword As String = "",
    Optional sDestPassword As String = "", _
    Optional sSourceTableName As String = "",
```

LISTING 6.1 Continued

```
        Optional sDestTableName As String = "", _
        Optional sExistingSource As String = "", _
        Optional sExistingDest As String = "", _
        Optional bAllowIdentityInserts As Boolean = False, _
        Optional lDataPumpOptions As Long = 0, _
        Optional sDestinationSQLStatement As String = "", _
        Optional sExceptionFileColumnDelimiter As String = "|", _
        Optional sExceptionFileName As String = "", _
        Optional dtsExceptionFileOptions As dtsExceptionFileOptions = 1, _
        Optional sExceptionFileRowDelimiter As String = "{CR}{LF}", _
        Optional sExceptionFileTextQualifier As String = "", _
        Optional dtsFastLoadOptions As dtsFastLoadOptions = 2, _
        Optional lFetchBufferSize As Long = 1, _
        Optional vFirstRow As Variant = 0, _
        Optional vLastRow As Variant = 0, _
        Optional sInputGlobalVariableNames As String = "", _
        Optional lInsertCommitSize As Long = 0, _
        Optional lMaximumErrorCount As Long = 0, _
        Optional lProgressRowCount As Long = 1000, _
        Optional sSourceSQLStatement As String = "", _
        Optional bUseFastLoad As Boolean = True) As String

On Error GoTo ProcErr

Dim conSource As DTS.Connection2
Dim conDest As DTS.Connection2
Dim stp As DTS.Step2
Dim tsk As DTS.Task
Dim cus As DTS.DataPumpTask2


'Check to see if the selected Base name is unique
sBaseName = fctFindUniqueBaseName(pkg, sBaseName)

If sExistingSource = "" Then
    'Create connection for Source
    Set conSource = pkg.Connections.New("SQLOLEDB")
    With conSource
        .ID = fctNextConnectionID(pkg)
        .Name = "conSource" & sBaseName
        .Description = "Source" & sBaseName
```

LISTING 6.1   Continued

```
        .DataSource = sSourceDataSource
        .Catalog = sSourceCatalog

        .UserID = sSourceUserID
        .Password = sSourcePassword

        'If User ID is empty string, use trusted connection
        If sSourceUserID = "" Then
          .UseTrustedConnection = True
        Else
          .UseTrustedConnection = False
        End If

    End With
    pkg.Connections.Add conSource
Else
    Set conSource = pkg.Connections(sExistingSource)
End If

If sExistingDest = "" Then
    'Create connection for Source
    Set conDest = pkg.Connections.New("SQLOLEDB")
    With conDest
        .ID = fctNextConnectionID(pkg)
        .Name = "conDest" & sBaseName
        .Description = "Dest" & sBaseName
        .DataSource = sDestDataSource
        .Catalog = sDestCatalog

        .UserID = sDestUserID
        .Password = sDestPassword

        'If User ID is empty string, use trusted connection
        If sDestUserID = "" Then
          .UseTrustedConnection = True
        Else
          .UseTrustedConnection = False
        End If

    End With
    pkg.Connections.Add conDest
Else
```

LISTING 6.1   Continued

```
    Set conDest = pkg.Connections(sExistingDest)
End If


'Create task and custom task
Set tsk = pkg.Tasks.New("DTSDataPumpTask") 'DTSBulkInsertTask
Set cus = tsk.CustomTask
With cus

    'Set ConnectionIDs
    .SourceConnectionID = conSource.ID
    .DestinationConnectionID = conDest.ID

    'Properties supplied to the procedure
    .Name = "tsk" & sBaseName
    .SourceObjectName = sSourceTableName
    .DestinationObjectName = sDestTableName
    .Description = sBaseName
    .AllowIdentityInserts = bAllowIdentityInserts
    .DataPumpOptions = lDataPumpOptions
    .DestinationSQLStatement = sDestinationSQLStatement
    .ExceptionFileColumnDelimiter = sExceptionFileColumnDelimiter
    .ExceptionFileName = sExceptionFileName
    .ExceptionFileOptions = dtsExceptionFileOptions
    .ExceptionFileRowDelimiter = sExceptionFileRowDelimiter
    .ExceptionFileTextQualifier = sExceptionFileTextQualifier
    .FastLoadOptions = dtsFastLoadOptions
    .FetchBufferSize = lFetchBufferSize
    .FirstRow = vFirstRow
    .InputGlobalVariableNames = sInputGlobalVariableNames
    .InsertCommitSize = lInsertCommitSize
    .LastRow = vLastRow
    .MaximumErrorCount = lMaximumErrorCount
    .ProgressRowCount = lProgressRowCount
    .SourceSQLStatement = sSourceSQLStatement
    .UseFastLoad = bUseFastLoad

End With


pkg.Tasks.Add tsk


'Create step for task
Set stp = pkg.Steps.New
With stp
    .Name = "stp" & sBaseName
    .Description = sBaseName
```

LISTING 6.1 Continued

```
    .TaskName = tsk.Name
End With
pkg.Steps.Add stp

fctCreateTransformDataTask = stp.Name

Set conSource = Nothing
Set conDest = Nothing
Set tsk = Nothing
Set cus = Nothing
Set stp = Nothing

ProcExit:
  Exit Function
ProcErr:
  MsgBox Err.Number & " - " & Err.Description
  fctCreateTransformDataTask = ""
  GoTo ProcExit

End Function
```

Creating Transformations in Code

You can create any type of transformation by using Visual Basic code. First you have to specify the type of transformation you are using. Then you set the particular properties that are needed for that type.

Choosing a Transformation Type in Code

You can query the TransformationInfos collection of the DTS Application object to obtain a list of the transformations that are registered on your computer. Here's the VBScript code for accessing that information:

```
Function Main()

dim app, info
set app = createobject("DTS.Application")

for each info in app.TransformationInfos
  msgbox "Description - " & info.Description & "    Name - " & info.Name
next

    Main = DTSTaskExecResult_Success
End Function
```

The `Name` property of the transformation in the `TransformationInfos` collection is used for the `TransformServerID` property of the `Transformation` object. This name is used when you create a new transformation in Visual Basic:

```
Dim cus As DTS.DataPumpTask2
Dim tran As DTS.Transformation2
Set tran = cus.Transformations.New("DTSPump.DataPumpTransformCopy")
```

You can use the `TransformServer` property to assign an object variable to a particular type of transformation. The `TransformServer` property works the same way for transformations as the `CustomTask` property does for tasks, as shown in the following VBScript. This code retrieves the text, language, and entry function for the ActiveX script used in a transformation:

```
Option Explicit

Function Main

Dim pkg, tsk, cus, tran, typ

Set pkg = DTSGlobalVariables.Parent
Set tsk = pkg.Tasks("tskArchiveFourthMonth")
Set cus = tsk.CustomTask
Set tran = cus.Transformations("tranProductInfo")
Set typ = tran.TransformServer

msgbox typ.Text
msgbox typ.Language
msgbox typ.FunctionEntry

    Main = DTSTaskExecResult_Success
End Function
```

Instead of creating an object variable for the transformation type, you can use the `TransformServerProperties` property, which contains a collection of the same properties. The following code does the same thing as the previous example. Note how an object variable for the transformation type is not needed:

```
Option Explicit

Function Main

Dim pkg, tsk, cus, tran, prp

Set pkg = DTSGlobalVariables.Parent
Set tsk = pkg.Tasks("tskArchiveFourthMonth")
Set cus = tsk.CustomTask
```

```
Set tran = cus.Transformations("tranProductInfo")
Set prp = tran.TransformServerProperties

msgbox prp("Text")
msgbox prp("Language")
msgbox prp("FunctionEntry")

    Main = DTSTaskExecResult_Success
End Function
```

NOTE

I usually reference transformation properties using this second method because it's
what DTS uses when a package is saved to Visual Basic.

There is one more property of the `Transformation` object that relates to transformation types.
The `TransformServerParameter` is used to send an initialization parameter to the transformation server for the particular transformation type. The particular value that's needed depends
on the transformation type. Some transformation types do not need an initialization parameter.

Creating the Transformation and Its Columns

It's useful to think of the code for the creation of a transformation in six parts:

1. Create a `Transformation` object of the appropriate transformation type:

   ```
   Set trn = cus.Transformations.New("DTSPump.DataPumpTransformCopy")
   ```

2. Give the transformation a name:

   ```
   trn.Name = "trnCopyAuthorName"
   ```

3. Set the other transformation properties.
4. Create the columns.
5. Set the `TransformServerProperties` needed for the particular type of transformation.
6. Add the `Transformation` to the `Transformations` collection for that custom task.

Steps #2 and #5 are different for each type of transformation. The other steps are basically the
same for all of them.

The code in Listing 6.2 creates a Copy Column transformation. There are no
`TransformServerProperties` for this type of transformation.

LISTING 6.2   Visual Basic Code That Creates a Copy Column Transformation

```
Public Sub subCopyColumn(ByVal cus As Object)

Dim trn As DTS.Transformation2
Dim prp As DTS.Properties
Dim col As DTS.Column

'#1. Create a transformation of the appropriate transformation type
Set trn = cus.Transformations.New("DTSPump.DataPumpTransformCopy")

'#2. Set the name of the transformation
trn.Name = "trnCopyAuthorName"

'#3. Set the other transformation properties.
trn.TransformFlags = 63
trn.ForceBlobsInMemory = False
trn.ForceSourceBlobsBuffered = 0
trn.InMemoryBlobSize = 1048576

'#4. Create the columns and set their properties.
Set col = trn.SourceColumns.New("LastName", 1)
col.Flags = 104
col.Size = 20
col.DataType = 129
col.Nullable = True

trn.SourceColumns.Add col
Set col = Nothing

Set col = trn.DestinationColumns.New("LastName", 1)
col.Flags = 104
col.Size = 20
col.DataType = 129
col.Nullable = True

trn.DestinationColumns.Add col
Set col = Nothing

'#5.Set the appropriate TransformServer Properties.
'No TransformServer Properties for the Copy Column transformation
Set prp = trn.TransformServerProperties

Set prp = Nothing
```

LISTING 6.2   Continued

```
'#6. Add the transformation to the transformations collection.
cus.Transformations.Add trn

Set trn = Nothing

End Sub
```

Copy Column, Uppercase, and Lowercase Transformations

The Copy Column, Uppercase, and Lowercase transformations are all similar in that they don't have any `TransformServer` properties. The code to create one `Transformation` object for each of these transformation types is as follows:

```
Set trnCopy = cus.Transformations.New _
      ("DTSPump.DataPumpTransformCopy")
Set trnUpper = cus.Transformations.New _
      ("DTSPump.DataPumpTransformUpperString")
Set trnLower = cus.Transformations.New _
      ("DTSPump.DataPumpTransformLowerString")
```

Trim String and Middle of String Transformations

The code to create these two types is as follows:

```
Set trnTrim = cus.Transformations.New _
      ("DTSPump.DataPumpTransformTrimString")
Set trnMid = cus.Transformations.New _
      ("DTSPump.DataPumpTransformMidString")
```

The Trim String transformation has `TransformServer` properties that remove whitespace from the string and set the string to uppercase and lowercase. All of these properties default to false:

```
prp("TrimLeadingWhiteSpace") = True
prp("TrimTrailingWhiteSpace") = True
prp("TrimEmbeddedWhiteSpace") = True
prp("UpperCaseString") = False
prp("LowerCaseString") = False
```

The Middle of String transformation uses all of the `TransformServer` properties that Trim String uses, plus these additional properties:

```
prp("CharacterStart") = 1
prp("CharacterCount") = 3
```

You set the point at which you want to start in the source string by setting the `CharacterStart` property. The default value is 1. You can cut off the first part of the string by setting it to a higher number.

The `CharacterCount` property limits the number of characters you want in the string. The default value is 0, which means there is no limit to the length of the string.

Read File and Write File Transformations

Here's the code to create Read File and Write File transformation objects:

```
Set trnRead = cus.Transformations.New _
     ("DTSPump.DataPumpTransformReadFile")
Set trnWrite = cus.Transformations.New _
     ("DTSPump.DataPumpTransformWriteFile")
```

The Read File transformation has the following `TransformServer` properties:

- `ErrorIfFileNotFound`—Defaults to True. An error is generated if the file indicated in the source column does not exist in the location specified by the `FilePath` property.

- `FilePath`—The location the files are read in.

- `UnicodeFile` and `OEMFile`—Both of these default to false, making ANSI the default file type. If either of these is set to true, that will become the file type. If you set both of these properties to true, Unicode will be the file type.

```
prp("ErrorIfFileNotFound") = True
prp("FilePath") = "C:\Temp"
prp("UnicodeFile") = False
prp("OEMFile") = False
```

The Write File transformation has the `UnicodeFile` and `OEMFile` `TransformServer` properties in common with Read File. When dealing with the Write File, the `FilePath` is the location where the new file will be saved.

There are three options if the file already exists in the location specified by the `FilePath`: create an error, append to the file, or overwrite the file. The two `TransformServer` properties used in code to set this option are `ErrorIfFileExists` and `AppendIfFileExists`. If you set them both to False, the overwrite option will be chosen, and if you set one of them to True, that option will be chosen. If you set both the error and append options to `True` in code, both of them will appear as being selected in the DTS designer. However, the error option overrides the append option.

In a Write File transformation, two source columns and no destination columns are included. One of the source columns specifies the name of the file to be created, and the other one has the text of the file. You can select which column you want to be the source of the filenames by setting the `FileColumnName` property:

```
prp("ErrorIfFileExists") = False
prp("AppendIfFileExists") = False
prp("FilePath") = "C:\Temp"
prp("FileColumnName") = "CommentFile"
prp("UnicodeFile") = False
prp("OEMFile") = False
```

DateTime Transformations

Here's the code to create a DateTime transformation:

```
Set trn = cus.Transformations.New _
        ("DTSPump.DataPumpTransformDateTimeString")
```

`DateTime` transformations have 43 `TransformServer` properties that you can set in code or in the DTS designer. There are properties for long and short month names, long and short day of the week names, `InputFormat`, `OutputFormat`, `AMSymbol`, `PMSymbol`, and `ShortYear2000Cutoff`.

- The `InputFormat` property specifies the format that a source date field is in. The example in the following code is in long month date, four-digit year format. If dates are not in the proper format, an error will be generated.

- The `OutputFormat` property specifies the format you want the dates to be in. In the example, the format is short month date, two-digit year.

- The `Month1LongName` property is set to "January" by default. You could change this value if, for instance, "January" is spelled incorrectly in the source data. Each month has a long name property and a short name property. Each day also has a long name and a short name. There are also properties for `AMSymbol` and `PMSymbol`.

- The `ShortYear2000Cutoff` property can be set to let you decide which 2-digit years are part of the 1900s and which are part of the 2000s. Its default is 30.

    ```
    prp("InputFormat") = "MMMM dd, yyyy"
    prp("OutputFormat") = "dd MMM yy"
    prp("Month1LongName") = "January"
    prp("Month1ShortName") = "Jan"
    prp("Day1LongName") = "Sunday"
    prp("Day1ShortName") = "Sun"
    prp("AMSymbol") = "AM"
    prp("PMSymbol") = "PM"
    prp("ShortYear2000Cutoff") = 30
    ```

ActiveX Transformations

Here's the code to create an ActiveX transformation:

```
Set trn = cus.Transformations.New _
        ("DTSPump.DataPumpTransformScript")
```

ActiveX scripts have three main `TransformServer` properties:

- `Text`—The content of the script.
- `Language`—The scripting language used. The default is VBScript.
- `FunctionEntry`—The name of the script function that the transformation calls. The default is Main. There are similarly named properties that are used with the Multiphase Data Pump (such as `BatchCompleteFunctionEntry`) that will be discussed in Chapter 9:

```
Dim txt As String
txt = "'*****************************************" & vbCrLf
txt = txt & "'  Visual Basic Transformation Script" & vbCrLf
txt = txt & "'*****************************************" & vbCrLf
txt = txt & "Option Explicit" & vbCrLf
txt = txt & "Function Main()" & vbCrLf
txt = txt & "   " & vbCrLf
txt = txt & "DTSDestination(""AreaCode"") = _
        left(DTSSource(""Phone""), 3)" & vbCrLf
txt = txt & "DTSDestination(""PhoneNumber"") = _
        Right(DTSSource(""Phone""), 8)" & vbCrLf
txt = txt & "   Main = DTSTransformStat_OK" & vbCrLf
txt = txt & "End Function"

prp("Text") = txt
prp("Language") = "VBScript"
prp("FunctionEntry") = "Main"
```

A Sample Application with All the Transformations

I have prepared a sample application that creates one of each of the nine types of transformations. The code for creating the transformations is in the Visual Basic module AddTransformations.bas, which is included in the Visual Basic project CreateTransformDataTask.vbp.

To execute this code, you have to do the following:

1. Open and execute the DTS package in CreateManagerTables.dts, which you can find in the directory for this chapter. This package will create a table named Manager in both the pubs and Northwind databases.

2. Copy the text files named SmithHistory.txt and JohnsonHistory.txt to C:\Temp. These files are used in the ReadFile transformation.

3. Execute the `CreateTransformDataTask` Visual Basic project. In the Create A Task dialog, enter the appropriate server and security information. Then choose pubs for the source database, Northwind for the destination database, and Manager for both the source and destination tables. Click the Create Task and Package button and then the Add Transformations button.

4. Refresh the list of Local Packages stored in SQL Server. Open the package that you have just created.

5. Examine the transformations in the package. When you execute the package, two new files named JohnsonComment.txt and SmithComment.txt will be created in C:\Temp.

Using the Transform Data Task as a FreeStanding Icon

When you use the Transform Data task in the Package Designer, it appears as a black arrow connecting two connections. This representation of the task clearly displays the movement of data from one connection to another.

But there are some problems with the black arrow icon:

- The representation of the Transform Data task is inconsistent with the representation of all the other tasks. Several tasks use connections, but none appear tied to the connections like the Transform Data task. The sharpest contrast is with the other two transformation tasks—the Data Driven Query task and the Parallel Data Pump task, both of which have their own freestanding icon that is not associated with connections.

- The representation of the precedence constraints is inconsistent. The precedence constraints set a relationship between the steps associated with the tasks, but when used with the Transform Data task, they appear to show a relationship to a connection icon.

- You can't copy a Transform Data task. The black arrow icon can't exist apart from its two connections, and you're not allowed to copy more than one DTS object at a time. This makes it difficult to move a single Transform Data task from one package to another or to create several Transform Data tasks that have minor differences. You can copy all the other tasks because they have freestanding icons.

SQL Server 2000 includes an alternative representation of the Transform Data task as a freestanding icon. This icon is not documented and is not directly available in the Package Designer interface. Figure 6.23 shows two Transform Data tasks, one with the black arrow icon and the other with the freestanding icon.

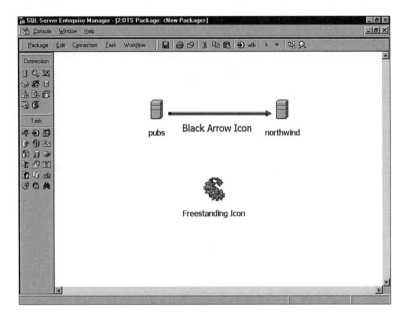

FIGURE 6.23

The Transform Data task can be represented in two different ways—the black arrow icon and the freestanding icon.

> **CAUTION**
>
> It's important to be careful when using undocumented features, such as the Transform Data task's freestanding icon. Undocumented features can be changed or removed when new versions of the software are released. If you have a problem when using an undocumented feature, you might not be able to receive help dealing with that problem.

The primary advantage of the freestanding icon is that it allows the Transform Data task to be copied. The task's transformations are copied, along with their collections of columns and the TransformServer properties, including the transformation scripts. You can use the icon to make a copy of the Transform Data task in the same package or in another package.

The one difficulty I have experienced in working with the freestanding icon is that you can't open the Transform Data Task Properties dialog if either of its connections is unavailable.

When you double-click the icon, the dialog flashes open and shut again. You have to fix the connection problem either in the Connection objects themselves or with Disconnected Edit. Then you can double-click on the icon and view the task's properties.

When you save a package with a freestanding Transform Data task icon to Visual Basic and then recreate the package, the freestanding icon is replaced with the regular black arrow icon pointing from the source connection to the destination connection. There is nothing different in the Visual Basic code that distinguishes one iconic representation of the task from the other.

You can find the Transform Data task's freestanding icon in a DTS template called FreeStandingIcon.dtt. You can use this template to start a new package or you can open the template and copy the icon to a different package. You can find the template by right-clicking on Data Transformation Services in the Enterprise Manager tree, and selecting Open Template from the All Tasks menu. The icon in the template has the `SourceConnectionID` property set to 1 and the `DestinationConnectionID` property set to 2. If you have valid connections with those Connection ID numbers in your package, you will be able to open the Transform Data Task Properties dialog from the icon and start setting the task's properties. You can view the `ConnectionID` property of your package's `Connection` objects by using Disconnected Edit.

If you want to convert the icon of an existing Transform Data task to the freestanding icon, you can do the following:

1. Create a new custom task. You can use any type of custom task except the Transform Data task.
2. Right-click on the Design Sheet and select Disconnected Edit. Find the name of the Transform Data task you want to convert. Enter that name as the `TaskName` property of the `Step` object associated with the new task you just created.
3. Double-click on the icon for the new task. The Properties dialog for your Transform Data task should appear. This step is shown in Figure 6.24.
4. Right-click on the icon for the new task. Select Copy from the pop-up menu.
5. Right-click on the Design Sheet and select Paste. You can do this in the same package or in any other package where you want to move the Transform Data task. The freestanding Transform Data task will appear.
6. Delete the duplicate copies of the Transform Data task, including the new task you created and the original black arrow icon, if you are creating the new Transform Data task in the same package.

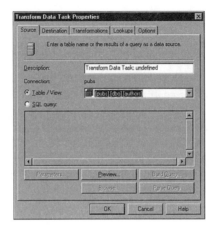

FIGURE 6.24

You can change your Transform Data tasks to the freestanding icon.

NOTE

Whenever you create a new task using the Package Designer, a step, a task, and an icon for the step/task are all created at the same time. The Package Designer creates the icon that is appropriate for the particular custom task.

After the point of creation, that icon is attached to the Step object and not the Task object. You can switch the task associated with the step to another task. (That's what you're doing when you change the Step's TaskName property.) You can remove the Task object from the Package's Tasks collection. The step will still be displayed in the Package Designer with the icon that was originally assigned to it.

The connection between step and icon remains when saving and loading the package from any type of storage except Visual Basic code. When you SaveToVB, none of the visual representation of the package is saved. When you recreate the package by executing the saved code, the default visual representation of the package is recreated. An icon is assigned to each step based on the task that is associated with that step in the VB code.

CAUTION

One more reminder. As far as I know, there is no Microsoft documentation regarding the freestanding Transform Data task icon or on any of the information I have presented in this section.

Conclusion

There's a lot to learn about the Transform Data task! This has been a long chapter, but there's still a lot more to learn about this task.

The next chapter, "Writing ActiveX Scripts for a Transform Data Task," shows you how to implement precise programmatic control in the row-by-row processing of your data.

Writing ActiveX Scripts for a Transform Data Task

IN THIS CHAPTER

Data transformation scripts give DTS its flexibility and versatility. These scripts allow you to manipulate the data in each field of every row. All the code in the transformation script is executed once for each record in the data source. Other tasks, like the Bulk Insert, and other transformations, like the Copy Column, certainly move data faster, but they can only be used in specific situations. The ActiveX Script transformation can be used in almost every data transformation situation—and it's usually fast enough.

The needs of data transformation can be very complex. You may need to transform a field in different ways depending on a number of specific circumstances. You can accomplish a lot of detailed data manipulation with SQL queries, but there are times when programmatic requirements overwhelm the set-based logic of SQL.

The ActiveX transformation in the Transform Data task is a Rapid Application Development (RAD) tool because it lets you use the complex logic you need to apply to your data while still achieving excellent performance.

> **NOTE**
>
> Before DTS was included with SQL 7.0, I used Transact-SQL cursors in stored procedures to do what I now accomplish with transformation scripts. I know some database developers who would never use a Transact-SQL cursor because of its poor performance. I also know some developers who have been reluctant to try script transformations in DTS because the processing of these scripts seems to be very similar to the operation of a cursor.
>
> An ActiveX Data Transformation script is quicker than a Transact-SQL cursor—a *lot* quicker. It's optimized for high-speed data movement. Yes, you can slow it down by writing complex code. But if you need complexity in your data transformations, transformation scripts are a great place to implement that complexity.

You can learn more about writing ActiveX scripts in Chapter 16, "Writing Scripts for an ActiveX Script Task." You can learn about debugging scripts in Chapter 27, "Handling Errors in a Package and Its Transformations."

When You Should Use the ActiveX Script Transformation

The basic rule of an ActiveX Script transformation is to use it when nothing else is going to work:

- If you can use a Bulk Insert or some other task, consider using them first.
- If you can use one of the other transformations, use them.

- If your transformation logic is too complex for anything else, use the ActiveX Script Transformation.

- If you could do the transformation some other way, but it would take too long and it would be too hard to work out the logic, use the ActiveX Script to get the job done on time.

Deciding Between One Task and Many

Sometimes it's possible to meet the data manipulation requirements in a couple of different ways:

- Write a transformation script in a Transform Data task.

- Create a Bulk Insert task followed by a couple of Execute SQL tasks. This way, you would get the data into SQL Server from a text file in the fastest possible way. You would use the rapid set-oriented processing of SQL to finish the detailed data manipulation—updating rows, deleting rows, and moving records to other tables.

Which strategy results in the quickest development time? Which one gives the best performance? Which one will be easier to maintain as additional transformation needs are discovered?

I can usually create a Transform Data task with a transformation script faster than setting up a Bulk Insert task and a couple of Execute SQL tasks. I can often achieve better performance by using the Bulk Insert with a couple of Execute SQL tasks. I usually find that a Transform Data task is a more maintainable solution because an additional change can be added in the programmatic logic where it is needed.

In general, transformation scripts become a better solution as the complexity of your data manipulation logic increases.

Using the Variety of Transformation Types

You didn't have much choice regarding transformation types in SQL Server 7.0. If you weren't doing a straight copy of fields from source to destination, you had to use an ActiveX Script transformation.

In SQL Server 2000, you can choose from the nine different transformation types. Basic date and string manipulation that would have required an ActiveX Script in the past can now be accomplished with another transformation type.

Use a specific transformation type to accomplish a specific job whenever you can. In fact, if you have a particular kind of transformation that you use frequently, the best way to improve its performance is to make it into a Custom Transformation. See Chapter 32, "Creating a Custom Transformation with VC++."

> **TIP**
>
> When I created a Transform Data task in SQL Server 7.0, I often put all the columns from the source and the destination in one ActiveX Script transformation. I'm moving away from that strategy in SQL Server 2000. I like using the new types of transformations, especially the one that transforms dates.
>
> My new strategy is to use one of each of the appropriate transformation types, dividing the columns into the appropriate types of transformations. With the date transformation type, I create one transformation for each combination of source and destination date formats that I'm using.

Transformation ActiveX Scripts Basics

The code in an ActiveX Script transformation is run repeatedly as a Transform Data task is executed. Here is the logical sequence of events:

1. The package executes the Transform Data task.
2. The Transform Data task (the data pump) runs the source query.
3. The values for the first record in the recordset returned by the source query are loaded into the transformation's collection of source columns.
4. The data pump executes the transformations in the order of their ordinal numbers in the Transformations collection. Each transformation can use the information from one or more of the source columns and may assign values to one or more of the destination columns.
5. Each script used in an ActiveX Script transformation must have an entry function. The default name for the entry function is Main. When the ActiveX Script transformation is executed, the data pump calls this entry function.
6. The code in the entry function is executed. Other functions in the script may be called. Any of the functions in the script may assign values to destination columns. The script can use information from the source columns, lookups defined for the task, and global variables defined for the package.
7. The entry function must return a transformation status code to the data pump. You can use this status code to insert a record, skip inserting a record, skip fetching a new record, return information, and/or return an error.
8a. If the last transformation executed for a record returns the transformation status code DTSTransformStat_OK, the values in the transformation's destination columns are loaded into the data destination. If you are not using Fast Load, the record is inserted

individually into the destination. If you are using Fast Load, the record is saved for loading later as a part of a batch. The values of the destination columns are set to null. The values for the next record from the data source are loaded into the transformation's source columns.

8b. If the last transformation executed for a record returns the transformation status code DTSTransformStat_SkipFetch, the processing is the same as for DTSTransformStat_OK, except that the values for the transformation's source columns are left unchanged.

8c. If the last transformation executed for a record returns the transformation status code DTSTransformStat_SkipInsert, a record is not inserted into the destination. The values for the next record from the data source are loaded into the transformation's source columns. The values in the transformation's destination columns are not set to null. They keep their values as the processing starts for the next source record.

9. Steps 3 through 7 are repeated for all the records returned by the source query.

10. If you are using the fast load option, the data pump loads the records into the data destination when the number of destination records specified by the InsertCommitSize property has been reached.

7

> **NOTE**
>
> You can reference the same destination column in two or more transformations. If you do this, you will receive a warning message from the DTS Designer:
>
> "Same destination column 'au_id' exists in two transformations, which may cause a potential problem. Do you still want to continue?"
>
> The potential problem is that if you assign a destination column twice, the second assignment will overwrite the first. This could present a confusing debugging situation.
>
> But there is also a potential benefit in doing this. If you add a transformation column that has already been assigned a value to an ActiveX Script transformation, you can use the assigned value in your programmatic logic.

The Transformation ActiveX Script Development Environment

Figure 7.1 shows the ActiveX Script Transformation Properties dialog, which opens when you create a new ActiveX transformation. You can also open the dialog by double-clicking the transformation's mapping line.

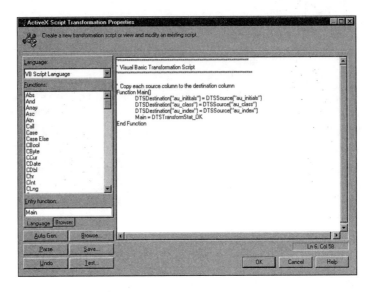

FIGURE 7.1

The ActiveX Script Transformation Properties dialog provides a simple user interface for creating transformation scripts.

When you first open the ActiveX Script Transformation Properties dialog, you see a default script that has been generated already. This default script gives you the same transformation result as a Copy Column transformation. Each field in the source is copied to the same field in the destination, based on the ordinal position of the fields in the two collections. The first field is copied to the first field in the destination, the second field is copied to the second field in the destination, and so on. The names of the fields are ignored in this mapping process.

Listing 7.1 is an example of a default script. The data source is the authors table from the pubs sample database. The data destination has fields with identical names as the source, except that the first field, au_id, is not included. The first eight fields in the source column collection have been mapped to the eight fields in the destination column collection.

LISTING 7.1 Sample Script Mapping Fields from a Source to a Destination

```
'*************************************************************************
'  Visual Basic Transformation Script
'  Copy each source column to the
'  destination column
'*************************************************************************

Function Main()
    DTSDestination("au_lname") = DTSSource("au_id")
```

LISTING 7.1 Continued

```
    DTSDestination("au_fname") = DTSSource("au_lname")
    DTSDestination("phone") = DTSSource("au_fname")
    DTSDestination("address") = DTSSource("phone")
    DTSDestination("city") = DTSSource("address")
    DTSDestination("state") = DTSSource("city")
    DTSDestination("zip") = DTSSource("state")
    DTSDestination("contract") = DTSSource("zip")
    Main = DTSTransformStat_OK
End Function
```

The default script is very useful when the fields have been lined up in the proper order. In a situation like this, however, it's not very helpful.

The dialog provides three ways to modify or create a transformation script:

- Automatically generate the script. The default script is generated when the ActiveX transformation is first created. If you want, you can regenerate the script in a different scripting language. You may also want to return to the original script after experimenting with some changes. You can re-create the default script by clicking the Auto Gen. button.

- Insert a script from a file. A Browse button is provided so you can choose the file.

- Write the script in the Script textbox.

The tabs on the left side of the ActiveX Script Transformation Properties dialog provide assistance in writing and editing the script:

- The first tab has a list box for choosing the scripting language. Prototypes of all the functions in the language you have chosen are available in the second list box. If you double-click on any of the functions, the prototype is copied into the text of your script at the point where you have placed the cursor. This tab also has a text box for choosing the entry function for your script.

- The second tab, shown in Figure 7.2, has a Package Object Browser. Source columns, destination columns, lookups, global variables, task constants, and step constants are all available for selection and insertion into your script.

- If you have enabled the Multiphase Option, you will have a third tab where you can name the entry function for each of the phases. The use of multiple phases is discussed in Chapter 9, "The Multiphase Data Pump."

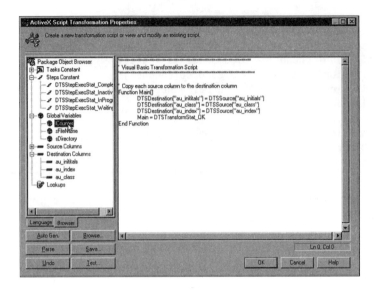

FIGURE 7.2

You can insert object references into your script using the Package Object Browser.

NOTE

The Package Object Browser is a great addition to SQL Server 2000 because you don't need to remember the names of lookups and global variables.

TIP

The script code will execute more quickly if you refer to the columns by their ordinal numbers rather than by their names, such as DTSDestination(1) instead of DTSDestination("au_lname"). Unfortunately, this is not an option in the automatically generated script.

CAUTION

The script code will execute more quickly if you refer to the columns by their ordinal numbers rather than by their names, such as DTSDestination(1) instead of DTSDestination("au_lname"). We have seen a 35% performance improvement when

> using 20 columns. But you have to be careful if you use this performance optimization strategy.
>
> The ordinal numbers of the columns used in a Transform Data task are changed every time you look at one of the column tabs in the Transformation Options dialog. This behavior makes it very risky to refer to the columns by ordinal numbers in the script. If anyone looks at the columns, saves the task, and saves the package, the script will be invalidated because the references to all the columns will be changed.
>
> Chapter 28, "High-Performance DTS Packages," has a pair of ActiveX scripts—one that programmatically changes all the column name references to ordinal references and the other that changes them all back.

7

WRITING ACTIVEX SCRIPTS

There are four other buttons that help you develop and manage your scripts:

- The Parse button checks the script's syntax. The parsing will find some errors, such as unterminated strings. Unfortunately, it does not find others, such as invalid column references.

- The Test button executes the script. This is the same test that can be run from the Transformation tab of the Data Transformation Properties dialog. The results of the script test are displayed on the screen and saved to a text file. You can find many errors by testing that you can't find by parsing.

- The Save button, a new addition to SQL Server 2000, saves the script to a .vbs or .bas file.

- The Undo button, also new in SQL Server 2000, lets you undo your recent script edits.

Choosing a Scripting Language

You can use any scripting language that is installed on your system for your transformation script. There are two scripting languages that are installed with SQL Server:

- Microsoft Visual Basic Scripting Edition (VBScript)
- Microsoft JScript

Microsoft has documented some performance differences in the use of the various scripting languages in DTS. VBScript runs approximately 10% faster than JScript, and JScript runs approximately 10% faster than PerlScript.

NOTE

We have chosen to use VBScript for all the ActiveX Script code samples in the book.

Setting the DTS Transformation Status

You set the DTS Transformation Status value to tell the data pump what it should do at the conclusion of a transformation script. Should the record be inserted into the destination table? Do you want to process the same source record again? Should the record be handled as an error? Should the entire Transform Data task be aborted because of what has happened in the processing of this record?

The status value is set as the return value from the Main function in your ActiveX transformation script. The following is the final line of code that appears in the default transformation script:

```
Main = DTSTransformStat_OK
```

This transformation status value reports that the script has completed successfully and that normal processing should continue.

All the values for this constant that can be used in transformation scripts for the Transform Data task are listed in this section. There are four additional Transformation Status values that can be used with data-driven queries. Those values are discussed in Chapter 8, "The Data Driven Query Task."

DTSTransformStat_OK

The transformation script was successful.

- Value 1
- There are no error messages.
- The data pump continues on with the next transformation for this record.
- The data pump inserts the record into the data destination, and the values of all the destination columns are set to null if this transformation status is received for the last transformation in the Transformations collection.
- The data pump continues processing with the next record from the data source if this transformation status is received for the last transformation in the Transformations collection.

DTSTransformStat_SkipRow

Skip all transformations for this row.

- Value 2
- There are no error messages.
- The data pump does not execute any more of the transformations for this row.

- No record is inserted into the data destination for this source record. The values of all the destination columns are set to null.

- The data pump continues processing with the next record from the data source.

DTSTransformStat_SkipFetch

Skip fetching the next row. You can use this status flag to create more than one record in the destination for one record in the source.

- Value   4
- There are no error messages.
- The data pump continues on with the next transformation for this record.
- The data pump inserts the record into the data destination, and the values of all the destination columns are set to null if this transformation status is received for the last transformation in the Transformations collection.
- The data pump stays on the same record in the data source and begins processing it, as if it were a new record, if this transformation status is received for the last transformation in the Transformations collection.

DTSTransformStat_SkipInsert

Skip the insert for this record.

- Value   8
- There are no error messages.
- The data pump continues on with the next transformation for this record.
- The data pump skips inserting the record into the data destination if this transformation status is received for the last ActiveX Script transformation in the Transformations collection. Values that have been assigned to destination columns are not set to null.
- The data pump continues processing with the next record from the data source if this transformation status is received for the last transformation in the Transformations collection.

DTSTransformStat_DestDataNotSet

This transformation status is used internally by the Write File transformation to indicate that the row was successfully processed, even though no data was sent to the destination.

- Value   512
- Processing similar to Skip Insert.

DTSTransformStat_Info

The transformation was successful, and there are information messages.

- Value   4096
- Writes the results of this transformation to the destination table.
- An error has not occurred, but there is information available in the error sink.
- This flag is usually not used by itself. It can be combined with OK or with Skip Row, as described below.

DTSTransformStat_OKInfo

Combine the functionality of DTSTransformStat_OK and DTSTransformStat_Info.

- Value   4097 (4096 + 1)
- Combination of OK and Info.

DTSTransformStat_SkipRowInfo

Combine the functionality of DTSTransformStat_SkipRow and DTSTransformStat_Info.

- Value   4098 (4096 + 2)
- Combination of Skip Row and Info.

DTSTransformStat_Error

This transformation status and the two following ones are closely related. All three do one or both of the following things:

- Increment the number of errors that have been recorded for the Transform Data task. When the number of errors reaches the number that has been set in Max Error Count, the task terminates and is treated as having failed.
- Write the source record to the exception file.

The DTSTransformStat_Error status causes both of these to happen. The DTSTransformStat_ErrorSkipRow status causes just the first. The DTSTransformStat_ExceptionRow causes just the second.

Here's the information about DTSTransformStat_Error:

- Value   8192
- An error has occurred. This error is counted in the maximum allowed number of errors for this Transform Data task.

- Skip the insert for this record.
- Information about the error is available in the error sink.
- The record is inserted into the exception file.
- No more transformations are executed for this record.
- No record is inserted into the data destination for this source record.
- The data pump continues processing with the next record from the data source.

DTSTransformStat_ErrorSkipRow

An error has occurred and the row should be skipped.

- Value 8194 (8192 + 2)
- An error has occurred. This error is counted in the maximum allowed number of errors for this Transform Data task.
- The behavior is identical to DTSTransformStat_Error, except that the error record is not written to the exception file.

DTSTransformStat_ExceptionRow

Handle this row as an exception.

- Value 8448 (8192 + 256)
- An exception has occurred. The behavior is identical to DTSTransformStat_Error, except that this exception does not count against the maximum allowed number of errors for this Transform Data task.
- An error record is written to the exception file.

DTSTransformStat_AbortPump

Abort the Transform Data task.

- Value 16384
- Do not insert any more records for this Transform Data task.
- Return the value DTSTransformExec_AbortPump as the result of the Transform Data task.

DTSTransformStat_NoMoreRows

There are no more rows in the data source.

- Value 32768
- Do not insert the current row into the data destination.

7

WRITING ACTIVEX
SCRIPTS

- Do not process any more rows.
- Terminate the Transform Data task with a value of `DTSTransformExec_OK`, indicating success.

Creating and Using Local Variables

You can declare local variables within an ActiveX Script. If a variable is declared inside the script but not inside a function, the scope of the variable is the entire script. If a variable is declared within a function, its scope is just that individual function.

Variables that are declared outside a function maintain their values from the processing of one record to the next. If you want to pass values between transformation scripts or between transformation tasks, you have to use global variables.

Variable Types

When you declare a local variable in VBScript, you are not allowed to specify a datatype. Here is an example of a variable declaration:

```
Dim sName
```

All variables in VBScript are variant variables. They can change their datatypes freely, depending on which value is assigned to the variable. You can change the datatype of a variant variable by using functions such as the following:

```
lCounter = CLng(lCounter)
```

This code changes the datatype of lCounter to Long. However, if there is a value assigned to lCounter that is not a numeric value, an error will be generated.

You can determine the variable type by using the `VarType` function. Here are some of the key values:

- 0—Empty
- 1—Null
- 2—Integer
- 3—Long
- 4—Single
- 5—Double
- 6—Currency
- 7—Date
- 8—String

- 11—Boolean

- 17—Byte

You can check whether or not a variable has been assigned a value by using the IsEmpty function, which returns a value of TRUE or FALSE:

```
If IsEmpty(sName) Then
    Msgbox "Name has not yet been assigned."
Else
    Msgbox "Name is " & sName
End If
```

> **NOTE**
>
> You will generate an error if you attempt to use an unassigned variable in a string, whether in creating text for a message box, a query, or a lookup. If there is any chance that a variable will be unassigned, use the IsEmpty function to avoid these errors.

Object Variables

You can use your local variables to hold a reference to a COM object. The object variable is created in one of two ways:

- By assigning it to an object that has a certain relationship to another object or to a collection.

  For example, if you need a variable with a reference to the DTS package in which a block of code is executing, you can use the Parent property of the DTSGlobalVariables collection:

  ```
  Dim pkg, stp
  Set pkg = DTSGlobalVariables.Parent
  ```

  Then, if you want to set a variable to one of the steps, you can specify a particular step in the Steps collection of the Package object:

  ```
  Set stp = pkg.Steps("NameOfTheStep")
  ```

- By using the CreateObject function. You have to use this function if you don't have a reference to an existing object. The CreateObject function requires you to specify the object library and the type of object you are creating.

To create an ADO Recordset object so that you can read data directly from a script:

```
Dim rst
Set rst = CreateObject("ADODB.Recordset")
```

To create a DTS Application object so that you can query the DTS system properties:

```
Dim app
Set app = CreateObject("DTS.Application")
```

Using Option Explicit

The default behavior of VBScript variables is that they do not have to be declared before they are used. To enforce the declaration of local variables before they are used, you must use Option Explicit in each of your scripts.

Unlike global variables, the names of local variables are not case sensitive.

Creating and Using Global Variables

You have to use global variables for many types of DTS package communication:

- Between ActiveX Script tasks and scripts in data transformation tasks.
- To fill parameters in the source query of a Transform Data task or the SQL query of an Execute SQL task.
- To store values retrieved from a query of an Execute SQL task.
- To send values into a package as it is executed with DTSRun.
- To send values from one package to another package when using the Execute Package task.

A global variable is usually referenced as a particular member of the `DTSGlobalVariables` collection:

```
DTSGlobalVariables("sManager").Value = "Smith"
```

You can also reference a global variable through the `GlobalVariables` collection:

```
Dim pkg, gv
Set pkg = DTSGlobalVariables.Parent
Set gv = pkg.GlobalVariables("sManager")
gv.Value = "Smith"
```

Creating Global Variables in the User Interface

You can create global variables in several places using the DTS Designer. One way is to do the following:

1. Select Properties from the main DTS Designer Package menu. Make sure no objects on the design sheet are selected when you make this selection, or else the properties of that object will be displayed rather than the properties of the package as a whole.

2. Select the Global Variables tab in the DTS Package Properties dialog.

3. Click the New button (or just start typing in the box).

4. Enter a name for the variable and choose a datatype.

5. You may also enter a value for the global variable, which will be the initial value that the global variable holds each time the package is executed. You have to enter an appropriate value for the global variable if you are choosing a non-string datatype.

> **NOTE**
>
> This last detail in #5 escaped me for quite a while. I always received an error message when I was trying to set the datatype of a global variable to an integer, a Boolean, or a date. You can't use other datatypes unless you set a value for the variable that is appropriate for the selected datatype. You can't leave the value as the default, an empty string.

The Global Variables tab of the DTS Package Properties dialog is shown in Figure 7.3. Note the Explicit Global Variables check box, which is used to require explicit declaration for all global variables.

FIGURE 7.3
Global variables can be created in the DTS Package Properties dialog and can be referenced throughout the package.

Creating Global Variables in an ActiveX Script

You can create global variables three different ways in ActiveX scripts.

> **NOTE**
>
> Usually, you wouldn't create a global variable in a transformation script. Instead, you would use an ActiveX Script task, a workflow script, or the Pre Source phase of a multiphase data transformation. I am discussing this topic here to keep the primary consideration of global variables in one place in the book.

These global variables exist only for the duration of the package's execution. Because these variables are not saved after the package is executed, you will not be able to view them in the Package Properties dialog.

> **NOTE**
>
> Global variables created during the execution of a package are destroyed after the package is run. But if you execute an individual step in the Package Designer, any global variables created during the execution of that step will persist and will be listed in the Package Properties dialog.
>
> If your script assigns an object reference to any of your global variables, you will not be able to save your package until those variables are deleted or the reference is changed to a different datatype.

Here are the three ways to create global variables in an ActiveX script:

- Create by reference. If you reference a global variable that does not exist, it will be created automatically:

```
DTSGlobalVariables("VarCreatedByRef").Value = 1
```

To prevent global variables from being created by reference, select the Explicit Global Variables check box in the Package Properties dialog. You can still use the other two methods of creating global variables in code.

- Create with the `AddGlobalVariable` method. This method of the `DTSGlobalVariables` collection allows you to create a new global variable and assign its initial value:

```
DTSGlobalVariables.AddGlobalVariable ("VarCreatedWithAddGlobalVariable"), 2
```

- Create with the `Add` method of the `GlobalVariables` collection. This is similar to the code that you would use to create a global variable in Visual Basic but requires a little more code:

```
Dim pkg, gv
Set pkg = DTSGlobalVariables.parent
Set gv = pkg.GlobalVariables.New("VarCreatedWithAdd")
gv.Value = 3
pkg.GlobalVariables.Add gv
```

When you create a global variable in the interface, you pick its datatype from a list. When you create a global variable in code, you cannot specify its datatype explicitly. The datatype will be assigned automatically depending on the type of data that you assign to the variable. The datatype of the global variable will be changed automatically when you assign data of another datatype to the global variable:

- Create a global variable with a string datatype:

```
DTSGlobalVariables("sVar").Value = "whatever"
```

- Create a global variable with an integer datatype:

```
DTSGlobalVariables("lVar").Value = 12345
```

- Create a global variable with a date datatype:

```
DTSGlobalVariables("dtVar").Value = #1/1/2002#
```

- Create a global variable with an object datatype:

```
DTSGlobalVariables("pkg").Value = DTSGlobalVariables.Parent
```

- Explicitly change a global variable from a string value to an integer value:

```
DTSGlobalVariables("StringToInteger").Value = _
    CLng(DTSGlobalVariables("StringToInteger").Value)
```

Case Sensitivity of Global Variables and Option Explicit

Global variables, unlike local ones, are case sensitive in Data Transformation Services, so it's easier to make a mistake in naming a variable. By using SQL Server 2000's capability to require Explicit Global Variables, you can avoid programming errors caused by using the wrong case in a variable name.

7

WRITING ACTIVEX
SCRIPTS

In the following code, two new global variables are created because of the different cases in the variable names. The message box will display a value of 1. The second line of this code will generate an error if you have selected Explicit Global Variables, allowing you to find and fix the problem:

```
DTSGlobalVariables.AddGlobalVariable "NewIdCount", 0
DTSGlobalVariables("NewIDCount").Value = 5
DTSGlobalVariables("NewIdCount").Value = _
    DTSGlobalVariables("NewIdCount").Value + 1
Msgbox DTSGlobalVariables("NewIdCount").Value
```

The Lock and Unlock Methods of the GlobalVariable2 Object

The extended GlobalVariable2 object in SQL Server 2000 has two new methods—Lock and Unlock. SQL Server Books Online states that the Lock method allows a task to acquire a global variable for exclusive use:

```
DTSGlobalVariables("Var1").Lock
```

Locking a global variable does not prevent its value from being read or changed by another task. However, it does prevent the global variable from being locked in another task until it has been unlocked in the first task:

```
DTSGlobalVariables("Var1").Unlock
```

An error will be generated if you lock a variable in a task, never unlock it, and then attempt to reference that global variable in a different task. An error will also occur if a global variable is locked in one task and the Unlock method is called for it in a different task.

You can use a timeout parameter with the Lock method. If the global variable is already locked, the method waits for the number of milliseconds specified and then generates an error:

```
DTSGlobalVariables("Var1").Lock 2000
```

Creating and Using Lookups

You can use a Lookup object to retrieve information from a separate data source during a transformation. Lookups are especially useful when you're inserting records into dimension tables in a star schema. If your source data contains abbreviations, you can use a lookup to replace those fields with their full text value. Lookups are also useful for checking the validity of your data.

You could open a recordset and retrieve values of fields directly in a transformation script, but this would be too time-consuming. That script could run thousands of times. With a lookup, only the data connection has to be made. Lookup values can be cached as they are retrieved, so if the same value is needed again, it's immediately available. The process is very efficient.

Creating Lookups with the User Interface

`Lookup` objects are made for a specific data transformation task. You can create them in the DTS Designer with the following steps:

1. Create the connection that the `Lookup` object is going to use, unless you are going to use an existing connection.
2. Select the Lookups tab in the Transform Data Task Properties dialog.
3. Click the Add button (or just type in the box).
4. Enter the lookup's name and choose a connection for it from the list.
5. Click the expand button for the lookup's query. The Data Transformation Services Query Designer dialog opens so you can create the query for the lookup. A lookup query usually returns one field, although it can be set up to return multiple fields. Include one or more parameters in the query by using question marks. Here is a typical lookup query that finds the name of the state when given the value of the state's abbreviation:

```
Select StateName from tblStateLookup where StateAbbreviation = ?
```

You may enter a value for the cache. This sets the value of the `MaxCacheRows` property of the `Lookup` object. If you don't enter a value, the default of 0 will be used and no rows will be cached for the lookup. The cache will be filled with rows as they are retrieved. When the assigned cache size is reached, each additional retrieval will cause one of the rows to be removed from the cache.

The Lookups tab of the Transform Data Task Properties dialog is shown in Figure 7.4.

FIGURE 7.4

You can create lookups to allow your transformation scripts to efficiently access information from other data sources.

Creating Lookup Objects in an ActiveX Script

You can also create `Lookup` objects in ActiveX scripts. Use the `AddLookup` method of the `Lookups` collection. You can find the examples in this section in a DTS package in a file called Lookups.dts.

> **NOTE**
>
> As with Global Variables, you would usually create a lookup in an ActiveX Script task, a workflow script, or the Pre Source phase of a multiphase data transformation.

The parameters for the `AddLookup` method are the `Name` of the lookup, the `Query`, the `ConnectionID`, and the `MaxCacheRows`:

```
Dim pkg, tsk, cus
Set pkg = DTSGlobalVariables.Parent
Set tsk = pkg.Tasks("tskLoadAddress")
Set cus = tsk.CustomTask
cus.Lookups.AddLookup "FindStateName", _
    "Select StateName from tblStateLookup where StateAbbr = ?", 3, 50
```

Using a Lookup in an ActiveX Script

You use the `Execute` method of the `Lookup` object to return the value for a lookup. This line of code will use the `Lookup` object to replace the state abbreviation from the source with the state name in the destination:

```
DTSDestination("StateName") = _
    DTSLookups("FindStateName").Execute(DTSSource("State"))
```

Here is how you reference a `Lookup` object that uses two or more parameters:

```
DTSDestination("StateNameFromStateAndCountry") = _
    DTSLookups("FindStateName").Execute(DTSSource("State"),_
    DTSSource("Country"))
```

If your lookup query selects more than one field, you can reference them as members of an array:

```
Dim arrayStateAndCountry
arrayStateAndCountry = DTSLookups("StateAndCountryFromStateAbbr")._
        Execute(DTSSource("State"))
DTSDestination("StateName") =  arrayStateAndCountry(0)
DTSDestination("Country") = arrayStateAndCountry(1)
```

Using a Lookup to Modify Data

One of the new features in SQL Server 2000 is the ability to use data modification queries in lookups. The ability to call inserts, updates, deletes, and stored procedures with lookups gives the Transform Data task functionality that is similar to the Data Driven Query task.

You can create a Transform Data task that inserts new records into a dimension table and also updates existing dimension records. The update would be implemented with a data modification lookup query that looks like this:

```
Update dimCustomer Set LastName = ? Where CustID = ?
```

A similar data modification lookup is implemented in the package in Lookups.dts:

```
Update tblAuthorAndStateName Set au_lname = ? Where au_id = ?
```

You don't return a value with a lookup that modifies data. Here's the code in the transformation script that calls the data modification lookup:

```
DTSLookups("updAuthorName").Execute(DTSSource("au_lname"), _
DTSSource("au_id"))
```

> **NOTE**
>
> One of the criticisms I have heard about DTS is that you can't divide a wide record containing many fields into several different tables. You could do so with a Data Driven Query, of course—at least, you could divide one record into four tables. Now you can also do it with a Transform Data task by using Insert lookup queries to fill as many different tables as you want.
>
> The problem with this strategy is that you lose the high-performance data manipulation that you normally have available in the Transform Data task. Using Fast Load as you move data into SQL Server, you can insert many rows at the same time. If you're using a lookup to do an insert, that insert query has to be called separately for each record. If you're doing inserts into several different tables, you could have a very slow data transformation.
>
> It would usually be faster to execute two separate Transform Data tasks, one to load each table, rather than executing one Transform Data task that uses an Insert lookup query to load a table.
>
> Also consider the possibility of using a Data Driven Query task or a Parallel Data Pump task.

Using ActiveX Scripts or Modifying the Source Query

Transformation scripts can be very simple or very complex. One of the best ways to improve the performance of basic data manipulation is to move it into the source query of the Transform Data task and switch to using a Copy Column transformation. See Chapter 28, "High-Performance DTS Packages," for an analysis of the performance of these scripts and source queries.

Most of the examples in this section can be found in a DTS package stored in SampleTransformations.dts in the section for Chapter 7 on the CD.

Simple Assignment of Fields

In the simplest script transformation, you assign the value of the destination column to the value of the source column, as is generated by the default ActiveX transformation script:

```
Function Main()
    DTSDestination("au_lname") = DTSSource("au_lname")
    DTSDestination("au_fname") = DTSSource("au_fname")

    Main = DTSTransformStat_OK
End Function
```

This transformation should be changed to a Copy Column transformation, which is 2 to 4 times faster.

String Manipulation

String manipulation can include formatting dates, extracting a portion of a string, changing from upper- to lowercase, and concatenating strings.

The new types of transformations take some of the string manipulation away from the transformation scripts, but there will still be many situations where your need for string manipulation does not match the existing transformation types. In those cases, you can do your string manipulation. You could join first and last names like this:

```
Function Main()
    DTSDestination("au_fullname") = _
    DTSSource("au_lname") & ", " & DTSSource("au_fname")
    Main = DTSTransformStat_OK
End Function
```

The data transformation would be quicker if the string manipulation could be pushed into the source query, especially when that would allow you to use a Copy Column transformation:

```
Select au_lname + ', ' + au_fname as au_fullname
from AuthorName
```

The only reason to use the script in a situation like this is if there are too many unusual situations to handle easily in a SQL query. Complex logic is easier in a procedural language such as VBScript than in a set-oriented language like SQL.

Handling Unknown Values

Here is how you could handle empty string or null values in the name fields by using programmatic logic in a transformation ActiveX Script:

```
Function Main()
'If Last Name is missing, insert "Unknown Name"
'If First Name is missing, insert Last Name
'If both names are present, concatenate them

If IsNull( DTSSource("au_lname") ) Or DTSSource("au_lname") = "" Then

  DTSDestination("au_fullname") = "Unknown Name"

Else

    If IsNull( DTSSource("au_fname") ) Or DTSSource("au_fname") = "" Then
        DTSDestination("au_fullname") = DTSSource("au_lname")
    Else
        DTSDestination("au_fullname") = _
            DTSSource("au_lname") & ", " & DTSSource("au_fname")
    End If

End If

    Main = DTSTransformStat_OK
End Function
```

To convert this logic into the source query, you have to use the Case statement in the Select clause:

```
select
    case
        when au_lname is null or au_lname = ''
            then 'Unknown Name'
        when au_fname is null or au_fname = ''
            then au_lname
```

```
    else
        au_lname + ', ' + au_fname
    end as au_fullname
from AuthorName
```

Looking Up an Unknown Value

When the primary source of data is inadequate, you may have an alternative source. In those situations, you can use a lookup to retrieve the value from the other table.

You can create a lookup called lkpAuthorName that has the following SQL query:

```
Select FullName from tblAuthorNameList Where au_id = ?
```

Your ActiveX Script would then look like this:

```
Function Main()
'If either name is missing, look up the value of the Full Name

If IsNull(DTSSource("au_lname") ) Or DTSSource("au_lname") = "" Or _
   IsNull(DTSSource("au_fname") ) Or DTSSource("au_fname") = "" Then

    DTSDestination("au_fullname") = _
        DTSLookups("lkpAuthorName").Execute(DTSSource("au_id"))

Else
    DTSDestination("au_fullname") = _
        DTSSource("au_lname") & ", " & DTSSource("au_fname")
End If

    Main = DTSTransformStat_OK
End Function
```

Usually, you can replace a lookup in a transformation script with a join in the source query:

```
select
    case
        when a.au_lname is null or a.au_lname = ''
          or a.au_fname is null or a.au_fname = ''
            then lkp.FullName
        else
            au_lname + ', ' + au_fname
    end as au_fullname
from AuthorName a
    inner join tblAuthorNameList  lkp
        on a.au_id = lkp.au_id
```

Using an Outer Join to Protect Against Missing Data

If you have to check for missing authors in the lookup table, modify the transformation script with the following embedded If block after the lookup:

```
If IsNull(DTSDestination("au_fullname")) Or _
    DTSDestination("au_fullname")  = "" Then
        DTSDestination("au_fullname") = "Unknown Value"
End If
```

If you are joining to the lookup table in the source query, you have to use an outer join if there's any chance that some author names might be missing in the lookup table. If you don't use an outer join, authors that don't have a match in the lookup table will be eliminated from the transformation:

```
select
    case
        when a.au_lname is null or a.au_lname = ''
          or a.au_fname is null or a.au_fname = ''
            then
                case
                    when lkp.FullName is null or lkp.FullName = ''
                        then 'Unknown Value'
                    else
                        lkp.FullName
                end
        else
            au_lname + ', ' + au_fname
    end as au_fullname
from AuthorName a
    left outer join tblAuthorNameList lkp
        on a.au_id = lkp.au_id
```

> **TIP**
>
> I think one of the key issues with using the set-oriented logic of SQL is the risk of los-
> ing records that don't match the join criteria. If there is any chance that your data is
> incomplete in one of the tables you are joining, you have to use an outer join so that
> records aren't lost altogether.

Merging Data from Two Sources with a Full Outer Join

You need to use a full outer join in the following situation:

- You're merging data from two tables, such as lists of customers that have been kept by two divisions within your organization.
- You have some matching records in the table that you can identify with a common key field.
- You have some records in each of the tables that do not match records in the other table.

A full outer join matches the matching records and keeps the unique records from both of the tables. In this query, priority is given to the information from CustomerList1 when it is available:

```
select
    case
        when c1.CustomerID is not null
            c1.CustomerID
        else
            c2.CustomerID
    end as CustomerID ,
    case
        when c1.CustomerName is not null
            c1.CustomerName
        else
            c2.CustomerName
    end as CustomerName,
    case
        when c1.CustomerAddress is not null
            c1.CustomerAddress
        else
            c2.CustomerAddress
    end as CustomerAddress,
from CustomerList1 c1
    full outer join CustomerList2 c2
        on c1.CustomerID = c2.CustomerID
```

Of course, you could keep both values in the query and use more sophisticated logic in the transformation script to determine which set of customer information is valid for each particular record. You might also want to store both sets of information in the destination table.

Separating Information from One Record into Several Records

You can use a transformation script to separate data from one record into several records. This needs to be done when you're eliminating repeated fields in the process of normalization.

> **TIP**
>
> You can often increase your ability to analyze data by splitting one record into multiple records. Once I worked on a project in which the database had a 128-character field with Y's and N's that indicated whether or not customers were participating in specific programs. It is hard to write efficient queries to retrieve multiple data elements encoded in one field.
>
> I separated out the field using the strategy described in this section, making one record for each Y in the field.

When you divide one record into multiple records, you set up a loop to process each of the source records:

1. You use a variable to keep track of the state of the loop. In the following example, a counter is incremented each time through the loop to keep track of where the process is.

2. The variable needs to be initialized in two places—before the first record and at the end of each record. I recommend using the Pre Source phase for the first initialization. I also recommend implementing the subsequent initializations at the end of the Main function for the Row Transform phase. (See Chapter 9, "The Multiphase Data Pump," for a discussion of the phases in an ActiveX transformation script.)

3. The variable is used to determine which data from the source record is to be used for each particular destination record. You can often use a `Case` statement in the code to do this.

4. You have to determine the appropriate transformation status:

   `DTSTransformStat_SkipFetch` inserts a destination record and stays on the same source record.

   `DTSTransformStat_OK` inserts a destination record and moves to the next source record.

   `DTSTransformStat_SkipInsert` doesn't insert a destination record and moves to the next source record. This is needed if you have reached the last pass through the data and you don't have a final record to insert.

5. If you don't find a record to insert for a particular pass through the data and you're not on the last pass, it's more efficient to move to the next possibility without reloading the source record. The example uses a `Do` loop to keep looking for the next possibility within the source record. The code breaks out of the loop when data to insert is found or when the last possibility has been checked.

Listing 7.2 shows the code for dividing one record into multiple records. You can find it in a DTS package on the CD, in a file called SeparateAndMerge.dts. This example uses the Orders table from the Northwind sample database. The three date fields in the table are divided into separate records in a new table called tblTransaction. This table has four fields:

- TransactionID—Identity field. Primary key of tblTransaction.
- OrderID—Copied from the Orders table.
- TranType—OrderDate, ShippedDate, or RequiredDate.
- TranDate—The date copied from the Orders table.

LISTING 7.2   An ActiveX Script That Divides One Record into Multiple Records

```
Dim lNormalizeTranCounter

Function PreSourceMain()

'Initialize Counter to 0 before first record is processed.
lNormalizeTranCounter = 0

    PreSourceMain = DTSTransformstat_OK
End Function


Function Main()

'Set the Order ID. It is always the same.
DTSDestination("OrderID") = DTSSource("OrderID")

'Loop until a record is found or the last possibility is checked.
'Always Exit Do Loop explicitly
Do While 1=1

    'Increment Counter to keep track of
    'which type of date we're processing
    'Starts at 0 for new record
    lNormalizeTranCounter = _
            lNormalizeTranCounter + 1

    'Set the TranDate and the TranType for this pass through the data
    Select Case lNormalizeTranCounter


        Case 1
            DTSDestination("TranDate") = DTSSource("OrderDate")
            DTSDestination("TranType") = "OrderDate"

        Case 2
            DTSDestination("TranDate") = DTSSource("ShippedDate")
```

LISTING 7.2 Continued

```
            DTSDestination("TranType") = "ShippedDate"

        Case 3
            DTSDestination("TranDate") = DTSSource("RequiredDate")
            DTSDestination("TranType") = "RequiredDate"

    End Select

    If lNormalizeTranCounter < 3 Then

        If IsNull(DTSSource("OrderDate")) Then

            'Didn't find a record to insert. Stay in loop to try again.

        Else

            'Insert destination row. Stay on the same source record
            Main = DTSTransformStat_SkipFetch
            Exit Do

        End if

    Else

        If IsNull(DTSSource("OrderDate")) Then

            'Don't insert destination row. Go on to next source record.
            Main = DTSTransformStat_SkipInsert

        Else

            'Insert row. Go on to next source record
            Main = DTSTransformStat_OK

        End if

        'Reset the counter
        lNormalizeTranCounter = 0

        'Always exit loop when the counter is 3
        Exit Do

    End If

Loop
End Function
```

Combining Information from Several Records into One

There are times when you might want to do the opposite of the last section by combining data into one record that is now located in several records. You can undo the work of the previous section with the following strategy:

1. Use a source query that puts all the records with the same OrderID in sequence together:

```
Select OrderID, TranType, TranDate
From tblTransaction
Order By OrderID
```

2. At the start of the ActiveX Script, examine the value of the OrderID in the destination column.

3. If the value of the OrderID in the destination column is null, this is either the first record being processed from the source query or the next record after a record has been inserted into the destination. Assign a value to the OrderID destination column and to the appropriate date column. Return a transformation status of DTSTransformStat_SkipInsert so that a record is not inserted into the destination and a new record will be retrieved from the source.

4. If OrderID is the same in the source and the destination, continue gathering the data by entering a value for the appropriate destination columns. Continue to use a transformation status of DTSTransformStat_SkipInsert.

5. If OrderID is different in the source and the destination, don't assign any of the destination columns. Return a transformation status of DTSTransformStat_SkipFetch. The values already assigned to the destination columns will be inserted into the destination. The same source record will be reloaded for the next execution of the script. In that next execution, all the destination columns will be null—ready to start collecting the values for the next OrderID.

6. There is no way of knowing when you're processing the last record in a Transform Data task, so the information for the last Transform Data task has to be inserted in a special script. You could do this with a data modification lookup in the Post Source Data phase. Here's the lookup query you could use:

```
INSERT INTO tblOrderDates
    (OrderID, OrderDate, ShippedDate, RequiredDate)
VALUES
    (?, ?, ?, ?)
```

The code for this example is shown in Listing 7.3. It is on the CD in a package stored in the SeparateAndMerge.dts file.

LISTING 7.3   ActiveX Transformation Script That Merges Several Records into One Record

```
Function Main()

If DTSSource("OrderID") = DTSDestination("OrderID") Or _
        IsNull(DTSDestination("OrderID")) Then

    'Assign value to OrderID
    DTSDestination("OrderID")  = DTSSource("OrderID")

    'Load data from the current source record into the destination column
    Select Case DTSSource("TranType")

        Case "OrderDate"
            DTSDestination("OrderDate") = DTSSource("TranDate")

        Case "ShippedDate"
            DTSDestination("ShippedDate") = DTSSource("TranDate")

        Case "RequiredDate"
            DTSDestination("RequiredDate") = DTSSource("TranDate")


    End Select

    'Assign Transformation Status to skip insert
    Main = DTSTransformStat_SkipInsert

Else

    Main = DTSTransformStat_SkipFetch

End If

End Function

Function PostSourceMain()
On Error Resume Next

DTSLookups("InserttblOrderDates").Execute _
        DTSDestination("OrderID"), _
        DTSDestination("OrderDate"), _
        DTSDestination("ShippedDate"), _
        DTSDestination("RequiredDate")

If Err.Number <> 0 Then
    Msgbox Err.Number & " " & Err.Description
```

7

WRITING ACTIVEX
SCRIPTS

LISTING 7.3   Continued

```
    PostSourceMain = DTSTransformstat_Error
Else
    PostSourceMain = DTSTransformstat_OK
End If

End Function
```

Conclusion

You have a great deal of flexibility when using a transformation ActiveX script in a Transform Data task. You have even more options when using a Data Driven Query task, multiple phases, or a Parallel Data Pump task. Those are the topics of the following chapters.

The Data Driven Query Task

IN THIS CHAPTER

Data transformation is the process of moving data. The most common result of the transformation is the insertion of records into the data destination.

But there are also times when a data transformation results in an updating or a deletion of a record in the data destination. The Data Driven Query task gives you the opportunity to define up to four different possibilities for the result of a data transformation. You can insert records, but you can also update records, delete records, and run stored procedures. The queries can all modify data in the same table or in different tables.

You might want to do this when loading a dimension table in a data mart. You can insert new dimension records and update existing dimension records, doing both operations in one Data Driven Query task.

You define these different transformation results by writing up to four different data-driven queries. You then write a transformation script that programmatically determines which of the queries should be used for a particular record being transformed.

NOTE

The query is labeled "data-driven" because the data in each individual record is used to drive the decision as to which query is executed.

Here is the flow of events in the execution of a Data Driven Query task:

1. The source query is executed.
2. The ActiveX Script transformation is executed for each of the records returned by the source query.
3. The script assigns values to the destination columns which, in the Data Driven Query task, are called columns of the bindings table.
4. The ActiveX Script return a transformation status that indicates which one, if any, of the four parameter queries is to be run.
5. The parameter query fills its parameters with the assigned values from the fields of the bindings table. The query is run.

NOTE

Much of the functionality of the Data Driven Query task is similar to that of the Transform Data task. This chapter explains the parts of the task that are different. In order to use the capabilities of the Data Driven Query task, you also need to be familiar with the material in Chapter 6, "The Transform Data Task," and Chapter 7, "Writing ActiveX Scripts for a Transform Data Task."

When to Use the Data Driven Query Task

You should use the Data Driven Query task when you need the flexibility of choosing among the four parameterized queries.

For example, you could have a destination table that contains a current list of products. Your source table could be a list of changes to the products, with some source records requiring that product records be added, others that product records be deleted, and others that product records be updated. A Data Driven Query task would allow you to look at each source record and run the appropriate data modification query.

For most of the times that you can use a Data Driven Query task, you can also use a Transform Data task. In the Data Driven Query, you can define four distinct queries to be executed and choose which one will be executed at the end of the ActiveX script. You can only define a single result for an ActiveX in the Transform Data task—an insertion of a new record in the data destination. But you can use multiple data modification lookup queries with one Transform Data task.

Here are the factors you should consider when deciding whether to use a Data Driven Query task or a Transform Data task:

- You cannot use the SQL Server Fast Load capability with the Data Driven Query task. Our testing indicates that the Transform Data task with Fast Load can insert records about 100 times faster than the Data Driven Query task. When the Transform Data task is used without Fast Load, the two tasks have nearly the same performance.

- Our testing indicates that update queries executed in a Data Driven Query task are about 30% faster than updates executed by a lookup in a Transform Data task.

- The process of creating and using the four queries in a Data Driven Query task is easier than the process of creating multiple data modification lookup queries in a Transform Data task.

- If you need to have more than four data modification results from a transformation task, you can define as many data modification lookup queries as you need. You can use these lookups in either the Transform Data task or the Data Driven Query task.

If you are primarily inserting records with your transformation task and you can use Fast Load, you should use the Transform Data task. If you are primarily updating records or you cannot use Fast Load with the Transform Data task, you should consider using the Data Driven Query task.

You can find more information about the relative performance of various DTS tasks in Chapter 28, "High Performance DTS Packages."

Creating a Data Driven Query Task

You can create the Data Driven Query task in the Package Designer and in code. The last section of this chapter explains how to create the task in code.

The Data Driven Query Task Properties dialog in the Package Designer has six tabs, as shown in Figure 8.1. The first and second tabs are used to set the information for the data source and the bindings table.

FIGURE 8.1

The second tab of the Data Driven Query Task Properties dialog is used to set the bindings table.

NOTE

In SQL Server 7.0, the second connection involved in a Data Driven Query task was called the data destination. I think the change in terminology from "destination" to "bindings" is very helpful.

Data isn't inserted or modified in the bindings table. This table is used as the model for the values that are used in the parameter queries.

The ActiveX script starts with the values as they exist in the data source. The script can modify those values before they are assigned to the fields of the Binding table. This design allows you to programmatically modify the data before it is used in the parameter queries.

Even though the name has been changed in the interface, the custom task's properties still refer to the data destination—`DestinationConnectionID`, `DestinationObjectName`, `DestinationSQLStatement`, `DestinationCommandProperties`, and `DestinationColumnDefinitions`.

Most of the properties of the Data Driven Query task are the same as the properties of the Transform Data task. See Chapter 6, "The Transform Data Task," for a discussion of those properties.

The Transform Data task has five properties that are not available with the Data Driven Query task. Four of these are properties connected with the Fast Load option, which is not available with the Data Driven Query:

- `UseFastLoad`
- `FastLoadOptions`
- `AllowIdentityInserts`
- `InsertCommitSize`

The other property that is not available with the Data Driven Query task is the `DataPumpOptions` property.

The Data Driven Query task has eight additional properties, all related to the parameter queries used with the task. These are assigned on the Queries tab of the Data Driven Query Task Properties dialog.

You start creating a parameter query by choosing one of the four query types—Insert, Update, Delete, or Select (see Figure 8.2). You then write the parameter query, using question marks for each of the parameters. If you want, you can click the Build button and create the query in the Data Transformation Services Query Designer.

After creating the query, choose the Parse/Show Parameters button. If the query can be parsed successfully, the parameters will be listed on the right in the order they appear in the query. For each parameter, you select one of the columns from the Binding table (see Figure 8.3).

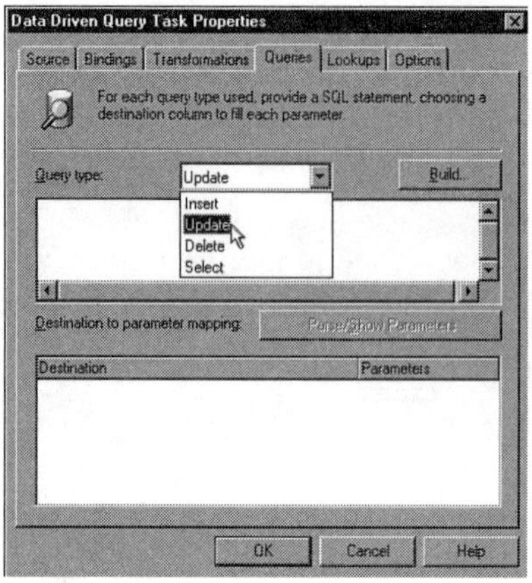

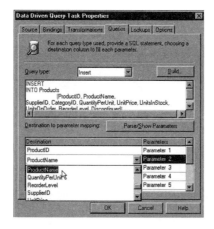

FIGURE 8.2

You assign the queries and their parameters on the Queries tab of the Data Driven Query Task Properties dialog.

FIGURE 8.3

You assign one of the columns from the Binding table to each of the parameters in the query.

The queries are assigned with the following properties of the DataDrivenQueryTask object:

- InsertQuery
- UpdateQuery
- DeleteQuery
- UserQuery—The Select query

> **NOTE**
>
> The only difference between the four types of queries is that you use a different transformation constant to call each of them. You don't have to create a query that matches the query type. If you want, you can create four different insert queries, four update queries, four delete queries, or four stored procedures.

The task has a collection of columns to fill the parameters for each of the four queries. The columns are used for the parameters in the order of their ordinal positions in the collections. The collections can be referenced as the following properties of the task:

- `InsertQueryColumns`
- `UpdateQueryColumns`
- `DeleteQueryColumns`
- `SelectQueryColumns`—The collection of columns for the UserQuery

Transformation Status Constants for the Data Driven Query Task

You can use the transformation status returned by the entry function to determine which of the parameter queries is executed. The four constants reference the four types of queries by their names:

- `DTSTransformStat_UpdateQuery`

  Value of constant—32

- `DTSTransformStat_InsertQuery`

  Value of constant—16

- `DTSTransformStat_DeleteQuery`

  Value of constant—64

- `DTSTransformStat_UserQuery`—Execute the Select query

  Value of constant—8

You can also use all of the transformation status constants that are used with the Transform Data task, except for `DTSTransformStat_OK`.

Here are some of the constants you might want to use with a Data Driven Query task:

- `DTSTransformStat_SkipFetch`—Use this with one of the parameter query status constants to execute a query and stay on the record so that another query can be executed.
- `DTSTransformStat_SkipInsert`—Do not execute a query.
- `DTSTransformStat_Error`—An error has occurred. Do not execute a query and handle the record as an error.

You can only execute one of the queries each time the transformation script is executed. If you want to execute two of them, you have to add `Skip Fetch` with one of the other four execution constants so that the ActiveX script will be executed twice for the same source record.

A Data Driven Query Example

The DataDrivenQuerySample.dts file on the CD has a sample package with a Data Driven Query task labeled "Modify Products" that uses all four parameter queries. This package creates a database called DDQSample that has three tables:

- Products—Copied from the Products table in Northwind.
- ProductChange—Contains insertions, updates, and deletions for the Products table.
- ProductChangeError—Records errors that take place during the execution of the Data Driven Query task.

Every record in the ProductChange table specifies an insertion, update, or deletion for the Products table. The ProductChange table has a field called ProductChangeType that specifies the type of data modification.

The Insert parameter query uses the values in ProductChange to insert data into all the fields of the Products table:

```
INSERT INTO Products (ProductID, ProductName,
SupplierID, CategoryID, QuantityPerUnit, UnitPrice, UnitsInStock,
UnitsOnOrder, ReorderLevel, Discontinued)
VALUES     (?, ?, ?, ?, ?, ?, ?, ?, ?, ?)
```

In a similar way, the Update query updates all the fields in the Products table. The record to update is chosen by a value for ProductID, the primary key:

```
UPDATE     Products
SET ProductID = ?, ProductName = ?, SupplierID = ?,
CategoryID = ?, QuantityPerUnit = ?, UnitPrice = ?, UnitsInStock = ?,
UnitsOnOrder = ?,  ReorderLevel = ?, Discontinued = ?
WHERE (ProductID = ?)
```

The Delete query removes a record that has a particular ProductID:

```
DELETE FROM Products WHERE (ProductID = ?)
```

The Select query is used for inserting a record into the error table when an error occurs in the transformation script. The sample package has one record that will fail with a data type error:

```
INSERT INTO tblProductChangeError
(ErrorDateTime, ErrorNumber, ErrorDescription, ErrorField, ErrorValue,
ProductChangeID, ProductChangeType, ProductID, ProductName,
SupplierID, CategoryID, QuantityPerUnit, UnitPrice, UnitsInStock,
UnitsOnOrder, ReorderLevel, Discontinued)
VALUES      (?, ?, ?, ?, ?, ?, ?, ?, ?, ?, ?, ?, ?, ?, ?, ?, ?)
```

A portion of the ActiveX Script for this Data Driven Query task is shown in Listing 8.1. The code has four sections:

- The values of the source columns are assigned to the values of the destination columns. If there is an error in assigning any of the columns, the error handler is called.

- The ProductChangeType field is used in a Select Case statement to determine which of the parameter queries is to be run.

- If an error has occurred, the Select parameter query is chosen, overruling the previous choice.

- A separate function, fctErrHandler, sets appropriate values for an error situation. All fields that had an error are set to NULL in the destination. The error table shows the name and value of the last field that generated an error.

LISTING 8.1 The ActiveX Script for the Sample Data Driven Query Task

```
Option Explicit

Dim bError

Function Main()
On Error Resume Next

'Initialize variable that indicates whether or not an error occurred
bError = CBool(FALSE)

'Assign values to the destination columns
DTSDestination("ProductChangeID") = DTSSource("ProductChangeID")
If Err.Number <> 0 Then
```

LISTING 8.1 Continued

```
    fctErrHandler("ProductChangeID")
End If


DTSDestination("ProductChangeType") = DTSSource("ProductChangeType")
If Err.Number <> 0 Then
    fctErrHandler("ProductChangeType")
End If


'Continue on with the assignment of all the other columns

'Select the appropriate parameter query.
Select Case DTSSource("ProductChangeType")
    Case "Insert"
        Main = DTSTransformstat_InsertQuery
    Case "Update"
        Main = DTSTransformstat_UpdateQuery
    Case "Delete"
        Main = DTSTransformstat_DeleteQuery
End Select


'If an error has occurred, run the Select query
If bError = True Then
    Main = DTSTransformstat_UserQuery
End If


End Function


Function fctErrHandler(sErrorField)

    DTSDestination("ErrorDateTime") = Now
    DTSDestination("ErrorNumber") = Err.Number
    DTSDestination("ErrorDescription") = Err.Description
    DTSDestination("ErrorField") = sErrorField
    DTSDestination(sErrorField) = Null

    IF IsNull(DTSSource(sErrorField)) Then
        DTSDestination("ErrorValue") = Null
    Else
        DTSDestination("ErrorValue") = CStr(DTSSource(sErrorField))
    End If

    bError = CBool(True)
    Err.Clear

End Function
```

> **NOTE**
>
> The error handling in this script only deals with errors in the transformation script. Data modification errors are not recorded in the error table. You can insert data modification errors into a table with a lookup query in the On Insert subphase of a Data Driven Query. See Chapter 9, "The Multiphase Data Pump."

> **NOTE**
>
> In real-life situations, there's usually much more logic needed for determining whether a particular source record should cause an insertion, an update, or a deletion.

Creating a Data Driven Query Task in Visual Basic

I have created a Visual Basic procedure, `fctCreateDataDrivenQueryTask`, that creates two connections, a step, a task, and a custom task for a Data Driven Query task. The basic properties of the task can be set with this procedure. You can find the code for it in the directory for Chapter 8 on the book's CD as a Visual Basic Project, with files CreateDataDrivenQueryTask.vbp, CreateDataDrivenQueryTask.frm, and CreateDataDrivenQueryTask.bas.

The code for `fctCreateDataDrivenQueryTask` is shown in Listing 8.2. The procedure needs some utility functions that are included with the code listings on the CD. The project requires references to the Microsoft DTSPackage Object Library and the Microsoft DTSDataPump Scripting Object Library.

LISTING 8.2   The Code to Create a Data Driven Query Task with Its Basic Properties

```
Option Explicit

Public Function fctCreateDataDrivenQueryTask( _
    pkg As DTS.Package2, _
    Optional sBaseName As String = "DataDrivenQueryTask", _
    Optional sSourceDataSource As String, _
    Optional sDestDataSource As String, _
    Optional sSourceCatalog As String, _
    Optional sDestCatalog As String, _
    Optional sSourceUserID As String, _
    Optional sDestUserID As String, _
```

LISTING 8.2 Continued

```
        Optional sSourcePassword As String, _
        Optional sDestPassword As String, _
        Optional sSourceTableName As String, _
        Optional sDestTableName As String, _
        Optional sExistingSource As String, _
        Optional sExistingDest As String)
On Error GoTo ProcErr
Dim conSource As DTS.Connection2
Dim conDest As DTS.Connection2
Dim stp As DTS.Step2
Dim tsk As DTS.Task
Dim cus As DTS.DataDrivenQueryTask2

'Check to see if the selected Base name is unique
sBaseName = fctFindUniqueBaseName(pkg, sBaseName)

If sExistingSource = "" Then
    'Create connection for Source
    Set conSource = pkg.Connections.New("SQLOLEDB")
    With conSource
        .ID = fctNextConnectionID(pkg)
        .Name = "conSource" & sBaseName
        .Description = "Source" & sBaseName
        .DataSource = sSourceDataSource
        .Catalog = sSourceCatalog

        .UserID = sSourceUserID
        .Password = sSourcePassword

        'If User ID is empty string, use trusted connection
        If sSourceUserID = "" Then
          .UseTrustedConnection = True
        Else
          .UseTrustedConnection = False
        End If

    End With
    pkg.Connections.Add conSource
Else
    Set conSource = pkg.Connections(sExistingSource)
End If

If sExistingDest = "" Then
    'Create connection for Source
    Set conDest = pkg.Connections.New("SQLOLEDB")
```

LISTING 8.2 Continued

```
    With conDest
        .ID = fctNextConnectionID(pkg)
        .Name = "conDest" & sBaseName
        .Description = "Dest" & sBaseName
        .DataSource = sDestDataSource
        .Catalog = sDestCatalog

        .UserID = sDestUserID
        .Password = sDestPassword

        'If User ID is empty string, use trusted connection
        If sDestUserID = "" Then
          .UseTrustedConnection = True
        Else
          .UseTrustedConnection = False
        End If

    End With
    pkg.Connections.Add conDest
Else
    Set conDest = pkg.Connections(sExistingDest)
End If


'Create task and custom task
Set tsk = pkg.Tasks.New("DTSDataDrivenQueryTask")
Set cus = tsk.CustomTask
With cus

    'Set ConnectionIDs
    .SourceConnectionID = conSource.ID
    .DestinationConnectionID = conDest.ID

    'Properties supplied to the procedure
    .Name = "tsk" & sBaseName
    .SourceObjectName = sSourceTableName
    .DestinationObjectName = sDestTableName
    .Description = sBaseName

    'Other properties
    'Set to values provided by the Package Designer

    .DestinationSQLStatement = ""
    .ExceptionFileColumnDelimiter = "|"
    .ExceptionFileName = ""
```

LISTING 8.2 Continued

```
    .ExceptionFileOptions = 1 'DTSExcepFile_SingleFile70
    .ExceptionFileRowDelimiter = "{CR}{LF}"
    .ExceptionFileTextQualifier = ""
    .FetchBufferSize = 1
    .FirstRow = 0
    .InputGlobalVariableNames = ""
    .LastRow = 0
    .MaximumErrorCount = 0
    .ProgressRowCount = 1000
    .SourceSQLStatement = ""

End With


pkg.Tasks.Add tsk


'Create step for task
Set stp = pkg.Steps.New
With stp
    .Name = "stp" & sBaseName
    .Description = sBaseName
    .TaskName = tsk.Name
End With
pkg.Steps.Add stp

fctCreateDataDrivenQueryTask = stp.Name

Set conSource = Nothing
Set conDest = Nothing
Set tsk = Nothing
Set cus = Nothing
Set stp = Nothing

ProcExit:
  Exit Function
ProcErr:
  MsgBox Err.Number & " - " & Err.Description
  GoTo ProcExit
End Function
```

Conclusion

The Data Driven Query task is a useful tool when you need to specify multiple results for a data transformation. The next chapter explains how to use multiple phases with the transformation tasks.

The Multiphase Data Pump

IN THIS CHAPTER

The multiphase data pump option allows you to write code at several different points in the data transformation process. You can use this option with the Transform Data task, the Data Driven Query task, and the Parallel Data Pump task.

If you haven't enabled the multiphase data pump, you can write code for only one point of the data transformation process—the point at which each row is being transformed. After enabling this option, you can write code for all these phases and subphases:

- Pre Source Phase—Before the source query is executed.
- Row Transform Phase—Each row of data is processed.
- On Transform Failure—Subphase of the Post Row Transform phase. Occurs when there is an error in the transformation.
- On Insert Failure—Subphase of the Post Row Transform phase. Occurs when a record fails to be inserted.
- On Insert Success—Subphase of the Post Row Transform phase. Occurs when a record is successfully inserted.
- Batch Complete Phase—A batch of records is successfully inserted.
- Post Source Data Phase—The rows have all been processed.
- Pump Complete Phase—The transformation task has completed its work.

Enabling the Multiphase Data Pump

The last section of this chapter explains how to create a multiphase data pump in code. In the DTS Designer, you can enable the multiphase data pump by doing the following:

1. Right-click on the Data Transformation Services node in the Enterprise Manager.
2. Select Properties from the pop-up menu.
3. Select Show multi-phase pump in DTS Designer on the Package Properties dialog, as shown in Figure 9.1.

After selecting the multiphase option, you will see a Phases filter on the Transformation tab of the Transform Data Task Properties dialog, as shown in Figure 9.2. Each transformation can implement one or more of the phases. By selecting one of the phases, you can see which transformations have implemented a particular phase.

The Phases tab of the ActiveX Script Transformation Properties dialog shows the eight phases and subphases where you can write code, as shown in Figure 9.3. You enable a phase by selecting the check box beside it. You can set the default entrance function and create the default code for all the phases you have selected by clicking the Auto Gen button.

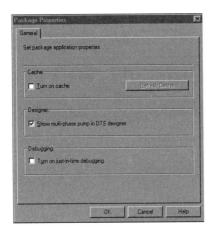

FIGURE 9.1
You select the multiphase data pump option in the Package Properties dialog.

FIGURE 9.2
You can use the Phases filter to show the transformations that are using a particular phase.

9

NOTE

Even if you remove the multiphase option from the Package Designer, multiple phases in a transformation will remain. However, you will not be able to view all the properties of those transformations in the Package Designer without using Disconnected Edit. If any of your transformations do not include a Row Transform phase, you will not be able to access that phase in the Transform Data Task Properties dialog.

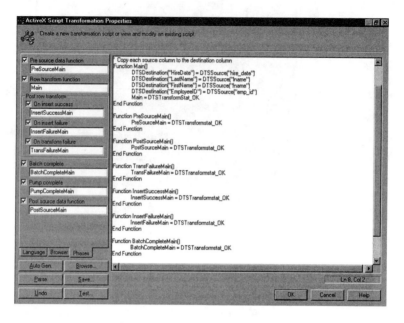

FIGURE 9.3

You can choose which phases you want to use in the ActiveX Script Transformation Properties dialog.

You can enable the multiphase data pump option in code by using the Application object. Here's the VBScript code to do so:

```
Function Main
Dim app

Set app = CreateObject("DTS.Application")
app.DesignerSettings = DTSDesigner_ShowMultiPhaseTransforms

    Main = DTSTaskExecResult_Success
End Function
```

Programmatic Flow with Multiple Phases

Figure 9.4 shows the programmatic flow of the phases and subphases as the Transform Data task is executed. You can choose to implement one, all, or any combination of these phases and subphases. When you implement a phase, the specified entry function is called and the code in that function is executed.

The Pre Source phase is usually executed just once. You can execute it more than once by setting DTSTransformStat_SkipFetch as the return value from the entry function.

The Row Transform phase is executed once for each record in the data source.

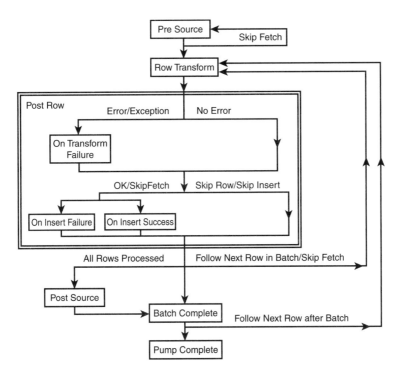

FIGURE 9.4

The programmatic flow in the multiphase data pump.

The Post Row Transform phase is often executed once for each record in the data source. It is not executed if the Row Transform phase is completed successfully, and it does not attempt to insert a record into the destination.

The Transform Failure subphase is executed whenever there is an error in the Row Transform phase.

Either the Insert Success subphase or the Insert Failure subphase is executed after an attempt to insert a record into the destination. These subphases are mutually exclusive.

The On Batch Complete phase is executed once each time a batch of records is committed. This phase is only used when Fast Load is being used.

The Post Source Data and Pump Complete phases are each executed once after all the records have been processed.

Information about the progress of the transformation is available through the properties of the DTSTransformPhaseInfo object. This object can be referenced both from the code of the transformation and from code in a transformation ActiveX script.

All six properties of the `DTSTransformPhaseInfo` object are read-only. They are as follows:

- `CurrentPhase`—The phase whose code is currently being executed. This property uses the values of the `DTSTransformPhaseEnum`, which are listed in the last section of this chapter.

- `CurrentSourceRow`—The number of the source row currently being processed. The source rows are numbered consecutively, beginning with 1.

- `DestinationRowsComplete`—The number of rows that have been successfully inserted into the data destination. For a Data Driven Query task, the value in this property is the number of data-driven queries that have been executed.

- `ErrorRows`—The number of rows that have generated an error.

- `ErrorCode`—The error code returned by the phase immediately preceding the current phase.

- `TransformStatus`—The transformation status returned by the transformation immediately preceding the current transformation, when that transformation was executed on the same row of source data.

Three of these properties (CurrentSourceRow, DestinationRowsComplete, and ErrorRows) use the vt_decimal data type. When you reference these properties in VBScript, you have to convert them to long integers:

```
lCurrentSourceRow = CLng(DTSTransformPhaseInfo.CurrentSourceRow)
```

Listing 9.1 shows a function that uses several of these properties to record the state of the transformation at the time of an error. You can find this code in a file called UseAllPhases.dts on the book's CD.

LISTING 9.1   The Properties of the DTSTransformPhaseInfo Object Can Help Determine What Happened at the Time of an Error

```
Function fctError
    Dim msg, sPhase

    sPhase = fctPhaseName
    If bDisplayErrMsg Then
        msg =  "Error in " & sPhase & vbCrLf
        msg = msg & Err.Number & " " & Err.Description
        msgbox msg
    End If

    If bRecordErr Then
        DTSLookups("InserttblOrderErrors").Execute _
```

LISTING 9.1 Continued

```
        DTSSource("OrderID"), _
        DTSSource("TranType"), _
        DTSSource("TranDate"), _
        DTSDestination("OrderID"), _
        DTSDestination("OrderDate"), _
        DTSDestination("RequiredDate"), _
        DTSDestination("ShippedDate"), _
        DTSTransformPhaseInfo.CurrentPhase, _
        CLng(DTSTransformPhaseInfo.CurrentSourceRow) , _
        DTSTransformPhaseInfo.ErrorCode, _
        CLng(DTSTransformPhaseInfo.DestinationRowsComplete) , _
        DTSTransformPhaseInfo.TransformStatus, _
        Now, _
        Err.Number, _
        Err.Description
    End If

End Function
```

Using the Phases

The phases and subphases differ in their access to the source and destination columns. They also have different return values that are valid for the entry function. Table 9.1 has an overview of these differences. (Where my testing varies from Books Online, the information from Books Online appears in parentheses.)

TABLE 9.1 The Columns and the Return Values Available for Each of the Phases

Phase/Subphase	Source Columns	Destination Columns	Return Values
Pre Source	None	Write	All
Row Transform	Read	Write	All
Transform Failure	Read	Write	All
Insert Failure	Read	Write(None)	OK or AbortPump
Insert Success	Read	Write(None)	OK or AbortPump
Batch Complete	Read(None)	Read(None)	OK or AbortPump
Post Source Data	None	Write	All
Pump Complete	Read(None)	Read(None)	OK or AbortPump

9

THE MULTIPHASE DATA PUMP

Books Online states that the Pre Source phase, the Transform Failure subphase, and the Post Source Data phase can use all the transformation values that can be returned from a Row Transform phase.

> **NOTE**
>
> The transformation statuses have some different behavior when used for the various phases:
>
> DTSTransformStat_SkipFetch can be used as the return value for the Pre Source phase, the Transform Failure subphase, and the Post Source Data phase, as well as for the Row Transform phase. For all of these phases, this transformation status causes the phase's entry function to be called again immediately.
>
> DTSTransformStat_SkipInsert has the same effect as DTSTransformStat_OK when used for the Pre Source phase, the Transform Failure subphase, and the Post Source Data phase.
>
> DTSTransformStat_SkipRow can be used only for the Row Transform phase. It generates an error when used for any other phase.

Chapter 7, "Writing ActiveX Scripts for a Transform Data Task," has a transformation script example that uses two of the transformation phases. I have extended that example here to use all eight of the phases and subphases. You can find it on the CD in a file called UseAllPhases.dts.

The transformation script has a function called fctPhase that displays a message box telling which phase is currently active. The message is only displayed if the user sets the value of the variable bDisplayPhase to TRUE in the Pre Source phase. This function calls another function, fctPhaseName, which finds the current phase number and converts it into a phase name. These functions are shown in Listing 9.2.

LISTING 9.2   Functions That Display the Current Phase

```
Function fctPhase
    Dim msg

    If bDisplayPhase = True Then
        msg = fctPhaseName
        msgbox msg
    End If


End Function
```

LISTING 9.2   Continued

```
Function fctPhaseName
    dim sName

    Select Case DTSTransformPhaseInfo.CurrentPhase

        Case 1
           sName = "Pre-Source Data Phase"
        Case 2
            sName = "Post-Source Data Phase"
        Case 4
            sName = "Row Transform Phase"
        Case 8
            sName = "On Transform Failure Phase"
        Case 16
            sName = "On Insert Success Phase"
        Case 32
            sName = "On Insert Failure Phase"
        Case 64
            sName = "Batch Complete Phase"
        Case 128
            sName = "Pump Complete Phase"

    End Select

    fctPhaseName = sName

End Function
```

Pre Source Phase

You can use the Pre Source phase to initialize variables that are used throughout the script. You can use either global variables or script variables declared outside a function for this purpose. If you use script variables, they will be visible only to functions in this particular script. They will not be visible outside the task or to other transformations in the same task.

If you are using a text file as the destination for your transformation, you could use the Pre Source phase to write a header to the file.

If you want to execute the code in this phase more than once, you can return the `DTSTransformStat_SkipFetch` transformation value from the entry function of the Pre Source phase.

You cannot access any of the transformation's source columns in this phase. You do have access to the destination columns, however. Any values that you assign to the destination columns will remain until they are overwritten or until the first record is inserted into the destination.

> **NOTE**
>
> You can change the source for the Transform Data task in the Pre Source phase, but that change does not go into effect until the next time the task is executed. Even though the Pre Source phase occurs before the first data is processed, the source query has already been executed when this phase occurs, so changing the query has no effect on the current execution of the task.
>
> If you want to dynamically modify the source query for a Transform Data task, you can do so in a Dynamic Properties task or an ActiveX Script task before the execution of the Transform Data task. You could also modify the source query in a Workflow ActiveX Script for the step associated with the Transform Data task.

Listing 9.3 shows the script variable declarations and the code for the Pre Source phase of the UseAllPhases example. In the Pre Source phase, you have the option of setting the display and recording options for the task. You can display message boxes that show the current phase, the transformation progress, or the transformation errors. You can record the progress in tblOrderProgress and the errors in tblOrderErrors. By default, the message boxes are disabled and the recording is enabled.

LISTING 9.3   The Pre Source Phase from the UseAllPhases Task

```
Option Explicit

Dim bDisplayProgressMsg, bRecordProgress
Dim bDisplayErrMsg, bRecordErr
Dim bDisplayPhase
Dim lLastInsertSuccessKey

Function PreSourceMain()

    'Set Display and Recording Options
    bDisplayProgressMsg = CBool(False)
    bRecordProgress = CBool(True)
    bDisplayErrMsg = CBool(False)
```

LISTING 9.3 Continued

```
bRecordErr = CBool(True)
bDisplayPhase = CBool(False)

'Initialize
lLastInsertSuccessKey = 0

Call fctPhase
Call fctProgress

PreSourceMain = DTSTransformstat_OK
```

End Function

Row Transform Phase

The Row Transform phase is the default transformation phase. Writing scripts for this phase is the topic of Chapter 7, "Writing ActiveX Scripts for a Transform Data Task."

You are required to have a Row Transform phase in at least one of the transformations defined for a transformation task. All the other phases are optional.

You can modify the values in the transformation's destination columns in most of the phases. This is the only phase where you can actually insert rows into the data destination.

Post Row Transform Phase

You cannot write code for the Post Row Transform phase. Instead, you write code for one or more of the subphases associated with this phase:

- On Transform Failure
- On Insert Failure
- On Insert Success

Zero, one, or two of these subphases will be called for each record being transformed. None of the subphases will be called if the Row Transform phase is successful but returns a transformation status of DTSTranformStat_SkipInsert or DTSTransformStat_SkipRow. On Insert Failure and On Insert Success are mutually exclusive—one and only one will be called for each attempted insert into the data destination.

On Transform Failure Subphase

If the Row Transform phase returns an error (DTSTransformStat_Error or
DTSTransformStat_ExceptionRow), the On Transform Failure subphase will be called.

You have read access to the source columns and write access to the destination columns in this
phase. The UseAllPhases task uses this subphase to call fctError, which creates a record to
store the values of all the source and destination columns (see Listing 9.4).

LISTING 9.4   The On Transform Failure Subphase from the UseAllPhases Task

```
Function TransFailureMain()

    Call fctPhase
    Call fctError

    TransFailureMain = DTSTransformstat_OK

End Function
```

On Insert Failure Subphase

The Row Transform phase may be completed successfully, but the insertion of a record into the
data destination may fail. The insert failure could be a result of one of the following:

- Violation of a Primary Key constraint
- Violation of a Foreign Key constraint
- Violation of a Unique constraint
- Violation of a Check constraint

> **NOTE**
>
> An insert failure is not usually caused by a data type conversion error. Those errors
> usually cause a transform failure.

You have read access to the transformation's source columns and write access to the destination columns during this phase. It doesn't do much good to write to these destination columns,
though, because they will be set to Null before the next execution of the Row Transform
phase.

> **CAUTION**
>
> My testing indicates that this subphase is never executed when Fast Load is used. Fast Load greatly improves the performance of the Transform Data task. The inability to use this subphase with Fast Load significantly reduces its value.
>
> This problem only occurs with this subphase—On Transform Failure and On Insert Success are executed whether or not Fast Load is being used.

The UseAllPhases task also uses this subphase to call `fctError`, as shown in Listing 9.5.

LISTING 9.5   The On Insert Failure Subphase from the UseAllPhases Task

```
Function InsertFailureMain()

    Call fctPhase
    Call fctError

    InsertFailureMain = DTSTransformstat_OK
End Function
```

On Insert Success Subphase

Whenever a record is successfully inserted into the data destination, the On Insert Success subphase is executed. As with the On Insert Failure subphase, you have read access to the transformation's source columns and write access to the destination columns during this subphase.

This subphase can be used to keep track of the progress of a data transformation when you are not using Fast Load. You would normally use the On Batch Complete phase to do this, but On Batch Complete is not executed when Fast Load is not being used.

This subphase can also be used for maintaining aggregations. As each new record is inserted into the destination, the aggregated value can be updated. It is usually possible (and much more efficient) to calculate aggregations after all the records have been processed.

The UseAllPhases task uses this subphase to store the value of the most recent OrderID that has been inserted (see Listing 9.6). This value is used in the On Batch Complete phase as additional information on the progress of the transformation for the report.

LISTING 9.6   The On Insert Success Subphase from the UseAllPhases Task

```
Function InsertSuccessMain()2

    Call fctPhase

    'Save the Value for use in fctProgress.
    lLastInsertSuccessKey = DTSDestination("OrderID")

    InsertSuccessMain = DTSTransformstat_OK
End Function
```

On Batch Complete Phase

The On Batch Complete phase occurs when a batch is committed to the destination. This phase is not executed when Fast Load is not being used.

Books Online states that neither the source nor the destination columns are available in this phase. My testing indicates that they are both available for reading but not writing.

The On Batch Complete phase is useful for keeping track of the progress of a data transformation. The UseAllPhases task uses the phase for that purpose, as shown in Listing 9.7.

LISTING 9.7   The On Batch Complete Phase and the `fctProgress` Function from the UseAllPhases Task

```
Function BatchCompleteMain()

    Call fctPhase
    Call fctProgress

    BatchCompleteMain = DTSTransformstat_OK
End Function

Function fctProgress
    Dim msg, sProgress, sPhase, lCurrentSourceRow, lDestRowsComplete

    lCurrentSourceRow = CLng(DTSTransformPhaseInfo.CurrentSourceRow)
    lDestRowsComplete = CLng(DTSTransformPhaseInfo.DestinationRowsComplete)

    Select Case DTSTransformPhaseInfo.CurrentPhase

        Case DTSTransformPhase_PreSourceData
            sProgress = "Start"
        Case DTSTransformPhase_OnBatchComplete
```

LISTING 9.7   Continued

```
                sProgress = "Batch Completed"
        Case DTSTransformPhase_OnPumpComplete
                sProgress = "Finished"
    End Select

    If bDisplayProgressMsg Then
        sPhase = fctPhaseName
        msg =   "Currently in " & sPhase & vbCRLF
        msg = msg & "Progress: " & sProgress  & vbCRLF
        msg = msg & "Current Source Row: " & lCurrentSourceRow & vbCRLF
        msg = msg & "Destination Rows Complete: " & _
            lDestRowsComplete & vbCRLF
        msgbox msg
    End If

    If bRecordProgress Then
        DTSLookups("InserttblOrderProgress").Execute _
        lLastInsertSuccessKey, _
        sProgress, _
        lCurrentSourceRow, _
        lDestRowsComplete, _
        CLng(DTSTransformPhaseInfo.ErrorRows), _
        Now
    End If


End Function
```

Post Source Data Phase

The Post Source Data phase occurs after all the records have been processed. This phase is executed only once, unless you use the DTSTranformStat_SkipFetch transformation value to execute it repeatedly.

You can access the data in the transformation's destination columns, but not in the source columns.

You can use this phase for any final processing that needs to be accomplished on the final row of data. The UseAllPhases task uses this phase for this purpose. The last record is inserted into the destination, using a data modification lookup query (see Listing 9.8).

LISTING 9.8   The Post Source Data Phase from the UseAllPhases Task

```
Function PostSourceMain()
On Error Resume Next

    Call fctPhase

    'Insert last record
    DTSLookups("InserttblOrderDates").Execute _
            DTSDestination("OrderID"), _
            DTSDestination("OrderDate"), _
            DTSDestination("ShippedDate"), _
            DTSDestination("RequiredDate")

    If Err.Number <> 0 Then
        Call fctError
    End If

    PostSourceMain = DTSTransformstat_OK

End Function
```

CAUTION

If you specify a value for MaxRows that is less than the number of rows in the data source, the Post Source Data phase code will not be executed.

NOTE

It appears that the final On Batch Insert phase usually occurs before the Post Source Data phase.

Pump Complete Phase

The Pump Complete phase is the last phase of the data transformation. It executes only once and cannot be called to execute again.

Books Online states that there is no access to either the source or destination columns from this phase, but my testing indicates that there is access to both of them.

You would use the Pump Complete phase in much the same way as the Post Source Data phase. The UseAllPhases task uses this phase to write one final record to report on the progress of the task (see Listing 9.9).

LISTING 9.9 The Pump Complete Phase from the UseAllPhases Task

```
Function PumpCompleteMain()

    Call fctPhase
    Call fctProgress

    PumpCompleteMain = DTSTransformstat_OK
End Function
```

Creating a COM Object with Visual C++ to Program the Phases

If you want the best possible performance from your multiphase data pump, you should consider creating a COM object with Visual C++. When you have registered your COM object, you will be able to choose it from the list of available transformations in the Create New Transformation dialog.

> **NOTE**
>
> You cannot use Visual Basic to create a custom transformation because the data pump library has not been made available to Visual Basic.
>
> You can create custom tasks with Visual Basic, though.

See Chapter 32, "Creating a Custom Transformation with VC++," for more information.

Creating a Multiphase Data Pump in Code

Most of the work in creating a multiphase data pump is writing the ActiveX script code for the various phases. There are two additional things you have to do when you are creating a task with phases using Visual Basic code—setting the TransformPhases property and setting the properties that determine the entrance functions.

The TransformPhases Property

The TransformPhases property is the only extended property for the Transformation2 object in SQL Server 2000. This property contains a bitmap that indicates which phases are enabled for that particular transformation. The values for the DTSTransformPhaseEnum constants are as follows:

- 0—DTSTransformPhase_None
- 1—DTSTransformPhase_PreSourceData

- 2—DTSTransformPhase_PostSourceData
- 4—DTSTransformPhase_Transform
- 8—DTSTransformPhase_OnTransformFailure
- 16—DTSTransformPhase_OnInsertSuccess
- 32—DTSTransformPhase_OnInsertFailure
- 64—DTSTransformPhase_OnBatchComplete
- 128—DTSTransformPhase_OnPumpComplete
- 255—DTSTransformPhase_All

> **NOTE**
>
> If you set the TransformPhases property to DTSTransformPhase_None, your script will never be called. Also, you will not be able to view this script in the Transform Data Task Properties dialog because it won't show up for any of the phase filters.

Setting the Entrance Functions

You have to specify the name of the entrance function for each of the phases that you are using. This is the function that is called when the programmatic flow reaches the point for the particular phase. The entrance function also returns a value that determines the result of the phase.

The entrance functions can be referenced through the TransformServerProperties of the Transformation object, as shown in Listing 9.10.

LISTING 9.10   VBScript Code to Reference the Names of the Entrance Functions

```
Option Explicit
Function Main

Dim pkg, tsk, cus, trn, trnprp

Set pkg = DTSGlobalVariables.Parent
Set tsk = pkg.Tasks("tskAllPhases")
Set cus = tsk.CustomTask
Set trn = cus.Transformations("trnAllPhases")
Set trnprp = trn.TransformServerProperties
Msgbox trnprp("PreSourceDataFunctionEntry")
Msgbox trnprp("FunctionEntry") 'The Row Transform Phase
```

LISTING 9.10   Continued

```
Msgbox trnprp("TransformFailureFunctionEntry")
Msgbox trnprp("InsertFailureFunctionEntry")
Msgbox trnprp("InsertSuccessFunctionEntry")
Msgbox trnprp("BatchCompleteFunctionEntry")
Msgbox trnprp("PostSourceDataFunctionEntry")
Msgbox trnprp("PumpCompleteFunctionEntry")

    Main = DTSTaskExecResult_Success
End Function
```

Conclusion

The multiphase data pump option allows you to extend the capabilities of your transformation tasks. It is especially useful for error handling and monitoring the progress of the task.

The next chapter introduces the new transformation task in SQL Server 2000—the Parallel Data Pump.

The Parallel Data Pump Task

IN THIS CHAPTER

The Parallel Data Pump task allows you to transform hierarchical rowsets, OLE DB objects in which individual columns can themselves be rowsets. This task is very similar to the Transform Data task or the Data Driven Query task. But instead of having one collection of Transformation objects for a task, the Parallel Data Pump task has multiple collections—one for each separate rowset embedded in the hierarchical rowset. Each of these collections of transformations is called a TransformationSet object.

NOTE

The Parallel Data Pump task is a new feature in SQL Server 2000. It's so new, in fact, that it doesn't have a user interface yet. You have to create your Parallel Data Pump tasks completely in code. That's unfortunate, especially for a task that is more complex than any of the other tasks included with DTS.

I have developed a strategy for using portions of the existing Package Designer interface for building a Parallel Data Pump task. This strategy is described in the last section of this chapter, "A User Interface for the Parallel Data Pump Task."

CAUTION

When you double-click on a Parallel Data Pump task icon, the default Custom Task Properties dialog opens with the task's properties. You can modify the task's properties as long as your source and destination queries are under 269 characters. If they are longer than that, the queries will be truncated when you click the OK button.

You can edit all the properties of a Parallel Data Pump task using Disconnected Edit. However, you can't view or edit any of the properties of the task's transformation sets or transformations.

CAUTION

The Parallel Data Pump task is not correctly saved to VB. The Save operation does not generate an error and the task's properties are correctly saved, but none of the task's transformation sets or transformations are saved.

Hierarchical Rowsets

A *rowset* is a data object that has rows and named columns. A *hierarchical rowset* contains columns that are themselves rowsets. Instead of joining child tables to parent tables with relationships between foreign and primary keys, the child tables become a part of the parent table.

The Microsoft Data Shaping Service for OLE DB can be used to create a hierarchical rowset. Here is some of the terminology for hierarchical rowsets:

- Shape language—The language used to construct hierarchical rowsets.
- Column rowset—A rowset that is contained in a column.
- Subsets or chapters—The individual values of a column rowset.
- Parent rowset—A rowset that contains a column rowset.
- Child rowset—A rowset that is used as the source for a column rowset.
- Shape Append Command—The syntax used in creating a hierarchical rowset. This command uses the keywords SHAPE, APPEND, AS, RELATE, and TO.
- SHAPE—Keyword used at the beginning of a parent rowset.
- APPEND—Keyword used at the beginning of the definition of a column rowset.
- AS—Keyword used before the name that is being assigned to the column rowset.
- RELATE—Keyword used before the field in the column rowset that is being used to join the column rowset to the parent rowset.
- TO—Keyword used before the field in the parent rowset that is being used to join the column rowset to the parent rowset.

Listing 10.1 shows a simple query for a hierarchical rowset. The rowset contains a parent rowset with one column rowset. If this query were used as the source query in a Parallel Data Pump task, you would create two TransformationSet objects, one for each of the two rowsets. You can find all the queries referenced in this chapter in the file HierarchicalQueries.txt.

LISTING 10.1 A Query for a Simple Hierarchical Rowset, Based on the Pubs Sample Database

```
SHAPE
{SELECT stor_id, stor_name, city, state FROM stores}
APPEND
  (
  {SELECT stor_id, ord_num, ord_date, qty, title_id FROM sales}
  ) AS sales_chapters
RELATE stor_id = stor_id
```

Listing 10.2 shows a more complex hierarchical rowset query that includes four levels of embedded rowsets. Note how all the APPEND phrases come before the first AS phrase when you have column rowsets embedded inside of column rowsets.

LISTING 10.2   A Query for a Hierarchical Rowset Containing Five Column Rowsets Embedded to Four Levels

```
SHAPE
{SELECT stor_id, stor_name, city, state FROM stores}
APPEND
  (
    (
    SHAPE
    {SELECT stor_id, ord_num, ord_date, title_id FROM sales}
    APPEND
      (
        (
        SHAPE
        {SELECT title_id, title, type, pub_id FROM titles}
        APPEND
          (
            {SELECT pub_id, pub_name FROM publishers}
            AS publisher_chapters
            RELATE pub_id TO pub_id
          )
        )
    AS title_chapters
    RELATE title_id TO title_id
      )
    ,
      (
      {SELECT ta.title_id, a.au_id, a.au_lname FROM authors a
        INNER JOIN titleauthor ta
          ON a.au_id = ta.au_id}
      AS author_chapters
      RELATE title_id TO title_id
      )
    )
  AS sales_chapters
  RELATE stor_id TO stor_id
  )
```

When to Use the Parallel Data Pump Task

If you have a hierarchical rowset to transform, you need the Parallel Data Pump task.

XML contains the structure of a hierarchical rowset. As XML becomes more widely used, hierarchical rowsets will become a more prominent part of data transformation.

You can use the Parallel Data Pump task to transform three related tables from one database into three related databases in another database. You have to create separate hierarchical queries for the source tables and the destination tables. It would be a lot harder to create this one Parallel Data Pump task than it would be to create three separate Transform Data tasks, especially without having a user interface for the Parallel Data Pump task. But using the Parallel Data Pump would allow you to integrate the logic of the transformation of the three tables.

In a similar way, you can use the Parallel Data Pump task to transform one table into multiple tables. Listing 10.3 shows a hierarchical rowset query that includes records from just one table. With the Parallel Data Pump task, you can load two tables from this one table in a single task as long as you have a unique key value that can be used to relate the two tables.

LISTING 10.3 A Hierarchical Rowset Query Can Be Created from One Table (Example from Northwind Sample Database)

```
SHAPE
{SELECT CustomerID, CompanyName, ContactName, PostalCode
    FROM Customers}
APPEND
  (
  {SELECT DISTINCT PostalCode, Region, Country FROM Customers}
  ) AS Region_Chapters
RELATE PostalCode TO PostalCode
```

> **NOTE**
>
> You usually lose performance by replacing two Transform Data tasks with one Parallel Data Pump task. This is especially true if the Transform Data tasks are able to use Fast Load, which is not an option in the Parallel Data Pump task.
>
> What you gain with the Parallel Data Pump task is the ability to more closely tie together the transformation logic for the transformation of the set of tables.

The Collections and the Properties of the Parallel Data Pump Task

The Parallel Data Pump task has only three collections. Two of them, SourceCommandProperties and DestinationCommandProperties, are also collections of the Transform Data task and the Data Driven Query task.

The third collection, TransformationSets, is unique to the Parallel Data Pump task. The TransformationSet objects in this collection hold the other collections that are found in the Transform Data task and the Data Driven Query task—Transformations, Lookups, DestinationColumnDefinitions, InsertQueryColumns, UpdateQueryColumns, DeleteQueryColumns, and UserQueryColumns.

The properties of the Parallel Data Pump task are very similar to the properties of the Data Driven Query task. Some of these properties are used for the Parallel Data Pump task itself, while other properties are implemented for each TransformationSet object.

> **NOTE**
>
> Chapter 30 contains object model diagrams for the Transform Data task, the Data Driven Query task, and the Parallel Data Pump task. See Figures 30.4 through 30.7.

The Parallel Data Pump task has one extra property not contained in the other transformation tasks—the TransformationSetOptions property, which sets the task's transformation mode.

The Transformation Modes

The Parallel Data Pump task has three distinct modes of operation—hierarchical, flattened, and data driven query.

The choice of mode involves two factors:

- Whether a hierarchical transformation or a flattened transformation should be used.
- Whether the Parallel Data Pump task should function like a Transform Data task or a Data Driven Query task.

These factors are combined in the following ways:

- Hierarchical mode—Hierarchical transformation functioning like a Transform Data task.
- Flattened mode—Flattened transformation functioning like a Transform Data task.
- Data driven query mode—Flattened transformation functioning like a Data Driven Query task.

The fourth option, a hierarchical transformation functioning like a Data Driven Query task, is not implemented.

Hierarchical Mode

Hierarchical mode uses the natural form of a hierarchical rowset.

A hierarchical rowset is similar to an inner join between a parent table and a child table. Some of the records in a child table might not have matching records in the parent table. The non-matched child records are not retrieved by an inner join. Other child records might have several matching records in the parent table. Those child records will appear multiple times in the inner join's rowset.

In hierarchical mode, records are copied row by row. Records in the child rowset that do not appear in the column rowset will not be copied. Records in the child rowset that appear multiple times will be copied multiple times.

Flattened Mode

Flattened mode transforms all the records of the component rowsets of the hierarchical rowset without regard to their hierarchical structure.

Each component rowset is transformed as if it existed independently. If there are fields in a child rowset that are not used in the column rowset, they are still included in the transformation. If there are fields that are used multiple times in the column rowset, they are included only once in the transformation.

Data Driven Query Mode

Data driven query mode is identical to flattened mode except that the Parallel Data Pump task functions like the Data Driven Query task. You choose one of four queries in the ActiveX script to execute as a result of the transformation of each row of data.

The Parallel Data Pump task used in data driven query mode has more flexibility than the Data Driven Query task because you can create a set of four queries for each of the transformation sets.

The `TransformationSetOptions` Property

The mode of a Parallel Data Pump task is set with the `TransformationSetOptions` property. This property uses the three `DTSTransformationSetOptions` constants:

- 0—`DTSTranSetOpt_Flattened`
- 1—`DTSTranSetOpt_Hierarchical`
- 4—`DTSTranSetOpt_DataDrivenQueries`

> **NOTE**
>
> Books Online has some contradictory information about this property. In one place
> `TransformationSetOptions` is identified as a property of the `TransformationSet`
> object, but it is really a property of the Parallel Data Pump task object. You cannot
> use different modes in different transformation sets. You choose one mode for the
> whole task.

Creating a Parallel Data Pump Task in Visual Basic

I have created a Visual Basic procedure, `fctCreateParallelDataPumpTask`, that creates connections, a step, a task, and a custom task for a Parallel Data Pump task.

You can find the procedure in the directory for Chapter 10 as a Visual Basic Project, with files CreateParallelDataPumpTask.vbp, CreateParallelDataPumpTask.frm, CreateParallelDataPumpTask.frx, CreateParallelDataPumpTask.bas, and CreateParallelDataPumpTask.exe. This project also contains code that creates an ActiveX Script task in the package that can be used to create the task's transformation sets and transformations. This task is described in the "A User Interface for the Parallel Data Pump Task" section later in this chapter.

The code for `fctCreateParallelDataPumpTask` is shown in Listing 10.4. The procedure needs some utility functions that are included with the code listings on the CD. The project requires references to the Microsoft DTSPackage Object Library and the Microsoft DTSDataPump Scripting Object Library.

LISTING 10.4 The Visual Basic Code to Create a Parallel Data Pump Task

```
Public Function fctCreateParallelDataPumpTask( _
    pkg As DTS.Package2, _
    Optional sBaseName As String = "ParallelDataPumpTask", _
    Optional sSourceDataSource As String = "(local)", _
    Optional sDestDataSource As String = "(local)", _
    Optional sSourceCatalog As String = "", _
    Optional sDestCatalog As String = "", _
    Optional sSourceUserID As String = "", _
    Optional sDestUserID As String = "", _
    Optional sSourcePassword As String = "", _
    Optional sDestPassword As String = "", _
    Optional sDestinationObjectName As String = "", _
    Optional sSourceObjectName As String = "", _
```

LISTING 10.4 Continued

```
    Optional sDestinationSQLStatement As String = "", _
    Optional sSourceSQLStatement As String = "", _
    Optional sInputGlobalVariableNames As String = "", _
    Optional dtsDTSTransformationSetOptions _
        As DTSTransformationSetOptions = 0, _
    Optional sExistingSource As String = "", _
    Optional sExistingDest As String = "") As String

On Error GoTo ProcErr

Dim conSource As DTS.Connection2
Dim conDest As DTS.Connection2
Dim stp As DTS.Step2
Dim tsk As DTS.Task
Dim cus As DTS.ParallelDataPumpTask

'Check to see if the selected Base name is unique
sBaseName = fctFindUniqueBaseName(pkg, sBaseName)

If sExistingSource = "" Then
    'Create connection for Source
    Set conSource = pkg.Connections.New("MSDataShape")
    With conSource
        .ID = fctNextConnectionID(pkg)
        .Name = "conSource" & sBaseName
        .Description = "Source" & sBaseName
        .DataSource = sSourceDataSource
        .Catalog = sSourceCatalog
        .ConnectionProperties("Data Provider") = "SQLOLEDB"

        .UserID = sSourceUserID
        .Password = sSourcePassword

        'If User ID is empty string, use trusted connection
        If sSourceUserID = "" Then
          .UseTrustedConnection = True
        Else
          .UseTrustedConnection = False
        End If

    End With
    pkg.Connections.Add conSource
Else
```

LISTING 10.4   Continued

```
    Set conSource = pkg.Connections(sExistingSource)
End If

If sExistingDest = "" Then
    'Create connection for Source
    Set conDest = pkg.Connections.New("MSDataShape")
    With conDest
        .ID = fctNextConnectionID(pkg)
        .Name = "conDest" & sBaseName
        .Description = "Dest" & sBaseName
        .DataSource = sDestDataSource
        .Catalog = sDestCatalog
        .ConnectionProperties("Data Provider") = "SQLOLEDB"

        .UserID = sDestUserID
        .Password = sDestPassword

        'If User ID is empty string, use trusted connection
        If sDestUserID = "" Then
          .UseTrustedConnection = True
        Else
          .UseTrustedConnection = False
        End If

    End With
    pkg.Connections.Add conDest
Else
    Set conDest = pkg.Connections(sExistingDest)
End If


'Create task and custom task
Set tsk = pkg.Tasks.New("DTSParallelDataPumpTask")
Set cus = tsk.CustomTask
With cus

    'Set ConnectionIDs
    .SourceConnectionID = conSource.ID
    .DestinationConnectionID = conDest.ID

    'Properties supplied to the procedure
    .Name = "tsk" & sBaseName
    .Description = sBaseName
    .SourceObjectName = sSourceObjectName
    .DestinationObjectName = sDestinationObjectName
    .DestinationSQLStatement = sDestinationSQLStatement
    .SourceSQLStatement = sSourceSQLStatement
```

LISTING 10.4 Continued

```
        .InputGlobalVariableNames = sInputGlobalVariableNames
        .TransformationSetOptions = dtsDTSTransformationSetOptions

End With

pkg.Tasks.Add tsk

'Create step for task
Set stp = pkg.Steps.New
With stp
        .Name = "stp" & sBaseName
        .Description = sBaseName
        .TaskName = tsk.Name
End With
pkg.Steps.Add stp

fctCreateParallelDataPumpTask = stp.Name

Set conSource = Nothing
Set conDest = Nothing
Set tsk = Nothing
Set cus = Nothing
Set stp = Nothing

ProcExit:
  Exit Function
ProcErr:
  MsgBox Err.Number & " - " & Err.Description
  fctCreateParallelDataPumpTask = ""
  GoTo ProcExit
End Function
```

A User Interface for the Parallel Data Pump Task

I have developed a user interface for creating a Parallel Data Pump task that uses existing functionality of the Package Designer along with the CreateParallelDataPump application, described in the "Creating a Parallel Data Pump Task in Visual Basic" section of this chapter. Here are the steps in my strategy:

1. Use the CreateParallelDataPumpTask application to create a Parallel Data Pump task and its two connections in a new DTS package, as shown in Figure 10.1.

2. Open the package that was created. Add Transform Data tasks or Data Driven Query tasks for each of the rowsets in the hierarchical query, as shown in Figure 10.2. Create and test the transformations for those tasks.

3. Modify the ActiveX Script described as Make Transformation Sets. In the `Main` function, add a call to the `fctTaskToTranSet` function for each of the tasks. You must use the right order when calling the function so that the order of the transformation sets matches the order of the rowsets in the source and destination queries. Also insert the proper name for the Parallel Data Pump task into the script.

4. Right-click on the ActiveX Script task. Select Execute Step from the pop-up menu. This task creates a transformation set for each of the Transform Data or Data Driven Query tasks. Any existing transformation sets in the Parallel Data Pump task are deleted before the new ones are added.

5. Disable the Transform Data tasks or the Data Driven Query tasks, and then test the package.

6. If you want to modify the transformation sets in the future, you can modify the Transform Data tasks or the Data Driven Query tasks and rerun the ActiveX Script task. If you want to modify the properties of the Parallel Data Pump task itself, you can modify them in Disconnected Edit. If your queries are longer than 270 characters and you attempt to modify any properties in the default Properties dialog, your queries will be truncated.

The ActiveX Script task checks the mode of the Parallel Data Pump task. If data driven query mode is set, the code expects to load information only from Data Driven Query tasks. If one of the other modes is being used, the code expects to load information from all Transform Data tasks.

The only way you can examine the objects and properties of the Parallel Data Pump task you create with this procedure is by saving the package to Meta Data Services and using the Meta Data Browser, described in Chapter 29, "Integrating DTS with Meta Data Services."

NOTE

You will not be able to view the task's properties and objects in the DTS Browser, located under Meta Data in the DTS node of the Enterprise Manager. You have to use the Meta Data Browser, located in the Meta Data Services node of the server.

I have found one additional limitation of this task—I have been unable to use the Meta Data Browser to export the definition of the task or its transformation sets to XML. I have successfully exported `Transformation` objects from a Parallel Data Pump task to XML, though.

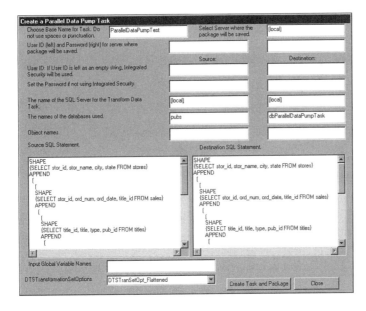

FIGURE 10.1
You can use the CreateParallelDataPumpTask application to begin creating a Parallel Data Pump task.

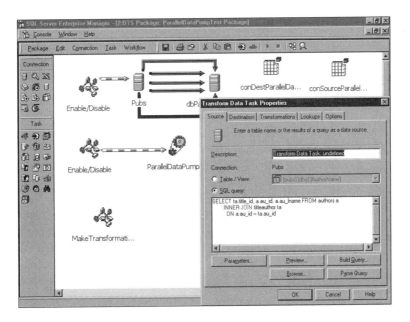

FIGURE 10.2
The five Transform Data tasks are used to create the five transformation sets for the Parallel Data Pump task.

CAUTION

I have tested this strategy for creating a Parallel Data Pump task and verified that it correctly creates the task with its transformation sets, its transformations, and their properties. However, I have not yet been able to test it extensively in a wide variety of situations. If you use it, I encourage you to verify that it has correctly created the Parallel Data Pump task.

I will also be posting any corrections or modifications to this strategy on the book's Web site.

The CD has a package in a file called ParallelDataPumpTaskSample.dts that was created using the process described in this section. The source query for this sample is the query in Listing 10.2. To use the sample, you have to open the package and right-click on the Create dbParallelDataPumpTask task to create the destination database.

The code for the MakeTransformationSets ActiveX Script task is shown in Listing 10.5.

LISTING 10.5   The Code for the ActiveX Script Task That Copies Transform Data Task Information into Parallel Data Pump Transformation Sets

```
Option Explicit

Dim pkg, tskPDP, cusPDP, transetPDP, tranPDP

Function Main()

Set pkg = DTSGlobalVariables.Parent

'***********************************************************************
'MODIFY FOLLOWING LINE WITH CORRECT PARALLEL DATA PUMP TASK NAME
Set tskPDP = pkg.Tasks("DTSTask_DTSParallelDataPumpTask_1")
'***********************************************************************

Set cusPDP = tskPDP.CustomTask

'Remove all current transformation sets
For Each transetPDP In cusPDP.TransformationSets
    cusPDP.TransformationSets.Remove transetPDP.Name
Next

'***********************************************************************
'MODIFY FOLLOWING LINES.
```

LISTING 10.5   Continued

```
'Use as many Transform Data tasks or Data Driven Query tasks
'    as there are rowsets
'Must call the procedure for each task, in the proper order
'The transformation sets will be created
'    with the ordinal number in this order
Call fctTaskToTranSet("DTSTask_DTSDataPumpTask_1")
Call fctTaskToTranSet("DTSTask_DTSDataPumpTask_2")
Call fctTaskToTranSet("DTSTask_DTSDataPumpTask_3")
Call fctTaskToTranSet("DTSTask_DTSDataPumpTask_4")
'*********************************************************************

    Main = DTSTaskExecResult_Success
End Function


Function fctTaskToTranSet(SourceTaskName)

Dim tskSource, cusSource, tranSource
Dim prop, col, lkp

DTSGlobalVariables("SourceTaskName").Value = SourceTaskName
Set tskSource = pkg.Tasks(DTSGlobalVariables("SourceTaskName").Value)
Set cusSource = tskSource.CustomTask

'Create transformation set and add to collection
set transetPDP = cusPDP.TransformationSets.New(SourceTaskName)
cusPDP.TransformationSets.Add transetPDP

'Derive the task name for the transformation set
transetPDP.Name = "TranSet_" & cusSource.Name

'Set other transformation set properties
transetPDP.Description = cusSource.Description
transetPDP.ExceptionFileColumnDelimiter = _
        cusSource.ExceptionFileColumnDelimiter
transetPDP.ExceptionFileName = cusSource.ExceptionFileName
transetPDP.ExceptionFileOptions = cusSource.ExceptionFileOptions
transetPDP.ExceptionFileRowDelimiter = _
        cusSource.ExceptionFileRowDelimiter
transetPDP.ExceptionFileTextQualifier = _
        cusSource.ExceptionFileTextQualifier
transetPDP.FetchBufferSize = cusSource.FetchBufferSize
transetPDP.FirstRow = cusSource.FirstRow
```

LISTING 10.5   Continued

```
transetPDP.LastRow = cusSource.LastRow
transetPDP.MaximumErrorCount = cusSource.MaximumErrorCount

'Set properties specific for data driven query mode
If cusPDP.TransformationSetOptions = _
        DTSTranSetOpt_DataDrivenQueries Then
    transetPDP.DeleteQuery = cusSource.DeleteQuery
    transetPDP.InsertQuery = cusSource.InsertQuery
    transetPDP.UpdateQuery = cusSource.UpdateQuery
    transetPDP.UserQuery = cusSource.UserQuery
End If

'Add lookups
For Each lkp In cusSource.Lookups
    transetPDP.Lookups.AddLookup lkp.Name, lkp.Query, _
            lkp.ConnectionID, lkp.MaxCacheRows
Next

'Add transformations
For Each tranSource In cusSource.Transformations

    Set tranPDP = _
        transetPDP.Transformations.New(tranSource.TransformServerID)

    'Copy all properties except TransformServerID,
    '        which is already assigned
    For Each prop in tranSource.Properties
        If prop.Name <> "TransformServerID" Then
            tranPDP.Properties(prop.Name).Value = prop.Value
        End If
    Next

    'Add column collections
    For Each col in tranSource.SourceColumns
        tranPDP.SourceColumns.AddColumn col.Name, col.Ordinal
    Next

    For Each col in tranSource.DestinationColumns
        tranPDP.DestinationColumns.AddColumn col.Name, col.Ordinal
    Next

    'Add transform server properties
    For Each prop in tranSource.TransformServerProperties
        tranPDP.TransformServerProperties(prop.Name).Value = _
```

LISTING 10.5   Continued

```
                prop.Value
    Next


    'Add collections specific for data driven query mode
    If cusPDP.TransformationSetOptions = _
            DTSTranSetOpt_DataDrivenQueries Then

        For Each col in tranSource.InsertColumns
            tranPDP.InsertColumns.AddColumn col.Name, col.Ordinal
        Next

        For Each col in tranSource.UpdateColumns
            tranPDP.UpdateColumns.AddColumn col.Name, col.Ordinal
        Next

        For Each col in tranSource.DeleteColumns
            tranPDP.DeleteColumns.AddColumn col.Name, col.Ordinal
        Next

        For Each col in tranSource.UserColumns
            tranPDP.UserColumns.AddColumn col.Name, col.Ordinal
        Next

    End If

    'Add the transformation
    transetPDP.Transformations.Add tranPDP

Next

End Function
```

Conclusion

The Parallel Data Pump task extends the power of DTS to the transformation of hierarchical rowsets. It's hard to use a task that doesn't have a user interface, but it's possible. Hopefully, the task will soon have a convenient interface.

Other Data Movement and Manipulation Tasks

IN THIS PART

The Bulk Insert Task

IN THIS CHAPTER

SQL Server provides the capability to bulk insert records, but only from a text file and only into a SQL Server database table. You can use this capability in four different ways:

- With the bcp command line utility.
- In Transact-SQL, with the BULK INSERT statement.
- In DTS, with the Bulk Insert task.
- In DTS, with the Transform Data task set to Fast Load.

The first three methods of bulk inserting have very similar parameters. It's convenient to use the DTS Bulk Insert task because it can be integrated into a DTS Package with a variety of other types of tasks. As I discuss the properties of the Bulk Insert task in this chapter, I will provide a cross-reference to the parameters used in bcp and the BULK INSERT statement.

The Bulk Insert task is implemented with the BULK INSERT statement. The task and the statement are both significantly faster than the other two bulk copying methods. See Chapter 28, "High-Performance DTS Packages," for more performance information.

The bcp utility uses the ODBC bulk copy API. Data is loaded into the database using the Insert Bulk command. The Insert Bulk command is also used by the Transform Data task when Fast Load is enabled.

Microsoft changed most of the DTS tasks in SQL 2000, but the Bulk Insert task has stayed the same. The Bulk Insert Task Properties dialog has a few changes (see Figure 11.1), most notably the addition of a Generate command button.

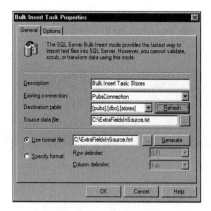

FIGURE 11.1

The Generate button provides an easy way to create a format file.

When to Choose the Bulk Insert Task Over the Transform Data Task

You will often use the Transform Data task to load data into SQL Server. But there are times when you should use the Bulk Insert task.

The main advantage of the Bulk Insert task is speed. This task provides the quickest way to import records from a text file into SQL Server. I have observed a three-fold increase in speed in using the Bulk Insert task over a Transform Data Copy transformation.

> **TIP**
>
> Don't expect to get the best possible speed from Bulk Insert without becoming familiar with the properties on the Options tab, which will be discussed later. Some of these settings can greatly increase the speed of a bulk insert. The most important performance setting is the Table Lock option.

But the Bulk Insert task is inflexible, and there are many situations when you can't use this task. Here are the limitations of the Bulk Insert task:

- It can only be used with a text file source.
- It can only be used with a SQL Server destination.

> **NOTE**
>
> Bcp can be used to move data from SQL Server to a text file, but that's not possible with the DTS Bulk Insert task.

- You cannot transform the data as it is being moved.
- You cannot generate an error file for records that fail to be imported.
- You can use the Transform Data task to automatically generate a destination table, which is useful in situations where you have field names in the first row of the file. You can't do this with the Bulk Insert task.

> **TIP**
>
> If the best import speed is not required, you can use a Transform Data task to import your text files into SQL Server. The Transform Data task is also fast, and in many situations, it's fast enough. Consider the advantages of Rapid Application Development—an easier graphical user interface, the ability to transform the data as it's being imported, and better options for error handling.

Creating a Bulk Insert Task

In the DTS Designer, you can create a Bulk Insert task with the following steps:

1. Create a DTS connection to the SQL Server database that will be used as the destination for the bulk insert.
2. Select the Bulk Insert task from the list of available tasks and make the appropriate selections.

You cannot create a Bulk Insert task with the DTS Import/Export Wizard.

You can find the code for creating a Bulk Insert task using Visual Basic at the end of this chapter.

The Destination for a Bulk Insert Task

A DTS connection must be used for the data destination of a Bulk Insert task. This connection must be to a SQL Server database. You will get an error if you start creating a Bulk Insert task before you have created a SQL Server connection.

After you have selected the connection, choose the destination table from that SQL Server database. You are given a list of all the user-defined tables and views from the database.

> **TIP**
>
> It's often easiest to reconcile the differences between the fields in the source text file and the destination table by using a view for the bulk insert. The use of views for this purpose is discussed later in this chapter.

The connection choice is assigned by DTS as the ConnectionID property of the Bulk Insert task, which references the ID of the selected connection. The table choice is the DestinationTableName property.

The Source for a Bulk Insert

The source for the Bulk Insert task must be a data file, which you can select from a file browsing dialog by clicking the expand button on the first tab. This data file may be either fixed-length or delimited.

Fixed-Length Text Files

If you are using a fixed-length text file, you must use a format file. The format file is needed to specify the number of characters in each field. The creation and use of format files is discussed later in this chapter.

Delimited Text Files

With delimited text files, you can pick the correct row delimiter and column delimiter from the lists or type in a different delimiter. The default values are a line feed character and a tab character. If you are using a format file, you can use the browsing dialog to select it.

> **NOTE**
>
> You have to use a format file when you're using a fixed-length text file. You may also choose to use a format file for a delimited text file to change the order or number of the fields in the bulk insert.

The choices discussed in this section are implemented in the bulk insert tools as follows:

Bulk Insert Task Property	BULK INSERT Statement	Bcp
DataFile	"FROM" clause	"in" clause
FormatFile	FORMATFILE	-f
RowTerminator	ROWTERMINATOR	-r
FieldTerminator	FIELDTERMINATOR	-t

Format Files

Format files allow you to bulk insert fixed-length text files. They also provide a way to control the fields that are being bulk copied. The same format file can be used for the Bulk Insert task, the BULK INSERT statement, and bcp.

Using the Bulk Insert Task the Easy Way

This and the next section discuss format files and how to reconcile differences between the source and destination of a Bulk Insert task. Please don't get the impression that it's always a hassle to set up a bulk insert. You don't even need these two sections if you are able to follow these guidelines:

1. Use delimited text files for the source, with a delimiter that will not appear in any field.

2. Do not use a text qualifier (such as double quotes) in your source.

3. Create a table for your destination that has the same number of fields, in the same order, as the source. Use this table as a working table for your data load.

4. Use the varchar data type for all the fields in your destination table. Make sure each of these fields is long enough for your source.

5. On the second tab of the Bulk Insert Task Properties dialog, select the Table Lock Option and set Insert Commit Size to 10000.

6. After you have bulk inserted the data into SQL Server, use Execute SQL tasks, Transform Data tasks, or Data Driven Query tasks to handle data cleansing and to move the data into the tables where you really want it.

If you use the Bulk Insert task like this, you won't have to use format files, you will rarely have errors, and your data will load quickly.

There are two problems with this strategy:

- Sometimes you can't specify what kind of text files you're going to use.

- After the bulk insert, you still have to spend time processing your data. For this quickest processing speed, you should use format files to move your data directly into the table where the data needs to be.

For those situations, read these two sections about format files and handling source/destination conflicts.

Format File Structure

Listing 11.1 shows a SQL Server 7.0 format file created with the fields in the stores table from the pubs sample database.

LISTING 11.1   The Basic Layout of a SQL Server 7.0 Format File Used for a Bulk Insert

```
7.0
6
1         SQLCHAR         0       4       " "       1       stor_id
2         SQLCHAR         0       40      " "       2       stor_name
3         SQLCHAR         0       40      " "       3       stor_address
4         SQLCHAR         0       20      " "       4       city
5         SQLCHAR         0       2       " "       5       state
6         SQLCHAR         0       5       " "       6       zip
```

Listing 11.2 shows a SQL Server 2000 format file created with the same fields from the same table.

LISTING 11.2   The Basic Layout of a SQL Server 2000 Format File Used for a Bulk Insert

```
8.0
6
1       SQLCHAR       0       4       " "       1       stor_id         SQL_Latin1_General_CP1_CI_AS
2       SQLCHAR       0       40      " "       2       stor_name       SQL_Latin1_General_CP1_CI_AS
3       SQLCHAR       0       40      " "       3       stor_address    SQL_Latin1_General_CP1_CI_AS
4       SQLCHAR       0       20      " "       4       city            SQL_Latin1_General_CP1_CI_AS
5       SQLCHAR       0       2       " "       5       state           SQL_Latin1_General_CP1_CI_AS
6       SQLCHAR       0       5       " "       6       zip             SQL_Latin1_General_CP1_CI_AS
```

A format file for a bulk insert has the following elements:

- A SQL Server version number at the top—8.0 is used for SQL Server 2000.
- The number of fields in the source data file is on the second line—in this case, 6.
- There is one row of information for each of the fields in the source data file—in this case, 6 rows.
- The first five columns specify information about the source data file: field order, field data type, prefix length, maximum data length, and delimiter.
- The next two columns specify information about the destination: column order and column name.
- The last column, found only in version 8.0, specifies the column collation.

> **NOTE**
>
> Both SQL Server 7.0 and SQL Server 2000 files can be used with the Bulk Insert task in SQL Server 2000. You use the two types of format files interchangeably in this chapter.
>
> In the release version of SQL Server 2000, the bcp utility generates a SQL Server 2000 format file, while the Bulk Insert task generates a SQL Server 7.0 format file.

Generating a Format File

You have two ways to generate a format file:

- Use the Generate button on the Bulk Insert Task Properties dialog.
- Use interactive bcp from the command line.

The Generate button takes you through a number of screens where you can choose:

- The data file being used as the basis for the generated format file.
- The filename of the format file that is to be generated.
- Whether the source file is fixed-length or delimited.
- The delimiters for a delimited file.
- The row length and the column widths for a fixed-length file.

The screen for setting the column widths is displayed in Figure 11.2.

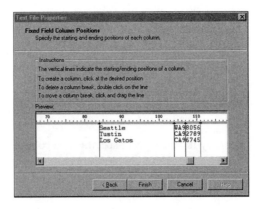

FIGURE 11.2

You have a convenient interface for selecting fixed-column widths when you generate a format file.

> **TIP**
>
> This will work fine as long as the source and destination columns match. If not, you will get the disheartening error "Unable to create format file. The number of columns in the source file and destination table do not match." You have to start all over, possibly having wasted a lot of time.

Using Format Files

When you try to do a bulk insert using a fixed-length data file with no row delimiter, the generate button creates a format file with an "\r\n" delimiter in the last row. It should be a "" delimiter.

> **CAUTION**
>
> One of the screens for generating a format file gives you the option of specifying the text qualifier used in the source data file. You have three choices—double quote, single quote, and none.
>
> If there are text qualifiers in your source file and you select the qualifier, the text qualifier will be properly removed in the onscreen display of your source data. Figure 11.3 shows the display of data in a comma-delimited text file with double quote text qualifiers. These text qualifiers are needed because commas have also been used in the fields.
>
> Unfortunately, the format file that is created will not reflect the existence of those text qualifiers. When you bulk insert the data, the text qualifier characters will be inserted into the destination data as if they were part of the data. If the addition of these two extra characters causes the string to exceed the permitted length of the destination field, an overflow error will be generated.
>
> You could try to work around this problem by editing the format file. You could add the text qualifiers as part of the delimiters. This solution will not work, though, if the first or last fields in the file have text qualifiers or if double quotes are used as the text qualifier.
>
> Here's my advice:
>
> 1. Get rid of text qualifiers and use non-occurring delimiters in the source data files, if you can.
>
> 2. If not, skip the Bulk Insert task and use a Transform Data task with a Copy Column transformation to move your text file data into SQL Server. The Transform Data task handles text qualifiers properly.

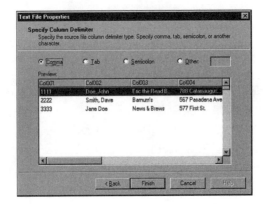

FIGURE 11.3

Text qualifiers are needed when commas occur in the data of a comma-delimited text file. Use the Transform Data task for these files.

The second way to create a format file is to use the bcp utility interactively.

Open a Command Prompt and type in a bcp command. The following command could be used to generate the format file in Listing 11.1:

```
bcp pubs.dbo.stores out c:\temp\stores.txt -Usa
```

The bcp utility will ask you a number of questions about the fields in this bulk copy. One of the last questions you will be asked is whether or not you want to create a format file. If you say yes, you will be asked for the host filename, which is used as the name of the format file that will be created.

Reconciling Differences Between the Source and the Destination

By default, a bulk insert takes data from the fields of a source file and puts it into the same number of fields, using the same order, in the data destination. If you don't have the same number of fields or if the fields are in a different order, you usually have three options:

- Use a view in place of the destination table. Create the view so that its fields line up with the fields of the source text file. This is usually the easiest option to implement.
- Use a format file. This option is usually harder to implement, but it gives the most flexibility.
- Change the destination table so its fields match the fields in the text file.

Extra Fields in the Data Destination Table

You may have fields in the destination table that do not exist in the source text file, as shown in the following example.

The destination is the Stores table in the Pubs database, which has the following fields:

```
stor_id, stor_name, stor_address, city, state, zip
```

The source text file is missing the last three fields:

```
1110Eric the Read Books          788 Catamaugus Ave.
2220Barnum's                     567 Pasadena Ave.
3330News & Brews                 577 First St.
```

You could use the following view as the destination for this Bulk Insert task:

```
create view vwStoresForBulkInsertFewerFields
as
select stor_id, stor_name, stor_address from stores
```

This code and the code for the following create table and create view items are on the book's CD as BulkInsertCreateQueries.sql.

If you use this view, you still need to use a format file because it's a fixed-length text file. You could use the format file as it is generated by the DTS Designer.

You could also use the table as the destination for the Bulk Insert task. To do that, you would have to create a special format file like this:

1. Create a temporary table that has the same structure as the source data file:

   ```
   create table tmpStoresForBulkInsertFewerFields
       (
       [stor_id] [char] (4)NOT NULL ,
       [stor_name] [varchar] (40)  NULL ,
       [stor_address] [varchar] (40) NULL
       )
   ```

2. Generate a format file using the temporary table as the destination for the Bulk Insert task. Your generated format file will look like this:

   ```
   8.0
   3
   1   SQLCHAR   0   4    " "    1   stor_id        SQL_Latin1_General_CP1_CI_AS
   2   SQLCHAR   0   40   " "    2   stor_name      SQL_Latin1_General_CP1_CI_AS
   3   SQLCHAR   0   40   "\r\n" 3   stor_address   SQL_Latin1_General_CP1_CI_AS
   ```

3. Add the missing fields in the order they appear in the destination, using 0 for the column length and 0 for the column order field.

4. If you have a row delimiter (in the example, the new line character), move that to the last line.

5. Change the number in the second row of the format file to the number of fields in the destination table.

When you are done, your format file should look like Listing 11.3.

LISTING 11.3   This Format File Accommodates Extra Fields in the Data Destination Table

```
  8.0
6
1   SQLCHAR   0   4    " "   1   stor_id       SQL_Latin1_General_CP1_CI_AS
2   SQLCHAR   0   40   " "   2   stor_name     SQL_Latin1_General_CP1_CI_AS
3   SQLCHAR   0   40   " "   3   stor_address  SQL_Latin1_General_CP1_CI_AS
4   SQLCHAR   0   0    " "   0   city          SQL_Latin1_General_CP1_CI_AS
5   SQLCHAR   0   0    " "   0   state         SQL_Latin1_General_CP1_CI_AS
6   SQLCHAR   0   0    "\r\n" 0  zip           SQL_Latin1_General_CP1_CI_AS
```

The files for this example are on the book's CD as FewerFieldsInSource.txt and FewerFieldsInSource.fmt.

Rearranging Fields When Moving from Source to Destination

It's easier when you have the same fields in the source and the destination, but they're in a different order.

For example, you could have a text file to import into stores that has the correct six fields, but the field order in this text file is stor_name, stor_id, stor_address, city, state, zip:

```
Eric the Read Books 1100788 Catamaugus Ave. Seattle    WA98056
Barnum's             2200567 Pasadena Ave.   Tustin     CA92789
News & Brews         3300577 First St.       Los Gatos CA96745
```

The view that you could create to use as the destination table is as follows:

```
create view vwStoresForBulkInsertRearrange
as
select stor_name, stor_id, stor_address, city, state, zip from stores
```

If you want to do the rearranging with a format file, start by generating the normal file, which will look like Listing 11.4.

LISTING **11.4**   A Generated Format File

```
7.0
6
1       SQLCHAR         0       40      " "     1       stor_name
2       SQLCHAR         0       4       " "     2       stor_id
3       SQLCHAR         0       40      " "     3       stor_address
4       SQLCHAR         0       20      " "     4       city
5       SQLCHAR         0       2       " "     5       state
6       SQLCHAR         0       5       " "     6       zip
```

The rows describing the fields in the format file must be in the order that those rows appear in the source text file. But the numbers in the sixth column must reflect the actual order of those fields in the destination table. Listing 11.5 shows a format file adjusting the order of fields that differ in the source and destination tables.

LISTING **11.5**   Switching the Numbering in Column 6 Reorders Fields as They Enter the Destination Table

```
7.0
6
1       SQLCHAR         0       40      " "     2       stor_name
2       SQLCHAR         0       4       " "     1       stor_id
3       SQLCHAR         0       40      " "     3       stor_address
4       SQLCHAR         0       20      " "     4       city
5       SQLCHAR         0       2       " "     5       state
6       SQLCHAR         0       5       " "     6       zip
```

The files for this example are on the book's CD as RearrangeFields.txt and RearrangeFields.fmt.

Extra Fields in the Source Text File

If the text file being used as the source for a Bulk Insert task has more fields than the destination, using a view is not an option. The easiest way to handle this situation is to create the extra fields in the destination table. If you don't want to do that, you can use a format file.

In this example, your source text file has the six fields for the Stores table but also has three extra fields—stor_type, stor_descript, and manager_name:

```
1111,John Doe,Eric the Read Books,788 Catamaugus Ave.,Seattle,
    WA,98056,discount,good books
2222,Dave Smith,Barnum's,567 Pasadena Ave.,Tustin,
    CA,92789,historical,better books,
3333,Jane Doe,News & Brews,577 First St.,Los Gatos,
    CA,96745,current events,best books
```

You could follow these steps:

1. Create a temporary table that has the same structure as the source data file:

```
create table tmpStoresForBulkInsertExtraFields
    (
    [stor_id] [char] (4)  NOT NULL,
    [manager_name] char(40) NULL,
    [stor_name] [varchar] (40)   NULL,
    [stor_address] [varchar] (40)   NULL,
    [city] [varchar] (20)   NULL,
    [state] [char] (2)   NULL,
    [zip] [varchar] (50)   NULL,
    [stor_type] char(40) NULL,
    [stor_descript] char(40) NULL
    )
```

2. Generate a format file using the temporary table as the destination for the Bulk Insert task. Your generated format file will look like this:

```
7.0
9
1    SQLCHAR    0    4     ","      1    stor_id
2    SQLCHAR    0    40    ","      2    manager_name
3    SQLCHAR    0    40    ","      3    stor_name
4    SQLCHAR    0    40    ","      4    stor_address
5    SQLCHAR    0    20    ","      5    city
6    SQLCHAR    0    2     ","      6    state
7    SQLCHAR    0    5     ","      7    zip
8    SQLCHAR    0    40    ","      8    stor_type
9    SQLCHAR    0    40    "\r\n"   9    stor_descript
```

3. Renumber the destination column order to reflect the actual order of fields in the destination. Set the value to 0 for those fields that don't exist in the destination.

When you're done, the format file should look like Listing 11.6.

LISTING 11.6   Adding Additional Fields with a Format File

```
7.0
9
1    SQLCHAR    0    4     " "      1    stor_id
2    SQLCHAR    0    40    " "      0    manager_name
3    SQLCHAR    0    40    " "      2    stor_name
4    SQLCHAR    0    40    " "      3    stor_address
5    SQLCHAR    0    20    " "      4    city
6    SQLCHAR    0    2     " "      5    state
7    SQLCHAR    0    5     " "      6    zip
8    SQLCHAR    0    40    " "      0    stor_type
9    SQLCHAR    0    40    " "      0    stor_descript
```

The files for this sample are on the book's CD as ExtraFieldsInSource.txt and
ExtraFieldsInSource.fmt.

Other Properties of the Bulk Insert Task

The Bulk Insert task has many additional properties. Most of them can be set on the Options
tab of the Bulk Insert Task Properties dialog, as shown in Figure 11.4.

FIGURE 11.4
Many settings on the Options tab of the Bulk Insert Task Properties dialog greatly affect performance.

The code sample at the end of this chapter shows how to set all these properties in Visual Basic
code.

Check Constraints

When this option is selected, the data is checked for compliance with all constraints as it is
added to the destination table. By default, constraints are ignored when adding records with a
Bulk Insert:

> Default value: `False`
>
> Effect on performance: Decreases performance when selected
>
> Object property: `CheckConstraints`
>
> Equivalent parameter of the Bulk Insert command: `CHECK_CONSTRAINTS`
>
> Equivalent parameter of bcp: `-h "CHECK_CONSTRAINTS"`

You enable constraints in Transact-SQL code with the `CHECK` parameter in the `ALTER TABLE`
statement. You can disable them with the `NO CHECK` parameter. Selecting or not selecting this
property implements identical behavior for the Bulk Insert task, although other data modifications taking place at the same time will still have those constraints enforced.

The Bulk Insert task runs more quickly if the constraints are not checked. You can create an Execute SQL task that checks for and processes any records that have been entered into the table that violate the table's constraints. Set this Execute SQL task to take place upon the successful completion of the Bulk Insert task.

> **NOTE**
>
> Triggers are never fired during the Bulk Insert task. You can activate the triggers when using the other two bulk copy tools:
>
> > Bulk Insert command parameter: `FIRETRIGGERS`
> >
> > Bcp parameter: `-h "FIRE_TRIGGERS"`
>
> If you want to check constraints and fire triggers after a Bulk Insert task, you can use the following command:
>
> `Update tblCustomer set PhoneNumber = PhoneNumber`
>
> This command does not modify any data, but it does cause all the table's constraints to be enforced and all the update triggers to fire. The command will fail if any record in the table violates one of the constraints.
>
> All the update triggers will be run by this command. If you take all your insert triggers and also make them update triggers, this code activates all the triggers that were missed during the Bulk Insert. If any of the triggers fails to be successfully completed, this update command will also fail.
>
> You need more complex code to clean up the data if it fails this constraint and trigger test.

Keep Nulls

Selecting this option causes null values to be inserted into the destination table wherever there are empty values in the source. The default behavior is to insert the values that have been defined in the destination table as defaults wherever there are empty fields.

Default value: `False`

Effect on performance: Improves performance when selected

Object property: `KeepNulls`

Equivalent parameter of the Bulk Insert command: `KEEPNULLS`

Equivalent parameters of bcp: `-k`

A Bulk Insert task that keeps nulls could run faster. You can create an Execute SQL task after the Bulk Insert that will apply the table's defaults. Here is a SQL statement that puts the default value into all the PhoneNumber fields that have empty values:

```
Update tblCustomer set PhoneNumber = Default where PhoneNumber = Null
```

This strategy assumes that there are no records in the PhoneNumber field where you intentionally want to place a Null value.

Enable Identity Insert

This option allows the insertion of values into an Identity column in the destination table.

> Default value: False
>
> Effect on performance: Negligible
>
> Object property: KeepIdentity
>
> Equivalent parameter of the Bulk Insert command: KEEPIDENTITY
>
> Equivalent parameters of bcp: -E

There are three possible ways to handle a Bulk Insert into a table that has an identity column:

- If you want to ignore the values for the identity column in the source data file, leave the default setting of False for this property. The table's identity column will be filled with automatically generated values, as in a normal record insert.

- If you want to keep the values for the identity column that are in your source data file, select this option. SQL Server sets the IDENTITY_INSERT option on for the Bulk Insert and writes the values from the text file into the table.

- If your text file does not have a field for the identity column, you must use a format file. This format file must indicate that the identity field is to be skipped when importing data. The table's identity column will be filled with the automatically generated values.

Table Lock

SQL Server has a special locking mechanism that is available for bulk inserts. Enable this mechanism either by selecting this property or using sp_tableoption to set the "table lock on bulk load" option to True.

> Default value: False
>
> Effect on performance: Significantly improves performance when selected
>
> Object property: TableLock
>
> Equivalent parameter of the Bulk Insert command: TABLOCK
>
> Equivalent parameters of bcp: -h "TABLOCK"

When this special locking mechanism is enabled, a bulk insert acquires a bulk update lock. This lock allows other bulk inserts to take place at the same time but prevents any other processes from accessing the table.

If this property is not selected and the "table lock on bulk load" option is set to False, the Bulk Insert will acquire individual record locks. This significantly reduces the speed of the Bulk Insert task.

Sorted Data

By default, the Bulk Insert task processes the records in the data file as if they were in no particular order. Setting this property to true improves the performance of a bulk insert if the following three requirements are met:

- A clustered index exists on the table.
- The data file is in the same order as that clustered index.
- The order specified by the SortedData property matches the ordering of the table's clustered index.

    Default value: Not selected. Empty string for property value.

    Effect on performance: Improves performance when selected, but only if all the requirements for its proper use are met.

    Object property: SortedData, which holds the string specifying the sort order.

    Equivalent parameter of the Bulk Insert command: ORDER

    Equivalent parameters of bcp: -h "ORDER (<Ordering String>)"

If the table does not have a clustered index, or an ordering other than the clustered index is specified, this property is ignored.

The ordering string is constructed in the same way as the syntax of the ORDER BY clause in a SQL statement. If the ordering of customers were alphabetical by city and oldest to youngest within a city, the ordering string would be

```
City, Age DESC
```

Code Page

This option specifies the code page that has been used for the data in the source file. This property affects the Bulk Insert only in cases where there are characters with values less than 32 or greater than 127.

    Default value: OEM

    Other possible values: ACP, RAW, Specific code page number

Effect on performance: Usually none

Object property: `CodePage`

Equivalent parameter of the Bulk Insert command: `CODEPAGE`

Equivalent parameters of bcp: `-C`

Data File Type

There are two choices to make in this property—the choice between `char` and native data types, and the choice between regular character fields and Unicode character fields.

If you have Unicode data in your data, you must use `widechar` or `widenative` to bulk insert your data.

`Char` and `widechar` are used for inserting data from a file that has character fields. `Native` and `widenative` use a variety of data types in their fields. These `native` files must be created by bulk copying data out of SQL Server with bcp. If you are using text files to transfer data between two SQL Server databases, using `native` mode improves performance.

Default value: `char`

Here are all the possible values, with their constants:

Constant	Value
DTSBulkInsert_DataFileType_Char	0
DTSBulkInsert_DataFileType_Native	1
DTSBulkInsert_DataFileType_WideChar	2
DTSBulkInsert_DataFileType_WideNative	3

Effect on performance: Using `native` and `widenative` improves performance when you're using a text file to transfer data from one SQL Server to another.

Object property: `DataFileType`

Equivalent parameter of the Bulk Insert command: `DATAFILETYPE`

Equivalent parameters of bcp: `-s` for native, `-w` for wide character

Insert Commit Size

By default, all records are inserted into the destination table as a single transaction. This property allows for fewer records to be included in each transaction. If a failure takes place during the Bulk Insert, all inserts in the current transaction are rolled back. If some batches have already been committed, those records stay in the destination database.

> Default value: Not selected. Batch size is 0, indicating that all records are to be inserted in one batch.
>
> Effect on performance: Import speed increases as the batch size is increased, unless there are limiting factors such as inadequate space for the transaction log.
>
> Object property: `BatchSize`
>
> Equivalent parameter of the Bulk Insert command: `BATCHSIZE`
>
> Equivalent parameters of bcp: `-b`

This is one of the places where the Bulk Insert properties do not exactly match the parameters of the Bulk Insert Transact-SQL command. Two parameters are available in the Transact-SQL command that are not available when you're doing a Bulk Insert task. `KILOBYTES_PER_BATCH` and `ROWS_PER_BATCH` are both used by SQL Server to perform the Bulk Insert more efficiently.

Maximum Errors

This property specifies the maximum number of allowable errors before the Bulk Insert task is terminated. (It is not possible to set this property in the interface. It must be done in code or with Disconnected Edit.)

> **NOTE**
>
> I have not been able to use this property with the Bulk Insert task. No matter what values I set for the `MaximumErrors` property and the `BatchSize` property, the task still fails with the first error.

> Default value: 10
>
> Effect on performance: None
>
> Object property: `MaximumErrors`
>
> Equivalent parameter of the Bulk Insert command: `MAXERRORS`
>
> Equivalent parameters of bcp: `-m`

Only Copy Selected Rows, Starting with Row, and Stopping at Row

These properties allow you to choose to include only a particular range of records from the source data file in your bulk insert.

Default values: Not selected, 0, and 0. All the records in the file are included in the bulk insert.

Effect on performance: None

Object Properties: FirstRow and LastRow

Equivalent parameters of the Bulk Insert command: FIRSTROW and LASTROW

Equivalent parameters of bcp: -F and -L

Creating a Bulk Insert Task in Visual Basic

I have created a Visual Basic procedure, fctCreateBulkInsertTask, that creates a connection, a step, a task, and a custom task for a Bulk Insert task.

You can find the code for this procedure in several forms on the book's CD in the directory for Chapter 11:

- In a Visual Basic Project, with files CreateBulkInsertTask.vbp, CreateBulkInsertTask.frm, and CreateBulkInsertTask.bas

- Modified for VBScript as CreateBulkInsertTask.scr.

- In a DTS Package, CreateBulkInsertTask.dts. Load this package into the Package Designer and execute it. The package will be saved in SQL Server storage. Open that package and you will see the Bulk Insert task. The package can be run repeatedly to create more Bulk Insert tasks. The new tasks will not be visible in the Package Designer until you close the Package and then reopen it.

The code for fctCreateBulkInsertTask is shown in Listing 11.7. The procedure needs some utility functions, which are included with the code listings on the CD. The project requires a reference to the Microsoft DTSPackage Object Library.

LISTING 11.7   The Visual Basic Code to Create a Bulk Insert Task

```
Option Explicit

Public Function fctCreateBulkInsertTask( _
    pkg As DTS.Package2, _
    Optional sBaseName As String = "BulkInsertTask", _
    Optional sDataSource As String = "(local)", _
    Optional sConnectionUserID As String = "", _
    Optional sConnectionPassword As String = "", _
    Optional sCatalog As String = "pubs", _
    Optional sDestinationTableName As String = "stores", _
    Optional sDataFile As String = "", _
    Optional sExistingConnection As String = "", _
    Optional lBatchSize As Long = 0, _
```

LISTING 11.7   Continued

```
        Optional bCheckConstraints As Boolean = False, _
        Optional sCodepage As String = "", _
        Optional lDataFileType As Long = 0, _
        Optional sFieldTerminator As String = "\t", _
        Optional sRowTerminator As String = "\n", _
        Optional sFormatFile As String = "", _
        Optional lFirstRow As Long = 0, _
        Optional lLastRow As Long = 0, _
        Optional bKeepIdentity As Boolean = False, _
        Optional bKeepNulls As Boolean = False, _
        Optional lMaximumErrors As Long = 10, _
        Optional sSortedData As String = "", _
        Optional bTableLock As Boolean = False) As String

On Error GoTo ProcErr

Dim con As DTS.Connection2
Dim stp As DTS.Step2
Dim tsk As DTS.Task
Dim cus As DTS.BulkInsertTask

'Check to see if the selected Base name is unique
sBaseName = fctFindUniqueBaseName(pkg, sBaseName)

If sExistingConnection = "" Then
    'Create connection for Bulk Insert Destination
    Set con = pkg.Connections.New("SQLOLEDB")
    With con
        .ID = fctNextConnectionID(pkg)
        .Name = "con" & sBaseName
        .DataSource = sDataSource
        .Catalog = sCatalog

        .UserID = sConnectionUserID
        .Password = sConnectionPassword

        'If User ID is empty string, use trusted connection
        If sConnectionUserID = "" Then
          .UseTrustedConnection = True
        Else
          .UseTrustedConnection = False
        End If

    End With
    pkg.Connections.Add con
```

LISTING 11.7   Continued

```
Else
    Set con = pkg.Connections(sExistingConnection)
End If

'Create task and custom task
Set tsk = pkg.Tasks.New("DTSBulkInsertTask")
Set cus = tsk.CustomTask
With cus

    'Set ConnectionID
    .ConnectionID = con.ID

    'Properties
    .Name = "tsk" & sBaseName
    .Description = sBaseName
    'Set to values provided by the Package Designer
    .DataFile = sDataFile
    .DestinationTableName = sDestinationTableName
    .FormatFile = sFormatFile
    .FieldTerminator = sFieldTerminator 'Tab
    .RowTerminator = sRowTerminator 'New line character
    .CheckConstraints = bCheckConstraints 'False
    .KeepNulls = bKeepNulls 'False
    .KeepIdentity = bKeepIdentity 'False
    .TableLock = bTableLock 'False
    .SortedData = sSortedData 'Not sorted
    .Codepage = sCodepage
    .DataFileType = lDataFileType 'char
    .BatchSize = lBatchSize
    .MaximumErrors = lMaximumErrors
    .FirstRow = lFirstRow
    .LastRow = lLastRow

End With
pkg.Tasks.Add tsk

'Create step for task
Set stp = pkg.Steps.New
With stp
    .Name = "stp" & sBaseName
    .Description = sBaseName
    .TaskName = tsk.Name
End With
```

LISTING 11.7   Continued

```
pkg.Steps.Add stp
fctCreateBulkInsertTask = stp.Name

Set con = Nothing
Set tsk = Nothing
Set cus = Nothing
Set stp = Nothing

ProcExit:
  Exit Function
ProcErr:
  MsgBox Err.Number & " - " & Err.Description
  fctCreateBulkInsertTask = ""
  GoTo ProcExit
End Function
```

Conclusion

You can't use the Bulk Insert task in every situation. If you don't need the extra speed, it's often not worth the effort to make it work. But you'll find that when you need to load large text files into SQL Server, this task provides the best combination of speed and convenience.

The Execute SQL Task

IN THIS CHAPTER

Microsoft has significantly improved and extended the value of the Execute SQL task in SQL Server 2000. You can now do the following:

- Use global variables to dynamically modify the query used in the task.
- Use global variables to receive the value of fields for one record returned by a SELECT query.
- Use a global variable to receive a reference to the recordset returned by a SELECT query. This recordset can then be referenced in ActiveX scripts as if it were an ADO recordset.

When to Use the Execute SQL Task

The transformation tasks allow you to perform rapid row-by-row processing of your data. The Execute SQL task gives you the power of SQL-oriented set processing, which will usually be even faster. If you can write your data transformation as a SQL statement and you don't need to use special processing for individual rows, you can usually use an Execute SQL task.

You can use the Execute SQL task for executing a wide variety of queries, as long as you are using a user account with sufficient permissions:

- Individual statements or batches of SQL statements.
- Data retrieval queries—SELECT.
- Data modification queries—INSERT, UPDATE, and DELETE.
- Queries that load data from one table into another—INSERT...SELECT and SELECT INTO.
- Data definition queries—CREATE, DROP, and ALTER.
- Date access control queries—GRANT, DENY, and REVOKE.
- Stored procedures.
- DTS packages, by using SQL Server's OLE Automation stored procedures.

Creating the Execute SQL Task

You can create an Execute SQL task in the Package Designer or with code. The last section of this chapter shows how to create an Execute SQL task using code.

The Import/Export Wizard creates a variety of Execute SQL tasks. It uses these tasks to drop tables, create tables, and delete data from tables. You cannot use the wizard to create Execute SQL tasks for other purposes.

The Package Designer's Execute SQL Task Properties dialog is shown in Figure 12.1. It gives you three ways to set the SQL Statement:

- Write it in the SQL Statement box.
- Use the Browse button to load the query from a file.
- Use the Build Query button to create a query using a visual interface.

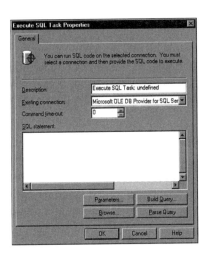

FIGURE 12.1
The Execute SQL Task Properties dialog gives you several ways to create a query.

> **TIP**
>
> When I'm developing queries for a SQL Server database, I usually use the Query Analyzer to create my SQL statements. The Query Designer in SQL Server 2000 provides an excellent development environment for creating and testing queries. After the query or query batch is working the way I want it to, I load it into the Execute SQL Task Properties dialog.

You have to select a DTS connection that has been previously defined in the package. You can provide a description and a value for the command timeout. You also have buttons for parsing the query and providing parameters for it.

The Execute SQL task has very few properties. Besides the Name and Description properties, the ExecuteSQLTask object in SQL Server 7.0 has only these four properties:

- SQLStatement—The text of the query.
- ConnectionID—The ID of the connection used for the query.
- CommandTimeout—The length of time in seconds that the task waits for a response from the connection. The default value is 0, which causes the task to wait forever.
- CommandProperties—A pointer to the collection of OLE DB properties for the connection.

The extended SQL Server 2000 object, ExecuteSQLTask2, has three additional properties, which implement the ability to use parameters with the Execute SQL task:

- InputGlobalVariableNames—A semicolon-delimited list of the names of the global variables used as parameters in the query.
- OutputAsRecordset—The name of the global variable that is to be assigned an object reference to the recordset returned by the query.
- OutputGlobalVariableNames—A semicolon-delimited list of the names of the global variables that are to receive the data values returned by the query.

The SQLStatement property has been modified in ExecuteSQLTask2 so that it can include question marks, which act as placeholders for the input parameters.

Writing Queries for Different Database Systems

You have to write the query for the Execute SQL task using the SQL dialect of the data connection. If you are using the task with an Oracle database, for example, you have to use SQL that can be understood by Oracle.

You can check the syntax of the query as you are creating it by using the Parse Query button. The task does no parsing of the query itself. Rather, it passes the query to the OLE DB provider for parsing.

You cannot use the Execute SQL task with connections that do not support SQL, such as text files.

Using Input Parameters in Execute SQL Tasks

SQL Server 2000 allows you to use parameters in your SQL statement. These parameters are filled with values from global variables. By using parameters, you can easily modify the text of a query as the DTS package is executing.

The most common use of input parameters is to provide values for filters in a WHERE clause. In the following example from the Northwind sample database, orders shipped by a particular carrier in a particular time period are loaded into a separate table for analysis. The time period and

shipper are set with parameters. The DTS package for this example is on the CD in
DemoInputParameters.dts:

```
Insert tblShipperReview
    Select * From orders
        Where ShippedDate >= ?
            And ShippedDate < DateAdd(d,1,?)
            And ShipVia = ?
```

Figure 12.2 shows the Parameter Mapping dialog, which you use to map these parameters to
the appropriate global variables. If the global variables don't exist, you can open the Global
Variables dialog to create them.

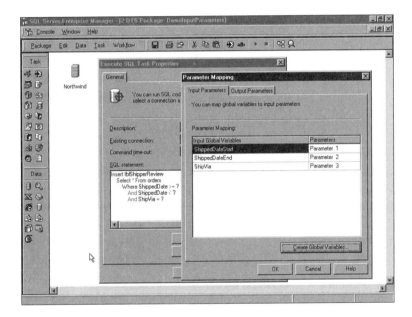

FIGURE 12.2

You map the input parameters to the appropriate global variables in the Parameter Mapping dialog.

After mapping the global variables, you can look at the InputGlobalVariableNames using
Disconnected Edit. The value of this property will be the following string:

```
ShippedDateStart;ShippedDateEnd;ShipVia
```

You can set the value of the input global variables in a variety of ways:

- In a Dynamic Properties task (perhaps from values in a text file or an .INI file, or from
  values retrieved by a query).
- In an ActiveX Script task.

12

THE EXECUTE
SQL TASK

- In a transformation ActiveX script, based on values found in the data being transformed.
- As output parameters from another Execute SQL task.
- Manually by selecting Properties on the Package menu, choosing the Global Variables tab, and typing in a value for the parameter.
- From another DTS package with the Execute Package task.
- In the parameters of the DTSRun command line that executes the package.

The sample application uses an ActiveX Script to check if the three global variables have valid values. If they do not, values are assigned to them.

A DTSRun command that could be used to execute the package from SQL Server storage with selected values for the global variables would be as follows:

```
DTSRun /S "(local)" /N "DemoInputParameters" /A
➥"ShippedDateStart":"7"="2/1/1997" /A "ShippedDateEnd":"7"="7/1/2000"  /A
➥"ShipVia":"2"="1" /W "0" /E
```

This file is on the CD in a batch file called DemoInputParameters.bat.

NOTE

You can use input parameters in several SQL statements in the same task. However, the statements with parameters have to be at the beginning of the script being used in the Execute SQL task. If other queries are used first, the parameterized queries generate syntax errors.

Using Output Parameters for Row Values

The Parameter Mapping dialog has a second tab that you can use to set output parameters for the Execute SQL task, as shown in Figure 12.3.

Each field in the record returned by a SELECT query can be assigned to a global variable. You can map none, some, or all of the fields. You capture the values of the fields by mapping them to global variables.

When you use output parameters for row values, you can only capture values from one record. The next section of this chapter will show you how to capture the whole recordset in a global variable.

FIGURE 12.3
You capture values from particular fields by mapping them to output parameters.

If you have multiple queries in a batch, the Execute SQL task will use the first SQL statement that returns a result as the source for the output parameters. If you want, you can gather values together in local variables and assign them at the end of the batch, as in this example from Northwind:

```
Declare @cAvgPriceBeforeUpdate money
Declare @cAvgPriceAfterUpdate money
Set NoCount on

Set @cAvgPriceBeforeUpdate =
    (Select AVG(UnitPrice) As AvgUnitPrice From Products)

Update Products
    Set UnitPrice = UnitPrice * 1.05
    Where UnitsInStock <= 10 And UnitsInStock > 5
Update Products
    Set UnitPrice = UnitPrice * 1.1
    Where UnitsInStock <= 5

Set @cAvgPriceAfterUpdate =
    (Select AVG(UnitPrice) As AvgUnitPrice From Products)

Select @cAvgPriceBeforeUpdate As AvgPriceBeforeUpdate,
       @cAvgPriceAfterUpdate As AvgPriceAfterUpdate
```

> **NOTE**
>
> This example will not work without NoCount turned on. If you don't do this, the Execute SQL task will consider the report of rows modified by the first UPDATE statement as the query that should be used to set the output parameters.

The DTS package for this example is on the CD in DemoOutputParameters.dts.

> **NOTE**
>
> There are ways around the limitation of output parameters capturing values from only one record. For a SQL Server connection, you could open a cursor and assign the values of different records to different variables and return those values. Or, as in the following code sample, you could return three of the distinct values found in a particular field:
>
> ```
> Declare @sName1 varchar(30), @sName2 varchar(30), @sName3 varchar(30)
>
> set @sName1 =
>     (
>     select top 1 au_lname from authors
>     )
>
> set @sName2 =
>     (
>     select top 1 au_lname from authors
>     where au_lname <> @sName1
>     )
>
> set @sName3 =
>     (
>     select top 1 au_lname from authors
>     where au_lname <> @sName1
>     and au_lname <> @sName2
>     )
>
> Select @sName1, @sName2, @sName3
> ```
>
> I wouldn't recommend that you use this strategy—the rowset output parameter would normally be better.

Using an Output Parameter for the Rowset

You can also capture the entire rowset returned by an Execute SQL task in a single global variable. You set the rowset parameter in the Parameter Mapping dialog, as shown in Figure 12.4. This global variable can then be used as an object reference to a disconnected ADO recordset. You can browse this recordset in an ActiveX script.

FIGURE 12.4
You can capture the output of an Execute SQL query as a disconnected ADO recordset.

For example, if you wanted to examine the suppliers in the Northwind sample database with the most sales during a particular time period, you could use the following query:

```
select top 5 s.SupplierID, s.CompanyName,
    Convert(Numeric(15,2),
        SUM(od.UnitPrice * od.Quantity * od.Discount)) As TotalSales
from Suppliers s
    inner join Products p
        on s.SupplierID = p.SupplierID
    inner join [Order Details] od
        on p.ProductID = od.ProductID
    inner join Orders o
        on od.OrderID = o.OrderID
where o.OrderDate >= ?
    and o.OrderDate < DateAdd(d,1,?)
group by s.SupplierID, s.CompanyName
order by
    SUM(od.UnitPrice * od.Quantity * od.Discount) DESC
```

12

THE EXECUTE
SQL TASK

If you assigned the output parameter for the rowset to a global variable named rstTopSupplier, you could reference this data in an ActiveX script with the following code:

```
Option Explicit
Function Main
Dim rst, fld, msg

Set rst = GlobalVariables("rstTopSupplier").Value
rst.MoveFirst

Do Until rst.EOF = TRUE

    msg = ""
    For Each fld in rst.Fields
        msg = msg & fld.Name & vbTab &  fld.Value & vbCrLf
    Next

    Msgbox msg
    rst.MoveNext

Loop

    Main = DTSTaskExecResult_Success
End Function
```

The DTS package for this example is on the CD in DemoOutputRowset.dts.

Dynamically Modifying the SQL Statement

The use of parameters has greatly increased the flexibility and usefulness of the Execute SQL task, but sometimes it is still useful to modify a task's SQL statement directly with code. For instance, you might want to execute the same SQL code on two tables that have the same definition but different names. You cannot change a table name in the SQL statement with a parameter, but you can dynamically change the text of the SQL statement as the package is being executed.

The three most likely ways to change the SQL statement are as follows:

- Use an ActiveX Script task to construct the new statement, and set the SQLStatement property of the Execute SQL task in that ActiveX script. This was the only way to dynamically modify the SQLStatement property in SQL Server 7.0.
- Use an ActiveX task to construct the new statement, but actually assign it to the SQLStatement property by using the Dynamic Properties task.
- Use the Dynamic Properties task to assign the new SQLStatement property to the text in a particular file.

Here's an ActiveX Script that creates a new SQLStatement and assigns it to the SQLStatement property of the Execute SQL task:

```
Option Explicit
Function Main

Dim pkg, tsk, cus
Dim sql

Set pkg = DTSGlobalVariables.Parent
Set tsk = pkg.Tasks("DTSTask_DTSExecuteSQLTask_1")
Set cus = tsk.CustomTask

sql = "Select Top 5 * from " & DTSGlobalVariables("TableName")
cus.SQLStatement = sql

    Main = DTSTaskExecResult_Success
End function
```

This code is on the CD in a DTS package called DynamicModify.dts.

Using the Execute SQL Task to Execute a DTS Package from a Remote Server

One of the challenges in executing DTS packages is to ensure that the execution takes place on the appropriate server. If you are running a large data transformation, you normally want that task to be executed on the database server so that a large amount of data is not pulled across the network.

You can use the Execute SQL task in one DTS package to execute a second DTS package on a particular server. You can use this technique to ensure that a large volume data transformation is run on the server, no matter where the calling DTS package is executed.

The tools you use to execute a DTS package from an Execute SQL task are a set of extended stored procedures that encapsulate the functionality of OLE Automation:

- sp_OACreate
- sp_OAMethod
- sp_OAGetProperty
- sp_OASetProperty
- sp_OAGetErrorInfo
- sp_OAStop
- sp_OADestroy

Listing 12.1 contains an example of code that executes a package with a Transform Data task on a particular database server. Information about the transformation is captured in the calling package by using Execute SQL task output parameters. You can find this example on the CD in a file called RemoteExecutionCall.dts. Before running this task, you have to open the package in PackageExecutedRemotely.dts and save that package in SQL Server storage on the local server. You also have to set the appropriate security to call this package in the Execute SQL task.

You can find a more developed version of this code in Chapter 18, "The Execute Package Task." The use of the OLE Automation stored procedures is discussed in Chapter 26, "Managing Packages with Visual Basic and Stored Procedures."

LISTING 12.1   Executing a Package from an Execute SQL Task

```
--Declare local variables that need to be set by user.
DECLARE @sServerName varchar(255)
DECLARE @sServerUserName varchar(255)
DECLARE @sServerPassword varchar(255)
DECLARE @sPackageName varchar(255)
DECLARE @sStepName varchar(255)

--Set name of package to be executed.
SET @sPackageName =  'PackageExecutedRemotely'

--Set step name for which information will be returned.
SET @sStepName =  'stpLoadTable'

--Set server where package is located. (SQL Server storage assumed.)
SET @sServerName = '(local)'

--Set security information for accessing package.
--  Use empty string for integrated security.
SET @sServerUserName = ''
SET @sServerPassword =  ''

--Query used to set output parameter names for Execute SQL task.
--    Must not ever be actually run.
--    Prevent it from running by looking for 1=2
IF 1=2
BEGIN
    SELECT 1 as HResult, 1 As Source, 1 As [Description], 1 As Info,
        1 As RowsComplete, 1 As RowsInError, 1 As ExecutionTime
END

--Declare local variables that do not need to be set by user.
DECLARE @hPkg int, @hStp int, @hTsk int, @hCus int
```

LISTING 12.1   Continued

```
DECLARE @sMethod varchar(500), @sProperty varchar(500)
DECLARE @lFlags int
DECLARE @sTaskName varchar(255)
DECLARE @lRowsComplete int, @lRowsInError int, @nExecutionTime real
DECLARE @hResult int, @src varchar(255), @desc varchar(255)

--Initialization
SET @lRowsComplete = 0
SET @lRowsInError = 0
SET @nExecutionTime = 0

--Create package
EXEC @hResult = sp_OACreate 'DTS.Package', @hPkg OUT

--Set integrated security if user name is empty string or null
IF @sServerUserName = '' OR @sServerUserName IS NULL
  SET @lFlags = 256
ELSE
  SET @lFlags = 0

--Load package.
SET @sMethod = 'LoadFromSQLServer'
EXEC @hResult = sp_OAMethod @hPkg, @sMethod, NULL,
    @ServerName = @sServerName,
    @ServerUserName = @sServerUserName,
    @ServerPassword = @sServerPassword,
    @Flags = @lFlags,
    @PackageName = @sPackageName

--Always check for error after calling method or property
IF @hResult <> 0
BEGIN
   EXEC sp_OAGetErrorInfo @hPkg, @src OUT, @desc OUT
   SELECT hResult =
     @hResult, Source=@src, Description=@desc, _
       Info = 'Method - ' + @sMethod, 0, 0, 0
   RETURN
END

--Get object reference to the step through package's Steps collection
SET @sProperty = 'Steps("' + @sStepName + '")'
EXEC @hResult = sp_OAGetProperty @hPkg, @sProperty, @hStp OUT
IF @hResult <> 0
BEGIN
```

LISTING 12.1   Continued

```
    EXEC sp_OAGetErrorInfo @hPkg, @src OUT, @desc OUT
    SELECT hResult =@hResult, Source=@src, Description=@desc, _
        Info = 'Property - ' + @sProperty, 0, 0, 0
    RETURN
END

--Get value of step's TaskName property
SET @sProperty = 'TaskName'
EXEC @hResult = sp_OAGetProperty @hStp, @sProperty, @sTaskName OUT
IF @hResult <> 0
BEGIN
    EXEC sp_OAGetErrorInfo @hStp, @src OUT, @desc OUT
    SELECT hResult =@hResult, Source=@src, Description=@desc, _
        Info = 'Property - ' + @sProperty, 0, 0, 0
    RETURN
END

--Get object reference to task through package's Tasks collection.
SET @sProperty = 'Tasks("' + @sTaskName + '")'
EXEC @hResult = sp_OAGetProperty @hPkg, @sProperty, @hTsk OUT
IF @hResult <> 0
BEGIN
    EXEC sp_OAGetErrorInfo @hPkg, @src OUT, @desc OUT
    SELECT hResult =@hResult, Source=@src, Description=@desc, _
        Info = 'Property - ' + @sProperty, 0, 0, 0
    RETURN
END

--Get object reference to custom task through task's CustomTask property.
SET @sProperty = 'CustomTask'
EXEC @hResult = sp_OAGetProperty @hTsk, @sProperty, @hCus OUT
IF @hResult <> 0
BEGIN
    EXEC sp_OAGetErrorInfo @hPkg, @src OUT, @desc OUT
    SELECT hResult =@hResult, Source=@src, Description=@desc, _
        Info = 'Property - ' + @sProperty, 0, 0, 0
    RETURN
END

--Execute the package
SET @sMethod = 'Execute'
EXEC @hResult = sp_OAMethod @hPkg, @sMethod, NULL
IF @hResult <> 0
BEGIN
    EXEC sp_OAGetErrorInfo @hPkg, @src OUT, @desc OUT
```

LISTING 12.1   Continued

```
    SELECT hResult =@hResult, Source=@src, Description=@desc, _
        Info = 'Method - ' + @sMethod, 0, 0, 0
    RETURN
END


--Read the custom task's RowsComplete property
SET @sProperty = 'RowsComplete'
EXEC @hResult = sp_OAGetProperty @hCus, @sProperty, @lRowsComplete OUT
IF @hResult <> 0
BEGIN
    EXEC sp_OAGetErrorInfo @hCus, @src OUT, @desc OUT
    SELECT hResult =@hResult, Source=@src, Description=@desc, _
        Info = 'Property - ' + @sProperty, 0, 0, 0
    RETURN
END


--Read the custom task's RowsInError property
SET @sProperty = 'RowsInError'
EXEC @hResult = sp_OAGetProperty @hCus, @sProperty, @lRowsInError OUT
IF @hResult <> 0
BEGIN
    EXEC sp_OAGetErrorInfo @hCus, @src OUT, @desc OUT
    SELECT hResult =@hResult, Source=@src, Description=@desc, _
        Info = 'Property - ' + @sProperty, 0, 0, 0
    RETURN
END


--Read the custom task's ExecutionTime property
SET @sProperty = 'ExecutionTime'
EXEC @hResult = sp_OAGetProperty @hStp, @sProperty, @nExecutionTime OUT
IF @hResult <> 0
BEGIN
    EXEC sp_OAGetErrorInfo @hStp, @src OUT, @desc OUT
    SELECT hResult =@hResult, Source=@src, Description=@desc, _
        Info = 'Property - ' + @sProperty, 0, 0, 0
    RETURN
END


--Release package object variable
EXEC sp_OADestroy @hPkg

--Set output parameters
Select hResult = 0, Source = 'None', Description = 'No Error',
    Info =
    'Rows Complete - ' + convert(varchar(10), @lRowsComplete)
```

LISTING 12.1 Continued

```
    + CHAR(10) +
'Rows In Error - ' + convert(varchar(10), @lRowsInError)
    + CHAR(10) +
'Execution Time In Seconds ' + convert(varchar(10), @nExecutionTime),
RowsComplete = @lRowsComplete,
RowsInError = @lRowsInError,
ExecutionTime = convert(numeric(10, 3), @nExecutionTime)
```

Creating an Execute SQL Task in Visual Basic

I have created a Visual Basic procedure, fctCreateExecuteSQLTask, which creates a connection, a step, a task, and a custom task for an Execute SQL Task. All the properties of the task can be set with this procedure.

You can find the code for this procedure in the directory for Chapter 12 on the book's CD as a Visual Basic Project, with files CreateExecuteSQLTask.vbp, CreateExecuteSQLTask.frm, CreateExecuteSQLTask.frx, and CreateExecuteSQLTask.bas.

The code for fctCreateExecuteSQLTask is shown in Listing 12.2. The procedure needs some utility functions that are included with the code listings on the CD. The project requires a reference to the Microsoft DTSPackage Object Library.

LISTING 12.2 The Visual Basic Code to Create an Execute SQL Task

```
Option Explicit

Public Function fctCreateExecuteSQLTask( _
    pkg As DTS.Package2, _
    Optional sBaseName As String = "ExecuteSQLTask", _
    Optional sCatalog As String = "", _
    Optional sDataSource As String = "(local)", _
    Optional sUserIdConnection As String = "", _
    Optional sPasswordConnection As String = "", _
    Optional lCommandTimeout As Long = 0, _
    Optional sSQLStatement As String = "Select 1", _
    Optional sInputGlobalVariableNames As String = "", _
    Optional sOutputGlobalVariableNames As String = "", _
    Optional bOutputAsRecordset As Boolean = False, _
    Optional sExistingConnectionName As String = "") As String
On Error GoTo ProcErr

Dim con As DTS.Connection2
Dim stp As DTS.Step2
```

LISTING 12.2 Continued

```
Dim tsk As DTS.Task
Dim cus As DTS.ExecuteSQLTask2

'Check to see if the selected Base name is unique
sBaseName = fctFindUniqueBaseName(pkg, sBaseName)

If sExistingConnectionName = "" Then
    'Create connection for Execute SQL Task
    Set con = pkg.Connections.New("SQLOLEDB")
    With con
        .ID = fctNextConnectionID(pkg)
        .Name = "con" & sBaseName
        .DataSource = sDataSource
        .Catalog = sCatalog

        .UserID = sUserIdConnection
        .Password = sPasswordConnection

        'If sUserID is empty string, use trusted connection
        If sUserIdConnection = "" Then
          .UseTrustedConnection = True
        Else
          .UseTrustedConnection = False
        End If

    pkg.Connections.Add con
    End With
Else
    Set con = pkg.Connections(sExistingConnectionName)
End If

'Create task and custom task
Set tsk = pkg.Tasks.New("DTSExecuteSQLTask")
Set cus = tsk.CustomTask

With cus

    .Name = "tsk" & sBaseName
    .Description = sBaseName

    'Set ConnectionID
    .ConnectionID = con.ID

    .CommandTimeout = lCommandTimeout
    .OutputAsRecordset = bOutputAsRecordset
```

LISTING 12.2   Continued

```
     If sSQLStatement <> "" Then
         .SQLStatement = sSQLStatement
     End If

     If sInputGlobalVariableNames <> "" Then
         .InputGlobalVariableNames = sInputGlobalVariableNames
     End If

     If sOutputGlobalVariableNames <> "" Then
         .OutputGlobalVariableNames = sOutputGlobalVariableNames
     End If

End With

pkg.Tasks.Add tsk

'Create step for task
Set stp = pkg.Steps.New
With stp
     .Name = "stp" & sBaseName
     .Description = sBaseName
     .TaskName = tsk.Name
End With
pkg.Steps.Add stp

fctCreateExecuteSQLTask = stp.Name

Set tsk = Nothing
Set cus = Nothing
Set stp = Nothing

ProcExit:
  Exit Function
ProcErr:
  MsgBox Err.Number & " - " & Err.Description
  fctCreateExecuteSQLTask = ""
  GoTo ProcExit

End Function
```

Conclusion

Take the time to learn about the Execute SQL task's capability to use parameters. This capability allows the task to dynamically interact with the other tasks in the DTS package, as well as with other packages.

The Copy SQL Server Objects Task

IN THIS CHAPTER

When to Use the Copy SQL Server Objects Task

The Copy SQL Server Objects task moves data and/or database objects between SQL Server databases that are version 7.0 or later. It generates Transact-SQL scripts, which it then uses to move the database objects.

Consider using this task if the following are true:

- You don't want to copy a whole database. (If you do, consider using the Transfer Databases task.)

- You don't want to manipulate data as it is being moved. (If you do, you have to use one of the transformation tasks.)

- You want to move database objects, not just data. You can create database objects with Execute SQL tasks, but the Copy SQL Server objects task gives you a highly efficient development environment for doing that.

- You're using SQL Server 7.0 or SQL Server 2000 as the source and the destination for the object copy. The Copy SQL Server Objects task does not support any other data sources or destinations.

TIP

Out testing indicates that the Copy SQL Server Objects task is much slower than the Transform Data task using Copy Column transformations and Fast Load. This appears to be true both for large and small tables. See Chapter 28, "High-Performance DTS Packages," for the results of our testing.

We used the SQL Server Profiler to examine the commands the two tasks are sending to the database engine. Both use the Insert Bulk command to load the data. The Copy SQL Server task uses many additional commands in its processing.

One of the reasons that the Copy SQL Server task takes longer than the Transform Data task is that it writes both script files and log files during its operation.

If you're concerned about performance, you should probably create your tables with Execute SQL tasks and use Transform Data tasks to move your data.

If you just want to move tables and their data, you should usually use the Transfer Data task rather than the Copy SQL Server Objects task.

You can choose to transfer all, a selected subset, or none of the following types of SQL Server objects with this task:

- Tables, with or without the data in them
- Indexes
- Referential integrity constraints
- Triggers
- Views
- Stored procedures
- Rules
- Defaults
- User-defined data types
- Database users
- SQL Server logins
- Object-level permissions
- Full text indexes

You can create this task in both the Package Designer and the DTS Import/Export Wizard. The process is the same with both tools, and it takes about the same length of time. The last section of this chapter shows how to create the task in code using the TransferObjectsTask2 object.

The Source and the Destination

The source and destination databases are set on the first two tabs of the Copy SQL Server Objects Tasks Properties dialog, as shown in Figure 13.1. You cannot use DTS connections for the source and destination. You have to enter the information specifically for use in this task. The connection information is saved in a set of task properties:

- SourceServer and DestinationServer
- SourceDatabase and DestinationDatabase
- SourceLogin and DestinationLogin
- SourcePassword and DestinationPassword
- SourceUseTrustedConnection and DestinationUseTrustedConnection

FIGURE 13.1

You have to enter source and destination database information specifically for this Copy SQL Server Objects Task.

Transfer Choices

You have five primary choices for copying objects with a Copy SQL Server Objects task. You make most of these choices by checking boxes on the Copy tab of the Copy SQL Server Objects Task Properties dialog, as shown in Figure 13.2.

FIGURE 13.2

The primary choices for copying data are made on the Copy tab.

Creating Destination Objects

Your first choice is whether or not you want to create objects in the destination database. If you choose to create objects, you are given two additional choices:

- Do you want to drop destination objects first?
- Do you want to create (or drop and create) all dependent objects?

There are several logical possibilities regarding the existence of tables in the destination database:

- They don't exist. If this is the case, you have to choose the Create Destination Objects option. If you don't, the task will generate an error for each nonexistent table and data will not be loaded into them.
- They exist and they have different names than the tables in the source database. If this is the case, you can't use this task. Use the Transform Data task instead, where you can match tables that have dissimilar names with each other.
- They exist, they have the same names, and you want to drop and create them. Select the first two boxes.
- They exist, they have the same names, and you want to add new data to the existing tables. Select the first box and unselect the second.

These choices are implemented with three properties of the Copy SQL Server task. By default, the Package Designer sets all three properties to TRUE:

- CopySchema
- DropDestinationObjectsFirst
- IncludeDependencies

> **CAUTION**
>
> It's important to use this option carefully. When you choose to drop destination objects first, you are choosing to completely overwrite those objects. Any modifications that you or any other developer has made to those destination objects will be lost. And if you also choose to include all dependent objects, you will be overwriting objects even when you don't select them individually.
>
> Remember—by default, IncludeDependencies is set to TRUE.

Copying Data

The second choice is whether or not you want to copy data from the source to the destination. If you do not select this box, you will copy the database objects to the destination database but you will not copy any data.

If you choose to transfer data, you then choose if you want to replace the existing data in the destination tables or append the new data.

These choices are implemented with the CopyData property, which can have these three values:

- 0—DTSTransfer_DontCopyData
- 1—DTSTransfer_ReplaceData
- 2—DTSTransfer_AppendData

The default choice is to copy the data, replacing the existing data.

Use Collation

The one new feature in the Copy SQL Server Objects Properties dialog for SQL Server 2000 is that you can choose whether or not to use collation when copying. This choice is implemented as the UseCollation extended property of the TransferObjectsTask2 object.

If you select this option, you can maintain column-level collation settings between SQL Server 2000 databases that are using the same code page. If you don't use this option, if different code pages are used, or if one of the servers is SQL Server 7.0, the collation settings are translated automatically.

Selecting this option can generate an error when SQL Server 7.0 servers are involved in the transfer. This option can also slow down performance when non-Unicode data types are used.

The default setting for this property is FALSE.

Copy All Objects

The next choice is whether or not you want to transfer all the objects in the database. The default choice is to select all. If you choose to transfer only some objects, the Select Objects button is enabled.

Figure 13.3 shows the Select Objects dialog.

You can select the various types of objects you want to consider for transferring with the check boxes at the top of the dialog. The objects in the list can be selected or unselected individually. You can also select all the objects in the list with the Select All button, or select a range of objects by pressing the Shift key while you are selecting two objects.

> **NOTE**
>
> In this box, you can't decide whether to include indexes, constraints, triggers, or security objects. You make those choices by setting options in the Advanced Transfer Options dialog.

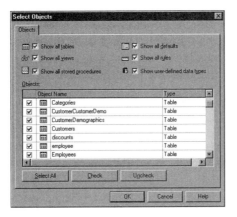

FIGURE 13.3
The Select Objects dialog is where you choose the objects you want to include in the Transfer SQL Server Objects task.

The choice of whether or not to select all the objects is implemented by the CopyAllObjects property. The selection of individual objects is implemented with a set of methods, which are described in the "Using Methods to Include Objects in the Transfer" section later in this chapter.

Use Default Options

You can choose to specify many additional details regarding the object transfer. If you uncheck the Use Default Options box, the Options button is enabled. This gives you access to the Advanced Copy Options dialog, as shown in Figure 13.4.

FIGURE 13.4
The Advanced Copy Options dialog opens with the default choices displayed.

13

THE COPY SQL
SERVER OBJECTS
TASK

If you examine this dialog box without making any changes, you can see what the default choice includes:

- Copy database users and database roles.
- Do not copy SQL Server logins.
- Copy object-level permissions.
- Copy indexes.
- Copy triggers.
- Do not copy full text indexes.
- Copy PRIMARY and FOREIGN keys.
- Do not generate scripts in Unicode.
- Use quoted identifiers when copying objects.

The first two of these advanced copy options are implemented with the IncludeUsers and IncludeLogins properties. The other options are implemented with a set of flags that are added together to set two properties—ScriptOption and ScriptOptionEx. SQL Server Books Online lists a total of 58 constants that can be used for these properties. You can have a good deal of control over these options by changing the choices on the Advanced Copy Options dialog. You can gain even greater control by setting these properties with Disconnected Edit or in code. Here are a couple of the additional possibilities:

- Through the interface, you can choose whether or not to transfer indexes. By using the individual flags, you can make separate choices whether or not to transfer clustered indexes, nonclustered indexes, and unique indexes.
- Through the interface, you can choose whether or not to transfer all the constraints. With the flags, you can specify whether or not to include each particular type of constraint—Primary Key Constraint, Unique Constraint, Foreign Key Constraint, Check Constraint, and/or Default Constraint.

Choose a Script File Directory

A number of files are generated when the Copy SQL Server Objects task is executed. These files include the following:

- Two files with an extension of .log, one each for the source and destination. These files have detailed error information about the transfer.
- A file with a .tab extension, containing the script that creates the new tables in the destination.
- Other files that contain the scripts to drop the objects or create the objects involved with the transfer.

You choose the directory where these files are created on the bottom of the Copy tab. This choice is implemented with the ScriptFileDirectory property.

Other Properties of the Copy SQL Server Objects Task

There are three other new properties implemented by the TransferObjectsTask2 object. You cannot set these properties in the Copy SQL Server Objects Properties dialog. You have to set them in Disconnected Edit or with code.

- SourceTranslateChar—Whether or not character data translation is performed on the source server. The default value is TRUE.
- DestTranslateChar— Whether or not character data translation is performed on the destination server. The default value is TRUE.
- DestUseTransaction— Whether or not the task's operations are performed within a transaction on the destination server. The default value is FALSE.

Using Methods to Include Objects in the Transfer

You can use three of the methods of the TransferObjectsTask object to manipulate the list of objects included for transferring. These methods are as follows:

- GetObjectForTransfer—Retrieve a particular object based on its index in the list of objects being transferred.
- AddObjectForTransfer— Add another object to the list of those being transferred.
- ResetObjectsList— Clear the list of objects being transferred.

The GetObjectForTransfer method has four parameters. The same parameters, with the exception of the first one, are also used for AddObjectForTransfer:

- Index—The index for the list of objects selected to be transferred. This list is 0-based.
- ObjectName—The name of the object.
- OwnerName—The owner name of the object.
- Type—The type of object, using values from the DTSSQLObjectType constants.

You have to use these methods if you want to manipulate the set of selected objects in code. They are not publicly exposed as a collection in the DTS object model. You cannot view or edit this list using Disconnected Edit.

The Visual Basic code in Listing 13.1 uses these three methods. The first function adds a new object to the list, the second displays the current list of objects, and the third clears the list. An additional procedure decodes the values of the DTSSQLObjectType constants for displaying in the message boxes.

LISTING 13.1 Using the Methods of the TransferObjectsTask to Add, Display, and Clear the List of Selected Objects

```
Option Explicit

Function fctAddObject(pkg As DTS.Package2, _
        cusTransferSQL As DTS.TransferObjectsTask2, _
        sObjectName As String, _
        lType As Long, _
        Optional sOwnerName As String = "dbo") As Boolean
On Error GoTo ProcErr

cusTransferSQL.AddObjectForTransfer sObjectName, sOwnerName, lType

ProcExit:
  Exit Function
ProcErr:
  MsgBox Err.Number & " - " & Err.Description
  GoTo ProcExit
End Function

Function fctListObjects(pkg As DTS.Package2, _
        cusTransferSQL As DTS.TransferObjectsTask2) As Boolean
On Error GoTo ProcErr

Dim msg As String
Dim lIndex As Long
Dim sObjectName As String
Dim sOwnerName As String
Dim lType As Long

'List all the objects being transferred.
'Start with an index value of 0
lIndex = 0

'We don't know how many objects there are, so
'   we end the loop by looking for an error.
On Error Resume Next

cusTransferSQL.GetObjectForTransfer lIndex, sObjectName, _
        sOwnerName, lType
```

LISTING 13.1   Continued

```
If Err.Number <> 0 Then
    MsgBox "There are no objects selected."
End If

Do Until Err.Number <> 0
    msg = "Object Index - " & CStr(lIndex) & vbCrLf
    msg = msg & "Object Name - " & sObjectName & vbCrLf
    msg = msg & "Owner Name - " & sOwnerName & vbCrLf
    msg = msg & "Object Type Constant - " & CStr(lType) & vbCrLf
    msg = msg & "Object Type - " & fctGetObjectType(lType)
    MsgBox msg
    lIndex = lIndex + 1
    cusTransferSQL.GetObjectForTransfer lIndex, sObjectName, _
            sOwnerName, lType
Loop

Err.Clear

ProcExit:
  Exit Function
ProcErr:
  MsgBox Err.Number & " - " & Err.Description
  GoTo ProcExit
End Function

Function fctClearObjectList(pkg As DTS.Package2, _
        cusTransferSQL As DTS.TransferObjectsTask2) As Boolean
On Error GoTo ProcErr

'Clear all the objects in the list
cusTransferSQL.ResetObjectsList

ProcExit:
  Exit Function
ProcErr:
  MsgBox Err.Number & " - " & Err.Description
  GoTo ProcExit
End Function

Function fctGetObjectType(lType As Long) As String
On Error GoTo ProcErr

Select Case lType
    Case 1
        fctGetObjectType = "User defined data type"
```

LISTING 13.1 Continued

```
Case 2
    fctGetObjectType = "System Tables"
Case 4
    fctGetObjectType = "Views"
Case 8
    fctGetObjectType = "User Tables"
Case 16
    fctGetObjectType = "Stored Procedures"
Case 64
    fctGetObjectType = "Defaults"
Case 128
    fctGetObjectType = "Rules"
Case 256
    fctGetObjectType = "Triggers"
Case 4096
    fctGetObjectType = "User-defined functions"
Case 4605
    fctGetObjectType = "User database objects"
Case 4607
    fctGetObjectType = "System and database objects"

End Select

ProcExit:
  Exit Function
ProcErr:
  MsgBox Err.Number & " - " & Err.Description
  GoTo ProcExit
End Function
```

Creating a Copy SQL Server Objects Task in Visual Basic

I have created a Visual Basic procedure, fctCreateTransferObjectTask, that creates a step, a task, and a custom task for a Transfer Objects task. All the properties of the task can be set with this procedure. You can find the code for it in the directory for Chapter 13 on the book's CD as a Visual Basic Project, with files CreateTransferObjectTask.vbp, CreateTransferObjectTask.frm, frmList.frm, AddObjectForTransfer.bas, and CreateTransferObjectTask.bas.

The code for fctCreateTransferObjectTask is shown in Listing 13.2. The procedure needs some utility functions that are included with the code listings on the CD. The project requires a reference to the Microsoft DTSPackage Object Library.

LISTING 13.2 The Visual Basic Code to Create a Transfer Object Task

```
Option Explicit
Public Function fctCreateTransferObjectTask( _
    pkg As DTS.Package2, _
    Optional sBaseName As String = "TransferObjectTask", _
    Optional bCopyAllObjects As Boolean = True, _
    Optional dtsCopyData As DTSTransfer_CopyDataOption = 1, _
    Optional bCopySchema As Boolean = True, _
    Optional sDestinationDatabase As String = "", _
    Optional sDestinationLogin As String = "", _
    Optional sDestinationPassword As String = "", _
    Optional sDestinationServer As String = "", _
    Optional bDestTranslateChar As Boolean = True, _
    Optional sSourceDatabase As String = "", _
    Optional sSourceLogin As String = "", _
    Optional sSourcePassword As String = "", _
    Optional sSourceServer As String = "", _
    Optional bSourceTranslateChar As Boolean = True, _
    Optional bDropDestinationObjectsFirst As Boolean = True, _
    Optional bIncludeDependencies As Boolean = True, _
    Optional bIncludeLogins As Boolean = False, _
    Optional bIncludeUsers As Boolean = True, _
    Optional sScriptFileDirectory As String = _
        "C:\Program Files\Microsoft SQL Server\80\Tools", _
    Optional lScriptOption As Long = -2147061505, _
    Optional lScriptOptionEx As Long = 4112, _
    Optional bDestUseTransaction As Boolean = False, _
    Optional bUseCollation As Boolean = False) As String

On Error GoTo ProcErr

Dim stp As DTS.Step2
Dim tsk As DTS.Task
Dim cus As DTS.TransferObjectsTask2

'Check to see if the selected Base name is unique
sBaseName = fctFindUniqueBaseName(pkg, sBaseName)

'Create task and custom task
Set tsk = pkg.Tasks.New("DTSTransferObjectsTask")
```

13

THE COPY SQL
SERVER OBJECTS
TASK

LISTING 13.2   Continued

```
Set cus = tsk.CustomTask

With cus

    .Name = "tsk" & sBaseName
    .Description = sBaseName

    .CopyAllObjects = bCopyAllObjects
    .CopyData = dtsCopyData
    .CopySchema = bCopySchema
    .DestinationDatabase = sDestinationDatabase
    If sDestinationLogin = "" Then
        .DestinationUseTrustedConnection = True
    Else
        .DestinationLogin = sDestinationLogin
        .DestinationPassword = sDestinationPassword
    End If
    .DestinationServer = sDestinationServer
    .DestTranslateChar = bDestTranslateChar
    .SourceDatabase = sSourceDatabase
    If sSourceLogin = "" Then
        .SourceUseTrustedConnection = True
    Else
        .SourceLogin = sSourceLogin
        .SourcePassword = sSourcePassword
    End If
    .SourceServer = sSourceServer
    .SourceTranslateChar = bSourceTranslateChar
    .DropDestinationObjectsFirst = bDropDestinationObjectsFirst
    .IncludeDependencies = bIncludeDependencies
    .IncludeLogins = bIncludeLogins
    .IncludeUsers = bIncludeUsers
    .ScriptFileDirectory = sScriptFileDirectory
    .ScriptOption = lScriptOption
    .ScriptOptionEx = lScriptOptionEx
    .DestUseTransaction = bDestUseTransaction
    .UseCollation = bUseCollation


End With

pkg.Tasks.Add tsk

'Create step for task
Set stp = pkg.Steps.New
```

LISTING 13.2 Continued

```
With stp
    .Name = "stp" & sBaseName
    .Description = sBaseName
    .TaskName = tsk.Name
End With
pkg.Steps.Add stp

fctCreateTransferObjectTask = stp.Name

Set tsk = Nothing
Set cus = Nothing
Set stp = Nothing

ProcExit:
  Exit Function
ProcErr:
  MsgBox Err.Number & " - " & Err.Description
  fctCreateTransferObjectTask = ""
  GoTo ProcExit
End Function
```

Conclusion

The Copy SQL Server Objects task gives you some special capabilities. It's usually not as fast as the Transform Data task, but it is the most convenient way to move objects from one SQL Server database to another.

The File Transfer Protocol (FTP) Task

IN THIS CHAPTER

The File Transfer Protocol (FTP) task allows you to retrieve files from network or Internet sites.

When to Use the File Transfer Protocol (FTP) Task

The FTP task can be used to move files or directories in your local network. It can also be used to get files from remote Internet sites. It cannot be used to send files to Internet sites.

When you're using the FTP task, it's important to recognize the possibilities for integration with the Dynamic Properties task and with the many ways you can use global variables. You can use the Dynamic Properties task to change the source, the destination, and the files involved with the FTP. You can set these values with global variables that have themselves been set with DTSRun, by another DTS package, by an Execute SQL task, or with an ActiveX Script task.

There are times when an ActiveX Script task is more convenient than an FTP task for moving files around your local network. See the discussion of using the FileSystemObject for file and directory manipulation in Chapter 16, "Writing Scripts for an ActiveX Script Task."

Creating the Task and Setting Its Properties

You can create the FTP task with the Package Designer or with code. The last section of this chapter has an example of creating the task with code.

The FTP Site tab of the File Transfer Protocol Task Properties dialog is shown in Figure 14.1. This is the place where you enter information about the site from which you want to FTP files.

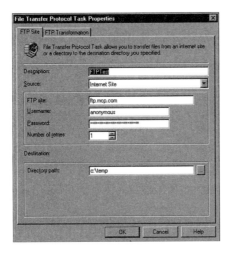

FIGURE 14.1
The FTP task allows you to move files from a local network or from an Internet site.

The primary choice you make on the FTP Site tab is the type of source location. You can choose either an Internet site or a network directory. This choice is implemented in code by setting the SourceLocation property to one of the DTSFTPSourceLocation constants:

- 0—DTSFTPSourceLocation_InternetSite (The default choice)
- 1—DTSFTPSourceLocation_Directory

Most of the other properties you set on the FTP Site fill in the details about the source of the FTP transfer:

- SourceSite—Must be used for an Internet source. The property is set to an FTP site name, such as ftp.mcp.com.
- SourceUserName—"Anonymous" is used as the default, which is the standard username for making a read-only connection to an Internet FTP site.

- SourcePassword—The email address of the user is often used when connecting as "anonymous."

- NumRetriesOnSource—The number of attempts to be made before the task terminates with a failure.

The other property you set on the FTP Site is the directory path, the DestSite property. You have to specify a local network directory for the destination of the FTP task.

The FTP Transformation tab, shown in Figure 14.2, lets you choose files from the source that you want to be transferred. The files appear in a list on the left side of the screen. You can move some or all of them over to the list on the right so that they will be included in the transfer.

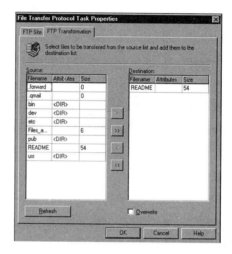

FIGURE 14.2

Choose files to transfer on the FTP Transformation tab.

These selections are implemented by the SourceFileName property. This property is a semi-colon-delimited string that contains the filenames, file paths, and file sizes in bytes. The string looks like this:

```
"'FileOne.dat';'ftp.mcp.com';'1234';'FileTwo.dat';'ftp.mcp.com';
➥'4312';'FileThre.dat';'ftp.mcp.com';'314';"
```

If you specify the site in the SourceSite property, you do not need to include the second parameter. Also, when you are creating this task programmatically, you do not need to specify the size of the file. You do still need to include the spaces for these values, however.

This string is equivalent to the preceding one if `ftp.mcp.com` is assigned to the `SourceSite` property:

```
"'FileOne.dat';'';'';'FileTwo.dat';'';'';'FileThre.dat';'';'';"
```

The only other choice you have on the FTP Transformation tab is a check box for specifying whether or not files with the same name should be overwritten. This choice is implemented with the `NonOverwritable` property. This property has a default value of `TRUE`, which means that files are not overwritten.

Creating the Task in Visual Basic

I have created a Visual Basic procedure, `fctCreateFTPTask`, which creates a step, a task, and a custom task for an FTP task. All the properties of the task can be set with this procedure. You can find the code for it in the directory for Chapter 14 on the book's CD as a Visual Basic Project, with files CreateFTPTask.vbp, CreateFTPTask.frm, and CreateFTPTask.bas.

The code for `fctCreateFTPTask` is shown in Listing 14.1. The procedure needs some utility functions that are included with the code listings on the CD. The project requires references to the Microsoft DTSPackage Object Library and the Microsoft DTS Custom Tasks Object Library.

LISTING 14.1 The Visual Basic Code to Create an FTP Task

```
Option Explicit

Public Function fctCreateFTPTask( _
    pkg As DTS.Package2, _
    Optional sBaseName As String = "FTPTask", _
    Optional sDestSite As String = "C:\Temp", _
    Optional lNumRetriesOnSource As Long = 0, _
    Optional sSourceFileName As String = "", _
    Optional lSourceLocation As Long = 0, _
    Optional sSourcePassword As String = "", _
    Optional sSourceSite As String = "", _
    Optional sSourceUserName As String = "anonymous", _
    Optional bNonOverwritable As Boolean = True) As String


On Error GoTo ProcErr

Dim stp As DTS.Step2
Dim tsk As DTS.Task
Dim cus As DTSCustTasks.DTSFTPTask
```

LISTING 14.1 Continued

```
'Check to see if the selected Base name is unique
sBaseName = fctFindUniqueBaseName(pkg, sBaseName)

'Create task and custom task
Set tsk = pkg.Tasks.New("DTSFTPTask")
Set cus = tsk.CustomTask

With cus

    .Name = "tsk" & sBaseName
    .Description = sBaseName

    .NonOverwritable = bNonOverwritable

    If sDestSite <> "" Then
        .DestSite = sDestSite
    End If

    If sSourceFileName <> "" Then
        .SourceFilename = sSourceFileName
    End If

    If sSourceSite <> "" Then
        .SourceSite = sSourceSite
    End If

    .SourceLocation = lSourceLocation
    If .SourceLocation = 0 Then

        If sSourcePassword <> "" Then
            .SourcePassword = sSourcePassword
        End If

        If sSourceUserName <> "" Then
            .SourceUsername = sSourceUserName
        End If

        .NumRetriesOnSource = lNumRetriesOnSource

    End If

End With

pkg.Tasks.Add tsk
```

LISTING 14.1 Continued

```
'Create step for task
Set stp = pkg.Steps.New
With stp
    .Name = "stp" & sBaseName
    .Description = sBaseName
    .TaskName = tsk.Name
End With
pkg.Steps.Add stp

fctCreateFTPTask = stp.Name

Set tsk = Nothing
Set cus = Nothing
Set stp = Nothing

ProcExit:
  Exit Function
ProcErr:
  MsgBox Err.Number & " - " & Err.Description
  fctCreateFTPTask = ""
  GoTo ProcExit

End Function
```

Conclusion

The FTP task is a helpful addition to DTS in SQL Server 2000. This task furthers the goal of creating an integrated, RAD environment for data movement and manipulation.

14

THE FILE
TRANSFER
PROTOCOL (FTP)
TASK

The Transfer Databases and Other Transfer Tasks

IN THIS CHAPTER

The five tasks described in this chapter are the ones used by the Copy Database Wizard to move databases and associated meta data from one SQL Server to a separate SQL Server 2000.

It's important to be able to move meta data along with the transfer of databases. SQL Server stores most of the meta data needed for database manipulation inside each individual database, but there is a significant amount of meta data that is stored in the Master and Msdb system databases.

Centralized meta data storage makes it possible for the meta data to be used by all the databases on a server. But the centralized meta data becomes a problem when you move an individual database to a new server. Unless you include all the needed meta data, the database will not operate properly on its new server.

Each of the four additional transfer tasks involves the movement of a particular kind of data:

- Logins, stored in master
- System stored procedures, stored in master
- Error messages, stored in master
- Jobs, stored in msdb

The most common difficulty I have seen in moving databases is getting all the logins moved properly. But all the meta data is important. Stored procedures, scheduled jobs, and batch processes can all fail if the proper meta data is missing.

When to Use the Transfer Databases and Other Transfer Tasks

The five transfer tasks are designed for two purposes:

- The specific purpose of upgrading a SQL Server 7.0 database to SQL Server 2000.
- The more general purpose of moving a database and associated meta data between database servers.

You can only use databases on SQL Server 7.0 or SQL Server 2000 as the source for these transfer tasks. The destination must be SQL Server 2000. One or more databases can be included in a database transfer. For each included database, you can choose to copy it or move it.

You cannot resolve most naming conflicts in the process of using these tasks. You need to resolve any conflicts before setting up these tasks, with the exception of conflicts in the naming of database storage files.

You can include or exclude individual items of meta data, such as particular stored procedures, logins, messages, and jobs. You cannot exclude any of the objects included in the databases being transferred. If you just want to transfer some objects in a database, you should consider using the Copy SQL Server Objects task. If you want to modify the data as it is being moved, you should consider using one of the transformation tasks.

These five tasks are the ones to use when you want to move or copy one or more whole databases.

Creating the Tasks and Setting Their Properties

The primary method of creating these tasks is to use the Copy Database Wizard, which is described in Chapter 25. You can also create the tasks in the Package Designer, although this is not as convenient as using the wizard.

It is possible to create these tasks in code, but the object model for these tasks is not as well documented as the object model for the other DTS tasks. Most of the properties for these objects are not displayed with Disconnected Edit. The last section of this chapter shows how to create the basic tasks in code.

The Source and the Destination for the Tasks

All five of the transfer tasks have similar properties for the source and destination. Figure 15.1 shows the Source tab for the Transfer Databases task.

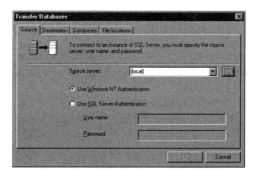

FIGURE 15.1
All five transfer tasks have the same tabs for entering source and destination server information.

The transfer tasks do not use DTS connections. Instead, the connection information must be entered for both source and destination in the task's properties dialog.

> **NOTE**
>
> This is one of the reasons why using the wizard is appealing. You enter the source and destination information once, and it is used for all of the tasks.

The Transfer Database Task

The Databases tab of the Transfer Databases dialog, shown in Figure 15.2, is the place where you choose which databases to copy and which databases to move.

FIGURE 15.2

The Transfer Databases dialog shows you which databases you are allowed to copy or move.

> **NOTE**
>
> If you move a database, that database won't be available on the source server after the step is executed.
>
> The database files on the source server are not removed, however. Whether you copy or move a database with the Copy Databases task, after the task is executed there will be a copy of all the database files on both the source and the destination.
>
> You could use the FileSystemObject in an ActiveX task to delete the source database files after the databases have been moved.

You are not allowed to transfer a database if

- The destination has a database with the same name.
- The database is involved in replication.

- The source is a SQL Server in Windows 2000 and the destination is a SQL Server in Windows 98.
- The database is unavailable because it is marked inaccessible, loading, offline, recovering, suspect, or in Emergency Mode.

Figure 15.3 shows the File Locations tab. You can change the destination file or directory if there are problems with filename conflicts. You can also move the files to a different directory if there is inadequate space to copy the database to the default data location.

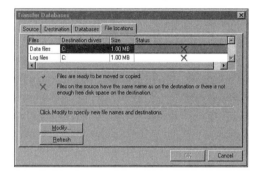

FIGURE 15.3

You can modify the destination files for the databases while you are creating the task.

The Transfer Logins Task

You have two basic options on the Logins tab of the Transfer Logins dialog:

- Include all server logins detected at package runtime.
- Include logins for selected databases.

The other meta data transfer tasks have similar options.

If you choose to include logins for selected databases only, the list of choices is enabled, as shown in Figure 15.4.

NOTE

When you're transferring databases, it's sometimes reasonable to include only the logins that are being used in those databases. After all, if certain logins aren't using those databases on the old server, why should those logins need to be transferred?

> On the other hand, when a server has a group of user logins, it's only a matter of time until more of those users are going to be given access to those particular databases. If you transfer all the logins, you will have an easier time giving database access permissions in the future.

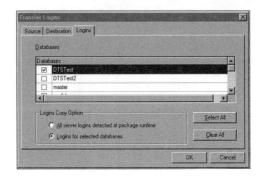

FIGURE 15.4
You can choose whether to transfer all of the logins or only some of them.

The Transfer Jobs Task

Figure 15.5 shows the Jobs tab of the Transfer Msdb Jobs dialog after the choice has been made to include selected jobs.

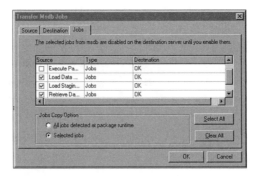

FIGURE 15.5
You can choose which jobs to include or exclude in the transfer.

Choosing to include only certain jobs probably makes sense, unless you are moving all the databases on a server. If a job involves a database that is not being moved, that job will fail if it is executed on a different server.

If you want to view details of the jobs you are considering transferring, they are listed in the Enterprise Manager tree under the Management\SQL Server Agent node.

The Transfer Master Stored Procedures Task

Figure 15.6 shows the Stored Procedures tab of the Transfer Master Stored Procedures dialog after the choice has been made to select individual stored procedures.

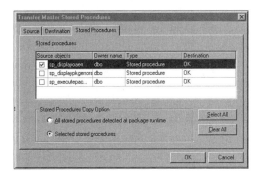

FIGURE 15.6
You choose which of the Master database's stored procedures to transfer.

If you create a stored procedure in the Master database and it is named with an sp_ prefix, that stored procedure can be executed from all the databases on a server as if it were local. A stored procedure created like this is called a system stored procedure.

There are many system stored procedures that are included with SQL Server. These procedures shouldn't cause any problems when a database is being transferred because they exist on all SQL Servers. But if users have defined their own customized system stored procedures, there can be problems. System stored procedures can be referenced from within a database's own stored procedures. An error will be generated if they don't exist on the local server.

TIP

In my opinion, it's usually best to transfer all the stored procedures. They won't hurt anything, even if they're never used.

The only reason for following another strategy is if there are naming conflicts between stored procedures on separate servers. If you have different stored procedures that have the same names, you will have to carefully examine how you can separate the two procedures and make them unique.

The Transfer Error Messages Task

Figure 15.7 shows the Error Messages tab of the Transfer Error Messages dialog after the choice has been made to select specific error messages.

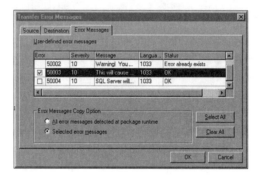

FIGURE 15.7

The error messages and numbers are displayed as you select the ones to transfer.

SQL Server stores all its error messages in a table called sysmessages in the master database. All the error numbers under 50000 are reserved for Microsoft's use. Error numbers starting with 50000 are user-defined error messages.

You can create user-defined error messages to send customized, application-specific error messages back to client applications. Many developers create a separate set of error messages for each of their database applications. When used, these messages become an essential part of the database application.

TIP

Moving user-defined error messages from one server to another can be a problem if the same error number is used for two separate messages. Careful modifications will have to be made to the code to make sure the wrong error message isn't called.

I have seen database developers who have used the numbers in the 50000 to 51000 range for their user-defined error messages. Using those numbers brings a high risk of error number conflicts.

I have seen other developers who use a 4-digit prefix for their database applications, which is assigned as a unique value for their organization, and another 4-digit value for each particular error. So altogether, the error numbers all have 8 digits. This system reduces the chance of conflict in error numbers.

Creating the Tasks in Visual Basic

I have created a Visual Basic procedure, `fctCreateTransferDatabaseTask`, which creates a step, a task, and a custom task for a Transfer Databases task. Only the properties exposed in Disconnected Edit are set by this procedure.

> **NOTE**
>
> Most of the properties and methods of the transfer tasks are undocumented. You can examine these other properties when working with the tasks in Visual Basic, but I have not included them in my examples here.

I have also created functions that create the other four tasks discussed in this chapter. You can find the code for these procedures in the directory for Chapter 15 on the book's CD as a Visual Basic Project, with files CreateTransferDatabaseTask.frm, CreateTransferDatabaseTask.bas, and CreateTransferDatabaseTask.vbp.

The code for `fctCreateTransferDatabaseTask` is shown in Listing 15.1. The procedure needs some utility functions that are included with the code listings on the CD. The project requires references to the Microsoft DTSPackage Object Library and the OMWCustomTasks 1.0 Type Library.

LISTING 15.1   The Visual Basic Code to Create a Transfer Databases Task

```
Public Function fctCreateTransferDatabaseTask( _
    pkg As DTS.Package2, _
    Optional sBaseName As String = "TransferDatabaseTask" _
    ) As String

On Error GoTo ProcErr

Dim stp As DTS.Step2
Dim tsk As DTS.Task
Dim cus As OMWTransferDatabases

'Check to see if the selected Base name is unique
sBaseName = fctFindUniqueBaseName(pkg, sBaseName)

'Create task and custom task
Set tsk = pkg.Tasks.New("OMWCustomTasks.OMWTransferDatabases")
Set cus = tsk.CustomTask
```

LISTING 15.1   Continued

```
With cus

    .Name = "tsk" & sBaseName
    .Description = sBaseName

End With

pkg.Tasks.Add tsk

'Create step for task
Set stp = pkg.Steps.New
With stp
    .Name = "stp" & sBaseName
    .Description = sBaseName
    .TaskName = tsk.Name
End With
pkg.Steps.Add stp

fctCreateTransferDatabaseTask = stp.Name

Set tsk = Nothing
Set cus = Nothing
Set stp = Nothing

ProcExit:
  Exit Function
ProcErr:
  MsgBox Err.Number & " - " & Err.Description
  fctCreateTransferDatabaseTask = ""
  GoTo ProcExit
End Function
```

Conclusion

The Transfer Databases task and the other transfer tasks are useful when you're moving data from one server to another. These tasks cannot be manipulated in code as easily as most of the other tasks because their properties and methods are not documented or displayed in Disconnected Edit.

The easiest way to use these tasks is through the Copy Database Wizard.

Control Tasks

IN THIS PART

Writing Scripts for an ActiveX Script Task

IN THIS CHAPTER

The ActiveX Script task allows you to include a block of scripting code anywhere in your DTS package.

Much of the information about how to use ActiveX scripts in DTS is presented in Chapter 7, "Writing ActiveX Scripts for a Transform Data Task." Chapter 27, "Handling Errors in a Package and Its Transformations," tells how to debug ActiveX scripts.

Most of the code for this chapter has been put into one DTS package. This package is stored in a file called ScriptSample.dts. You can find it on the book's CD.

When to Use an ActiveX Script Task

You can use an ActiveX Script task to accomplish a variety of programmatic goals:

- Read or modify the properties of DTS objects.
- Set the values of global variables.
- Read, write, create, delete, and move files and directories.
- Open and manipulate ADO recordsets.
- Manipulate a disconnected ADO recordset created as the output of an Execute SQL task.
- Write customized log records to the DTS task log.
- Execute other DTS packages.
- Access COM objects.

Most of these things can also be done with other DTS tasks, of course. It's usually better to use the other DTS tasks when you can because each one assists in automating the development process. Here are some of the alternatives to consider:

- Use the Dynamic Properties task to modify the properties of DTS objects or set the values of global variables. Use the ActiveX Script task to do this when you have to use some programmatic logic to determine the value you are going to assign.
- Use the FTP task to move files. Use the ActiveX script task for other file and directory manipulation.
- Use the Transform Data task to retrieve data, rather than opening ADO recordsets in an ActiveX script.
- Use the Execute Package task to execute other DTS packages. Consider executing a DTS package from an ActiveX script when you want to load it, modify its properties, and then execute it.

Creating an ActiveX Script Task

You can create an ActiveX Script task in the DTS Designer or in code. The last section of this chapter shows how to create the task in code.

Writing Scripts for an ActiveX Script Task

CHAPTER 16

347

16

WRITING SCRIPTS
FOR AN ACTIVEX
SCRIPT TASK

Figure 16.1 shows the ActiveX Script Task Properties dialog. The interface is very similar to the one used for creating ActiveX transformation scripts. In fact, the object browser lists the result constants for the Data Pump and the Data Driven Query next to the return constants for the ActiveX Script, even though only the ActiveX Script return constants can be used here.

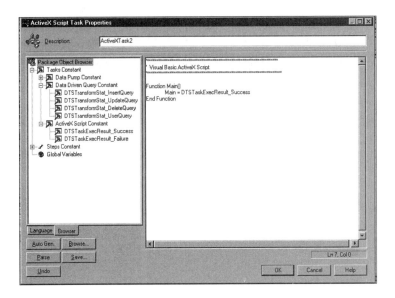

FIGURE 16.1
You can write your scripts in the ActiveX Script Task Properties dialog or load the scripts from a file.

The ActiveX Script task has very few properties:

- `Name` and `Description`

- `ActiveXScript`—The full text of the ActiveX script.

- `ScriptLanguage`—The scripting language used, such as VBScript or JScript. You can set this property on the Language tab in the ActiveX Script Task Properties dialog.

- `FunctionName`—The name of the entry function for the script. This is the function that is called by the package when the task is executed, and the function that returns the Execution Result to the package. The default value is Main. You can change this on the Language tab in the ActiveX Script Task Properties dialog.

- `AddGlobalVariables`—Whether or not the package's global variables can be accessed from inside the script. The default is `TRUE`, and you cannot change this value in the user interface.

There are only two possible result values from the entry function of a script used in an ActiveX Script task. The value returned determines whether the task is marked as a success or a failure:

- `DTSTaskExecResult_Success`—The task is a success.
- `DTSTaskExecResult_Failure`—The task failed.

Dynamically Modifying DTS Properties

Just about the only way to change properties during package execution in SQL Server 7.0 was to use the ActiveX Script task. In SQL Server 2000, it's easier to use the Dynamic Properties task for much of this property manipulation.

But there are still many situations in which you need to modify properties and the Dynamic Properties task cannot do the job. Here are a few examples:

- You want to construct the text of a message for a Send Mail task, with information about execution times and the number of records processed.
- You want to modify the name of the table in the FROM clause in the SQL Statement of an Execute SQL task. You want to set the name of this table with a parameter in the DTSRun command.
- You want to read the name of a file in a directory and set a text file connection to that particular name.

You can use ActiveX scripts to reference the properties of almost all the objects in DTS, and you can change almost all the read/write properties. All the code samples in the following sections are in one ActiveX Script task in the ScriptSample package.

Referencing a Package

First, you have to obtain a reference to the Package object before you can obtain a reference to any of the objects within a package. The easiest way to get that reference is by using the `Parent` property of the `DTSGlobalVariables` collection:

```
Dim pkg
Set pkg = DTSGlobalVariables.Parent
MsgBox pkg.Name
```

Referencing a Connection

You reference a connection by naming a particular member of the package's `Connections` collection:

Writing Scripts for an ActiveX Script Task

CHAPTER 16

349

16

WRITING SCRIPTS
FOR AN ACTIVEX
SCRIPT TASK

```
Dim con
Set con = pkg.Connections("conPubs")
MsgBox con.DataSource
```

You can also gain a reference to the connection by using the ordinal number of that connection in the Connections collection. This method is unreliable, though, because if any connection is modified, its ordinal number is changed to the last in the collection:

```
Set con = pkg.Connections(2) 'You shouldn't do this!
```

For the Connections collection, and almost all other collections in the DTS object model, you can loop through all the objects using For Next syntax. Remember that in VBScript, you always use the word Next by itself:

```
For Each con in pkg.Connections
    msgbox con.Name
Next
```

Referencing a Global Variable

DTS exposes the package's GlobalVariables collection in a special way as the DTSGlobalVariables collection. You can reference DTSGlobalVariables directly, without first referencing the Package object. This is the easiest and most common way of referencing a global variable:

```
Msgbox DTSGlobalVariables("TopSellingProduct").Value
```

You can also reference a GlobalVariable the same way you reference a connection, by naming the specific member of the package's GlobalVariables collection:

```
Dim gv
Set gv = pkg.GlobalVariables ("TopSellingProduct")
Msgbox gv.Value
```

Referencing Steps, Tasks, and Custom Tasks

You can reference steps and tasks as members of the package's collections:

```
Dim stp, tsk

Set stp = pkg.Steps("stpLoadAuthors")

Msgbox stp.ExecutionStatus

Set tsk = pkg.Tasks("tskLoadAuthors")

Msgbox tsk.Description
```

The description of a task is displayed in the Package Designer's user interface. The name of the task is not displayed, except in Disconnected Edit. The name of the step is displayed on the second tab of the Workflow Properties dialog. You can gain a reference to the task object without knowing its name, if you know the name of the step:

```
Dim stp, tsk
Set stp = pkg.Steps("stpLoadAuthors")
Set tsk = pkg.Tasks(stp.TaskName)
```

After you have established a reference to the task, you can then reference the custom task:

```
Dim cus
Set cus = tsk.CustomTask
```

Most of the properties of DTS tasks are specific to the custom task that is being used. You can reference these specific properties as properties of the CustomTask object or as members of the Properties collections of the Task object. You cannot reference any custom task specific properties directly as properties of the Task object:

```
Dim pkg, tsk, cus
Set pkg = DTSGLobalVariables.Parent
Set tsk = pkg.Tasks("tskUpdateAuthors") 'An Execute SQL task
Set cus = tsk.CustomTask
Msgbox cus.SQLStatement 'One way to reference custom task properties.
Msgbox tsk.Properties("SQLStatement").Value 'The other way.
Msgbox tsk.SQLStatement 'This Will Not Work!
```

Referencing the Collections and Objects in a Transform Data Task

You can continue in a similar way through the object hierarchy. The transformation tasks are more complex than most of the other tasks because there are collections inside of collections. Here's how you could retrieve the Size property of one of the Source Columns:

```
Dim pkg, tsk, cus, trn, col
Set pkg = DTSGlobalVariables.Parent
Set tsk = pkg.Tasks("tskLoadAuthors")
Set cus = tsk.CustomTask
Set trn = cus.Transformations(1)
Set col = trn.SourceColumns("au_id")
Msgbox col.Size
```

Referencing the DTS Application Object

You can also reference the DTS Application object and all its collections from inside a package. The Application object is referenced independently of the package. You have to use the CreateObject method to initialize it:

```
Dim DTSApp, info
Set DTSApp = CreateObject("DTS.Application")
For Each info in DTSApp.ScriptingLanguageInfos
    Msgbox info.Name
Next
```

Objects and Properties That You Cannot Directly Reference

Some tasks have objects and properties that cannot be referenced from an ActiveX Script, or can only be referenced in certain ways. Some custom task properties can only be referenced as members of the `Properties` collection of the `Task` object.

When developers create their own custom tasks, the properties of those tasks may or may not be accessible to ActiveX scripts. See Chapter 31, "Creating a Custom Task with VB," for more details about creating custom tasks.

The collection of objects to be copied in the Copy SQL Server Objects task cannot be obtained by directly referencing the collection. Instead, there are methods that can be used to work with the elements of the collection.

The Transfer Databases task and the four tasks that transfer database meta data also have collections that cannot be directly referenced.

Building a Utility to Limit Rows Processed

When you're testing a DTS package, it is often useful to limit the number of rows that are processed. If you have a lot of transformation tasks, it can be a chore to manually limit the number of records for each one of them.

With a knowledge of the DTS object model, you can automate jobs like this. You can loop through all the objects in the package and modify each of them in an appropriate way.

Listing 16.1 shows the code for a simple utility that limits the rows processed for all Transform Data tasks, Data Driven Query tasks, Parallel Data Pump Tasks, and Bulk Insert tasks. The code loops through all the tasks in the package and modifies the LastRow property for the four types of tasks. You can change the value of `lNumRows` to the value that works best in your situation. Setting `lNumRows` to 0 removes the restriction for all of the tasks in the package. The source code for this example is in the directory for Chapter 16 on the book's CD in a file called RowLimiting.dts.

LISTING 16.1   You Can Use the DTS Object Model to Automate Processes Such as Setting the Number of Rows to Be Processed

```
Option Explicit
Function Main()

dim pkg,tsk,cus, lNumRows

Set pkg = DTSGlobalVariables.Parent

'How many rows you want to process, 0 processes all rows.
lNumRows = 10

'Give a message box if user is limiting rows.
If lNumRows > 0 Then
    msgbox "You are going to process " & lNumRows& " rows."
End if

For each tsk in pkg.Tasks

    Set cus = tsk.CustomTask

    Select Case tsk.CustomTaskID

        Case  "DTSDataPumpTask", "DTSDataDrivenQueryTask", "DTSBulkInsertTask"
            cus.LastRow = lNumRows

        Case "DTSParallelDataPumpTask"

            For Each transet in cus.TransformationSets
                transet.LastRow = lNumRows
            Next

    End Select

Next

    Main = DTSTaskExecResult_Success
End Function
```

Programming a Loop in a DTS Package

You can create a loop in your DTS package by modifying the properties of the Step objects. This can be useful if you want to repeat the same action for many different objects, such as importing several files that have the same structure but different names.

Figure 16.2 shows a package with a simple loop that can be used as a template for looping code in other packages. This template is on the CD in a file called LoopingTemplate.dtt.

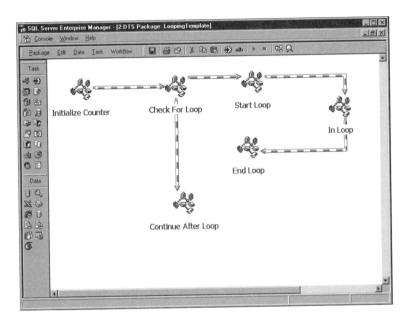

FIGURE 16.2
Properties of the steps can be modified to implement looping in a DTS package.

To use this template, do the following:

1. Right-click on Data Transformation Services in the Enterprise Manager. Select All Tasks and Open Template. Select LoopingTemplate.dtt.
2. Add the logic for controlling the loop in the fctLoopAgain function of the Check For Loop task.
3. Add any initialization of looping variables in Initialize Counter.
4. Replace the In Loop task with the tasks or set of tasks you want to execute repeatedly.
5. Set precedence constraints so that everything you want to do before the loop happens before Initialize Counter.
6. Set precedence constraints so that everything you want to do after the loop happens after Continue After Loop.
7. Leave Start Loop, End Loop, and Continue After Loop in your package unchanged.

The Check For Loop task is shown in Listing 16.2. The task has two functions. The Main function sets the step properties so that either the loop executes again or the package continues on with other tasks. The `fctLoopAgain` function has the logic that determines whether or not the looping should continue. When you use the template, the `Main` function should be left unchanged, while the `fctLoopAgain` function should be modified to reflect your looping criteria.

LISTING 16.2   The Code in the Check For Loop Task Determines Whether or Not to Continue Looping

```
Option Explicit
Function Main()

Dim pkg, stpStart, stpContinue
Dim bLoopAgain

Set pkg = DTSGlobalVariables.parent
Set stpStart = pkg.Steps("stpStartLoop")
Set stpContinue = pkg.Steps("stpContinueAfterLoop")

'Call fctLoopAgain to determine whether to continue or terminate loop.
bLoopAgain = fctLoopAgain

'Check for looping condition
If bLoopAgain = TRUE Then

    stpStart.DisableStep = False
    stpStart.ExecutionStatus = DTSStepExecStat_Waiting

    stpContinue.DisableStep = True
Else
    stpStart.DisableStep = True

    stpContinue.DisableStep = False
    stpContinue.ExecutionStatus = DTSStepExecStat_Waiting
End If

    Main = DTSTaskExecResult_Success
End Function

Function fctLoopAgain
'Replace the code in this function with your looping criteria

'Check for looping condition
If DTSGlobalVariables("LoopCount").Value < _
        DTSGlobalVariables("LoopTotal").Value Then

    'Increment the counter
    DTSGlobalVariables("LoopCount").Value = _
```

Writing Scripts for an ActiveX Script Task

CHAPTER 16

355

16

WRITING SCRIPTS
FOR AN ACTIVEX
SCRIPT TASK

LISTING 16.2 Continued

```
        DTSGlobalVariables("LoopCount").Value + 1
    fctLoopAgain = CBool(True)
Else
    fctLoopAgain = CBool(False)
End If

End Function
```

The code in the End Loop task, shown in Listing 16.3, sets the execution status of the Check For Loop task so that it will execute again.

LISTING 16.3 The Code in the End Loop Task Causes the Check For Loop Task to Execute Again

```
Option Explicit

Function Main()
Dim pkg, stp

Set pkg = dtsGlobalVariables.Parent
Set stp = pkg.Steps("stpCheckForLoop")

'Set the execution status to Waiting so the
'Check for Loop task will execute again.
stp.ExecutionStatus = DTSStepExecStat_Waiting

    Main = DTSTaskExecResult_Success
End Function
```

Using ADO Recordsets

Listing 16.4 shows the code to open an ADO recordset in an ActiveX Script task. This task checks the number of records in the Orders table before the new records are imported. A similar task can be executed after the import to verify the number of records that have been added. This code is on the CD in a separate ActiveX Script task in the ScriptSample package.

LISTING 16.4 A VBScript That Opens and Retrieves Information Using an ADO Recordset

```
Option Explicit
Function Main()
Dim ADOcon, ADOrst
```

LISTING 16.4   Continued

```
Dim str, sql

Set ADOcon = CreateObject("ADODB.Connection")
Set ADOrst = CreateObject("ADODB.Recordset")

ADOcon.Provider = "sqloledb"

' Set SQLOLEDB connection properties.
ADOcon.Properties("Data Source").Value = "(local)"
ADOcon.Properties("Initial Catalog").Value = "Northwind"
ADOcon.Properties("Integrated Security").Value = "SSPI"
'ADOcon.Properties("User ID").Value = UserName
'ADOcon.Properties("Password").Value = Password

' Open the database.
ADOcon.Open

sql = "Select count(*) As OrderCount from Orders"
ADOrst.Open sql, ADOcon

ADOrst.MoveFirst

DTSGlobalVariables("OrderCountBeforeImport").Value = _
    ADOrst.Fields("OrderCount")

'Msgbox DTSGlobalVariables("OrderCountBeforeImport").Value

        Main = DTSTaskExecResult_Success
End Function
```

> **TIP**
>
> I personally prefer to use a Transform Data task for this situation. The source query for the Transform Data task would be the query that was used to open the recordset. I would not use any destination fields. The ActiveX Script transformation would assign the value of the source field to the global variable, like this:
>
> ```
> DTSGlobalVariables("OrderCountBeforeImport").Value = DTSSource("OrderCount")
> ```
>
> I don't mind writing code, but sometimes it's easier when I don't have to write as much of it.

Manipulating Files and Directories

You can manipulate files and directories by using the `FileSystemObject` from the Scripting library, as shown in Listing 16.5. This code is in the ScriptSample package.

LISTING 16.5   VBScript Code for Working with Files and Directories

```
Dim fso, fld, fil, txtstr
Dim msg

Set fso = CreateObject("Scripting.FileSystemObject")
fso.createtextfile "c:\temp\HelloWorld.txt"
Set fil = fso.getfile("c:\temp\HelloWorld.txt")
set txtstr= fil.OpenAsTextStream(2)

txtstr.Write "Hello World"
txtstr.Close
set txtstr= fil.OpenAsTextStream(1)
msg = txtstr.ReadLine
msgbox msg
txtstr.Close

on error resume next
fso.CreateFolder "C:\Temp\HelloWorldDir"
fso.movefile "c:\temp\HelloWorld.txt", _
    "C:\Temp\HelloWorldDir\HelloWorld.txt"
on error goto 0

set fld = fso.getfolder("C:\Temp\HelloWorldDir")

for each fil in fld.files
    msg = ""
    msg = msg & "Name"  & vbTab & vbTab & vbTab  & fil.Name & vbCrLf
    msg = msg & "Date Created" & vbTab & vbTab  & _
        fil.DateCreated & vbCrLf
    msg = msg & "Date Last Modified" & vbTab & vbTab  & _
        fil.DateLastModified & vbCrLf
    msg = msg & "Date Last Accessed" & vbTab & vbTab  & _
        fil.DateLastAccessed & vbCrLf
    msg = msg & "Size" & vbTab &  vbTab & vbTab  & fil.Size & vbCrLf
    msgbox msg

next
```

Writing Task Log Records

Chapter 23, "The DTS Package and Its Properties," describes the package, step, and task logs that can be created when a DTS package is executed. The task log can have details about the execution of a task, but it has no records for most tasks. Of the standard DTS tasks, only the five transfer tasks write anything to the task log.

There are two ways that records can be written to the task log:

- Custom task developers can add code to their custom tasks that will write to the log.
- Code can be added to the script of an ActiveX script task to write to the log.

NOTE

You can't write to the task log from a transformation script or a workflow script. These methods only work in an ActiveX Script task.

There are two methods that can be used to write to the log. Both are methods of the DTSPackageLog object, which can be referenced directly in ActiveX Script tasks. In order to use these methods, you have to enable SQL Server logging in the Package Properties dialog. Here are the two methods:

- WriteStringToLog has only one parameter—the message that is placed in the log:

```
DTSPackageLog.WriteStringToLog "Written by WriteStringToLog."
```

- WriteTaskRecord has a parameter for an error code and another one for the message. The error code field can be used for any numeric value you choose:

```
DTSPackageLog.DTSPackageLog.WriteTaskRecord _
        1, "Written by WriteTaskRecord."
```

TIP

It appears that WriteStringToLog messages are always displayed in the task log as if they are errors. WriteTaskRecord messages also appear as errors, unless you set the error code to 1.

Writing Scripts for an ActiveX Script Task

359

CHAPTER 16

16

WRITING SCRIPTS
FOR AN ACTIVEX
SCRIPT TASK

> **NOTE**
>
> You can't execute an ActiveX Script task that references the `DTSPackageLog` by right-clicking on the task in the Package Designer and selecting Execute Step from the popup menu. If you do, you will receive an error stating that an object is required. You can reference the `DTSPackageLog` objects from ActiveX Script tasks if those tasks are executed as part of a package.

A script with these methods is also included in ScriptSample. Figure 16.3 shows the task log that is generated by running that script.

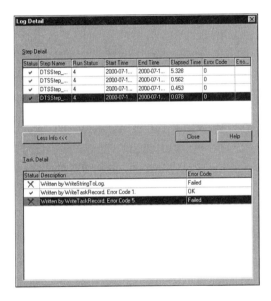

FIGURE 16.3
The task log displays messages written by `WriteStringToLog` *and* `WriteTaskRecord`.

Converting VB Code to VBScript

Usually, it's not very hard to take a block of Visual Basic code and convert it into VBScript for use inside an ActiveX Script task. There are a lot of little changes you have to make. This section contains a list of things that have to be modified. You can also use these same techniques when creating ActiveX transformation scripts, of course.

Variable Declaration

In Visual Basic, you can provide a datatype when you declare variables. In VBScript, you're not allowed to provide datatypes. Remove all the datatypes from your variable declarations.

Using `CreateObject` for Object Variables

Visual Basic allows the `CreateObject` syntax to create new object variables, but most VB programmers use the `New` syntax:

```
Declare pkg As New DTS.Package
```

or

```
Declare pkg As DTS.Package
Set pkg = New DTS.Package
```

Anytime you see `New` used to initialize an object variable, you have to replace it with the `CreateObject` statement in VBScript:

```
Dim pkg
Set pkg = CreateObject("DTS.Package")
```

For Next Loops

In Visual Basic, you can use a variable after the word `Next` in a `For Next` loop:

```
For Each tsk In Pkg.Tasks
    Msgbox tsk.Name
Next tsk
```

To convert to VBScript, you must remove the variable after `Next, if you have used one:`

```
For Each tsk In Pkg.Tasks
    Msgbox tsk.Name
Next
```

File Access

Replace any file access syntax with the `Scripting.FileSystemObject` syntax described earlier in this chapter.

GoTo and Line Labels

You can't use `GoTo commands` and line labels in VBScript. This could be the most difficult part of the conversion if you have a block of VB code that has a lot of `GoTo` commands.

Writing Scripts for an ActiveX Script Task

CHAPTER 16

361

16

WRITING SCRIPTS
FOR AN ACTIVEX
SCRIPT TASK

Error Handling

You can't use the `On Error GoTo ErrHandler` syntax because `GoTo` commands in general aren't allowed. You can use `On Error Resume Next` and then specifically check for errors at every point in the script where you expect an error could take place. Here's VBScript code you could use to check for an error:

```
If Err.Number <> 0 Then
    Msgbox Err.Number & vbTab & Err.Description
    Main = DTSTaskExecResult_Failure
    Exit Function
End If
```

API Calls

No direct Windows API calls are allowed in VBScript. You can wrap the functions that call the Windows API in COM objects and make method calls from your VBScript to the functions.

Using Code as an Entry Function

When you are converting VB code to VBScript in DTS, you will often have a VB function that you want to use as the entry function for an ActiveX Script or a transformation script. The entry function is the function called by the DTS package when a task is executed. If you are using your VB code as an entry function, you have to do two extra things:

- Make the task's entry function equal to the function's name. You could also, of course, change the function's name to the default entry function name Main.

- Set the appropriate return value for the entry function, such as:

  ```
  Main = DTSTaskExecResult_Success
  ```

Using VBScript Code in VB

You usually don't have to change anything in your VBScript code when you use it in Visual Basic. You may choose to take advantage of some of the features in Visual Basic that are missing in VBScript, of course, such as declaring variable types and `On Error GoTo` error handling.

Creating an ActiveX Script Task in Visual Basic

I have created a Visual Basic procedure, `fctCreateActiveXTask`, that creates a step, a task, and a custom task for an Active X Script task. All the properties of the task can be set with this procedure.

You can find the code for this procedure in the directory for Chapter 16 on the book's CD as a Visual Basic Project, with files `CreateActiveXTask.vbp`, `CreateActiveXTask.frm`, `CreateActiveXTask.frx`, and `CreateActiveXTask.bas`.

The code for `fctCreateActiveXTask` is shown in Listing 16.6. The procedure needs some utility functions that are included with the code listings on the CD. The project requires a reference to the Microsoft DTSPackage Object Library.

LISTING 16.6   The Visual Basic Code to Create an ActiveX Script Task

```
Public Function fctCreateActiveXTask( _
    pkg As DTS.Package2, _
    Optional sBaseName As String = "ActiveXTask", _
    Optional sActiveXScript As String = "", _
    Optional bAddGlobalVariables As Boolean = True, _
    Optional sFunctionName As String = "Main", _
    Optional sScriptLanguage As String = "VBScript") As String

On Error GoTo ProcErr

Dim stp As DTS.Step2
Dim tsk As DTS.Task
Dim cus As DTS.ActiveScriptTask

'Check to see if the selected Base name is unique
sBaseName = fctFindUniqueBaseName(pkg, sBaseName)

'Create task and custom task
Set tsk = pkg.Tasks.New("DTSActiveScriptTask")
Set cus = tsk.CustomTask

With cus

    .Name = "tsk" & sBaseName
    .Description = sBaseName

    .AddGlobalVariables = bAddGlobalVariables

    If sActiveXScript <> "" Then
        .ActiveXScript = sActiveXScript
    End If

    If sFunctionName <> "" Then
        .FunctionName = sFunctionName
```

Writing Scripts for an ActiveX Script Task

Chapter 16

363

16

WRITING SCRIPTS
FOR AN ACTIVEX
SCRIPT TASK

LISTING 16.6 Continued

```
    End If

    If sScriptLanguage <> "" Then
        .ScriptLanguage = sScriptLanguage
    End If

End With

pkg.Tasks.Add tsk

'Create step for task
Set stp = pkg.Steps.New
With stp
    .Name = "stp" & sBaseName
    .Description = sBaseName
    .TaskName = tsk.Name
End With
pkg.Steps.Add stp

fctCreateActiveXTask = stp.Name

Set tsk = Nothing
Set cus = Nothing
Set stp = Nothing

ProcExit:
  Exit Function
ProcErr:
  MsgBox Err.Number & " - " & Err.Description
  fctCreateActiveXTask = ""
  GoTo ProcExit
End Function
```

Conclusion

There's been a lot in this chapter about dynamically changing properties in a DTS package. The Dynamic Properties task is the topic of the next chapter, where you will learn the possibilities of doing those modifications through a graphical user interface.

The Dynamic Properties Task

IN THIS CHAPTER

You can use the Dynamic Properties task to modify the properties of your packages, its tasks, its steps, and its global variables while the package is executing.

> **NOTE**
>
> I don't think I can accomplish anything with a Dynamic Properties task that I couldn't also do with code in an ActiveX Script task. But the Dynamic Properties task is almost always more convenient, and in some situations it greatly reduces the amount of programming needed in a package.

When to Use the Dynamic Properties Task

There are many situations in which it is useful to be able to dynamically modify the objects in a DTS package:

- Assigning a SQL statement for the source of a Transform Data task or for the query of an Execute SQL task.
- Assigning the text of an email for a Send Mail task.
- Assigning the package name to be called by an Execute Package task.
- Assigning the files to be retrieved for an FTP task.
- Assigning a filename for a text file data source.
- Modifying the ExecutionStatus property of a step so that you can execute the step many times in one execution of a package.
- Changing the properties that control the package logging behavior.

> **TIP**
>
> When you're thinking about possibilities for the Dynamic Properties task, I think it's important to remember that you can use the DTSRun utility to send global variables into a DTS package. You can modify any property of any task by sending the package a value for that property in a global variable and then using a Dynamic Properties task to assign that value to the appropriate property.

You can retrieve the values to be used by the Dynamic Properties task from several different sources:

- Global variables
- SQL queries
- Data files
- INI files
- Environment variables
- Constants

> **TIP**
>
> Many people execute DTS packages from VB or VC++ rather than executing the package directly. If you're executing a package programmatically, the Dynamic Properties task is less useful. After you have loaded the package, you can modify any of its properties from code before you execute it.
>
> When you're executing a package from the SQL Server interface or from a command line, you can't make changes between loading and execution. You have to modify the package during its actual execution, and that's the purpose of the Dynamic Properties task.

Creating the Task and Assigning Its Properties

You can create the Dynamic Properties task in the Package Designer or in code. It is not created by either of the wizards. The last section of this chapter shows how to create the task in code.

The Dynamic Properties task has only three properties—Description, Name, and Assignments. When you open the Dynamic Properties Task Properties dialog, as shown in Figure 17.1, you see only a place to edit the task's description and a button to add a new assignment.

Making a New Assignment

After you add a Dynamic Properties task to your package, you can begin making property assignments. A property assignment has two parts:

- The identification of the specific DTS object property that you want to modify.
- A specification of how to find the value to assign to that property.

FIGURE 17.1

A Dynamic Properties task does not take effect until you add assignments.

The assignments are implemented in the DTS object model with the following objects and collection:

- The `Assignments` property of the task points to the `DynamicPropertiesTaskAssignments` collection.
- The `DynamicPropertiesTaskAssignments` collection is made up of `DynamicPropertiesTaskAssignment` objects.
- The properties of the `DynamicPropertiesTaskAssignment` object are used to define the particular assignment.

Choosing the Object and Property to Be Assigned

When you select the Add button, the Dynamic Properties Task: Package Properties dialog opens, as shown in Figure 17.2. The left side of this dialog has a tree that displays all the DTS objects and collections. The right side displays the property names and values for the object that is selected on the left.

You might choose to do any of the following:

- Modify the `Description` property of the `Package` object.
- Change the `Server` property of a `Connection` object.
- Change the `Value` property of a `GlobalVariable` object.

- Modify the `SourceQuery` property of a Transform Data task.
- Change the type of precedence used in a precedence constraint from `OnSuccess` to `OnCompletion`. You would do this by modifying the `PrecedenceBasis` and `Value` properties of the `PrecedenceConstraint` object.

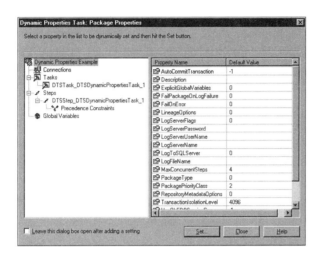

FIGURE 17.2
You can modify properties of any of the DTS objects.

You start making a property assignment by finding the appropriate object in the tree on the left side of the dialog. Next, you select the property you want to modify. Finally, you select the Set button, which brings you to the dialog that allows you to choose the type of data for the assignment.

> **NOTE**
>
> The Dynamic Properties Task: Package Properties dialog looks very similar to the dialog for Disconnected Edit. However, there are many properties you can change in Disconnected Edit that you are not allowed to change with the Dynamic Properties task.
>
> One example is the names of tasks and steps. You can change them in Disconnected Edit, but you cannot change them in this task.
>
> The unavailable properties are not displayed in the interface for the Dynamic Properties task.

The destination of the assignment is set in one property of the `DynamicPropertiesTask` `Assignment` object—the `DestinationPropertyID`. The value for this property is a complex string. It's complex because it has to be able to identify every point in the DTS object hierarchy. The string is delimited by semicolons. Each portion of the string identifies a particular part of the object hierarchy.

NOTE

SQL Server Books Online incorrectly states that three back ticks (```) are used for the delimiter in the `DestinationPropertyID` string.

If you want to modify the `Size` property of the `au_lname` column, which is being used in a Transform Data task, the `DestinationPropertyID` string would have the following components:

- String constants that are used to reference DTS collections. The specific case-sensitive string values that you are required to use for each collection are documented in Books Online. For this example, these are the collections—Tasks, Transformations, SourceColumns, and Properties.
- The name of the object you are selecting—au_lname.
- The names of parent objects—DTSTask_DTSDataPumpTask_1 and DTSTransformation__1.
- The name of the property you are assigning—Size.

The completed string looks like this:

```
'Tasks';'DTSTask_DTSDataPumpTask_1';'Transformations';
'DTSTransformation__1';'SourceColumns';'au_id';'Properties';'Size'
```

Choosing the Source of Data for the Assignment

You can open the Add/Edit Assignment dialog by highlighting a property and clicking the Set button or by double-clicking on the property. You choose the source of the data for an assignment in this dialog. The first step is to select one of the six ways of making an assignment from the drop-down list box. The appearance of the Add/Edit Assignment dialog is modified as you select each different source type. Figure 17.3 shows the dialog when a SQL query has been selected as the source.

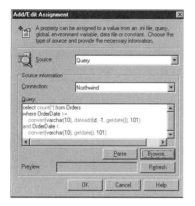

FIGURE 17.3

The Add/Edit Assignment dialog changes depending on what type of source is being used.

The type of assignment is set with the SourceType property of the DynamicPropertiesTask Assignment object. This property uses the DynamicPropertiesTaskSourceType constants:

- 0—DTSDynamicPropertiesSourceType_IniFile
- 1—DTSDynamicPropertiesSourceType_Query
- 2—DTSDynamicPropertiesSourceType_GlobalVariable
- 3—DTSDynamicPropertiesSourceType_EnvironmentVariable
- 4—DTSDynamicPropertiesSourceType_Constant
- 5—DTSDynamicPropertiesSourceType_DataFile

For each of the types of sources for the assignment, you enter different information in the Add/Edit Assignment dialog. This information is stored in additional properties of the DynamicPropertiesTaskAssignment object.

You will find a DTS package in a file on the CD called TaskAssignments.dts, which has an ActiveX script that creates one of each of the six types of assignments. The code for each assignment is listed in the following sections. There are two files, IniFileExample.ini and SQLExample.txt, that need to be copied from the CD to C:\Temp in order to make the package run successfully.

> **NOTE**
>
> If you execute the TaskAssignments DTS package repeatedly, you will see that duplicated assignments are created. The DTS object model provides a New and an Add

method to create new assignments, but does not provide a `Delete` method to remove assignments from the collection.

The only way I have found to remove dynamic assignments from the collection is to do it through the Package Designer interface or to programmatically delete the entire task.

Global Variables

You choose the name of the global variable, which is stored in the `SourceGlobalVariable` property. The dialog shows you the current global variables and lets you create a new one. When you select a global variable, you can click the Refresh button to see that global variable's current value.

Here's how to add a property assignment in VBScript that uses a global variable:

```
Dim pkg, tsk, cus, dpta

Set pkg = DTSGlobalVariables.Parent
Set tsk = pkg.Tasks("tskDynamicProperties")
Set cus = tsk.CustomTask

set dpta = cus.Assignments.New
dpta.DestinationPropertyID = "'Properties';'Description'"
dpta.SourceType = 2 'DTSDynamicPropertiesSourceType_GlobalVariable
dpta.SourceGlobalVariable = "PackageDescriptionAssigner"
cus.Assignments.Add dpta
```

SQL Queries

You select one of the existing DTS connections and enter the text of the query. You can also load a query from a file. The property will be assigned the data from the first column of the first row returned by the query. Data from additional columns or rows is ignored.

This choice is implemented with two properties:

- `SourceQueryConnectionID`
- `SourceQuerySQL`

Here's how to add a property assignment in VBScript that uses a SQL Query:

```
set dpta = cus.Assignments.New
dpta.DestinationPropertyID = _
        "'Global Variables';'AuthorCount';'Properties';'Value'"
dpta.SourceType = 1 'DTSDynamicPropertiesSourceType_Query
```

```
dpta.SourceQueryConnectionID = 1
dpta.SourceQuerySQL = "Select Count(*) from authors"
cus.Assignments.Add dpta
```

Data Files

For data files, you need the name of the file, which is stored in the `SourceDataFileFileName` property. The property is assigned the full text that is located in that file.

Here's how to add a property assignment in VBScript that uses a data file:

```
set dpta = cus.Assignments.New
dpta.DestinationPropertyID = _
        "'Tasks';'tskExecuteSQL';'Properties';'SQLStatement'"
dpta.SourceType = 5 'DTSDynamicPropertiesSourceType_DataFile
dpta.SourceDataFileFileName = "C:\Temp\SQLExample.txt"
cus.Assignments.Add dpta
```

INI Files

First you choose the path of the INI file. Then you can select from list boxes that display the sections and keys that are available in that file, as shown in Figure 17.4. You have a Refresh button, so you can see the current value of the key you have selected.

FIGURE 17.4
The dialog gives you a listing of the sections in an INI file and then a listing of the keys within the section.

Your choice is implemented by three properties:

- `SourceIniFileFileName`
- `SourceIniFileSection`
- `SourceIniFileKey`

Here's how to add a property assignment in VBScript that uses an INI file:

```
set dpta = cus.Assignments.New
dpta.DestinationPropertyID = _
        "'Global Variables';'gIntegerValue';'Properties';'Value'"
dpta.SourceType = 0 'DTSDynamicPropertiesSourceType_IniFile
dpta.SourceIniFileFileName = "C:\Temp\IniFileExample.ini"
dpta.SourceIniFileSection = "MySectionName"
dpta.SourceIniFileKey = "MyKey"
cus.Assignments.Add dpta
```

Environment Variables

You can select any of the system environment variables, such as TEMP, WinDir, and USERName. All the variables that are available are displayed in a drop-down list. Your choice is stored in the `SourceEnvironmentVariable` property.

Here's how to add a property assignment in VBScript that uses an environment variable:

```
set dpta = cus.Assignments.New
dpta.DestinationPropertyID = "'Global
Variables';'TempDirectory';'Properties';'Value'"
dpta.SourceType = 3 'DTSDynamicPropertiesSourceType_EnvironmentVariable
dpta.SourceEnvironmentVariable = "Temp"
cus.Assignments.Add dpta
```

Constants

You can assign the property to any constant value. A list of DTS constants is available to assist you in your selection, as shown in Figure 17.5, but you can enter any constant value you choose. The value that you select is stored in the `SourceConstantValue` property.

FIGURE 17.5

You can view many of the DTS constants when you choose to use a constant for a property assignment.

Here's how to add a property assignment in VBScript that uses a constant:

```
Set dpta = cus.Assignments.New
dpta.DestinationPropertyID = _
        "'Tasks';'tskExecuteSQL';'Properties';'Description'"
dpta.SourceType = 4 'DTSDynamicPropertiesSourceType_Constant
dpta.SourceConstantValue = "This is the new description."
cus.Assignments.Add dpta
```

Creating a Dynamic Properties Task in Visual Basic

I have created a Visual Basic procedure, fctCreateDynamicPropertiesTask, that creates a step, a task, and a custom task for an FTP Task. All the properties of the task can be set with this procedure.

You can find the code for it in the directory for Chapter 17 on the book's CD as a Visual Basic Project, with files CreateDynamicPropertiesTask.vbp, CreateDynamicPropertiesTask.frm, and CreateDynamicPropertiesTask.bas.

The code for fctCreateDynamicPropertiesTask is shown in Listing 17.1. The procedure needs some utility functions that are included with the code listings on the CD. The project requires references to the Microsoft DTSPackage Object Library and the Microsoft DTS Custom Tasks Object Library.

LISTING 17.1   The Visual Basic Code to Create a Dynamic Properties Task

```
Option Explicit

Public Function fctCreateDynamicPropertiesTask( _
    pkg As DTS.Package2, _
    Optional sBaseName As String = "DynamicPropertiesTask" _
    ) As String

On Error GoTo ProcErr

Dim stp As DTS.Step2
Dim tsk As DTS.Task
Dim cus As DTSCustTasks.DynamicPropertiesTask


'Check to see if the selected Base name is unique
sBaseName = fctFindUniqueBaseName(pkg, sBaseName)

'Create task and custom task
Set tsk = pkg.Tasks.New("DTSDynamicPropertiesTask")
```

17

THE DYNAMIC
PROPERTIES TASK

LISTING 17.1   Continued

```
Set cus = tsk.CustomTask

With cus

    .Name = "tsk" & sBaseName
    .Description = sBaseName

End With

pkg.Tasks.Add tsk

'Create step for task
Set stp = pkg.Steps.New
With stp
    .Name = "stp" & sBaseName
    .Description = sBaseName
    .TaskName = tsk.Name
End With
pkg.Steps.Add stp

fctCreateDynamicPropertiesTask = stp.Name

Set tsk = Nothing
Set cus = Nothing
Set stp = Nothing

ProcExit:
  Exit Function
ProcErr:
  MsgBox Err.Number & " - " & Err.Description
  fctCreateDynamicPropertiesTask = ""
  GoTo ProcExit

End Function
```

Conclusion

The Dynamic Properties task improves the level of control within a DTS package. The next two chapters describe the two tasks that give you control between packages—the Execute Package task and the Message Queue task.

The Execute Package Task

IN THIS CHAPTER

The Execute Package task lets you execute one DTS package from another.

When to Use the Execute Package Task

Here are some reasons you might want to divide your DTS functionality between several packages:

- The packages have become too complex. They will be easier to understand if the tasks are divided between several packages.
- You have a task or group of tasks that performs a utility function. This functionality can be put into a separate package so that the same code can be used by several packages.
- Some of the DTS functionality needs to have a higher level of security. You can put that functionality into a separate package where it can be executed but not viewed or edited.

There are several ways to execute one package from another, in addition to using the Execute Package task. This task is the easiest way to execute another package, but some of the other ways have additional functionality. Here are the other possibilities:

- Use DTSRun from an Execute Process task. If you use an encrypted command line, you can hide all the parameters used in the execution, including the name of the server, package, and user.
- Use the DTS object model from an ActiveX Script task. You can change the properties of the package and its tasks before executing the package. You can read the values of global variables after executing the package.
- Use OpenRowset to query a package from an Execute SQL task. You can return a recordset from the child package when you use this strategy.
- Use the OLE Automation stored procedures from an Execute SQL task. This strategy allows you to execute a package from the context of a remote server. You can also modify the properties before executing and read the values of global variables after executing, as when you use the object model from an ActiveX Script task.

You can set the values of global variables in the child package when you use the Execute Package task and in all but one of the other strategies. Using OpenRowset from an Execute SQL task is the only method that does not allow you to set the values of global variables in the package you are executing.

You can only receive values back from a child package when you use the DTS object model in an ActiveX Script task or with the OLE Automation stored procedures in an Execute SQL task. You cannot receive values of global variables back from a child package when you use the Execute Package task.

One of the most important advantages of using the Execute Package task rather than one of the other methods is that you can include parent and child packages together in transactions. To enable transactions that span packages, you have to do the following:

- Ensure that transactions are enabled for the package as a whole. The package transaction properties are set on the Advanced tab of the DTS Package Properties dialog.
- In the Workflow Properties dialog for the step associated with the Execute Package task, select the Join Transaction If Present option.
- The Microsoft Distributed Transaction Coordinator client must be running on all the computers that are executing one of the packages.

There is more information about using transactions in DTS packages in Chapter 24, "Steps and Precedence Constraints."

Creating the Task and Setting Its Properties

You can create the Execute Package task in the Package Designer or in code. The last section of this chapter shows how to create the task in code. The Package Designer's Execute Package Task Properties dialog is shown in Figure 18.1.

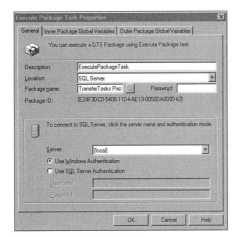

FIGURE 18.1
You choose package and connection information on the General tab of the Execute Package Task Properties dialog.

Most of the properties of the Execute Package task are concerned with package and connection information. You set these properties on the General tab of the Execute Package Task Properties dialog:

- `Description`—The description of the task.
- `FileName`—The file from which the DTS package is to be loaded. When the DTS package is not stored in a file, this property should be an empty string.
- `UseRepository`—If `FileName` is an empty string and this property is `TRUE`, the package is loaded from the repository. If `FileName` is an empty string and this property is `FALSE`, the package is loaded from SQL Server storage.
- `RepositoryDatabaseName`— The database that contains the instance of Meta Data Services from which the package is to be retrieved. This property is only used for a package loaded from the repository. If it is an empty string, the database that contains the default instance of Meta Data Services is used.
- `PackageName`, `PackageID`, `VersionID`— You choose the package and version from those available in the storage location you have specified. When you choose a package, the Execute Package task will always use the most current version of that package. If you choose a particular version of a package, the task will always use the same version, whether or not new versions are created. The value of these three properties is displayed in the interface. To change the Package or Version ID, you have to pick a new item in the Select Package dialog.
- `PackagePassword`— Either the owner password or the user password can be used to execute the package.
- `ServerName`— The server on which the DTS package is stored.
- `ServerUserName`, `ServerPassword`, and `UseTrustedConnection`—Connection information for the server on which the DTS package is stored.

Setting Values of Global Variables in the Child Package

You can pass information from the parent package to the child package by setting the values of global variables. There are two ways you can do this:

- With fixed values, where you set the values of the global variables at design time in the Execute Package task.
- With dynamic values, where the child package is sent the current values assigned to the global variables as the parent package is being executed.

You send global variables with the fixed values method by adding global variables on the Inner Package Global Variables tab of the Execute Package Task Properties dialog, as shown in Figure 18.2. You can choose the name, the datatype, and the value for the global variable.

FIGURE 18.2
You set fixed values for global variables on the Inner Package Global Variables tab.

The variables you set on this tab are not global variables in the parent package. They set the values of global variables in the child package.

You send global variables with the dynamic values method by adding global variables on the Outer Package Global Variables tab, as shown in Figure 18.3. This tab allows you to choose from the existing global variables in the parent package. These parent package global variables set the values of global variables in the child package to the parent package values at the time the Execute Package task is executed.

You can send global variables with both methods in the same Execute Package task. If you use the same name for both a fixed value and a dynamic value global variable, the global variable is sent with the fixed value.

The two types of global variables are received the same way in the child package. If a global variable with the specified name exists in the child package, the value sent from the parent package is assigned to it. If that global variable doesn't exist in the child package, a new global variable is created. This new global variable only persists during the execution of the child package.

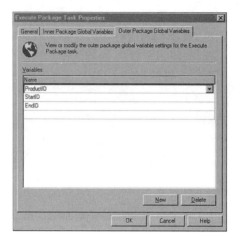

FIGURE 18.3

You choose existing global variables on the Outer Package Global Variables tab when you want to use the dynamic values method.

CAUTION

Global variable names are always case sensitive. If you are attempting to pass a variable and you do not match the case of all the letters in the name, a new variable will be created in the child package.

Also, a global variable passed to a child package overrules the option for required explicit declaration of global variables. A new global variable will be created in the child package when a global variable with the same name doesn't exist, even if explicit declaration of variables is required in that package.

The Execute Package task has a `GlobalVariables` collection that contains a collection of GlobalVariable objects. All of the fixed-value global variables that you pass to the child package are members of this collection.

The Execute Package task has an `InputGlobalVariableNames` property that contains a semicolon-delimited list of global variable names. These are the names of the dynamic value global variables that are being sent to the child package:

```
"GlobalVariableName1";"GlobalVariableName2";"GlobalVariablename3"
```

> **NOTE**
>
> It's hard to find the right terminology to talk about these two kinds of global variables. I am not satisfied with the Inner Package/Outer Package labeling that the interface gives to the two kinds of global variables, because both types become global variables in the inner package.
>
> I think it's better to focus on the function of the global variables.
>
> If you have fixed values that you always want to send to the child package, you create global variables that use the fixed value method. You specify the fixed value, along with the global variable name, on the Inner Package Global Variables tab.
>
> If you have dynamic values that you want to set while your parent package is executing, you create global variables with the dynamic value method. You create global variables in the parent package and send them to the child package on the Outer Package Global Variables tab.

The `NestedExecutionLevel` Property of the Package

The DTS `Package2` object has a property called `NestedExecutionLevel`. This read-only property reports the level of nesting that has been reached through the use of the Execute Package task.

This property returns a value of 0 for a package that is executed directly and a value of 1 for the first package called by the Execute Package task. If that called package calls another package, the `NestedExecutionLevel` property will return a value of 2 for the innermost package.

DTS has an absolute limit of 32 for the NestedExecutionLevel. If that level is reached and another Execute Package task is executed, the package will fail with the following error:

"Nested package execution limit of 32 was exceeded."

If you are calling DTS packages recursively with the Execute Package task, you can query the `NestedExecutionLevel` property to break out of the recursion before this error occurs:

```
Dim pkg, stp
Set pkg = DTSGlobalVariables.Parent
Set stp = pkg.Steps("stpExecutePackage")
If pkg.NestedExecutionLevel = 32 Then
    stp.DisableStep = True
End If
```

> **CAUTION**
>
> Books Online recommends against using the Execute Package task to call packages recursively because of the danger of a stack overflow shutting down the Enterprise Manager.

Creating and Calling a Utility DTS Package

In Chapter 12, "The Execute SQL Task," I described how to use OLE Automation procedures in an Execute SQL task to force a DTS package to execute on a particular server. I have encapsulated that somewhat complex code into a utility DTS package so that it can be called with the Execute Package task.

The name of the utility package is the Remote Execution Utility. You call it from an Execute Package task, and it runs the selected DTS package on any server you choose. The utility writes execution information to an INI file. The whole process is shown in Figure 18.4.

FIGURE 18.4

The Remote Execution Utility contains the functionality to execute a Called Package on any server and report the results to the Calling Package.

You can find the utility and a sample of a Calling Package and a Called Package in three files on the CD—CallingPackage.dts, RemoteExecutionUtility.dts, and CalledPackage.dts. To use these sample packages, you have to do the following:

1. Save the Remote Execution Utility and the Called Package to SQL Server. You can put them on any servers you like, as long as you reference those servers appropriately in the Execute Package task in the Calling Package.

2. The Calling Package has to be set to log to SQL Server. Check the logging settings in the Package Properties dialog.

3. In the Execute Package task of the Calling Package, you must choose the Remote Execution Utility as the package to be executed.

4. Set the global variables in the Execute Package task to appropriate values.

You are only required to send one value to the Remote Execution Utility—the PackageName. The utility will open the Called Package from SQL Server storage on the local computer using integrated security. The utility will execute the Called Package in the context of the local server, again using integrated security. You can override these default values by sending these global variables to the Remote Execution Utility:

- PackageStorageServer—The name of the server where the Called Package is stored using SQL Server storage.
- PackageStorageUserName and PackageStoragePassword.
- PackageExecutionServer—The name of the server where the Called Package is to be executed.
- PackageExecutionUserName and PackageExecutionPassword.
- ConnectionServer—You can change all the connections in the executed package to reference a particular server. If this parameter is an empty string, the connections will not be changed.
- ConnectionUserName and ConnectionPassword.

The Remote Execution Utility reports results in an INI file. The following global variables can be sent to the utility to set up the reporting:

- CallingPackageID—Any identification value from the Calling Server. I recommend sending the short lineage value for the current execution of the Calling Server. You could also use the full lineage value, the package ID, the package version ID, or the package name.
- ReportName—The name of the INI file used to report results. If not supplied, the name of the INI file will be set to RemoteExecutionReport.ini.
- ReportDirectory—The directory where the INI file is to be written. The default value is set in the Remote Execution Utility to the user's temporary directory.
- StepName—The step associated with a Transform Data task for which you want a complete report. If this is not set, no step will be given special reporting.

> **CAUTION**
>
> The initial version of SQL Server 2000 limits the headings used for INI files in the Dynamic Properties task to 255 characters. Because of this limitation, the Calling Package will not be able to read the values for the current package execution after 23 entries have been made into the INI file.

The Remote Execution Utility has a parameter called `TimeoutInSeconds`. The utility will terminate with an error if the Called Package does not complete execution within the specified period. By default, the Calling Package sets the timeout to 60 seconds.

> **CAUTION**
>
> Do *not* use message boxes in the Called Package. They will not be displayed and will prevent the Remote Execution Utility from completing. The timeout will not terminate the utility if an attempt is being made to display a message box. To end the package, you have to stop SQL Server or terminate the Enterprise Manager process.

The sample for the Calling Package, shown in Figure 18.5, has five steps:

- Set Calling Package ID—An ActiveX Script task that sets the Calling Package ID. In the sample package, the Short Lineage variable of the package's current execution is used. That value is set in a dynamic value global variable so that it will be sent to the utility. It is also set in the Dynamic Properties task so that the proper section of the INI file will be read for the report.
- Remote Execution—The Execute Package task that calls the Remote Execution Utility.
- Determine Reporting—An ActiveX Script task that sets the directory and name of the INI file used in reporting. If an empty string has been chosen for these values, this task disables the two reporting tasks.
- Find Results—A Dynamic Properties task that reads the values of the report INI file into global variables.
- Report Results—An ActiveX Script task that displays a message box reporting on those global variables. In a production environment, you could set this string as the message of a Send Mail task, which could then be sent to the appropriate recipients.

The Calling Package doesn't have to be this complicated, of course. If you use an unchanging value for `CallingPackageID`, you don't need the Set Calling package ID task. If you don't want to view the results in the package, you don't need the Find Results and Report Results tasks. The only thing you need to call the utility is a Dynamic Properties task.

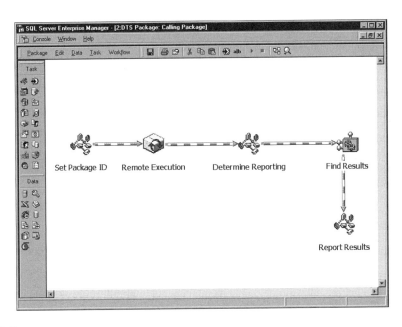

FIGURE 18.5
You only need a Dynamic Properties task to call the utility, but you may want to add other tasks to set global variables and report results.

Creating the Task in Visual Basic

I have created a Visual Basic procedure, `fctCreateExecutePackageTask`, that creates a step, a task, and a custom task for an Execute Package task. All the properties of the task can be set with this procedure. The procedure does not let you add any members to the `GlobalVariables` collection. You can add dynamic value global variables with the `InputGlobalVariableNames` property. You can find the code for it in the directory for Chapter 18 on the book's CD as a Visual Basic Project, with files CreateExecutePackageTask.vbp, CreateExecutePackageTask.frm, and CreateExecutePackageTask.bas.

The code for `fctCreateExecutePackageTask` is shown in Listing 18.1. The procedure needs some utility functions that are included with the code listings on the CD. The project requires a reference to the Microsoft DTSPackage Object Library.

LISTING 18.1   The Visual Basic Code to Create an Execute Package Task

```
Option Explicit

Public Function fctCreateExecutePackageTask( _
    pkg As DTS.Package2, _
    Optional sBaseName As String = "ExecutePackageTask", _
    Optional sFileName As String = "", _
    Optional sInputGlobalVariableNames As String = "", _
    Optional sPackageID As String = "", _
    Optional sPackageName As String = "", _
    Optional sPackagePassword As String = "", _
    Optional sRepositoryDatabaseName As String = "", _
    Optional sServerName As String = "(local)", _
    Optional sServerPassword As String = "", _
    Optional sServerUserName As String = "", _
    Optional bUseRepository As Boolean = False, _
    Optional sVersionID As String = "") As String

On Error GoTo ProcErr

Dim stp As DTS.Step2
Dim tsk As DTS.Task
Dim cus As DTS.ExecutePackageTask

'Check to see if the selected Base name is unique
sBaseName = fctFindUniqueBaseName(pkg, sBaseName)

'Create task and custom task
Set tsk = pkg.Tasks.New("DTSExecutePackageTask")
Set cus = tsk.CustomTask

With cus

    .Name = "tsk" & sBaseName
    .Description = sBaseName

    .FileName = sFileName
    .InputGlobalVariableNames = sInputGlobalVariableNames
    .PackageID = sPackageID
    .PackageName = sPackageName
    .PackagePassword = sPackagePassword
    .RepositoryDatabaseName = sRepositoryDatabaseName
    .UseRepository = bUseRepository
```

LISTING 18.1   Continued

```
    .ServerName = sServerName
    .VersionID = sVersionID

    If sServerUserName = "" Then
        .UseTrustedConnection = True
    Else
        .ServerPassword = sServerPassword
        .ServerUserName = sServerUserName
        .UseTrustedConnection = False
    End If

End With

pkg.Tasks.Add tsk

'Create step for task
Set stp = pkg.Steps.New
With stp
    .Name = "stp" & sBaseName
    .Description = sBaseName
    .TaskName = tsk.Name
End With
pkg.Steps.Add stp

fctCreateExecutePackageTask = stp.Name

Set tsk = Nothing
Set cus = Nothing
Set stp = Nothing

ProcExit:
  Exit Function
ProcErr:
  MsgBox Err.Number & " - " & Err.Description
  fctCreateExecutePackageTask = ""
  GoTo ProcExit
End Function
```

Conclusion

The Execute Package task gives you a convenient way to execute one package from another, which can help you organize your DTS processing more efficiently.

The biggest drawback of the task is the inability to return values from the child package to the parent package. Chapter 12, "The Execute SQL Task," and Chapter 26, "Managing Packages with Visual Basic and Stored Procedures," show you how to execute packages from one another in a way that allows for two-way communication.

The Message Queue Task

IN THIS CHAPTER

The Message Queue task uses message queuing to send and receive messages from DTS packages. You can send and receive simple string messages or messages that contain files or values for global variables.

You use the Message Queue task to coordinate the execution of two or more DTS packages. One package has a Message Queue task configured for sending. When that task executes, it adds a message to the specified queue. The other package has a Message Queue task configured for receiving. When that task is executed, it looks for an appropriate message in the queue. If it finds one, the task completes successfully. If it does not find the message, it continues checking until the message appears in the queue or the period of time specified by the ReceiveMessageTimeout property expires.

> **NOTE**
>
> If you don't have the MSMQ client installed on your computer, you will receive a warning message when you attempt to create a Message Queue task. You are allowed to create the task and set its properties. However, the task will not successfully execute unless you install the MSMQ client.

When to Use the Message Queue Task

Both the Message Queue task and the Execute Package task are used to coordinate the execution of two or more DTS packages. Here are the factors in deciding which one of these tasks to use:

- Use the Message Queue task when you need asynchronous processing of two or more packages. Use the Execute Package task to call one package from another in situations where both packages are available at the same time. You can use the Message Queue task in situations where one or more of the packages are executing on computers that are not always connected to the network.

- Use the Dynamic Properties task when you need the tasks of two or more packages to be joined in a transaction. The Message Queue task does not support transactions.

- You can use the Message Queue task to send string messages, global variables, or files from one package to another. You can send only global variables with an Execute Package task.

Here are some examples of situations where you could use a Message Queue task:

- One DTS package has tasks that shouldn't be executed before the successful execution of other packages. You can create the package with several Message Queue tasks for receiving messages. The other packages can add a message to the queue to signal when they have successfully completed execution. Each of the message-sending packages can send a string message, send a file, or set global variables in the receiving package.

- A complex DTS package could be divided into parts that are executed on different computers. The precedence constraints connecting steps can be replaced by a set of send and receive Message Queue tasks. Global variables that are used throughout the package can be sent back and forth with those tasks. The main limitation is that you can't bind all the packages together into a transaction, as you would be able to do if you were using Execute Package tasks.

- After creating a set of local cubes, the cube files could be sent throughout an organization with a Message Queue task. All the computers receiving the cube files could save the cube file to a local path without removing the message from the queue. When a new local cube was created, the sending package could remove the previous message from the queue before adding the message with the new cube.

Creating the Task and Setting Its Properties

The primary choice you make when creating a Message Queue task is whether its function is to send or receive. You make this choice in the Messages box of the Message Queue Task Properties dialog, shown in Figure 19.1. This dialog shows you a listing of all the messages that have been created when you are configuring the task to send.

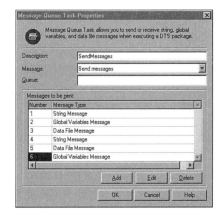

FIGURE **19.1**

The Properties dialog of the Message Queue task when sending a message.

The choice to send or receive messages is implemented with the custom task's TaskType property. This property uses the DTSMQType constants:

- 0—DTSMQType_Sender
- 1—DTSMQType_Receiver

You can also set the Description property for the task in the Message Queue Task Properties dialog. The Name property is set automatically.

Setting the Queue Path

Whether you are sending or receiving messages, you have to enter the path of the queue that you want the task to use. The queue path has the following syntax.

- For a private queue:

  computer_name\PRIVATE$\queue_name

- For a public queue:

  computer_name\\queue_name

- For a public queue on the local computer:

  .\\queue_name

The queue path is assigned with the QueuePath property of the custom task object.

Sending Messages

The Message Queue Task Properties dialog has buttons for adding, editing, and deleting messages from the task. The Add and Edit buttons call the Message Queue Message Properties dialog, shown in Figure 19.2.

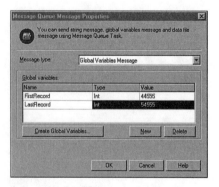

FIGURE 19.2

The Message Queue Message Properties dialog allows you to add or edit messages.

The primary choice in the Message Queue Message Properties dialog is the type of message to send—String Message, Data File Message, or Global Variables Message. Depending on which one you choose, the dialog presents an interface for typing in the string, picking the file, or adding the global variables.

The custom task object has a collection of messages called the DTSMQMessages collection. The DTSMQMessage object has the MessageType property, which uses one of these DTSMQMessageType values:

- 0—DTSMQMessageType_String
- 1—DTSMQMessageType_DataFile
- 2—DTSMQMessageType_GlobalVariables

The DTSMQMessage object also has a set of properties, one of which is used for each of the message types:

- MessageString—The text of the string message being sent.
- MessageDataFile—The path and filename of the data file being sent.
- MessageGlobalVariables—A semicolon-delimited list of the names of the global variables being sent:

  'NameVar1';'NameVar2';'NameVar3';

> **NOTE**
>
> The DTSMQMessage object has two additional properties that cannot be set in the Message Queue Message Properties dialog and are only partially documented in Books Online—UseTransaction and WaitForAcknowledgement. You can view these properties with Disconnected Edit.

Receiving Messages

If you choose to create a Message Queue task for receiving, you choose one of the three options in the Message Types box of the Message Queue Task Properties dialog. All of these types give you choices for filtering the messages.

The message type choice is implemented with the ReceiveMessageType property of the Message Queue custom task. This property uses the same DTSMQMessageType values that are used by the Message object's MessageType property.

Receiving a String Message

Figure 19.3 shows the choices for filtering a string message. You can choose to accept all messages from a particular queue. You can also choose to filter the messages with a filter string. There are three ways that the filter string can be used:

- As an exact match.
- As an exact match, except for ignoring case.
- As a substring, where any message that contains the filter string will be accepted.

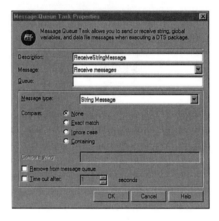

FIGURE 19.3

The choices in the Message Queue Task Properties dialog when receiving a string message.

The StringCompareValue property is used for the filter string. The type of comparison is implemented with the StringCompareType property, which uses the DTSMQStringMessageCompare constants:

- 0—DTSMQStringMessageCompare_None—No string comparison is used. This is the default value for the task.
- 1—DTSMQStringMessageCompare_Exact—Exact match.
- 2—DTSMQStringMessageCompare_IgnoreCase—Exact match, except for case.
- 3—DTSMQStringMessageCompare_Contains—Message contains string.

Receiving a Data File Message

Figure 19.4 shows the choices you have when you are configuring the Message Queue task to receive a data file message. You choose the filename and path where you want to save the file, and whether to overwrite an existing file with that name. You can also filter messages based on the sending DTS package. These filtering choices are discussed in the "Filtering a Data File or a Global Variables Message" section later in this chapter.

FIGURE 19.4
The choices in the Message Queue Task Properties dialog when receiving a data file message.

The filename is set with the `SaveDataFileName` property. The overwriting choice is stored in the `DataFileNonOverwritable` property.

Receiving a Global Variables Message

Figure 19.5 shows the choices when you are receiving a global variables message. The sending package filtering, discussed in "Filtering a Data File or a Global Variables Message," is the only additional configuration you have for this type of message.

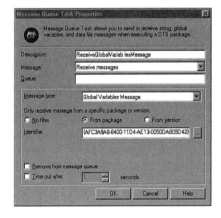

FIGURE 19.5
The choices in the Message Queue Task Properties dialog when receiving a global variables message.

Filtering a Data File or a Global Variables Message

You can filter data file and global variable messages based on the identity of the package sending the message. You can filter on either a particular package or a particular version of a package. A second Message Queue Task Properties dialog opens when you click on the expand button by the Identifier box on the Message Queue Task Properties dialog. This dialog allows you to choose a package from SQL Server, SQL Server Meta Data Services, or structured file storage. After selecting one of those options, you can click on the expand button beside the Package name box. In the Select Package dialog, shown in Figure 19.6, you can select the desired package or package version.

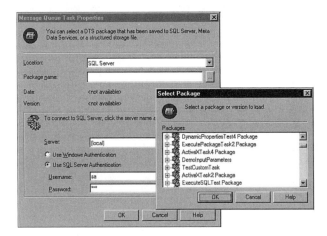

FIGURE 19.6
The Message Queue Task Properties dialog and the Select Package dialog give you the choices for filtering the message source.

The package and package version filtering are implemented with the DTSMessagePackageID and DTSMessageVersionID properties. These properties both have a string data type and a default value of "Not specified".

CAUTION

If you choose to filter messages on a package version, any change to the sending package will require a change in the value of DTSMessageVersionID. Whenever you save a DTS package, a new version of that package is created.

> **NOTE**
>
> The DTSMQMessage object also has a property called DTSMessageLineageID, which cannot be set in the Message Queue Task Properties dialog.

Removing the Message from the Queue

For all the message types, you can also choose whether or not to remove the message from the queue after it has been received. Messages are stored in a queue in a particular order. You will not be able to view the next message until you remove the first one. The Boolean RemoveFromQueue property is used for this choice. The default value is FALSE, which leaves the message in the queue.

> **NOTE**
>
> If you use the Message Queue task to send a message to a single DTS package, you will most likely remove the message from the queue after reading it. But if you send a message to several DTS packages, you will have to leave the message in the queue.
>
> Let's say you are distributing a local cube file or a report with the Message Queue task. You could have a package send the current version of the file each day. As it was received, each Message Queue task would leave it in the queue so that others could receive it. The file could be removed by the sending package in a Message Queue task executed immediately before the Message Queue task that sent the new version.

> **NOTE**
>
> You can use a Message Queue task to loop through a set of messages in a queue. In order to do this, you have to remove each message as you receive it. If you don't, you will never be able to receive the next message in the queue.

Message Timeout

You can enter the length of time in seconds that you want the Message Queue task to wait for the message. If the message is not found in the queue before the timeout expires, the Message Queue task finishes with an error.

The timeout is implemented with the `ReceiveMessageTimeout` and `ErrorIfReceiveMessageTimeOut` properties. The default values for these properties are 0 and `FALSE`, which means that that task will never time out. If you check the Time out after box in the Message Queue Task Properties dialog, the `ReceiveMessageTimeout` property is set to 1 and the `ErrorIfReceiveMessageTimeOut` property is set to `TRUE`. You can then change the `ReceiveMessageTimeout` property to the desired value.

Creating the Task in Visual Basic

I have created a Visual Basic procedure, `fctCreateMessageQueueTask`, which creates a step, a task, and a custom task for a Message Queue task. All the properties of the task can be set with this procedure. However, the procedure does not let you add any messages to the task.

If you look at the Message Queue Task Properties dialog for a task created by this procedure, the visual display will be incorrect. If you select OK in the dialog and open it again, it will appear correctly.

You can find the procedure in the directory for Chapter 19 as a Visual Basic Project, with files CreateMessageQueueTask.vbp, CreateMessageQueueTask.frm, CreateMessageQueueTask.frx, and CreateMessageQueueTask.bas.

The code for `fctCreateMessageQueueTask` is shown in Listing 19.1. The procedure needs some utility functions that are included with the code listings on the CD. The project requires references to the Microsoft DTSPackage Object Library and the Microsoft DTS Custom Tasks Object Library.

LISTING 19.1   The Visual Basic Code to Create a Message Queue Task

```
Option Explicit

Public Function fctCreateMessageQueueTask( _
        pkg As DTS.Package2, _
        sBaseName As String, _
        bDataFileNonOverwritable As Boolean, _
        sDTSMessageLineageID As String, _
        sDTSMessagePackageID As String, _
        sDTSMessageVersionID As String, _
        bErrorIfReceiveMessageTimeout As Boolean, _
        sQueuePath As String, _
        lReceiveMessageTimeout As Long, _
        dtsReceiveMessageType As Long, _
        bRemoveFromQueue As Boolean, _
        sSaveDataFileName As String, _
        dtsStringCompareType As Long, _
```

LISTING 19.1   Continued

```
        sStringCompareValue As String, _
        dtsTaskType As Long) As String

On Error GoTo ProcErr

Dim stp As DTS.Step2
Dim tsk As DTS.Task
Dim cus As DTSCustTasks.DTSMessageQueueTask

'Check to see if the selected Base name is unique
sBaseName = fctFindUniqueBaseName(pkg, sBaseName)

'Create task and custom task
Set tsk = pkg.Tasks.New("DTSMessageQueueTask")
Set cus = tsk.CustomTask
With cus

'Properties
    .Name = "tsk" & sBaseName
    .Description = sBaseName

'Specific Properties for this task

    If sQueuePath <> "" Then
        .QueuePath = sQueuePath
    End If

    .TaskType = dtsTaskType

    If .TaskType = 1 Then

        .ReceiveMessageType = dtsReceiveMessageType
        .ErrorIfReceiveMessageTimeout = bErrorIfReceiveMessageTimeout
        .ReceiveMessageTimeout = lReceiveMessageTimeout

        .RemoveFromQueue = bRemoveFromQueue

        Select Case .ReceiveMessageType

            Case 0 'String
                .StringCompareType = dtsStringCompareType
                If sStringCompareValue <> "" Then
```

LISTING 19.1 Continued

```
                    .StringCompareValue = sStringCompareValue
                End If

            Case 1 'Data file
                .DataFileNonOverwritable = bDataFileNonOverwritable
                If sSaveDataFileName <> "" Then
                    .SaveDataFileName = sSaveDataFileName
                End If
                If sDTSMessageLineageID <> "" Then
                    .DTSMessageLineageID = sDTSMessageLineageID
                End If
                If sDTSMessagePackageID <> "" Then
                    .DTSMessagePackageID = sDTSMessagePackageID
                End If
                If sDTSMessageVersionID <> "" Then
                    .DTSMessageVersionID = sDTSMessageVersionID
                End If

            Case 2 'Global variables
                If sDTSMessageLineageID <> "" Then
                    .DTSMessageLineageID = sDTSMessageLineageID
                End If
                If sDTSMessagePackageID <> "" Then
                    .DTSMessagePackageID = sDTSMessagePackageID
                End If
                If sDTSMessageVersionID <> "" Then
                    .DTSMessageVersionID = sDTSMessageVersionID
                End If

        End Select

    End If

End With

pkg.Tasks.Add tsk

'Create step for task
Set stp = pkg.Steps.New
With stp
    .Name = "stp" & sBaseName
    .Description = sBaseName
    .TaskName = tsk.Name
```

LISTING 19.1 Continued

```
End With
pkg.Steps.Add stp

fctCreateMessageQueueTask = stp.Name

Set tsk = Nothing
Set cus = Nothing
Set stp = Nothing

ProcExit:
  Exit Function
ProcErr:
  MsgBox Err.Number & " - " & Err.Description
  fctCreateMessageQueueTask = ""
  GoTo ProcExit
End Function
```

Conclusion

The Message Queue task extends the ability of DTS packages to work with one another. You can use this task to coordinate packages on computers that are online or that are temporarily disconnected from the network.

The Send Mail Task

IN THIS CHAPTER

The Send Mail task provides an interface between your DTS package and your email system. This task is the same in SQL Server 2000 as it was in SQL Server 7.0.

When to Use the Send Mail Task

The primary role of the Send Mail task is to send a report regarding what has happened in the execution of a DTS package. Using the workflow objects, you can specify that an email will be sent only on failure, only on success, or no matter what the outcome of the DTS process.

In order to use the Send Mail task, the computer that is running the DTS package must have Microsoft's Messaging API (MAPI) installed and the user must have a valid user profile for the messaging system.

> **NOTE**
>
> Send Mail is the task I have seen fail most frequently when I move a DTS package from a development machine to the database server. Not all database servers have MAPI installed, and if they do, you still have to make sure that the user profile you are using is valid on the server.

I have seen these three strategies for integrating the Send Mail task into a DTS package:

- Prepare fixed messages ahead of time and decide whether or not to send those messages depending on what happens in the package. You create several Send Mail tasks. Each one has a different message. You set each one to execute on the completion, success, or failure of a particular task.
- Write the results of the package execution to a file, using an ActiveX Script task. Send that file as an attachment with a Send Mail task that executes as the last task of the package.
- Dynamically construct an email message in an ActiveX script task. Set that message as the MessageText property of a Send Mail task that executes as the last task of the package. Depending on the particular results of the package, you could also change the individuals who are set to receive the message.

There are code samples for both the second and third options in Chapter 16, "Writing Scripts for an ActiveX Script Task."

Using the properties of the DTS tasks and steps, you have access to the time each step starts and finishes, the duration of each step, the number of records that were successfully transformed, the number of records that generated an error, and the success or failure of each step. You can include all of this information when you report on the execution of the package.

Creating the Task and Setting Its Properties

You can create the Execute Process task in the DTS Designer or in code. Neither of the DTS wizards creates an Execute Process task.

The Send Mail Task Properties dialog is shown in Figure 20.1. The expand buttons by the To: and CC: boxes open up the Address Book on the local computer.

FIGURE 20.1
Creating a Send Mail task is very similar to sending a regular email message.

Almost all of the properties of the Send Mail task are the kinds of things you would expect when creating a regular email. The `Name`, `SaveMailInSentItemsFolder`, and `IsNTService` properties can only be viewed or modified with Disconnected Edit or with code.

- `Name`—The name of the task. Cannot be viewed or modified in the Send Mail Task Properties dialog.
- `Description`—The description of the task.
- `Profile`—The profile name used to send the email.
- `Password`—The password needed by the email system.
- `ToLine`—The recipient.
- `CCLine`—Additional recipients.
- `Subject`—The subject line of the email.
- `MessageText`—The full text of the body of the email.
- `FileAttachments`—The names of attached files.

- SaveMailInSentItemsFolder—A Boolean value that determines whether or not mail is saved in the sent items folder. The default is FALSE. Cannot be modified in the dialog.

- IsNTService—A Boolean value that indicates if the caller is running as an NT or Windows 2000 Service. The default is FALSE. Cannot be modified in the dialog.

The Methods of the Send Mail Task

The Send Mail task has a variety of methods that allow it to interact with the email system. Some of these methods, such as Logoff and Logon, are used during the execution of the package. Others, such as ShowAddressBook, are used at design time to help the user set the task's properties:

- GetDefaultProfileName
- InitializeMAPI and UnitializeMAPI
- Logoff and Logon
- ResolveName
- ShowAddressBook

Creating the Task in Visual Basic

I have created a Visual Basic procedure, fctCreateSendMailTask, that creates a connection, a step, a task, and a custom task for a Send Mail task. All the properties of the task can be set with this procedure.

The fctCreateSendMailTask function is used in the DTSPackageGenerator utility that is included with this book. You can also find the procedure in the directory for Chapter 20 as a Visual Basic Project, with files CreateSendMailTask.vbp, CreateSendMailTask.frm, and CreateSendMailTask.bas.

The code for fctCreateSendMailTask is shown in Listing 20.1. The procedure needs some utility functions that are included with the code listings on the CD.

LISTING 20.1   The Visual Basic Code to Create a Send Mail Task

```
Option Explicit

Public Function fctCreateSendMailTask( _
    pkg As DTS.Package2, _
    Optional sBaseName As String = "SendMailTask", _
    Optional sEMailPassword As String = "", _
    Optional sToLine As String = "", _
    Optional sProfile As String = "", _
```

LISTING 20.1   Continued

```
    Optional sMessageText As String = "", _
    Optional sCCLine As String = "", _
    Optional sFileAttachments As String = "", _
    Optional sSubject As String = "", _
    Optional bIsNTService As Boolean = False, _
    Optional bSaveMailInSentItemsFolder As Boolean = False)

On Error GoTo ProcErr

Dim stp As DTS.Step2
Dim tsk As DTS.Task
Dim cus As DTS.SendMailTask

'Check to see if the selected Base name is unique
sBaseName = fctFindUniqueBaseName(pkg, sBaseName)

'Create task and custom task
Set tsk = pkg.Tasks.New("DTSSendMailTask")
Set cus = tsk.CustomTask
With cus

'Properties
    .Name = "tsk" & sBaseName
    .Description = sBaseName
    .Password = sEMailPassword
    .SaveMailInSentItemsFolder = bSaveMailInSentItemsFolder
    .IsNTService = bIsNTService
    .Profile = sProfile
    .MessageText = sMessageText
    .CCLine = sCCLine
    .FileAttachments = sFileAttachments
    .Subject = sSubject
    .ToLine = sToLine

End With
pkg.Tasks.Add tsk

'Create step for task
Set stp = pkg.Steps.New
With stp
    .Name = "stp" & sBaseName
    .Description = sBaseName
    .TaskName = tsk.Name
End With
```

LISTING 20.1   Continued

```
pkg.Steps.Add stp
fctCreateSendMailTask = stp.Name

Set tsk = Nothing
Set cus = Nothing
Set stp = Nothing

ProcExit:
  Exit Function
ProcErr:
  MsgBox Err.Number & " - " & Err.Description
  fctCreateSendMailTask = ""
  GoTo ProcExit
End Function
```

Conclusion

The Send Mail task plays an important role in integrating DTS into an organization's information system. You can report the package's execution information to your users, if you take the time to dynamically construct messages. At a minimum, you can keep your users informed about the success and failure of the DTS package and its tasks.

The Analysis Services Tasks

IN THIS CHAPTER

When you install Microsoft Analysis Services on a server that has SQL Server installed, you will find two new custom tasks registered with DTS:

- The Analysis Services Processing task
- The Data Mining Prediction Query task

These two tasks were not included with SQL Server 7.0. In the middle of 1999, Microsoft made the OLAP Services Processing task available in the Data Transformation Services Task Kit 1. The Analysis Services Processing task contains the functionality of the OLAP Services Processing task, plus additional features for SQL Server 2000.

When to Use the Analysis Services Tasks

One of the most important management tasks when you're using Analysis Services is the processing of cubes and mining models. These business analysis tools need to be kept current. Processing is the operation that synchronizes the cubes and data mining models with the underlying data.

The purpose of the Analysis Services Processing task is to automate the processing of cubes and data mining models. After you have loaded new data into your database, you can update your cubes and data mining models with this task. You have all the processing options that are available in the Analysis Services Manager, including the time-saving incremental update.

The purpose of the Data Mining Prediction Query task is to use a mining model on a set of data to predict the value of a particular column. The mining model is trained to recognize particular patterns in the data. The prediction query applies those patterns to new data so that you can predict an unknown value.

The Analysis Services Processing task updates your cubes and data mining models so that they contain the most current data. The Data Mining Prediction Query task uses a data mining model to predict the most likely values for a particular set of data. Together, they allow you to automate your use of business analysis data.

> **NOTE**
>
> Chapter 31, "Creating a Custom Task in VB," has an example of a custom task that automates the process of creating local cubes. Local cubes are files that contain multidimensional data. You can use them when you're disconnected from a network. You can also use them to give individual users a particular subset of the available data. Local cubes, like Analysis Services cubes, need to be updated to reflect the current data. This custom task lets you automate that process.

Using the Analysis Services Processing Task

The Analysis Services Processing Task dialog, shown in Figure 21.1, gives you a tree structure for selecting the object or objects that are to be processed. The available processing options on the right side of the dialog change dynamically depending on what you choose in the tree.

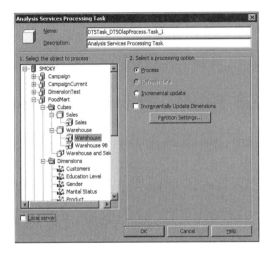

FIGURE 21.1
The Analysis Services Processing Task dialog.

You can only make one selection in the tree, but if you pick a node that has several objects within it, all those objects will be processed. The type of node you pick sets a custom task property called `ItemType`. The `ItemType` values are as follows:

- 1—Process all the objects in an Analysis Services database.
- 2—Process all the objects in a particular cube, dimension, or mining model folder.
- 3—Process a cube.
- 5—Process a virtual cube.
- 7—Process a partition.
- 9—Process a shared dimension.
- 11—Process a virtual dimension.
- 12—Process a mining model.

The particular object you pick is specified by the `TreeKey` property. For the Sales cube in the FoodMart 2000 database on the local computer, the value of this property is

```
LOCALHOST\FoodMart 2000\CubeFolder\Sales
```

Depending on the type of node you pick and the object's current processed state, you have one, two, or three choices for processing:

- When you process multiple objects, you don't have a choice. You always have to do a full process.

- When you pick a shared dimension, you have two choices—rebuild the dimension structure or do an incremental update.

- When you select a cube that is currently in a processed state, you have three choices—process, refresh data, or incremental update.

In addition to the processing choice, you can choose whether or not to incrementally update dimensions that are contained within a cube you are processing.

> **NOTE**
>
> A full discussion of cube and data mining model processing options is beyond the scope of this book, but there are some processing issues that become evident when you're using the Analysis Services Processing task.
>
> An incremental cube update is often much faster than a full cube process. This is especially true for large cubes. You can't do an incremental update on all the cubes in a database by picking the Cubes folder. You always do a full update when you select a folder. If you want to do an incremental update on all your cubes, you will have to create a separate task for each one.
>
> If you want to do an incremental update on all the dimensions in a cube, you also have to create a separate task for each one. If you select the Dimensions folder, you can process all the dimensions with one task, but you can only do a process that rebuilds the dimension structure. If you rebuild the dimension structure, you will invalidate all the cubes that use those dimensions, and you'll have to do a full process on all of them. That could take a lot of time, of course.

When you select the incremental update option for a cube, you are given the choice of a data source, a fact table, and a filter, as shown in Figure 21.2. An incremental update adds new data into a cube that already has data. You can choose to add data from a different fact table that can be from a different data source. If you choose to use an incremental update with the existing fact table, you have to specify a filter to limit the update to the data that is not already in the cube.

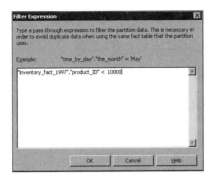

FIGURE 21.2
When you choose an incremental cube update in the Analysis Services Processing Task dialog, you can create a filter with the Filter Expression dialog.

The incremental update option uses three properties:

- `DataSource`
- `FactTable`
- `Filter`

CAUTION

Analysis Services does not check to see if you have defined your incremental update appropriately. An incremental update is an essential tool for efficient cube updating, but you have to guarantee that all the data is being entered into the cube once and only once.

One of the practical issues in using the Analysis Services Processing task is how to automate the setting of an appropriate filter for an incremental update. If this filter is based on a date, a key value, or a batch value, it will have to be updated every day. Here are three suggestions:

- I think the easiest solution is to not use a filter at all, but rather to use a view for the `FactTable` property. Use a WHERE clause in the view to limit the incremental update to the appropriate values. You can use the `ALTER VIEW` command to change the view dynamically during the execution of the package or before the package is executed.
- You can execute the package from Visual Basic and change the task's `Filter` property after the package is loaded but before it is executed.

- You can modify the property with the Dynamic Properties task while the package is being executed. If you do this, you have to set the Dynamic Properties task and the Analysis Services Processing task to execute on the main package thread. You can do this in the Workflow Properties dialog for the step associated with each of the tasks.

  Unlike the properties of other tasks, you cannot dynamically modify the properties of the Analysis Services Processing task in an ActiveX Script task.

You can set additional cube processing options in the Cube Processing Settings dialog (see Figure 21.3), which you open with the Cube Settings button. No DTS properties are set in this dialog. When you open the dialog, the current settings of these properties are loaded from the cube structure. When you click OK, the properties of the cube are changed to reflect your choices.

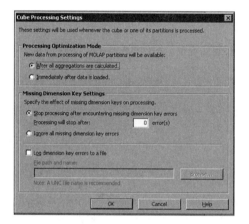

FIGURE 21.3
The Cube Processing Settings dialog gives you additional options.

The first section of this dialog allows you to make the processed cube available as soon as the data is loaded, before all the MOLAP aggregations have been calculated. If you choose this option, old aggregations can be presented to cube users when they're using new data. The advantage of using this setting is that it can give users quicker access to the new data. The two choices in this section correspond to the setting of Regular or Lazy Aggregations for the Processing Optimization Mode. You can set this property in the Analysis Manager, which is on the Advanced tab in the cube's Properties box.

The second section of the dialog gives you options for handling missing dimension keys. SQL Server 7.0 OLAP Services processing would fail if there were orphan records in the fact table—records with foreign key values that did not match the dimension table primary keys.

With SQL Server 2000 Analysis Services, you can choose what you want to do about missing dimension keys:

- You can stop processing when the first missing dimension key is found. This is the SQL Server 7.0 behavior.
- You can stop processing when a specified number of missing dimension keys are found.
- You can continue processing and ignore the orphan records.
- You can log the dimension key errors to a file.

In the Analysis Manager, you can make these choices on the Advanced tab in the cube's Properties box:

- Stop Processing On Key Errors
- Key Error Limit
- Key Error Log File

When you select a mining model, you can choose between a full process and refreshing the data. You also have the option of writing a training query, which is stored in the `TrainingQuery` property. Analysis Services will generate an appropriate query if you don't set the `TrainingQuery` property.

Using the Data Mining Prediction Query Task

There are three tabs in the Data Mining Prediction Query Task dialog. The first tab allows you to select a server, a database, and a mining model, as shown in Figure 21.4.

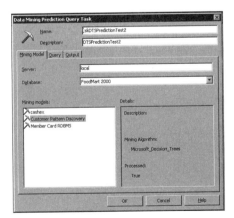

FIGURE 21.4
The Mining Model tab of the Data Mining Prediction Query Task dialog.

The Query tab of the dialog gives you a place to choose the data source for which you want to make a prediction and a box to write the prediction query. Prediction queries can be quite complex, as shown in Figure 21.5.

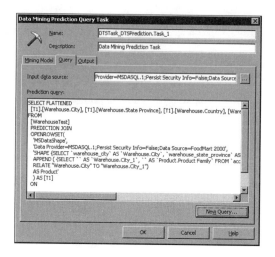

FIGURE 21.5

The Query tab of the Data Mining Prediction Query Task dialog shows the complexity of prediction queries.

Fortunately, the Query tab has a New Query button, which opens the Prediction Query Builder Wizard (see Figure 21.6). This can assist you in the process of writing a prediction query.

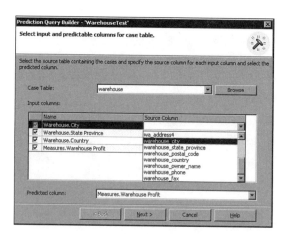

FIGURE 21.6

You can use the Prediction Query Builder Wizard to create a prediction query.

The following types of columns are displayed in the Prediction Query Builder Wizard:

- The key column is selected by default. It is grayed out, and you cannot remove it. You have to specify a source column from one of the case tables for the key column.
- You can choose whether or not to include any of the other input columns in the process of making the prediction. You have to specify a source column for all included input columns.
- You can choose the predicted column from the list of predicted columns that have been defined for this particular mining model.

The wizard presents one page for the case table and a page for each of the nested tables in the data mining model.

The Output tab lets you choose an output data source and an output table. The output table does not have to be an existing table. If it does not exist, the output table is created when the task is executed.

The properties of the Data Mining Prediction Query task all have descriptive names:

- `Name` and `Description` for the task as a whole.
- `Server`, `Database`, and `MiningModel` for the properties set on the first tab.
- `InputDatasource` and `PredictionQuery` for the second tab.
- `OutputDatasource` and `OutputTab` for the third tab.

NOTE

The behavior of the `MiningModel` property is a little unusual, but I don't think it's a problem.

This property is used as input information for the Prediction Query Builder Wizard. It does not affect the execution of the task at all. After you have built a prediction query, the name of the mining model is in the text of the query. Your chosen mining model will be used because it is specified in the query.

If you create a query with the wizard, select a different mining model on the first tab, and execute the step, the query that you have created will be executed. The new mining model that you have selected will be ignored. The new choice will only have an effect if you go back to the wizard to change the prediction query.

I've also noticed that you can't set the `MiningModel` property in Visual Basic code or in Disconnected Edit. The choice of a mining model is persistent, though, if you select it in the DTS Designer interface.

Creating the Analysis Services Processing Task in Visual Basic

You can find the code for fctCreateAnalysisServicesProcessingTask in the directory for Chapter 21 of the book's CD as a Visual Basic Project, with files CreateAnalysisServicesProcessingTask.vbp, CreateAnalysisServicesProcessingTask.frm, and CreateAnalysisServicesProcessingTask.bas.

The code for fctCreateAnalysisServicesProcessingTask is shown in Listing 21.1. The procedure needs some utility functions that are included with the code listings on the CD. The project requires references to the Microsoft DTSPackage Object Library and DTSOLAPProcess.

LISTING 21.1 The Visual Basic Code to Create an Analysis Services Processing Task

```
Option Explicit

Public Function fctCreateAnalysisServicesProcessingTask ( _
    pkg As DTS.Package2, _
    Optional sBaseName As String = "AnalysisServicesProcessingTask", _
    Optional sDataSource As String = "", _
    Optional sFactTable As String = "", _
    Optional sFilter As String = "", _
    Optional bIncrementallyUpdateDimensions As Boolean = False, _
    Optional iItemType As Integer = 0, _
    Optional iProcessOption As Integer = 0, _
    Optional sTrainingQuery As String = "", _
    Optional sTreeKey As String = "", _
    Optional sExistingConnectionName As String = "") As String

On Error GoTo ProcErr

Dim stp As DTS.Step2
Dim tsk As DTS.Task
Dim cus As DTSOlapProcess.Task

'Check to see if the selected Base name is unique
sBaseName = fctFindUniqueBaseName(pkg, sBaseName)

'Create task and custom task
Set tsk = pkg.Tasks.New("DTSOlapProcess.Task")
Set cus = tsk.CustomTask

With cus

    .Name = "tsk" & sBaseName
    .Description = sBaseName
```

LISTING 21.1   Continued

```
    .DataSource = sDataSource
    .FactTable = sFactTable
    .TreeKey = sTreeKey
    .Filter = sFilter
    .IncrementallyUpdateDimensions = bIncrementallyUpdateDimensions
    .ItemType = iItemType
    .ProcessOption = iProcessOption
    .TrainingQuery = sTrainingQuery


End With

pkg.Tasks.Add tsk

'Create step for task
Set stp = pkg.Steps.New
With stp
    .Name = "stp" & sBaseName
    .Description = sBaseName
    .TaskName = tsk.Name
End With
pkg.Steps.Add stp

fctCreateAnalysisServicesProcessingTask = stp.Name

Set tsk = Nothing
Set cus = Nothing
Set stp = Nothing

ProcExit:
  Exit Function
ProcErr:
  MsgBox Err.Number & " - " & Err.Description
  fctCreateAnalysisServicesProcessingTask = ""
  GoTo ProcExit

End Function
```

Creating the Data Mining Prediction Query Task in Visual Basic

You can find the code for fctCreateDataMiningQueryTask in the directory for Chapter 21 of the book's CD as a Visual Basic Project, with files CreateDataMiningPredictionTask.vbp, CreateDataMiningPredictionTask.frm, and CreateDataMiningPredictionTask.bas.

The code for fctCreateDataMiningQueryTask is shown in Listing 22.2. The procedure needs some utility functions that are included with the code listings on the CD. The project requires references to the Microsoft DTSPackage Object Library and DTSPrediction.

LISTING 21.2   The Visual Basic Code to Create a Data Mining Prediction Query Task

```
Option Explicit

Public Function fctCreateDataMiningQueryTask( _
    pkg As DTS.Package2, _
    Optional sBaseName As String = "DataMiningQueryTask", _
    Optional sCatalog As String = "", _
    Optional sDataSource As String = "local", _
    Optional sInputDataSource As String = "", _
    Optional sMiningModel As String = "", _
    Optional sOutputDatasource As String = "", _
    Optional sOutputTable As String = "Prediction Results", _
    Optional sPredictionQuery As String = "", _
    Optional sExistingConnectionName As String = "") As String
On Error GoTo ProcErr

Dim stp As DTS.Step2
Dim tsk As DTS.Task
Dim cus As DTSPrediction.Task

'Check to see if the selected Base name is unique
sBaseName = fctFindUniqueBaseName(pkg, sBaseName)

'Create task and custom task
Set tsk = pkg.Tasks.New("DTSPrediction.Task")
Set cus = tsk.CustomTask

With cus

    .Name = "tsk" & sBaseName
    .Description = sBaseName
    .Database = sCatalog
    .InputDatasource = sInputDataSource

    .OutputDatasource = sOutputDatasource
    .OutputTable = sOutputTable
    .PredictionQuery = sPredictionQuery
    .Server = sDataSource
```

LISTING 21.2   Continued

```
      .MiningModel = sMiningModel
End With

pkg.Tasks.Add tsk

'Create step for task
Set stp = pkg.Steps.New
With stp
      .Name = "stp" & sBaseName
      .Description = sBaseName
      .TaskName = tsk.Name
End With
pkg.Steps.Add stp

fctCreateDataMiningQueryTask = stp.Name

Set tsk = Nothing
Set cus = Nothing
Set stp = Nothing

ProcExit:
  Exit Function
ProcErr:
  MsgBox Err.Number & " - " & Err.Description
  fctCreateDataMiningQueryTask = ""
  GoTo ProcExit

End Function
```

Conclusion

If you're using Microsoft's Analysis Services, you will probably want to use the two tasks described in this chapter. They're convenient tools for automating the processing of cubes and mining models, as well as the running of prediction queries.

The Execute Process Task

IN THIS CHAPTER

The Execute Process task is one of the least complex of all the DTS tasks. Its only purpose is to run an executable program or a batch file.

When to Use the Execute Process Task

The importance of the Execute Process task is in the way it integrates DTS packages with other applications and batch processes. Many companies have existing programs that transfer data. You can use DTS as a control panel to run all of your data transformation applications. You can use the various DTS tasks when you want to manipulate data in a new way. You can use the Execute Process task to coordinate your existing data manipulation applications with the rest of what you are doing with DTS.

Consider the following specific ways of using the Execute Process task.

Bulk Copying from SQL Server to a Text File

If you are creating a new bulk copy operation to load SQL Server, I suggest that you use the Bulk Insert task. But you can't use it if you want to bulk copy data out of SQL Server. However, you can integrate that bulk copy into DTS by using the Execute SQL task. Use the bcp command-line utility to do the bulk copying.

Here's a sample of how to do that. Use the following values in the Execute Process Task dialog:

- Win32 Process—bcp
- Parameters—out "SELECT au_lname, au_fname as FullName FROM pubs..authors ORDER BY au_lname" queryout C:\Authors.txt -c -S(local) -T

Figure 22.1 shows the Execute Process Task Properties dialog with the properties set to execute this bulk copy.

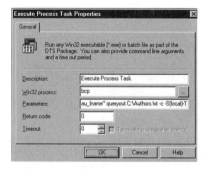

FIGURE 22.1

You can use the Execute Process task to bulk copy data out of SQL Server into a text file.

Executing a Batch File Containing osql and/or bcp Commands

If you have existing bcp commands in batch files, whether moving data into or out of SQL Server, you can keep on using those batch files with your DTS package by calling them from the Execute Process task.

You can also use osql, the SQL Server command-line utility for executing SQL commands, in these batch files. For example, you could write a batch file that creates a view, uses that view to bulk copy data out of SQL Server, and then drops the view. The file would look like this:

```
osql /S(local) /E /dpubs /Q"create view dbo.vwAuthorName(fullname)
➥as select au_fname + ' ' + au_lname from pubs.dbo.authors"
bcp "pubs.dbo.vwAuthorName" out C:\Temp\AuthorName.txt /c /T /S(local)
osql /S(local) /E /dpubs /Q"drop view dbo.vwAuthorName"
```

If you save this batch file as c:\temp\testdts.bat, you would then enter that filename in the Win32 Process of the Execute Process task. You would not use any parameters for the task.

Running Other Data Movement or Manipulation Applications

You may have external programs that you need to run before or after some of your DTS tasks, such as

- Specialized FTP processes that cannot easily be adapted to the DTS FTP task.
- Programs that unzip text files.
- Applications that convert binary files to text.
- Batch files that call OLTP systems to export data.
- Programs that process large text files, such as SyncSort.
- Customized parsing programs.

Executing DTSRun

You can execute DTS packages from the Execute Process task by using the DTSRun command-line utility:

```
DTSRun /E /N PackageName /F c:\temp\LoadEmployee.dts
```

> **NOTE**
>
> You have greater control in executing one package from another when you use the Execute Package task.

Creating the Task and Setting Its Properties

You can create the Execute Process task in the DTS Designer or in code. Neither of the DTS wizards creates an Execute Process task.

The Execute Process Task Properties dialog has only one tab. The dialog lets you set five of the task's seven properties. You have to use code or Disconnected Edit to view or modify the Name and FailPackageOnTimeout properties.

The Execute Process Task Properties

Here are the task's properties:

- Name—The name of the task. Cannot be viewed or modified in the Execute Process Task Properties dialog.

- Description—The description of the task.

- ProcessCommandLine—The command line that is executed. You enter the command line in two boxes in the dialog—the Win32 Process and the parameters. The DTS Designer concatenates the two values to create the value for this property.

- SuccessReturnCode—The code that is expected for a successful execution of the application. If the application returns a different code, the Execute Process task is marked as failed. The default return code is 0.

- Timeout—The number of seconds that the Execute Process task waits for a return code from the application. If no return code is received within this time period, the task is marked as failed. The default timeout value is 0, which means that the task will wait indefinitely.

- TerminateProcessAfterTimeout—If you specify a value for a time out, you can also choose to terminate the application that was executed when that timeout occurs. Whether or not you terminate the application on timeout, the DTS package will continue its execution. The default value for this property is FALSE.

- FailPackageOnTimeout—This property causes the whole DTS package to be terminated if a timeout occurs in the Execute Process task. This value cannot be set or viewed in the dialog. The default value is FALSE.

The GetExpandedProcessCommandLine Method of the CreateProcess2 Object

In code, the Execute Process task is implemented by the CreateProcess2 object. This object inherits all the properties of the CreateProcess object.

The `CreateProcess2` object adds no new properties, but it does add one method. This method, `GetExpandedProcessCommandLine`, can be used to return a command line with all parameter variables expanded.

For example, you could have a `ProcessCommandLine` property of

```
bcp pubs.dbo.authors out %TEMP%\authors.txt /c /T /S(local)
```

The `GetExpandedProcessCommandLine` method would return a value like this:

```
bcp pubs.dbo.authors out C:\Temp\authors.txt /c /T /S(local)
```

Creating the Task in Visual Basic

I have created a Visual Basic procedure, `fctCreateExecuteProcessTask`, that creates a connection, a step, a task, and a custom task for an Execute Process task. All the properties of the task can be set with this procedure.

The `fctCreateExecuteProcessTask` function is used in the DTSPackageGenerator utility that is included with this book. You can also find the procedure in the directory for Chapter 22 as a Visual Basic Project, with files CreateExecuteProcessTask.vbp, CreateExecuteProcessTask.frm, and CreateExecuteProcessTask.bas.

The code for `fctCreateExecuteProcessTask` is shown in Listing 22.1. The procedure needs some utility functions that are included with the code listings on the CD.

LISTING 22.1   The Visual Basic Code to Create an Execute Process Task

```
Option Explicit

Public Function fctCreateExecuteProcessTask( _
    pkg As DTS.Package2, _
    Optional sBaseName As String = "ExecuteProcessTest", _
    Optional sProcessCommandLine As String = "", _
    Optional lSuccessReturnCode As Long = 0, _
    Optional lTimeout As Long = 0, _
    Optional bTerminateProcessAfterTimeout As Boolean = False, _
    Optional bFailPackageOnTimeout As Boolean = False)

On Error GoTo ProcErr

Dim stp As DTS.Step2
Dim tsk As DTS.Task
Dim cus As DTS.CreateProcessTask2
```

LISTING 22.1   Continued

```
'Check to see if the selected Base name is unique
sBaseName = fctFindUniqueBaseName(pkg, sBaseName)

'Create task and custom task
Set tsk = pkg.Tasks.New("DTSCreateProcessTask")
Set cus = tsk.CustomTask
With cus

    .Name = "tsk" & sBaseName
    .Description = sBaseName
    .ProcessCommandLine = sProcessCommandLine
    .SuccessReturnCode = lSuccessReturnCode
    .Timeout = lTimeout
    .TerminateProcessAfterTimeout = bTerminateProcessAfterTimeout
    .FailPackageOnTimeout = bFailPackageOnTimeout

End With

pkg.Tasks.Add tsk

'Create step for task
Set stp = pkg.Steps.New
With stp
    .Name = "stp" & sBaseName
    .Description = sBaseName
    .TaskName = tsk.Name
End With
pkg.Steps.Add stp

fctCreateExecuteProcessTask = stp.Name

Set tsk = Nothing
Set cus = Nothing
Set stp = Nothing

ProcExit:
  Exit Function
ProcErr:
  MsgBox Err.Number & " - " & Err.Description
  fctCreateExecuteProcessTask = ""
  GoTo ProcExit
End Function
```

Conclusion

The Execute Process task is simple, but it is a key player in the integration of DTS with your other data manipulation applications.

This is the last chapter discussing the DTS tasks. Part V continues with a discussion of the DTS package as a whole and the steps that control the flow of the tasks.

DTS Packages and Steps

PART V

The DTS Package and Its Properties

IN THIS CHAPTER

The package is at the highest level in the DTS object hierarchy. You can't create tasks, steps, connections, or global variables outside of a package. It's the DTS level that is used for saving, loading, and executing a particular set of DTS steps that have their associated tasks.

As with many of the DTS tasks, the DTS `Package` object has a new implementation in SQL Server 2000 as the `Package2` object. This object inherits the properties and methods of the `Package object` and adds several new ones.

This chapter describes several facets of the DTS package as a whole. See Chapter 24, "Steps and Precedence Constraints," for a discussion of transactions and thread execution in a DTS package and its steps.

Identifying DTS Packages

A DTS package, like most other DTS objects, has a `Name` property and a `Description` property. The name is set when the package is first created and cannot be changed. You can change the description as often as you like.

Every time a DTS package is saved, a new version of the package is created. You can view the version history of a DTS package stored in the repository or in SQL Server by right-clicking on the name of the package in the Enterprise Manager and selecting Versions. The DTS Package Versions dialog is shown in Figure 23.1.

FIGURE 23.1

The DTS Package Versions dialog shows all the versions that have been created for a particular DTS package.

This dialog gives you the option of opening any version of the package for editing. For packages saved in SQL Server, you also have the option of deleting any of the versions.

> **NOTE**
>
> When you choose a particular version of a DTS package for editing and then save your changes, you don't overwrite the previous version. Instead, a new version is saved. The only way you can get rid of previous versions is by explicitly deleting them.

You can delete particular versions of a package saved in the repository or in SQL Server by using the `RemoveFromRepository` method or the `RemoveFromSQLServer` method. These methods remove one version of a package. If the version to be removed is not specified, the most recent one is removed.

Packages and their versions are identified by 16-byte globally unique identifiers (GUIDs). The Package GUID and Version GUID are displayed on the General tab of the DTS Package Properties dialog (see Figure 23.2).

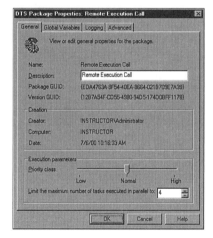

FIGURE 23.2
The DTS Package Properties dialog displays all the identification information for a package.

When a package is first created, the two GUID values will be the same. When later versions are created, the Package GUID remains the same and the Version GUID is always changed.

Either the Package GUID or the Version GUID can be used to identify a package for retrieval or deletion. When the Package GUID is used by itself, only the most recent version of the package is referenced. If the Version GUID is used, any of the package's versions can be referenced.

These values are implemented as the PackageID and VersionID properties of the Package object. These are read-only properties that use the 128-bit uniqueidentifier data type.

Storing DTS Packages

DTS packages can be saved in four different locations, each of which has its advantages:

- SQL Server storage provides the fastest saving and retrieval speed.
- Meta Data Services storage provides the ability to save and track meta data.
- File system storage allows DTS packages to be easily shared between users.
- Visual Basic storage provides programmatic access to DTS objects and properties.

The Save DTS Package dialog has a list box with the four DTS package storage options. The other choices you make in this dialog change as you choose a different storage location. Figure 23.3 shows the dialog as it appears when you are saving to Meta Data Services.

FIGURE 23.3

The Save DTS Package dialog presents choices to the user that differ depending on which storage method is selected.

You can save, retrieve, and delete packages in the different storage locations by using methods of the Package object. There is also one method, SaveAs, that is not implemented in the interface but can be used programmatically. This method saves a package with a new name but does not store this new package in any form of persistent storage. The SaveAs method has one parameter—NewName.

Saving DTS Packages to SQL Server

The definition of a package saved to SQL Server is stored in the sysdtspackages table in the msdb system database. The image data type is used to save the package.

Here are the details on saving and retrieving packages when saving to SQL Server:

- Packages saved to one instance of SQL Server must have unique names.
- You can assign a User password, an Owner password, or both to the package.
- Users must have permission to access the msdb database to save or retrieve the DTS package.

DTS packages are saved to the SQL Server with the SaveToSQLServer method of the Package object. SaveToSQLServer has the following parameters:

- ServerName—The server where the package should be stored.
- ServerUserName—The logon name for the server specified in ServerName.
- ServerPassword—The password for the ServerUserName logon.
- Flags—Security choice. Described below.
- PackageOwnerPassword—Password needed to view or edit package structure.
- PackageOperatorPassword—Password needed to execute package.
- PackageCategoryID—Not currently being used.
- pVarPersistStgOfHost—Pointer to the screen layout information for the package.
- bReusePasswords—Whether or not package passwords are allowed to be reused.

> **NOTE**
>
> The save and load methods of the package object both have a parameter called pVarPersistStgOfHost, which is a pointer to the screen layout of the package as it appears in the Package Designer. This pointer cannot be used when saving packages from VBScript, Visual Basic, or Visual C++. It is only available for internal use by the Package Designer.
>
> The visual representation of a package is always lost when you save a package programmatically. That's unfortunate if you've gone to a lot of work making all the tasks and precedence constraints appear in a logical arrangement. The next time you load the package, the Package Designer will apply the default arrangement, which often is not very visually appealing—especially if there are a lot of tasks.
>
> There are hints that Microsoft might give developers the ability to save and re-create the visual representation in the future. For now, don't spend too much time making your packages look nice if you're planning on saving them programmatically.

23

THE DTS PACKAGE AND ITS PROPERTIES

Table 23.1 contains two storage flags, which present the choice between using SQL Server authentication (the default) or a trusted connection.

TABLE 23.1 Constants Used for the `Flags` Parameter of the `SaveToSQLServer` Method

Constant	Value	Meaning
DTSSQLStgFlag_Default	0	Use SQL Server Security
DTSSQLStgFlag_UseTrustedConnection	256	Use Trusted Connection

The `Package2` object has a new method called `SaveToSQLServerAs` that is used to save a package with a new name and a new Package ID. This method has the same parameters as `SaveToSQLServer`, except for an additional first parameter called `NewName`.

The `LoadFromSQLServer` method is used to retrieve a package that is stored in SQL Server. The `RemoveFromSQLServer` method is used to delete a package from SQL Server storage. Their parameters are similar to those used by the saving methods:

- `ServerName`
- `ServerUserName`
- `ServerPassword`
- `Flags`—Optional parameter. Uses the constants in Table 23.1
- `PackagePassword`—Not used for `RemoveFromSQLServer`.
- `PackageGUID`—Optional. Not needed if a `PackageVersionGUID` or a `PackageName` is provided.
- `PackageVersionGUID`—Optional. If the `PackageVersionGUID` is not provided, the most recent version of the package is loaded or removed.
- `PackageName`—Optional. Not needed if either of the GUID parameters is provided.
- `pVarPersistStgOfHost`—Pointer to the screen layout information for the package. Not used for `RemoveFromSQLServer`.

Listing 23.1 has a sample of Visual Basic code that creates a package, saves it in SQL Server storage, loads it from SQL Server, changes its description, and saves it to SQL Server with a different name. The original package is then deleted. You can find this code on the CD in a file called SaveAndRetrieveMethods.bas. To use it in a VB project, you have to include a reference to the Microsoft DTSPackage Object Library.

LISTING 23.1 Code That Illustrates How to Work with Packages Stored in SQL Server

```
Sub subDTSSaveAndRetrieveMethods()
Dim pkg As New DTS.Package2
Dim FirstPackageID As String
```

LISTING 23.1   Continued

```
pkg.Name = "Test Save And Retrieve Methods"

'Save to the local server
'Use integrated security
pkg.SaveToSQLServer "(local)", , , DTSSQLStgFlag_UseTrustedConnection

pkg.LoadFromSQLServer "(local)", , , _
    DTSSQLStgFlag_UseTrustedConnection, , , _
    , "Test Save And Retrieve Methods"
FirstPackageID = pkg.PackageID

pkg.Description = "Description to be saved in second package."
pkg.SaveToSQLServerAs "Renamed Package", "(local)", , , _
    DTSSQLStgFlag_UseTrustedConnection

pkg.RemoveFromSQLServer "(local)", , , _
    DTSSQLStgFlag_UseTrustedConnection, _
    FirstPackageID

Set pkg = Nothing
End Sub
```

Saving DTS Packages in Meta Data Services

Microsoft Meta Data Services provides a standard method for different products to share information. The package's characteristics are available through the interfaces provided by the repository's information models. See Chapter 29, "Integrating DTS with Meta Data Services."

Here are the details on saving and retrieving packages when using the repository:

- As with packages saved to SQL Server, packages saved to a single instance of Meta Data Services must have unique names.
- When saving to Meta Data Services, there is a button on the Save DTS Package dialog to bring up the Scanning Options dialog. These options are also discussed in Chapter 29.
- DTS package encryption is not available for packages saved to Meta Data Services.
- By default, Meta Data Services is located in the SQL Server msdb database. If you create a package using Visual Basic, you can specify a different Meta Data Services database.
- Users must have permission to access the database that is hosting the instance of Meta Data Services that is being used.

23

THE DTS
PACKAGE AND ITS
PROPERTIES

The methods for working with Meta Data Services packages are similar to those for SQL Server packages:

- SaveToRepository
- SaveToRepositoryAs
- LoadFromRepository
- RemoveFromRepository

Here are the parameters of the SaveToRepository method:

- RepositoryServerName—The server where this instance of Meta Data Services is stored.
- RepositoryDatabaseName—The database where this instance of Meta Data Services is located.
- RepositoryUserName—The logon name for the server specified in RepositoryServerName.
- RepositoryUserPassword—The password for the RepositoryUserName logon.
- Flags—Security choice. Same as SaveToSQLServer, except the constants used are DTSReposFlag_Default and DTSReposFlag_UseTrustedConnection.
- CategoryID—Not currently being used.
- pVarPersistStgOfHost—Pointer to the screen layout information for the package.

Storing DTS Packages in the File System

DTS can save one or more packages in a single COM-structured storage file. Each saved package can have one or more versions, all stored in the same file.

Packages stored in files are not displayed in the Enterprise Manager, as are the packages stored in SQL Server or in the default Meta Data Services location. To retrieve a package from a file, right-click on Data Transformation Services in the Console Tree and choose Open Package. A Select File dialog appears. After you have selected a *.dts file, the packages and versions in that particular file are displayed in the Select Package dialog, as shown in Figure 23.4.

FIGURE 23.4

The Select Package dialog showing the packages and their versions.

Here are the details on saving and retrieving packages when saving to a file:

- The naming rules are different for DTS packages stored in files. You can have many packages with the same name in one file. This is in addition to having different versions of one package, of course. The different packages are distinguished by their Package GUID.
- If you want the package to be encrypted, you can provide an Owner password, a User Password, or both.
- To use a package stored in a file, a user must have the appropriate file system permissions.

There is no method to delete a package or a version of a package from a file. The other methods are similar to the SQL Server and Meta Data Services options:

- `SaveToStorageFile`
- `SaveToStorageFileAs`
- `LoadFromStorageFile`

`SaveToStorageFile` has fewer parameters than the comparable methods for the other storage types:

- `UNCFile`—File name to be used in saving the package. Microsoft recommends using a Uniform Naming Convention (UNC) filename, but that is not required.
- `OwnerPassword`— Password needed to view or edit package structure.
- `OperatorPassword`—Password needed to execute package.
- `pVarPersistStgOfHost`—Pointer to the screen layout information for the package.
- `bReusePasswords`—Determines whether or not package passwords can be reused.

Saving DTS Packages as Visual Basic Files

The fourth way to save a DTS package is to save it as a Visual Basic code module. This type of saving is very different from the other three:

- There is no versioning capability.
- There are no security options unless you apply file-level security.
- You don't have any methods to restore a package from this type of storage. If you store a package as a Visual Basic code file, you have to load that file into Visual Basic to re-create it.
- You don't even have a method to save the package. The Package Designer implements the save to VB internally without using the DTS object model.

> **CAUTION**
>
> If you are developing a package with the Package Designer and choose Save To VB, the package will be saved to the code file. If that file already exists, you will receive a message asking if you want to overwrite the previous file.
>
> The next time you select the Save button, nothing happens. For the other three saving choices, a new version is created. But when you save to VB, the Save button does not work. It appears that the Save operation is completed successfully. No error is returned. But the current version of the package is not saved at all.
>
> You have to select Save As, and if you then select Save to VB or any of the other choices, your package will again be saved.

Storage in a Visual Basic file has several advantages:

- It allows you to use a text editor to modify names throughout a package.
- It gives you a starting point for creating, modifying, and executing DTS packages from Visual Basic.
- It can help you understand the programmatic structure of your package.

The structure of the Visual Basic file that Save to VB generates is discussed in Chapter 26, "Managing Packages with Visual Basic and Stored Procedures."

> **NOTE**
>
> Save to VB is a new feature in SQL Server 2000. It is based on a utility called ScriptPkg.exe that was included on the installation CD with SQL Server 7.0.

Encrypting DTS Packages

DTS package security differs depending on the package storage location. A DTS package saved to SQL Server or to a file can be given an Owner password, a User password, or both passwords. If one or both of the passwords is assigned, the package is encrypted. The encryption includes all the objects, collections, and properties in the packages except for Name, Description, PackageID, VersionID, and CreationDate, which are used to identify packages for retrieval.

When a person attempts to retrieve an encrypted package, he must supply the password. The two passwords give the following permissions:

- The Owner password gives the right to execute the package, as well as the right to view and edit the package's objects and properties.
- The User password gives the right to execute the package, but not to view or edit its objects and properties.

Retrieving Information About Packages

You can retrieve information programmatically about the packages that are stored on a particular SQL Server, in a particular instance of Meta Data Services, or in a particular storage file without opening the packages at all. This is useful, especially when you want to obtain a list of names, versions, and IDs of all the available DTS packages.

The DTS `Application` object is used to provide a variety of information about the system and DTS packages:

- Chapter 30, "Programming with the DTS Object Model," discusses the system information available through this object.
- The next section in this chapter, "Package Logs and Error Files," describes how to retrieve package logging information.
- Chapter 29, "Integrating DTS with Meta Data Services," describes how to retrieve lineage information.
- This section discusses how you can use the `Application` object to retrieve information about SQL Server and Meta Data Services packages.

The `SavedPackageInfos` collection of the `Package2` object is used to retrieve information about the packages stored in a particular storage file. Since saving a package to VB creates a separate file with no versioning, there are no comparable strategies for packages saved in that way.

Package Stored in SQL Server

By using the `Application` object, you can gain a reference to the `PackageInfo` object for each version of every package stored on a particular SQL Server. The `PackageInfo` object contains this subset of the `Package2` object's properties:

- `Name` and `Description`
- `PackageID` and `VersionID`
- `Owner`

23

PACKAGE AND ITS
THE DTS
PROPERTIES

- `PackageType`
- `CreationDate`

The `PackageInfo` object contains additional information that is not contained in the `Package2` object properties:

- `PackageDataSize`—The amount of storage space taken up by the package.
- `IsOwner`—Whether or not the user currently accessing the information is the same as the user indicated by the `Owner` property.
- `Parent`—A reference to the parent of the `PackageInfo` object, i.e. the `PackageInfos` collection.

Obtaining a Reference to the `PackageInfo` Object

You obtain this information through the following steps, shown here in VBScript code that could be used in an ActiveX Script. This code is on the CD in a DTS package stored in a file called GetDTSInfo.dts.

1. Declare needed variables:

   ```
   Dim DTSApp, PkgSQL, PkgInfos, info, prp, msg
   ```

2. Create the `Application` object:

   ```
   Set DTSApp = CreateObject("DTS.Application")
   ```

3. Use the `GetPackageSQLServer` method to log on to a specific SQL Server and obtain a reference to a `PackageSQLServer` object. Four parameters are required—`ServerName`, `UserName`, `Password`, and `ConnectionFlags`:

   ```
   Set PkgSQL = DTSApp.GetPackageSQLServer("(local)", "", "". _
           DTSSQLStgFlag_UseTrustedConnection)
   ```

4. Use the `EnumPackageInfos` method of the `PackageSQLServer` object to build a `PackageInfos` collection. This method is discussed in more detail below. To retrieve all packages and versions on a Server, you would use the following syntax:

   ```
   Set PkgInfos = PkgSQL.EnumPackageInfos("", True, "")
   ```

5. Use the `Next` method of the `PkgInfos` collection to reference each of the `PackageInfo` objects. You can use `For Each` to examine all the properties of each of the objects:

   ```
   Set info = PkgInfos.Next

   Do Until PkgInfos.EOF
       msg = ""
       For Each prp in info.Properties
           msg = msg & prp.Name & vbTab & prp.Value & vbCrLf
   ```

```
        Next
        Msgbox msg,, "PackageInfo information for " & info.Name
        set info = PkgInfos.Next
    Loop
```

Using the `EnumPackageInfos` Method and the `PackageInfos` Collection

The `EnumPackageInfos` method adds the desired `PackageInfo` objects into the `PackageInfos` collection. You have several options regarding the content of this collection. You make these choices in the parameters of the `EnumPackageInfos` method:

- `PackageName`—You can limit the `PackageInfos` collection to information about one package by specifying a name.

- `ReturnLatest`—If `TRUE`, a `PackageInfo` object will be created for the most recent package version. If `FALSE`, separate `PackageInfo` objects will be created for each version.

- `PackageID`—You can also limit the `PackageInfos` collection to information about one package by specifying a package ID.

You are required to include all the parameters. You can use an empty string for the `PackageName` or `PackageID`. If you use an empty string for both `PackageName` and `PackageID`, the collection will include `PackageInfo` objects for all the SQL Server packages on the server.

You can only move forward through the `PackageInfos` collection. You cannot reference the members of the `PackageInfos` collection by their positions in the collection.

The collection has one method, `Next`, and one property, `EOF`. Instead of using the `For Next` syntax illustrated above, you could use this property and method to look at each of the `PackageInfo` objects:

```
Set info = PkgInfos.Next
Do Until PkgInfos.EOF
    Msgbox info.Name
    Set info = PkgInfos.Next
Loop
```

Finding a Unique Name for a New Package

Listing 23.2 shows a sample of VB code that uses the `PackageInfos` collection to find a unique name for a new DTS package. If the desired name already exists, a number is appended to the name and that name is checked. The process is repeated until a unique name is found. You can find this code on the CD in a file called UniquePackageName.bas. To use it in a VB project, you have to include a reference to the Microsoft DTSPackage Object Library.

LISTING 23.2   This Code Generates a Unique Package Name by Appending an Appropriate Number on a Base Name

```
Private Function fctFindUniquePackageName( _
        sBaseName As String, sServer As String, _
        sUserID As String, sPassword As String) As String
On Error GoTo ProcErr

Dim DTSApp As New DTS.Application
Dim PkgSQL As DTS.PackageSQLServer
Dim PkgInfos As DTS.PackageInfos
Dim info As DTS.PackageInfo

Dim lSuffix As Long
Dim sModifiedBaseName As String
Dim bDupeFound As Boolean

'Get PackageSQLServer object
If sUserID = "" Then
    Set PkgSQL = DTSApp.GetPackageSQLServer(sServer, _
        sUserID, sPassword, DTSSQLStgFlag_UseTrustedConnection)
Else
    Set PkgSQL = DTSApp.GetPackageSQLServer(sServer, _
        sUserID, sPassword, DTSSQLStgFlag_Default)
End If

'Initialize
sModifiedBaseName = sBaseName
lSuffix = 0

'Check for duplicate. If found, increment suffix and try again.
Do

    'Must reinitialize the list each time.
    Set PkgInfos = PkgSQL.EnumPackageInfos("", False, "")
    bDupeFound = False

    For Each info In PkgInfos

        If info.Name = sModifiedBaseName Then
            lSuffix = lSuffix + 1
            sModifiedBaseName = sBaseName & CStr(lSuffix)
            bDupeFound = True
```

LISTING 23.2   Continued

```
        Exit For
    End If

Next info

Set info = Nothing
Set PkgInfos = Nothing

Loop Until bDupeFound = False

fctFindUniquePackageName = sModifiedBaseName

ProcExit:
  Exit Function
ProcErr:
  MsgBox Err.Number & " - " & Err.Description
  fctFindUniquePackageName = ""
  GoTo ProcExit
End Function
```

> **TIP**
>
> When I was writing the code in Listing 23.2, I discovered that it was very important to set the `PackageInfo` and `PackageInfos` variables to `Nothing` before using the `EnumPackageInfos` a second time. Without this assignment to `Nothing`, the code worked but ran very slowly.

Package Stored in Meta Data Services

Obtaining information about packages stored in a particular instance of Meta Data Services is very similar to obtaining the properties for a package stored in a particular instance of SQL Server. You have the same `PackageInfos` collection, `PackageInfo` object, and properties of the `PackageInfo` object.

Instead of using the `GetPackageSQLServer` method, you use the `GetPackageRepository` method. Instead of using the `PackageSQLServer` object, you use the `PackageRepository` object. Here is the VBScript code for retrieving information about packages stored in a particular instance of Meta Data Services. You can find this code in GetDTSInfo.dts:

```
Dim DTSApp, PkgRepos, PkgInfos, info, prp, msg

Set DTSApp = CreateObject("DTS.Application")

'Parameters - ServerName, DatabaseName, UserName, _
    'Password, ConnectionFlags
'Must supply Meta Data Services database name, if it is not msdb.
Set PkgRepos = DTSApp.GetPackageRepository("(local)", "", "", "", _
    DTSReposFlag_UseTrustedConnection)

'Retrieve all versions of all packages
Set PkgInfos = PkgRepos.EnumPackageInfos("", True, "")

'Code is identical after here
Set info = PkgInfos.Next

Do Until PkgInfos.EOF
    msg = ""
    For Each prp in info.Properties
        msg = msg & prp.Name & vbTab & prp.Value & vbCrLf
    Next
    Msgbox msg,, "PackageInfo information for " & info.Name
    set info = PkgInfos.Next
Loop
```

Package Stored in Files

You don't use the Application object to get information about packages stored in files. Instead, you can use the Package2 object to query the contents of any particular file being used to store DTS packages. Here is how you can access the information using an ActiveX Script inside DTS. You can find this code in GetDTSInfo.dts.

1. Declare variables:

   ```
   Dim pkg, PkgInfos, info, msg
   ```

2. Obtain a reference to a DTS Package object. You do not have to load a package:

   ```
   set pkg = CreateObject("DTS.Package2")
   ```

3. Use the GetSavedPackageInfos method to obtain a reference to the SavedPackageInfos collection for a specific storage file. The only parameter for the method is the path of the file:

   ```
   On Error Resume Next
   Set PkgInfos = pkg.GetSavedPackageInfos("c:\temp\GetDTSInfo.dts")
   If Err.Number <> 0 Then
       msgbox "The file c:\temp\GetDTSInfo.dts does not exist."
   End If
   ```

4. Use `For Each` to obtain a reference to each `SavedPackageInfo` object in the collection. The object does not have a `Properties` property, so you have to reference each property by name to retrieve its value. All the properties are retrieved in this code sample:

```
for each info in PkgInfos
    msg = ""
    msg = msg & "Name" & vbTab & info.PackageName & " Package" & vbCrLf
    msg = msg & "Description" & vbTab & info.Description & vbCrLf
    msg = msg & "IsVersionEncrypted" & vbTab & _
                    info.IsVersionEncrypted & vbCrLf
    msg = msg & "PackageCreationDate"  & vbTab & _
                    info.PackageCreationDate & vbCrLf
    msg = msg & "PackageID"  & vbTab &  info.PackageID & vbCrLf
    msg = msg & "PackageName"  & vbTab & info.PackageName & vbCrLf
    msg = msg & "VersionID"  & vbTab & info.VersionID & vbCrLf
    msg = msg & "VersionSaveDate"  & vbTab & info.VersionSaveDate
    Msgbox msg,, "SavedPackageInfo information for " & info.PackageName
next
```

You can also use the `Item` method of the `SavedPackageInfos` collection to retrieve each object by its index number. The collection also has a `Count` property so you know how many objects are in the collection.

```
For idx = 1 to PkgInfos.Count
    Set info = PkgInfos.Item(idx)
    msgbox info.PackageName
Next
```

Package Logs and Error Files

DTS allows you to log information about the execution of your packages. This information has three components:

- Package information—Package and version identification, time of execution, and error conditions.

- Step information—Name and description of each step, time of execution, and success or failure.

- Task information—Additional information about the task. There can be one, many, or no records for one execution of a task.

You can save this log information for your packages no matter where those packages are stored.

> **NOTE**
>
> A portion of the information saved in the package log is also stored if you save a package to Meta Data Services and the LineageOptions property is set to write the execution information to Meta Data Services. Storing and retrieving this information is discussed in Chapter 29, "Integrating DTS with Meta Data Services."

Listing 23.3 shows what the log information looks like. This is an example of the execution of a package with two steps. The first step succeeded and the second failed. The tasks for both steps wrote additional information to the log.

LISTING 23.3   A Sample of the DTS Log Information

```
The execution of the following DTS Package failed:

Error Source: Microsoft Data Transformation Services (DTS) Package
Error Description:Package failed because
        Step 'CDW Databases Task Step' failed.
Error code: 80040428\Error Help File:sqldts80.hlp
Error Help Context ID:700

Package Name: CDW_Server1_Server2_3
Package Description: Copy Database Wizard Package
Package ID: {AE741877-0433-43C2-A5DB-09BC33ECD47A}
Package Version: {DA771A77-B889-41C1-8ECB-E34E474B8905}
Package Execution Lineage: {C7F11DBB-FAFB-42CD-BDC8-09FAFC6E7176}
Executed On: Server2
Executed By: Administrator
Execution Started: 7/13/2000 12:57:01 PM
Execution Completed: 7/13/2000 12:57:34 PM
Total Execution Time: 32.907 seconds

Package Steps execution information:

Step 'CDW Errors Task Step' succeeded
Step Execution Started: 7/13/2000 12:57:10 PM
Step Execution Completed: 7/13/2000 12:57:12 PM
Total Step Execution Time: 1.297 seconds
Progress count in Step: 0
Task Log for this step:
-----Start Task Log-----

Error = 1 (00000001), Description = Script    Error    50003
Error = 1 (00000001), Description = Script    Error    50004
```

LISTING 23.3   Continued

```
Error = 1 (00000001), Description = Transfer    Error    50003
Error = 1 (00000001), Description = Transfer    Error    50004

-----End Task Log-----
Step 'CDW Databases Task Step' failed

Step Error Source: Microsoft Data Transformation Services (DTS) Package
Step Error Description:Unspecified error

Step Error code: 80004005
Step Error Help File:sqldts80.hlp
Step Error Help Context ID:1100

Step Execution Started: 7/13/2000 12:57:12 PM
Step Execution Completed: 7/13/2000 12:57:34 PM
Total Step Execution Time: 22.219 seconds
Progress count in Step: 0
Task Log for this step:
-----Start Task Log-----

Error = 1 (00000001), Description =
        Begin to copy the database DTSTest
Error = 1 (00000001),
        Description = Put the database DTSTest in single user mode
Error = 1 (00000001), Description =
        Try to detach the database DTSTest
Error = 1 (00000001), Description =
        Successfully detached the database DTSTest
Error = 0 (00000000), Description =
        Failed to copy file \\Server1\DATA\DTSTest_Data.MDF
Error = 1 (00000001), Description =
        Successfully attach the database DTSTest on source
-----End Task Log-----
```

You can save the log information in three different places. You can choose none, one, all, or any combination of these options. The same logging information is stored for each option:

- You can write the information to the Windows NT/Windows 2000 Event log.
- You can write the information to an error file.
- You can log the package execution to SQL Server.

The logging choices are made on the Logging tab of the DTS Package Properties dialog, shown in Figure 23.5.

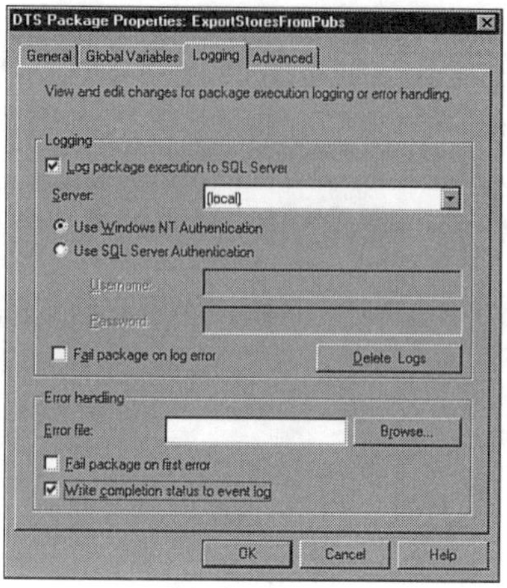

FIGURE 23.5

You can choose where the execution of a package is logged.

In addition to choosing where the logging takes place, you have two other choices on this tab:

- Whether or not a failure in the logging process should stop the execution of a package with a failure.

- Whether or not a failed task should terminate the execution of the package.

Logging to SQL Server

When you choose to log package execution to SQL Server, you can also choose which server should be used for the logging. The default choice is to log to the local server, but it could be convenient to consolidate the logging of all the servers in a central location.

The logging information is implemented with a set of Package2 properties. All of these properties are set by the choices on the Logging tab:

- LogToSQLServer—Boolean value that determines whether or not the SQL Server logging is enabled.

- LogServerName—The server used for the logging.

- LogServerUserName—Username for accessing that server.

- LogServerPassword—Password for LogServerUserName.

- LogServerFlags—One of the DTSSQLServerStorageFlags flags— DTSSQLStgFlag_Default (0) or DTSSQLStgFlag_UseTrustedConnection (256).

- FailPackageOnLogFailure—Boolean value that determines whether or not the package execution should be terminated with an error if the SQL Server logging process fails.

The log information is stored in three tables in the msdb database on the selected server:

- sysdtspackagelog—One record for each execution of a package.
- sysdtssteplog—One record for each execution of a step.
- sysdtstasklog—One record for each of the task log records.

> **TIP**
>
> The format of the information in these three tables is straightforward. Microsoft warns against using system tables or system stored procedures directly because these system objects might be changed at any time in the future.
>
> But if you want to look at the log records as a set, the easiest way to analyze them is to use SQL queries to access the tables directly or use these stored procedures in the msdb database—sp_enum_dtspackagelog, sp_enum_dtssteplog, and sp_enum_dtstasklog.

Viewing the SQL Server Logs

You can view the log for a particular package in the Enterprise Manager. Right-click on the Local Packages node in the tree. Select Package Logs. The DTS Packages Logs dialog, shown in Figure 23.6, will open.

FIGURE 23.6
To view logs, you pick the name of the package, the version, and the particular execution time.

You can choose to examine the logs for any package that has logs stored on this particular SQL Server, no matter where that package is executed or where it is stored. You can pick a package by name from a drop-down list box on the top of the form.

After you have selected a package, you are given a tree that has the different versions of the package and the separate log records. There is one log record for each time the package has been executed and the logging was activated.

When you select a log, you are given the details about the execution of each step in the Log Detail dialog. Select a step and choose More Info, and you will see the task detail records for that step, as shown in Figure 23.7. This additional information includes all the records that are stored for this task in sysdtstasklog.

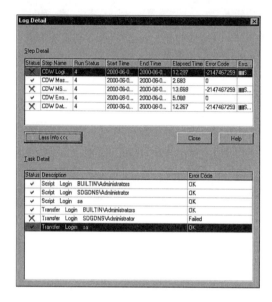

FIGURE 23.7

The More Info button displays the information from the task log.

Accessing the SQL Server Logs Programmatically

You can retrieve log information through the Application object by using the PackageLogRecord, StepLogRecord, and TaskLogRecord objects. These objects give you programmatic access to all the information stored in the msdb logging tables.

The code for accessing the package, step, or task log records is very similar to the code for enumerating the packages, as shown in Listing 23.4. This code is in the GetDTSInfo.dts file.

LISTING 23.4   VBScript Code for Displaying the Package Log Records for One Package

```
Dim DTSApp, PkgSQL, PkgLogs, StpLogs, TskLogs, log
Dim sPackageName, prp, msg

sPackageName = "Test Logging"
Set DTSApp = CreateObject("DTS.Application")
Set PkgSQL = DTSApp.GetPackageSQLServer("(local)","","",256)

'Enumerate all package log records for selected package
Set PkgLogs = _
    PkgSQL.EnumPackageLogRecords(sPackageName, False, "", "", "")
Set log = PkgLogs.Next

Do Until PkgLogs.EOF

    msg = ""

    For Each prp in log.Properties
        msg = msg & prp.Name & vbTab & prp.Value & vbCrLf
    Next

    Msgbox msg, , "Package Log Record"

    'Get next package log record
    Set log = PkgLogs.Next

Loop
```

You filter the log records that are returned by using parameters. For each of the methods, you have to decide on which level you want to do this filtering.

For EnumPackageLogRecords and EnumPackageStepRecords, only the lowest level of filtering specified will have any effect on the log records that are returned. In other words, if you specify values for PackageID and VersionID, the value for PackageID will be ignored.

When you use the methods, though, you still have to specify a value for all the parameters. If you want to use a higher level of filtering, you have to supply the proper non-value for the lower-level parameters. In most cases this is an empty string, but it can also be NULL or 0, as specified below.

You can return all the log records by setting all the parameters for no filtering. The number of records returned could be difficult to process, however.

EnumPackageLogRecords has five parameters:

- PackageName—Only returns log records for packages with this package name. Using this filter could return log records for packages with the same name from different storage locations or different servers.

  Use an empty string to skip filtering on this parameter.

- ReturnLatest—If TRUE, returns only the log record with the latest date that qualifies based on whichever other filters are selected. If FALSE, returns all log records based on the other filtering choices.

- PackageID—Only returns log records with this package ID. This value uniquely identifies one package no matter where it is stored.

  Use an empty string to skip filtering on this parameter.

- VersionID—Only returns records for this particular version of the package.

  Use an empty string to skip filtering on this parameter.

- LineageFullID—Only returns the one record for this specific execution of the package.

  Use an empty string to skip filtering on this parameter.

EnumStepLogRecords has two parameters:

- LineageFullID— Only returns records for this specific execution of a package.

  Use an empty string to skip filtering on this parameter.

- StepExecutionID—Only returns the one record for this specific execution of the step.

  Use NULL to skip filtering on this parameter.

EnumTaskLogRecords has two parameters:

- StepExecutionID— Only returns the records for this specific execution of a step.

  Use NULL to skip filtering on this parameter.

- SequenceID—Only returns the one record that has this SequenceID and stepExecutionID.

  Use 0 to skip filtering on this parameter.

There is a DTS package on the CD in a file called TestLogging.dts. This package has an ActiveX Script task that retrieves all of the package, step, and log records for a package. It has another ActiveX Script task that finds the lineage variables of an executing package, as described in the next section.

Finding the Lineage Variables of a Package Execution in Progress

You can use the EnumPackageLogRecords method to obtain the lineage variables of a package execution that is in progress. All packages stored in Meta Data Services have lineage variables that uniquely identify the time when a package was executed. When you log a package in SQL Server, lineage variables are also generated for that package even though it is stored outside of Meta Data Services.

The lineage variables are useful because you can use them to positively identify each execution of a package.

You can access these variables while the package is still executing because DTS writes the package log information to the log tables in two parts. A new record is inserted into the logging table when the package starts execution. That record is updated with additional information when the package execution is completed.

If you use the `EnumPackageLogRecords` method while the package is executing and you ask for the most recent package execution, you will receive the log record for the execution that is in progress. That log record has both of the lineage variables. Listing 23.5 has a VBScript that you can use to put those values into global variables.

LISTING 23.5   VBScript Code for an ActiveX Script Task That Finds the Lineage Variables of the Package Execution in Progress

```
Option Explicit

Function Main()

Dim pkg
Dim DTSApp, PkgSQL, PkgLogs, log, msg, lLineageShort, sLineageFull

Set pkg = DTSGlobalVariables.Parent
Set DTSApp = CreateObject("DTS.Application")
Set PkgSQL = DTSApp.GetPackageSQLServer("(local)","","",256)
Set PkgLogs = _
    PkgSQL.EnumPackageLogRecords("", True, pkg.PackageID, "", "")

Set log = PkgLogs.Next

sLineageFull = log.LineageFullID
lLineageShort = log.LineageShortID

'Display the lineage variables
msg = ""
msg = msg & "Here are the lineage variables for the current" & vbCrLf
msg = msg & "execution of this package:" & vbCrLf & vbCrLf
msg = msg & "Lineage Short" & vbTab & CStr(lLineageShort) & vbCrLf
```

LISTING 23.5   Continued

```
msg = msg & "Lineage Full" & vbTab & CStr(sLineageFull)
Msgbox msg

'Write the lineage variables to the Task Log
DTSPackageLog.WriteTaskRecord 1, _
    "Lineage Short" & vbTab & CStr(lLineageShort)
DTSPackageLog.WriteTaskRecord 1, _
    "Lineage Full" & vbTab & CStr(sLineageFull)

        Main = DTSTaskExecResult_Success
End Function
```

DTS Packages as Data Sources

A DTS package can be used as a data source, in which case it returns records to the application that is calling the package rather than sending data to a data destination.

Here are some of the ways you can use DTS packages as data sources:

- The Transact-SQL OPENROWSET statement can be used to query a DTS package.
- OPENROWSET can be used with FOR XML to return XML from a Transform Data task.
- You can register a DTS package as a linked server.

All these topics will be discussed in this section.

The Data Provider DTSPackageDSO

A DTS package is used as a data source through an OLE DB data provider called the DTSPackageDSO (Data Transformation Services Package Data Source Objects, or PDSO) provider. When the PDSO provider is called by a client application, it executes the requested DTS package and returns the resulting rowset to the client.

Setting Up a DTS Package to Be a Data Source

Only the results of a Transform Data task can be used as a data source. You make a DTS package into a data source by selecting the DSO rowset provider box on the Options tab of the Workflow properties dialog (see Figure 23.8) for a particular Transform Data task.

In code, you set this option with the IsPackageDSORowset property of the Step object. This is a Boolean property with a default value of FALSE.

FIGURE 23.8
Select the DSO rowset provider check box to make a DTS package a data source.

This selection has the following results when the DTS package is called through the PDSO data provider:

- No records are added to the data destination.
- The records that would normally have been added to the data destination are now returned as the result set to the application that called the DTS Package.
- Data modifications for other tasks in the package do not take place.

To use a DTS Package as a row source, you must call it through the PDSO provider. If you have a Transform Data task marked as a row source, you can still execute the package in other ways without using the PDSO provider, but it will behave differently. Here is the behavior:

- The task that is marked as a row source is not executed.
- Other tasks are executed unless they are dependent on the tasks marked as row sources.

NOTE

The DSO rowset provider option only makes sense with the Transform Data task. The box is available on the Workflow Properties dialog for other types of tasks. If it is selected for one of those other tasks, that task will be completed successfully but will block the execution of any tasks dependent on it. If the package is called with the PDSO provider and the DSO rowset provider box is checked on one of the other tasks, an error is returned by the PDSO provider to the client application.

Querying a DTS Package with OPENROWSET

A recordset can be returned from a DTS package by using the Transact-SQL statement
OPENROWSET. This command can be used to link to any data source for which an OLE DB
provider is available.

The following three parameters are used with OPENROWSET when it is used to return a recordset
from a DTS package:

- Provider_name—This is always 'DTSPackageDSO' when querying DTS packages.
- Provider_string—Any combination of the switches that are used with DTSRun to load
  a package can also be used with OPENROWSET. The use of DTSRun is documented toward
  the end of Chapter 1, "A Quick Look at DTS." Various forms of this string, used to
  retrieve packages from different modes of storage, are shown below.
- Query—The query that is to be executed.

> **NOTE**
>
> When I heard that I was going to be able to pass parameters into a DTS package with
> DTSRun, I was hoping that I would be able to do the same thing with OPENROWSET.
> Unfortunately, that does not seem to be the case. The switches that can be included
> in the provider_string include storage server, storage location type, and security
> information.

The query that is used in the OPENROWSET statement has four forms. The first three are equivalent. You must use the fourth when you are using OPENROWSET with a DTS Package that has
more than one Transform Data task marked as a DSO rowset source:

- 'SELECT *'
- 'SELECT * FROM ALL'
- 'SELECT * FROM <Package Name>'
- 'SELECT * FROM <Step Name>'

This is an example of an OPENROWSET statement used to return a rowset from a DTS package
stored in the file c:\MSSQL7\dts\salesimport.dts:

```
SELECT * FROM OPENROWSET
    (
    'DTSPackageDSO',
```

```
'/FC:\MSSQL7\dts\salesimport.dts',
'Select *'
)
```

If this package had more than one Transform Data task marked with the DSO rowset provider option, the query parameter would have to be changed to explicitly reference the step related to the task that had the desired rowset:

```
SELECT * FROM OPENROWSET

    (
    'DTSPackageDSO',
    '/F C:\MSSQL7\dts\salesimport.dts',
    'Select * FROM DTSStep_DTSDataPumpTask_5'
    )
```

The next example shows OPENROWSET being used to return a rowset from a DTS package stored in SQL Server. A trusted connection (/E) is being used:

```
SELECT * FROM OPENROWSET

    (
    'DTSPackageDSO',
    '/E /S Server1 /N SalesImport',
    'Select *'
    )
```

The last example shows OPENROWSET used to return a rowset from a DTS package stored in the repository. The user ID and password are being supplied (/Usa /P). A package ID (/G) is specified:

```
SELECT * FROM OPENROWSET

    (
    'DTSPackageDSO',
    '/Usa /P /S Server1 /G {9F99EE87-FE2F-11D2-91A8-00E0980134A1}',
    'SELECT * FROM ALL'
    )
```

Registering a DTS Package as a Linked Server

If a rowset is going to be returned from a DTS package on an occasional basis, using the OPENROWSET statement is the easiest method. But if you are frequently querying a DTS package, it would be easier to register the package as a linked server. After it is registered, it can be referenced in queries as easily as if it were another table in your database.

Linked servers are registered using the system stored procedure sp_addlinkedserver. This procedure requires four parameters:

- The linked server name. This is the name you want to use when you refer to the linked server in SQL statements. You can set this to any string, as long as it is different from all the linked servers that have been registered previously.

- The product name. This parameter must be included in the procedure call, but the content does not affect the result. Use any string value.

- The provider name. For DTS packages, this must be 'DTSPackageDSO'.

- The location. Use the same string as you would use for the OPENROWSET provider string, as described above.

Here is an example of the use of sp_addlinkedserver, registering the same package as was accessed by the first OPENROWSET statement above:

```
sp_addlinkedserver
    'SalesDTSLinkedServer',
    'Whatever',
    'DTSPackageDSO',
    '/FC:\MSSQL7\dts\salesimport.dts'
```

After the DTS package is registered as a linked server, you can reference it in SQL statements as if it were any other server. Either the package name or the step name can be used for the table name in the SQL statement. The name of the database and the name of the object owner are omitted for a <Linked Server name>...<Package or Step Name> syntax:

```
SELECT * FROM SalesDTSLinkedServer...DTSStep_DTSDataPumpTask_5
```

Using the DTSPackageDSO Provider to Return XML from a Transform Data Task

One of the new features in SQL Server 2000 is the use of FOR XML with SELECT statements to return data in XML format. You can use this capability with the OPENROWSET command to return the results of a Transform Data task as XML:

```
SELECT * FROM OPENROWSET
    (
    'DTSPackageDSO',
    '/E /S Server1 /N SalesImport',
    'Select *'
    )
    FOR XML AUTO
```

You can use DTS as a simple conversion utility to convert text files into XML by using a text file as the source for a Transform Data task and then using OPENROWSET with FOR XML.

> **TIP**
>
> OPENROWSET...FOR XML could be used from a Web page to return data in XML format to a Web browser.
>
> DTS is optimized for transforming large amounts of data. It might not be the most efficient tool for delivering results interactively to Internet users.
>
> However, if the request for data can be limited to a small enough recordset, and if there is a need to transform the data in some way as it is being returned from storage to the Internet user, DTS might be an excellent tool for the task. It could be used to convert data from a variety of data sources to XML.
>
> It would be more convenient to implement these solutions if we could use parameters to set global variables when using OPENROWSET. The source query of the Transform Data task could use these global variables to filter the records processed so that the XML data could be returned more quickly.
>
> It is possible to set global variables from outside a package in other ways, of course, but none would be as convenient as setting them directly in the OPENROWSET statement.

Other DTS Package Object Properties and Methods

The DTS package properties are presented in a variety of different places in this book:

- ExplicitGlobalVariables is covered in Chapter 7, "Writing ActiveX Scripts for a Transform Data Task."

- NestedExecutionLevel is covered in Chapter 18, "The Execute Package Task."

- AutoCommitTransaction, TransactionIsolationLevel, and UseTransaction are covered in the section on transactions in Chapter 24, "Steps and Precedence Constraints."

- MaxConcurrentSteps and PackagePriorityClass are covered in the section on threads and priority of execution in Chapter 24, "Steps and Precedence Constraints."

- LineageOptions and RepositoryMetadataOptions are covered in Chapter 29, "Integrating DTS with Meta Data Services."

- PackageID, VersionID, Name, and Description are covered in the section on DTS Package versions in this chapter.

23

THE DTS
PACKAGE AND ITS
PROPERTIES

- LogServerFlags, LogServerName, LogServerPasword, LogServerUserName, LogToSQLServer, and FailPackageOnLogFailure are covered in the section on package logging in this chapter.
- FailOnError, LogFileName, and WriteCompletionStatusToNTEventLog are covered in the section on error handling in this chapter.

The remaining package properties are covered in this section.

CreationDate, CreatorComputerName, and CreatorName

These three read-only properties provide information about the creation of the package. CreatorName uses the Windows NT formatting that combines the domain name and the user name: Domain/Username. This property may not have a value if the package is created on a computer running Microsoft Windows 95, Windows 98, or Windows ME.

These three values are all displayed in the Creation box on the General tab of the DTS Package Properties dialog.

PackageType

PackageType is an extended property of the Package2 object. You can query this property to determine the tool that was used to create the package. It's a read/write property. The DTSPackageType constants are used as the values for this property:

- 0—DTSPkgType_Default—Custom program or not set.
- 1—DTSPkgType_DTSWizard—DTS Import/Export Wizard.
- 2—DTSPkgType_DTSDesigner—DTS Designer.
- 3—DTSPkgType_SQLReplication—SQL Server 2000 replication function.
- 4—DTSPkgType_ActiveDirectory—Active Directory in Windows 2000.

> **NOTE**
>
> I have tested this property with the release version of SQL Server 2000. For packages created with Visual Basic, the DTS Designer, the DTS Import/Export Wizard, and the Copy Database Wizard, I have found that this property is always set to 0.

Parent

Each object in the DTS hierarchy has a Parent property. For members of a collection, the parent is the collection object. For collections, the parent is the object that contains that collection. For the package, the highest object in the hierarchy, the parent is itself.

UseOLEDBServiceComponents

This `Boolean` property is set on the Advanced tab of the DTS Package Property dialog. The default value is `TRUE`.

When this property is selected, the OLE DB components are instantiated using the OLE DB Service Components. When this property is set to `FALSE`, the data source objects are instantiated directly. This setting is ignored for the Data Transformation Services provider and for the SQL Server OLE DB Provider.

The `GetDTSVersionInfo` Method

All of the methods of the `Package` and `Package2` objects have already been discussed in this chapter, except for `GetDTSVersionInfo`. This method provides access to information about the current DTS version. Here's a Visual Basic code sample that shows how to use this method:

```
Dim pkg As New DTS.Package2
Dim msg As String
Dim lVersionMajor As Long
Dim lVersionMinor As Long
Dim lVersionBuild As Long
Dim sVersionComments As String

pkg.GetDTSVersionInfo lVersionMajor, lVersionMinor, _
        lVersionBuild, sVersionComments

msg = msg & "Version Major" & vbTab & lVersionMajor & vbCrLf
msg = msg & "Version Minor" & vbTab & lVersionMinor & vbCrLf
msg = msg & "Version Build" & vbTab & lVersionBuild & vbCrLf
msg = msg & "Version Comments" & vbTab & sVersionComments
MsgBox msg
```

Conclusion

The next chapter continues the discussion of the structure of the DTS package by presenting information on steps and precedence constraints. Some of the topics include thread execution and the use of transactions in steps and packages.

Steps and Precedence Constraints

CHAPTER

24

IN THIS CHAPTER

This chapter presents information about steps, the objects that control the execution of the tasks in a DTS package. It also presents information about two topics that involve both package and step properties—threading and transactions.

Steps, Tasks, and the DTS Package

Steps are the objects in a DTS package that determine whether or not a task is executed. They also determine the order in which the tasks are executed. DTS tasks define the work that is done. Steps control the execution of the tasks.

A step is created for you whenever you create a task in the DTS Package Designer. If you create a task using code, you have to explicitly create the step. The last section of this chapter explains how to create a step using Visual Basic.

A Step object has a variety of properties associated with it. Many of these properties can be set on the Options tab of the Workflow Properties dialog, shown in Figure 24.1. You can open the Workflow Properties dialog by right-clicking on any task icon and selecting Workflow, Workflow Properties. For a Data Transformation task, click on the black arrow and pick Workflow Properties.

FIGURE 24.1
You can set many of the properties of a step object on the Options tab of the Workflow Properties dialog.

The Name property of the Step object is assigned automatically. You cannot change it without using code or Disconnected Edit. You can view the step's name toward the top of the Options tab of the Workflow Properties dialog.

NOTE

I like to change the names of steps when I am going to reference them in code. I typically do this with Disconnected Edit.

You can have a problem if you change the name of a step when it is being used in a precedence constraint. It's easier if you delete all the precedence constraints before changing the name of a step.

Each task is normally associated with one step. You can associate one task with two or more steps, however. By doing this, you can execute the same task at more than one place in the execution of the package. A task is associated with a step through the `TaskName` property of the `Step` object. `TaskName` is not displayed in the interface, except in Disconnected Edit.

If you have a task in a package that is not associated with a step, that task will not be executed.

Steps have an `Execute` method, but this method is not usually used in code. When the DTS Package is executed, the `Execute` method of each of the steps is called automatically. Determining when and if the task associated with a step is actually executed is done by the precedence constraints.

CAUTION

It is possible to call the step's `Execute` method directly from Visual Basic code, but Microsoft does not support this practice and recommends against it.

If you want one step to execute more than once in a package, you can do so by modifying the step's `ExecutionStatus` property, as described in the next section.

Precedence Constraints

The `Step` object has a `PrecedenceConstraints` collection. The `PrecedenceConstraint` objects are used to set the ordering of the steps in the package's execution.

There are three significant factors in a precedence constraint:

- The step whose execution is dependent on the precedence constraint. This is the step that has the `PrecedenceConstraints` collection of which the `PrecedenceConstraint` is a member. It is called the destination step in the Workflow Properties dialog.

- The step that controls the execution. This step is determined by the StepName property of the PrecedenceConstraint. It is called the source step in the Workflow Properties dialog.

- The type of precedence—On Success, On Failure, or On Completion.

Each step can participate in many different precedence constraints. If you want to make one step dependent on 50 other steps, you can do so by creating 50 precedence constraints in that step's PrecedenceConstraints collection. Similarly, you can set the same step as the StepName for as many different precedence constraints as you like.

The Three Types of Precedence

You can choose from three types of precedence in the Package Designer: On Success, On Failure, or On Completion.

On Success

The destination step will not be executed until the source step has successfully completed. If the source step fails or is never executed, the destination step will not be executed.

You can serialize the flow of the tasks in your DTS Package by using On Success precedence. Each step waits for the successful completion of the previous step before starting its execution.

On Failure

The destination step will not be executed until the source step has failed. If the source step succeeds or is never executed, the destination step will not be executed.

You can use On Failure to trigger events that are to happen when tasks have failed. Perhaps you want to take some corrective action and then try the task again. You could also use On Failure to call a Send Mail task to inform an administrator of the problem.

On Completion

The destination step will not be executed until the source step has been completed, either successfully or with a failure. If the source step is never executed, the destination step will not be executed.

There are some tasks that need to be done whether or not the previous tasks have been successful. An Execute SQL task that creates a table is a good example. If the table creation task is successful, the processing can continue. If the table creation fails, that's probably because the table already exists, so the processing should be set to continue anyway. On Completion could also be used to create a report whether the previous step succeeds or fails.

Creating Precedence Constraints in the DTS Package Designer

You can create precedence constraints in a variety of ways using the DTS Package Designer:

- Select the icons for the tasks of the two steps included in the precedence constraint. You can select one, press the Shift key, and select the other. You can also draw a marquee around the two icons. In either case, the first one selected will be used as the controlling step.

- Select one of the three types of precedence—On Completion, On Success, or On Failure. You can do this from the Workflow menu, as shown in Figure 24.2. You can also right-click on either of the tasks, choose Workflow, and pick the type of precedence.

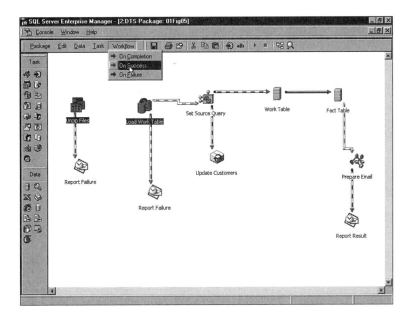

FIGURE 24.2
You can create a precedence constraint by selecting the two tasks involved and choosing the appropriate type of precedence from the Workflow menu.

Precedence constraints can also be created on the Precedence tab of the Workflow Properties dialog. When you use this method, you can create several precedence constraints for the same destination step. Here are the details of what you need to do:

- Open the dialog by right-clicking on the task associated with the step that you want to be dependent on the constraint. Select Workflow, Workflow Properties from the pop-up menu.

- Select the New button on the Precedence tab of the dialog. A new precedence constraint will be created, as shown in Figure 24.3.
- You can change the source step and the precedence. You cannot modify the destination step.

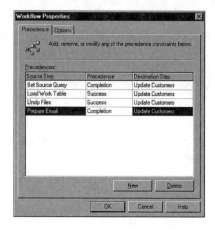

FIGURE 24.3
You can create many precedence constraints at the same time on the Precedence tab of the Workflow Properties dialog.

Creating Precedence Constraints in Code

The PrecedenceConstraint object has the following properties:

- StepName—The name of the source step. This property is also used as the name of the precedence constraint. You can use the step name to refer to a particular member of the PrecedenceConstraints collection:

  prc = stpDestination.PrecedenceConstraints("NameOfSourceStep")

- PrecedenceBasis and Value—The combined settings for these properties determine the type of precedence.
- Parent—A reference to the PrecedenceConstraints collection for this PrecedenceConstraint. The Parent of this collection is the destination step.

The PrecedenceBasis property determines whether the precedence should be based on the status of the source step or the result of the execution of the source step. The two values for this property are

- 0—DTSStepPrecedenceBasis_ExecStatus
- 1—DTSStepPrecedenceBasis_ExecResult

The Value property indicates the specific criteria used for determining the precedence. The value property uses either the DTSStepExecResult constants or the DTSStepExecStatus constants, depending on what has been chosen for the PrecedenceBasis property. The values for these two types of constants are shown in Table 24.1 and Table 24.2. These same constants are used as the values for the ExecutionResult and ExecutionStatus properties of the Step object.

TABLE 24.1 Constants Used for the Value Property of the PrecedenceConstraint Object When PrecedenceBasis Is Set to Result

Constant	Value	Type of Precedence
DTSStepExecResult_Failure	1	On Failure
DTSStepExecResult_Success	0	On Success

TABLE 24.2 Constants Used for the Value Property of the PrecedenceConstraint Object When PrecedenceBasis Is Set to Status

Constant	Value	Type of Precedence
DTSStepExecStat_Completed	4	On Completion
DTSStepExecStat_Inactive	3	
DTSStepExecStat_InProgress	2	
DTSStepExecStat_Waiting	1	

NOTE

When you use status for the PrecedenceBasis, the completed status is the only constant the Package Designer uses for the Value property. If you create a precedence constraint in code, you could set the status to one of the other three values—Inactive, In Progress, or Waiting.

I have tried using all these values for precedence constraints. I can't find a use for In Progress or Waiting, but Inactive could be useful. A precedence constraint set to a status of Inactive would allow you to set a step to execute as an alternate in situations where a particular step was inactivated by setting the IsDisabled property to TRUE.

24

STEPS AND PRECEDENCE CONSTRAINTS

Listing 24.1 shows the VBScript code that creates a new precedence constraint. The new step is created with the New method of the PrecedenceConstraints collection and added to the collection with the Add method. The PrecedenceBasis property is set to the execution result, and the Value property indicates that failure is the result that is to trigger the precedence.

LISTING 24.1   This ActiveX Script Creates a New On Failure Precedence Constraint

```
Option Explicit
Function Main()

Dim pkg, stpSource, stpDestination, prc

Set pkg = DTSGlobalVariables.Parent
Set stpSource = pkg.Steps("stpBulkInsert")
Set stpDestination = pkg.Steps("stpInsertCustomer")

Set prc = stpDestination.PrecedenceConstraints.New(stpSource.Name)

prc.PrecedenceBasis = DTSStepPrecedenceBasis_ExecResult
prc.Value = DTSStepExecResult_Failure

stpDestination.PrecedenceConstraints.Add prc

    Main = DTSTaskExecResult_Success
End Function
```

> **NOTE**
>
> If you create a precedence constraint with this code in an ActiveX Script task, the constraint will be in effect but will not be displayed in the Package Designer. In order for it to be displayed, you have to open the Workflow Properties dialog for the step and click OK.

The Execution Status of the Step

Steps execute when all of their precedence constraints have been met and the step has a status of DTSStepExecStat_Waiting. If the step has any other status, it will not be executed.

You can change the execution of a step by setting the ExecutionStatus property of the Step object in code:

- If a step has already been executed and you then set the ExecutionStatus property to DTSStepExecStat_Waiting, the step will be executed again.

- If a step is waiting to be executed and you set the ExecutionStatus to any of the constants listed in Table 24.2 besides DTSStepExecStat_Waiting, the step will not be executed. The status that makes the most sense to use for this purpose is DTSStepExecStat_Inactive.

> **NOTE**
>
> The ExecutionStatus property of the Step object is listed as a read-only property in the DTS Reference in Books Online. But there is a sample ActiveX script in Books Online that sets the property to DTSStepExecStat_Waiting for the purpose of executing a task in a loop.

Chapter 16, "Writing Scripts for an ActiveX Script Task," has an example of setting up a loop in a DTS package.

Threads and Priority of Execution

DTS is a multithreaded application. Many tasks can be executed simultaneously, each one with its own separate thread.

Package Level Thread Execution Parameters

There are two thread execution properties for the DTS package as a whole—Priority class and Limit the maximum number of tasks executed in parallel. These properties can be set on the General tab of the DTS Package Properties dialog, as shown in Figure 24.4. You can open this dialog by choosing Properties on the Package menu when no objects are currently selected in the Design Sheet.

The Priority Class

This setting determines the Microsoft Win32 process priority class for the DTS package when it is executed. The possible values are low, normal, and high.

In the object model, this setting is the PackagePriorityClass property of the Package object. The three allowed settings for this property are displayed in Table 24.3.

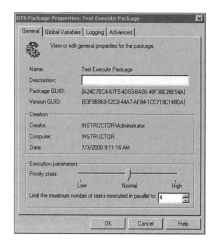

FIGURE **24.4**
The priority class and the maximum number of tasks executed in parallel are the two thread execution parameters that can be set for the DTS Package as a whole.

TABLE 24.3   Constants Used for the `PackagePriorityClass` of the `Package` Object

Constant	Value
DTSPackagePriorityClass_Low	1
DTSPackagePriorityClass_Normal	2
DTSPackagePriorityClass_High	3

The Maximum Number of Tasks Executed in Parallel

This setting limits the number of steps that are allowed to execute concurrently on separate threads. The default value for this setting is four.

This setting can affect the performance of a DTS package. Raising this value can increase the speed of a package's execution, especially when multiple processors are available. More steps can be executed simultaneously, as long as each step has had its precedence constraints satisfied. But if this value is raised too high, package execution can be slowed because of excessive switching between threads.

In code, this setting is the `MaxConcurrentSteps` property of the `Package` object.

Step Level Thread Execution Parameters

There are six settings in the Execution group on the Options tab of the Workflow Properties dialog:

- Task priority
- Execute on main package thread
- Close connection on completion
- DSO rowset provider
- Disable this step
- Fail package on step failure

Task Priority

The task priority gives a precise level of control over the execution priority of an individual task. The package priority class sets the overall thread priority class to low, normal, or high. The task priority sets the relative thread priority within each of the three priority classes.

The task priority is implemented as the `RelativePriority` property of the `Step` object. The five constants that can be used for this property are shown in Table 24.4.

TABLE 24.4   Constants Used for the `RelativePriority` Property of the `Step` Object

Constant	Value
DTSStepRelativePriority_Lowest	1
DTSStepRelativePriority_BelowNormal	2
DTSStepRelativePriority_Normal	3
DTSStepRelativePriority_AboveNormal	4
DTSStepRelativePriority_Highest	5

Execute on Main Package Thread

DTS normally spawns separate threads to execute different steps of the package. This setting changes that behavior for one particular step by forcing it to be executed on the main package thread.

These are the situations where it is necessary to execute a process on the main package thread:

- If the data provider is not free-threaded and does not support parallel execution of tasks. This is true for the Microsoft Jet OLE DB Provider, as well as the providers for Excel, dBase, Paradox, and HTML files. If more than one task is being executed with one of these providers at the same time, they should all be executed on the main package thread.
- If you are using custom tasks that have been created with Visual Basic.
- If you are executing a package from Visual Basic.
- If you want to debug multiple ActiveX Scripts with the script debugger provided with Microsoft Visual InterDev 6.0 or the Microsoft Windows NT 4.0 Option Pack.

24

STEPS AND
PECEDENCE
CONSTRAINTS

> **CAUTION**
>
> Errors can be generated if several tasks are being executed simultaneously using data sources or custom tasks that do not support parallel execution. Use the Execute on main thread option to avoid those problems.

The `ExecuteInMainThread` property of the `Step` object implements this option. This is a boolean property with a default value of FALSE.

Close Connection on Completion

The default behavior for opening and closing data connections is as follows:

- Do not open a connection until it is needed by a task.
- Do not close an open connection until the package completes its execution.

This default behavior is usually the most efficient because it minimizes the number of times that data connections have to be established.

The Close connection on completion option allows you to override the default behavior for a particular step by closing all of the step's connections when the step is finished.

There are several reasons to consider using this option:

- Some data providers have better performance if connections are not left open.
- If there are many connections in a package and inadequate memory resources, closing the connections could conserve memory and improve overall performance.
- You have to close a connection before dynamically modifying it. For example, you cannot change the file being used in a text file data source if that connection is open.

You can set this option in code with the `CloseConnection` property of the `Step` object. This is a boolean property with a default value of FALSE.

DSO Rowset Provider

This option allows a DTS package to return a recordset.

This option is the `IsPackageDSORowset` property of the `Step` object, a boolean value with a default value of FALSE. It is discussed in Chapter 23, "The DTS Package and Its Properties."

Disable This Step

When you choose this option, you block the execution of this step when the package is executed. As discussed in the section on precedence constraints, you can specify another task to run if, and only if, a particular task is disabled. You do this by using the DTSStepExecStat_ Inactive constant for the Value property and the DTSStepPrecedenceBasis_ExecStatus constant for the PrecedenceBasis property. Both of these are properties of the PrecedenceConstraint object.

This option is implemented with the DisableStep property of the Step object.

Fail Package on Step Failure

When this option is selected, the package is terminated with a failure if this step fails. By default, this option is not selected so that a step failure does not cause the package to fail.

This option is implemented with the FailPackageOnError property of the Step2 object. It is the only extended property of this object. It is a boolean property with a default value of FALSE.

NOTE

The package has a corresponding property called FailOnError. It is set on the Logging tab of the Package Properties dialog and is discussed in Chapter 23. If the package property FailOnError is set to True, the first error in any step will cause the package to terminate with failure. The step property FailPackageOnError causes the package to fail only if that particular step fails.

If both FailOnError and FailPackageOnError are set to FALSE (their default settings), all the steps in the package can fail and the package will still complete successfully.

Transactions in DTS Packages

Some or all of the tasks in a DTS package can be joined together into transactions. If you use a transaction in a package, an error in one task will cause all the data changes made by other tasks in the transaction to be rolled back. If you do not use transactions, data modifications remain that have already been completed, even if an error occurs that causes a task or the entire package to terminate with an error.

A package can have many transactions, but only one of them can be in effect at a time. Whether or not data modifications are successfully rolled back when a transaction fails depends on the transactional support of the OLE DB provider.

The transaction properties are set in two places—for the package as a whole and for each task.

24

STEPS AND
PRECEDENCE
CONSTRAINTS

Transaction Properties Set at the Package Level

You can set the three package transaction properties on the Advanced tab of the DTS Package Properties dialog. This tab is shown in Figure 24.5.

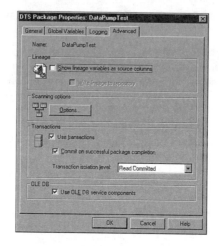

FIGURE 24.5

The transaction properties for the package as a whole can be set on the Advanced tab of the DTS Package Properties dialog.

Use Transactions

This option determines whether or not the DTS package will support a transaction. If this option is selected, you can configure steps to join the transaction. If no steps join the transaction, it doesn't make any difference whether or not this option is selected.

This option is the UseTransaction property of the Package object. It is a boolean property with a default value of True.

Commit On Successful Package Completion

If this option is selected and a transaction is in effect, that transaction will be committed automatically when the execution of the package is completed.

If this option is set to FALSE, a transaction that is in progress when the package completes its execution will be rolled back.

The AutoCommitTransaction property of the Package object sets this option. This is a boolean property with a default of True.

Transaction Isolation Level

The transaction isolation level can be set to one of five levels in the DTS Designer. These five levels are assigned using eight constants for the corresponding property, the TransactionIsolationLevel property of the Package object.

Here are some definitions of terms used in defining transaction isolation levels:

- Dirty read—Reading data that has been changed by another user, even though that change hasn't been committed and might still be rolled back.
- Non-repeatable read—Reading data that might be updated by another user before you read it again.
- Phantom read—You read a set of data and then another user adds data to that set. When you read it again, you see the phantoms, the new records that have been added.

DTSIsoLevel_Chaos

Chaos is not implemented in Transact-SQL.

- Value: 16
- ANSI SQL-92 Isolation Level 0
- At this isolation level, two different users may update the same data at the same time. (That's why it's called chaos.) This level is only appropriate for a database in single-user mode.

DTSIsoLevel_ReadUncommitted

Equivalent to Transact-SQL SET TRANSACTION ISOLATION LEVEL READ UNCOMMITTED.

- Value: 256
- ANSI SQL-92 Isolation Level 1
- Equivalent to constant DTSIsoLevel_Browse
- Allows dirty reads, non-repeatable reads, and phantom reads.
- This isolation level is useful for running complex decision support queries on data that is being updated. No locks are taken or honored when reading data at this isolation level.

DTSIsoLevel_ReadCommitted

Equivalent to Transact-SQL SET TRANSACTION ISOLATION LEVEL READ COMMITTED.

- Value: 4096
- ANSI SQL-92 Isolation Level 2
- Equivalent to constant DTSIsoLevel_CursorStability
- This is the default transaction isolation level in SQL Server and in DTS.

- Does not allow dirty reads.

- Allows non-repeatable reads and phantom reads.

- You are not allowed to read data modifications that have not been committed.

DTSIsoLevel_RepeatableRead

Equivalent to Transact-SQL SET TRANSACTION ISOLATION LEVEL REPEATABLE READ.

- Value: 65536

- ANSI SQL-92 Isolation Level 3

- Does not allow dirty reads or non-repeatable reads.

- Allows phantom reads.

- If you start a transaction in this isolation level and you read some data, you are guaranteed that the data you have read will not be changed until your transaction ends.

DTSIsoLevel_Serializable

Equivalent to Transact-SQL SET TRANSACTION ISOLATION LEVEL SERIALIZABLE.

- Value: 1048576

- ANSI SQL-92 Isolation Level 4

- Equivalent to constant DTSIsoLevel_Isolated.

- Does not allow dirty reads, non-repeatable reads, and phantom reads.

- Provides total isolation for the data being used in the transaction. You cannot read any data that other users have locked. No other users can change or update the data. No other users are allowed to put any locks on the data, including shared locks. Other users are not allowed to add new records to record sets that have been viewed by any queries in your transaction.

Transaction Settings for the Steps

You configure a step's participation in a transaction on the Options tab of the Workflow Properties dialog (see Figure 24.6).

Join Transaction If Present

If you select this option, the step will participate in the current transaction if the package's UseTransaction property is set to TRUE. If the UseTransaction property is set to FALSE, the request to participate in a connection will be ignored.

There can be only one transaction active in a package at a time. If one is currently active, this step will join it. If a transaction is not active, this step will start a new one.

In code, this option is implemented as the JoinTransactionIfPresent property of the Step object. This is a boolean property with a default value of FALSE.

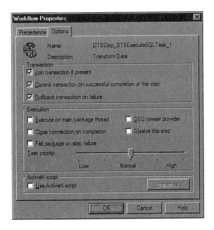

FIGURE 24.6
You have three choices regarding a step's involvement with a transaction.

Commit Transaction on Successful Completion of This Step

If this option is selected, the current transaction will be committed if this step completes successfully. All the data modifications made in this step, and in previous steps included in the transaction, will be committed.

You can select this option without choosing to have the step join the transaction.

After this step is completed and the transaction is committed, the next step that is set to join a transaction will start a new transaction.

This option is the CommitSuccess property of the Step object.

> **NOTE**
>
> The documentation for the CommitSuccess property in Books Online incorrectly states that this property specifies whether a step is committed upon successful completion. The whole transaction is committed, not just this particular step.

Rollback Transaction on Failure

If this option is selected, the current transaction will be rolled back if this step fails. All the data modifications made in this step, and in previous steps included in the transaction, will be rolled back.

You can select this option without choosing to have the step join the transaction.

If this step fails and the transaction is rolled back, the next step that is set to join a transaction will start a new transaction.

If this option is not selected, this step is included in a transaction, and the step fails, the transaction will continue without being committed or rolled back.

This option is the `RollbackFailure` property of the `Step` object.

Participation in Transactions by Connections and Tasks

Data connections and tasks have to be able to participate in distributed transactions, or else they are not allowed to join DTS transactions.

You can commit or roll back a DTS transaction based on the success or failure of any task. The task does not have to participate in the transaction for it to trigger the commit or the rollback.

Here are the tasks that can participate in DTS transactions:

- Transform Data
- Data Driven Query
- Execute SQL
- Bulk Insert
- Message Queue
- Execute Package

The following tasks cannot participate in a DTS transaction:

- Copy SQL Server Objects
- File Transfer Protocol
- Dynamic Properties
- ActiveX Script
- Execute Process
- Send Mail

If you select Join transaction if present for a step associated with one of these tasks, an error will be generated at runtime and the task and package will fail.

> **NOTE**
>
> Of course, non-DTS transactions can be started and managed by an ActiveX Script task, an Execute SQL task, or an application started with an Execute Process task. These transactions have no relationship with DTS transactions, though.

Connections using the following providers can participate in DTS transactions:

- The Microsoft OLE DB provider for SQL Server.
- OLE DB providers that implement ITransactionJoin.
- ODBC drivers that support SQL_ATT_ENLIST_IN_DTC.

If data is modified in a non-supported data connection as a part of a DTS transaction, a run-time error will be generated and the task and the package will fail. You can use a non-supported data connection as the source for a transformation without generating an error, however. Some examples of data sources that do not support DTS transactions include

- Microsoft Excel 2000 worksheets
- Microsoft Access 2000 tables
- Text files

A Transaction with Steps Executed in Sequence

The easiest way to structure a transaction in a DTS package is to set all the steps to execute in sequence, as shown in Figure 24.7. The DTS package with this transaction is on the CD in a file called SerialTransaction.dts.

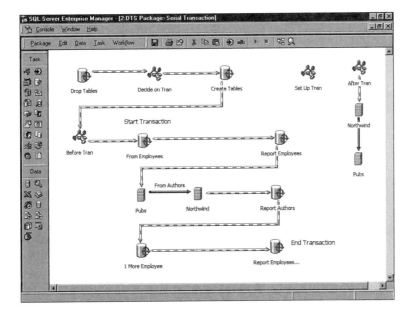

FIGURE 24.7
The easiest transactions have steps that execute sequentially.

Here's what you have to do to set up this simple transaction:

1. Select Use transactions and Commit on successful package completion on the Advanced tab of the DTS Package Properties dialog. These are the default choices.
2. Select Join transaction if present and Rollback on failure on the Options tab of the Workflow Properties dialog for all of the steps. Do not select Commit transaction on successful completion of this step for any of the steps.
3. Set precedence constraints so that the tasks are executed sequentially. Use On Success precedence.

As soon as an error occurs in this package, all the data modifications that have been previously made will be rolled back. The On Success precedence constraints will prevent any more steps from being executed.

You can set all the properties for this transaction programmatically by executing the script in Listing 24.2 as an ActiveX Script task. This script sets the precedence constraints to the appropriate type, but it does not create any new constraints.

LISTING 24.2   A VBScript to Set the Properties for a Simple Transaction

```
Option Explicit
Function Main

Dim pkg, stp, tsk, prc

Set pkg = DTSGlobalVariables.Parent

pkg.UseTransaction = True
pkg.AutoCommitTransaction = True

For Each stp in pkg.Steps

    Set tsk = pkg.Tasks(stp.TaskName)

    Select Case tsk.CustomTaskID

            Case "DTSDataPumpTask",  "DTSExecuteSQLTask",  _
                "DTSDataDrivenQueryTask",  "DTSBulkInsertTask",  _
                "DTSExecutePackageTask",  "DTSMessageQueueTask"

            stp.JoinTransactionIfPresent = True
            stp.RollbackFailure = True
            stp.CommitSuccess = False
```

LISTING 24.2   Continued

```
            For Each prc in stp.PrecedenceConstraints
                prc.PrecedenceBasis = DTSStepPrecedenceBasis_ExecResult
                prc.Value = DTSStepExecResult_Success
            Next

    End Select

Next

    Main = DTSTaskExecResult_Success
End Function
```

If you have some tasks that you want to run after the transaction, you can use the VBScript
code in Listing 24.3 in a Workflow ActiveX script. The code checks if any of the steps in the
transaction have failed or if all the steps in the transaction have been executed. The task is executed when one of these conditions is met.

LISTING 24.3   A Workflow ActiveX Script That Can Be Used to Watch for the Completion
of a Transaction

```
Option Explicit
Function Main()

Dim pkg, stp
Set pkg = DTSGlobalVariables.Parent

Main = DTSStepScriptResult_ExecuteTask

For Each stp In pkg.Steps

    If stp.JoinTransactionIfPresent = True Then

        If stp.ExecutionResult = DTSStepExecResult_Failure And _
            stp.ExecutionStatus = DTSStepExecStat_Completed Then
            Main = DTSStepScriptResult_ExecuteTask
            Exit For
        End If

        If stp.ExecutionStatus = DTSStepExecStat_Waiting Then
            Main = DTSStepScriptResult_RetryLater
```

LISTING 24.3 Continued

```
            Exit For
        End If

    End If

Next

'Initialize or increment variable used for timing out
If IsEmpty(DTSGlobalVariables("lCounter").Value) Then
    DTSGlobalVariables("lCounter").Value = 1
Else
    DTSGlobalVariables("lCounter").Value = _
        DTSGlobalVariables("lCounter").Value  + 1
End If

'Time out if we've run the Workflow script too many times
IF DTSGlobalVariables("lCounter").Value > 1000 Then
    Main = DTSStepScriptResult_DontExecuteTask
End If

End Function
```

A Transaction with Steps Executed in Parallel

Sometimes, for better performance, you may want to execute several steps in a transaction in parallel. Figure 24.8 shows a package with steps executing in parallel. The DTS package with this transaction is on the CD in a file called ParallelTransaction.dts.

If you use parallel execution in a transaction, you have to be aware of these issues:

- If you have two connections to the same instance of SQL Server 2000, one of them is being used, and a task using the second is set to join the transaction, the package will fail. One way to avoid this error is to use a single connection for each SQL Server 2000 that is accessed by your package. Only one task can use a connection at a time, so the tasks will actually be executed serially even if they're set to execute in parallel. If there are two connections to separate instances of SQL Server 2000, they can be successfully executed in parallel.

- It can be hard to prevent new transactions from starting after a transaction failure. For example, in Figure 24.8 a transaction could start and be joined by the first tasks on each of the three branches of the programmatic flow. If From Pubs fails and the other two steps are completed successfully, the data modifications made in all three steps will be rolled back. The problem is that a new transaction will be started with the Report Employees tasks. To avoid this problem, you can select Fail package on first error on the Logging tab of the Package Properties dialog.

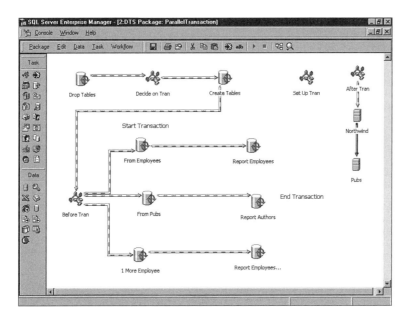

FIGURE 24.8
You can use a transaction with steps executed in parallel.

There may be times when you want to execute tasks in parallel and you don't want to fail the package on the first error. For example, you might want to send a message or do some other processing after the transaction has failed.

You can use an ActiveX Script task to commit or roll back a transaction after explicitly checking on the completion status of all the steps in the transaction. To implement this strategy, do the following:

1. Do *not* select Fail package on first error on the Logging tab of the Package Properties dialog.

2. Do *not* select Rollback on failure or Commit transaction on successful completion of this step for any of the steps in the transaction.

3. Create a new ActiveX Script task to be executed after all the tasks of the transaction have been completed. Figure 24.9 shows the package from Figure 24.8 with the ActiveX Script task added.

4. Do *not* select Join transaction if present for the ActiveX Script task. Select both Rollback transaction on failure and Commit transaction on successful completion of this step.

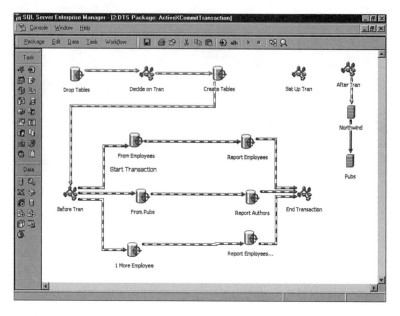

FIGURE 24.9

You can use an ActiveX Script task to commit or roll back a transaction executed in parallel.

5. Set all the precedence constraints to execute on completion.

6. The script for the ActiveX Script task is shown in Listing 24.4. This script assumes there is only one transaction in the package. If there were more than one, you would have to reference each step in the transaction explicitly, rather than looping through all the steps and examining all that were participating in a transaction.

LISTING 24.4   Code for an ActiveX Script Task to Commit or Roll Back a Transaction

```
Option Explicit
Function Main()

Dim pkg, stp
Set pkg = DTSGlobalVariables.Parent

Main = DTSTaskExecResult_Success

For Each stp In pkg.Steps

    If stp.JoinTransactionIfPresent = True Then

        If stp.ExecutionResult = DTSStepExecResult_Failure Then
            Main = DTSTaskExecResult_Failure
```

LISTING 24.4   Continued

```
        Exit For
    End If

  End If

Next

End Function
```

The DTS package with this transaction is on the CD in a file called
ActiveXCommitTransaction.dts.

Transactions Involving More Than One DTS Package

You can create a DTS transaction that includes steps from more than one package by doing
these two things:

1. Call another DTS package with the Execute Package task.
2. Select Join transaction if present for the step associated with that Execute Package task.

The transaction in the child package is called an *inherited transaction*. The events in the child
package can cause the transaction to be committed or rolled back, but not in the same way as a
normal DTS transaction:

- Select Join transaction if present for all steps in the child package that you want to
  include in the transaction. Data modifications will be committed immediately for steps
  that don't have this option selected.
- Rollback on failure and Commit transaction on successful completion of this step have
  no effect when selected for a step in an inherited transaction.
- If Rollback on failure is selected for the Execute Package task in the parent package and
  the child package terminates with failure, the whole transaction is rolled back. If you
  want to include all the steps of the child package in the transaction, select Join transaction if present for all the steps and select the option to fail the package on first error.
- If Commit transaction on successful completion of this step is selected for the Execute
  Package task in the parent package, and the child package terminates successfully, the
  whole transaction is committed.
- You can call another package from a child package that is participating in a transaction
  so that steps in additional packages are included in the transaction.

If you execute a package using the OLE Automation stored procedures in an Execute SQL task, using DTSRun in an Execute Process task, or using COM in an ActiveX Script task, you cannot include the called package in the DTS transaction.

Workflow ActiveX Scripts

A Workflow ActiveX Script is run at the beginning of a step's execution, before the task associated with that step is executed. The main purpose of the Workflow ActiveX Script is to determine whether or not the task should be executed.

You choose a Workflow ActiveX Script by selecting the Use ActiveX script box on the bottom of the Options tab of the Workflow Properties dialog (see Figure 24.10). You write the script by clicking the Properties button beside that check box. The Properties button opens the Workflow ActiveX Script Properties dialog, shown in Figure 24.11.

FIGURE 24.10
You choose a Workflow ActiveX Script on the Options tab of the Workflow Properties dialog.

The Workflow ActiveX Script Properties dialog is identical to the ActiveX Script Task Properties dialog, except that it doesn't have a box to enter a description for the task.

Script Result Constants

There are three script result constants that are used with workflow ActiveX scripts, each of which is described in this section. These values are assigned as the return value of the entry function:

```
Main = DTSStepScriptResult_ExecuteTask
```

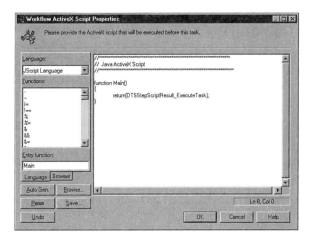

FIGURE 24.11
The scripts created in the Workflow ActiveX Script dialog determine whether or not a task is executed.

DTSStepScriptResult_ExecuteTask

Executes the task.

- Value   0

- Executes the task associated with this step immediately upon completion of the work-flow script.

- This is the default return value for a workflow script. It is also the return value when the Auto Gen. (auto generate) button is clicked.

DTSStepScriptResult_DontExecuteTask

Does not execute the task.

- Value   1

- The task associated with this step is not executed during the execution of the package.

DTSStepScriptResult_RetryLater

Retries the task later.

- Value   2

- The task associated with this step is not executed when the workflow script is completed. The execution method of the task is called again later in the execution of the package. When the step is retried, the workflow script is again executed before the task.

Using the Script Results for Looping

You can use the Retry Later Script Result to create a loop in the flow of the DTS Package. You could use this loop to check for the existence of a file, or to open a recordset to check on the state of data in a table. You could also use a loop to wait for the completion of other tasks, as shown in Listing 24.3:

1. You may want to use a Global Variable to serve as a counter. Increment the Global Variable each time the workflow script is run.

2. If the condition has not been met, the workflow script returns the Retry Later Script Result.

3. If everything is ready for the task to be run, the script returns the Execute Task Script Result.

4. You may want to terminate the loop with a return value of Don't Execute Task if the Global Variable reaches a certain value without the condition being met.

Step Properties for the Workflow Script

The workflow scripts are implemented with the following properties of the Step object:

- FunctionName—Specifies the entry function of the script. The default function name is *Main*.

- ActiveXScript—The text of the workflow ActiveX Script.

- ScriptLanguage—The scripting language used for the script.

- AddGlobalVariables—Determines whether or not global variables can be used in this workflow script. The default value is True.

Other Step Object Properties

The following Step object properties have already been discussed:

- AddGlobalVariables, ActiveXScript, ScriptLanguage, and FunctionName were covered in the section "Workflow ActiveX Scripts."

- CloseConnection, DisableStep, ExecuteInMainThread, and RelativePriority were covered in the section "Threads and Priority of Execution."

- IsPackageDSORowset was covered in Chapter 23, "The DTS Package and Its Properties".

- JoinTransactionIfPresent, CommitSuccess, and RollbackFailure were covered in the section "Transactions in DTS Packages."

- `Name` and `TaskName` were covered in the section "Steps."
- `ExecutionResult` and `ExecutionStatus` were covered in the section "Precedence Constraints."

The remaining step properties are discussed in this section.

StartTime, FinishTime, and ExecutionTime

`StartTime` and `FinishTime` are read-only properties with a date data type. `ExecutionTime` is a read-only integer, giving the duration of the task in seconds.

Description

The `Description` property on the `Step` object cannot be set in the DTS Designer, but it can be set in code. The description appears on the Options tab of the Workflow Properties dialog.

Parent

The `Parent` property of the `Step` object returns the `Steps` collection.

Creating a Step Using Visual Basic

I have created a Visual Basic procedure, `fctCreateStep`, that creates a step. All the properties of the step can be set with this procedure.

You can also find the code for `fctCreateStep` as a Visual Basic Project in the directory for Chapter 24 on the book's CD, with files CreateStep.vbp, CreateStep.frm, CreateStep.frx, and CreateStep.bas. This project creates a new package and associates the step with a Dynamic Properties task.

The code for `fctCreateStep` is shown in Listing 24.5.

LISTING 24.5 Code That Creates a Step and Sets All Its Properties

```
Public Function fctCreateStep( _
    pkg As DTS.Package2, _
    tsk As DTS.Task, _
    Optional sBaseName As String = "NewStep", _
    Optional sActiveXScript As String = "", _
    Optional bAddGlobalVariables As Boolean = True, _
    Optional bCloseConnection As Boolean = False, _
    Optional bCommitSuccess As Boolean = False, _
    Optional sDescription As String = "New Step", _
    Optional bDisableStep As Boolean = False, _
    Optional bExecuteInMainThread As Boolean = False, _
```

24

LISTING 24.5   Continued

```
        Optional sFunctionName As String = "", _
        Optional bIsPackageDSORowset As Boolean = False, _
        Optional bJoinTransactionIfPresent As Boolean = False, _
        Optional dtsRelativePriority As DTSStepRelativePriority = 3, _
        Optional bRollbackFailure As Boolean = False, _
        Optional sScriptLanguage As String = "VBScript", _
        Optional bFailPackageOnError As Boolean = False)


On Error GoTo ProcErr

Dim stp As DTS.Step2

'Check to see if the selected Base name is unique
sBaseName = fctFindUniqueBaseName(pkg, sBaseName)

'Create step for task
Set stp = pkg.Steps.New
With stp
    .Name = "stp" & sBaseName
    .Description = sBaseName
    .TaskName = tsk.Name
    .ActiveXScript = sActiveXScript
    .AddGlobalVariables = bAddGlobalVariables
    .CloseConnection = bCloseConnection
    .CommitSuccess = bCommitSuccess
    .DisableStep = bDisableStep
    .ExecuteInMainThread = bExecuteInMainThread
    .FunctionName = sFunctionName
    .IsPackageDSORowset = bIsPackageDSORowset
    .JoinTransactionIfPresent = bJoinTransactionIfPresent
    .RelativePriority = dtsRelativePriority
    .RollbackFailure = bRollbackFailure
    .ScriptLanguage = sScriptLanguage
    .FailPackageOnError = bFailPackageOnError
End With
pkg.Steps.Add stp

fctCreateStep = stp.Name

Set stp = Nothing

ProcExit:
  Exit Function
```

LISTING 24.5   Continued

```
ProcErr:
  MsgBox Err.Number & " - " & Err.Description
  GoTo ProcExit
End Function
```

Conclusion

Steps and their precedence constraints give you programmatic control over the execution of the tasks in your DTS package. The properties of the steps work together with the properties of the package to control transactions and priority of thread execution. As you work with objects in the Package Designer, the tasks seem more prominent but the steps are in control.

24

Rapid Development with the Copy Database Wizard and the DTS Import/Export Wizard

CHAPTER

25

IN THIS CHAPTER

The Copy Database Wizard and the DTS Import/Export Wizard automate and simplify the process of creating DTS packages. Wizards have two primary functions in a user interface:

- Organizing complex jobs into an orderly sequence of events so that a person who's unfamiliar with a piece of software can make all the necessary choices.
- Automating repetitive jobs so that they can be accomplished more quickly.

The Copy Database Wizard and the DTS Import/Export Wizard accomplish both of these goals. They provide an excellent learning tool for a person who is just learning about DTS, and they can also save an experienced user a lot of time in certain situations. The most significant time savings over using the DTS Designer comes in the following situations:

- You are transferring many tables, and the data destination has tables with the same names and field names. The Import/Export Wizard sets up all the data transformations automatically.
- You are transferring many tables, and you want to create new tables at the data destination. The Import/Export Wizard will automatically make Execute SQL tasks to create those tables.
- You are copying or moving a set of databases from one SQL Server to another SQL Server, and you want to include all the relevant metadata. The Copy Database Wizard selects all the metadata as the default choice.

Two Wizards with Three Levels of Granularity

The two DTS wizards offer three levels of granularity:

- Transferring whole databases.
- Copying SQL Server objects, such as tables and their data.
- Transforming data through row-by-row processing.

The Copy Database Wizard only offers the highest level of data movement—transferring whole databases. The other two levels of granularity are available in the Import/Export Wizard.

Transferring Databases with the Copy Database Wizard

The Copy Database Wizard allows you to copy or move a database from one SQL Server to another. Multiple databases may be moved or copied at one time, but during the process no changes may be made to those databases, objects within the databases, or the data itself.

One important application for this wizard is in upgrading databases from SQL Server 7.0 to SQL Server 2000. If you use the wizard for upgrading, you don't have to shut down any servers in the process. Also, metadata can be included in the upgrade procedure, and the upgrade can be scheduled for a convenient time.

The Copy Database Wizard is more restrictive than the Import/Export Wizard. You are limited to the following situations:

- Moving or copying a database from SQL Server 2000 to SQL Server 2000.
- Moving or copying a database from SQL Server 7.0 to SQL Server 2000.

In addition, you are not allowed to copy a database to SQL Sever 2000 running on Windows 98 when the source SQL Server is running on Windows 2000 or Windows NT.

Transferring SQL Server Objects with the Import/Export Wizard

Transferring SQL Server Objects with the Import/Export Wizard gives you more control than what is available with the Copy Database Wizard. You can choose to transfer or not transfer specific objects within a database. You can't modify any of the data in those objects.

You select the option to transfer SQL Server objects on the third screen of the Import/Export Wizard, as shown in Figure 25.1.

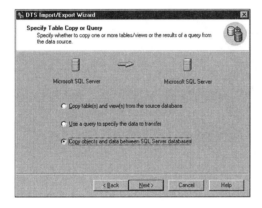

FIGURE 25.1
The Specify Table Copy or Query screen determines whether or not you are using the wizard to transfer SQL Server objects.

The transfer of SQL Server objects is slightly less restrictive than the transfer of databases. You can transfer the SQL Server objects between any SQL Server 7.0 and SQL Server 2000 databases.

25

Transforming Data with the Import/Export Wizard

You have the highest level of control when you use the Import/Export Wizard to transform data. When you select either of the first two choices on the third tab of the wizard, you can manipulate the data in each row as you transfer it.

RAPID DEVELOPMENT

You are much less restricted in your data sources and data destinations when you use the wizard in this way. You can use any data store with an OLE DB provider that works with DTS or an ODBC provider—SQL Server databases, Oracle databases, text files, Microsoft Access databases, and Excel spreadsheets, for example.

> **NOTE**
>
> One situation where I have often used the Import/Export Wizard is in upgrading an existing database in Btrieve, Paradox, or Microsoft Access to SQL Server (and occasionally to other destinations).
>
> It is very easy to create the connections to the existing database and to SQL Server, generate the code for the new tables, and create the transformations. In a few minutes, you can have a package set to move your database from any data source to any other data source that can connect to DTS.
>
> There are a couple of things you have to be careful about when doing this. Check if the destination datatypes are created as you want them to be. If they're not, you can do the following:
>
> 1. Use the Import/Export Wizard to create a package that creates all the new tables but does not transfer any data.
> 2. Script the database structure.
> 3. Make global changes in the script to replace the datatypes.
> 4. Re-create the database with the script.
> 5. Create another DTS package with the Import/Export Wizard to move the data.
>
> Also, constraints might be violated as the tables are loaded into the destination database. A new feature in the SQL Server 2000 Import/Export Wizard helps you work around this problem by allowing you to load the data first and then apply the constraints.

Calling the Wizards

The wizards are made available in a variety of ways, both inside and outside of SQL Server's Enterprise Manager.

The DTS Import/Export Wizard is easier to find than the DTS Designer. You can call the wizard from the Start menu by selecting Start, Programs, Microsoft SQL Server, Import and Export Data. You can also call it from the Enterprise Manager, from the DTSWiz command-line utility, or from Visual Basic using the SQL Namespace object model.

The Copy Database Wizard can be called either from the Enterprise Manager or from the command line.

From the Enterprise Manager

You can open the Copy Database Wizard in the Enterprise Manager by highlighting the SQL Server node and selecting Wizards from the Tools menu. The Copy Database Wizard is listed under the Management node in the Select Wizard dialog.

Here are the ways you can run the DTS Import/Export Wizard from inside the Enterprise Manager:

- Right-click on the Data Transformation Services folder, on the name of the server, on Databases, on any database, on Tables, or on any individual table. Select All Tasks. Select either Import Data or Export Data.
- Select any of the objects previously listed. Select the All Tasks item from the Action menu, and then select either Import Data or Export Data.
- Select Tools, Data Transformation Services from the menu. Select either Import Data or Export Data.
- Highlight the SQL Server node and select Wizards from the Tools menu. Select either the DTS Import Wizard or the DTS Export Wizard under the Data Transformation Services node in the Select Wizard dialog.

From the Command Line

The Copy Database Wizard can be run from the command line using the cdw command-line utility. The cdw utility does not have any parameters.

The DTS Wizard can be started from the command line using the DTSWiz command-line utility. DTSWiz has the following parameters, none of which are required:

- /n—Use Windows NT authentication. This is the default choice.
- /u—SQL Server login ID.
- /p—Password for the SQL Server login ID.
- /f—Name of the file to which the package will be saved. This parameter is documented in Books Online, but it is not available in the initial release of SQL Server 2000.
- /i—Call the wizard for import into SQL Server.
- /x—Call the wizard for export from SQL Server.
- /r—The name of the data provider, such as MSDASQL for the Microsoft OLE DB Provider for ODBC. This parameter is documented in Books Online, but it is not available in the initial release of SQL Server 2000.
- /s—The name of the SQL Server.

25

RAPID DEVELOPMENT

- /d—The name of the SQL Server database used in the import or export, if the /i or /x parameter is used.

- /y—Prevent the SQL Server system databases from being seen in the lists of source and destination databases.

- /?—Display the command prompt options.

- /m—Execute all steps on the main package thread. This option is discussed in Chapter 24, "Steps and Precedence Constraints."

Using `dtswiz /i /d Northwind /u sa /p 123` at the command prompt brings up the wizard for importing data into the Northwind database with a username of sa and a password of 123.

From Code

The SQL Namespace (SQL-NS) object model is a feature in SQL Server that lets programs call Enterprise Manager interface components.

I have included a sample Visual Basic program for calling the DTS Wizard. Only two objects and four methods from SQL-NS are needed in this program:

- The `SQLNamespace` object is the highest-level object in the SQL-NS object hierarchy.

- The Initialize method of the SQLNamespace object is used to connect to a particular SQL Server.

- The `SQLNamespaceObject` object can be used to execute commands that call various objects in the Enterprise Manager.

- The `GetRootItem` method of the `SQLNamespace` object returns a handle to the root object of the hierarchy. In this case, the root object is the SQL Server.

- The `GetSQLNamespaceObject` of the `SQLNamespace` object is used to create an `SQLNamespaceObject`. This method has one parameter—the level of the Enterprise manager Console Tree at which the `SQLNamespaceObject` is being created. For calling the DTS Wizard, the `SQLNamespaceObject` should be created at the SQL Server level of the hierarchy.

- The `ExecuteCommandByID` method of the `SQLNamespaceObject` calls one of the Enterprise Manager's interface components. This method has three parameters: a command ID constant, a handle to the application window, and a constant that determines whether or not the called object will be modal. The command ID constants for calling the DTS Wizards are `SQLNS_CmdID_DTS_Import` and `SQLNS_CmdID_DTS_Export`.

Listing 25.1 contains the code for the *Run DTS Wizards* application. You can also find this code on the book's CD in the folder for Chapter 25.

LISTING 25.1 A VB Application That Calls the Import/Export Wizard

```
Option Explicit

'Must include reference to Microsoft SQLNamespace Object Library
'This Object Library implemented in Mssql7\Binn\Sqlns.dll
Dim oSQLNS As SQLNamespace
Dim hServer As Long
'Create a SQLNamespaceObject object
'SQLNamespaceObject objects are used for executing Namespace commands
Dim oSQLNSObject As SQLNS.SQLNamespaceObject

Private Sub Form_Load()

  Dim oSQLNSObject As SQLNamespaceObject

  'Create the SQL Namespace object
  Set oSQLNS = New SQLNamespace

  'Initialize the SQLNameSpace object
  'Change Connection String as needed
  'For Trusted Connection, use "Server=.;Trusted_Connection=Yes;"
  oSQLNS.Initialize "RunDTSWiz", SQLNSRootType_Server, _
      "Server=.;UID=sa;pwd=;", hWnd

  'Get root object of type Server
  hServer = oSQLNS.GetRootItem

  Set oSQLNSObject = oSQLNS.GetSQLNamespaceObject(hServer)

  'Call the DTS Import wizard
  oSQLNSObject.ExecuteCommandByID SQLNS_CmdID_WIZARD_DTSIMPORT, _
      hWnd, SQLNamespace_PreferModal

  'Or call the DTS Export wizard
  oSQLNSObject.ExecuteCommandByID SQLNS_CmdID_WIZARD_DTSEXPORT, _
      hWnd, SQLNamespace_PreferModal

End Sub
```

Using the Copy Database Wizard

The Welcome screen of the Copy Database Wizard lists the things that the wizard allows you to choose:

- Pick source and destination server.
- Select databases to move or copy.

- Specify the file location for the databases.
- Create logins on the destination server.
- Move supporting shared objects, jobs, and error messages.
- Schedule the database migration.

Choosing the Source and Destination

The first two tabs of the Copy Database Wizard allow you to choose the source and the destination of the database transfer. Remember the limitations for the source and destination:

- The source must be SQL Server 7.0 or SQL Server 2000.
- You cannot transfer a database that is involved in replication.
- The destination must be SQL Server 2000.
- You cannot transfer from a SQL Server on Windows 2000 or Windows NT to a SQL Server on Windows 98.

There are also some security restrictions for the user who's executing the package that the wizard creates. The user must have the following:

- Sysadmin privileges on both SQL Servers involved in the transfer.
- Administrator privileges on the network.
- Exclusive use of all the files that are involved in the transfer.

Choosing the Databases and File Locations

The next screen gives you the choice of databases to transfer. The wizard lists all the databases on the source server, and it indicates which ones you are not allowed to transfer. You cannot transfer the following databases:

- System databases.
- Databases where the destination server has a database of the same name.

For each database you are transferring, you have the choice of moving or copying, as shown in Figure 25.2. If you move the database, it will be removed from the list of databases on the source server, but the database files will not be removed from the source server.

You also have a list box to specify the location of the data and log files to be used in the transfer. All the shared drives on the source server are included in the list.

The next screen of the wizard, shown in Figure 25.3, gives you the opportunity to view and change the destination files for the database transfer. If a file already exists with the same name in the default destination data directory, or if the default location doesn't have adequate disk space for the database transfer, a red X appears in the Status box.

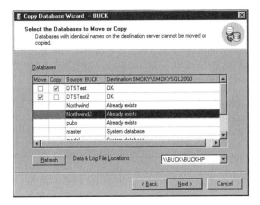

FIGURE 25.2
You can choose to move some databases and copy other databases.

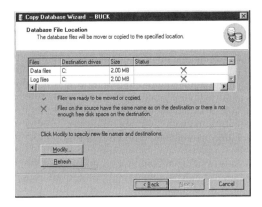

FIGURE 25.3
The wizard tells you if you have name conflicts or inadequate disk space on your destination directory.

You can change the destination filenames by clicking on the Modify button. If there is a conflict, you have to change the names before you can go on. You can always change the names if you prefer your data and log files to be placed in a different location, or if you want them to have different names than the ones that are automatically generated. The dialog for modifying the filenames is shown in Figure 25.4.

25

NOTE

The Copy Database Wizard lets you deal with conflicts caused by duplicate filenames. However, it does not let you change database names to deal with duplicate databases on the source and the destination. If you have a naming conflict, you can use the system stored procedure sp_renamedb to rename the source database before moving it.

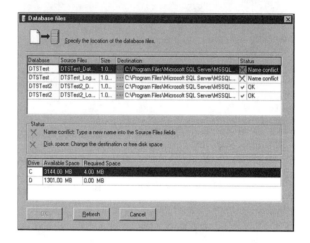

FIGURE 25.4
The wizard lets you resolve problems with the destination files.

Choosing Other Objects to Transfer

The next screen, shown in Figure 25.5, allows you to select other objects to transfer with the databases. All of these objects are stored in either the master or msdb system databases. If they are not transferred along with the database, it might not function properly in its new location. The four types of objects are

- Logins, which are stored in the master database.
- Shared stored procedures from the master database.
- User-defined error messages from the master database.
- Jobs from msdb.

The default choice is to select all the objects in all four of these categories. You can choose not to transfer any of the objects in any of the categories by unselecting the check box.

You can also choose to limit the number of objects selected. For the logins, you can choose to transfer only the logins for the specified databases. For the other three types of metadata, you can view a list for each one so you can make specific choices about which objects to transfer. The selection of user-defined error messages is shown in Figure 25.6.

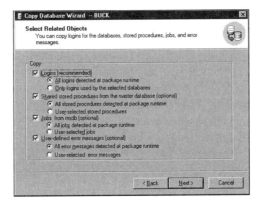

FIGURE 25.5
You can change the wizard's default transfer of all relevant metadata.

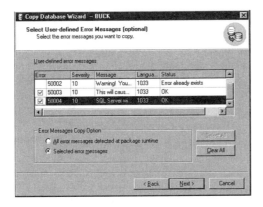

FIGURE 25.6
You can choose which of the user-defined error messages you want to transfer.

There is more information about transferring the various types of metadata in Chapter 15, "The Transfer Database and Other Transfer Tasks."

The DTS Package Created by the Copy Database Wizard

The last screen of the wizard lets you run the package immediately or schedule it to run at a later time. You cannot choose a name for the package. It is automatically named and saved on the destination server at the conclusion of the wizard.

The DTS package created by the wizard has one Transfer Databases task and one each of the other transfer tasks, if you have chosen to include the various types of metadata:

- Transfer Logins task
- Transfer Jobs task
- Transfer Master Stored Procedures task
- Transfer Error Messages task

You can edit the DTS package in the DTS Designer after you have created it, and you can change any of the choices you have made in the wizard. Figure 25.7 shows a package created with the Copy Database Wizard as it appears in the DTS Designer.

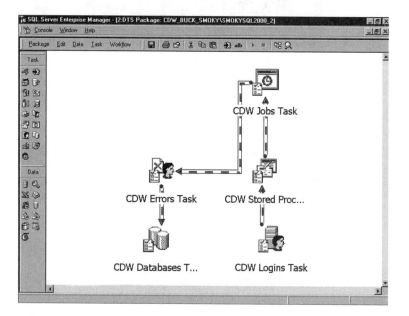

FIGURE 25.7

The DTS package created by the Copy Database Wizard has up to five tasks.

Creating Connections with the Import/Export Wizard

All the functionality for setting up connections in the DTS Designer (as discussed in Chapter 5) is available in the DTS wizard. The screens are almost identical to the ones in the DTS Designer, except that many of them are presented sequentially as the user moves through the wizard.

The wizard always requires you to set up two data connections, and *only* two. One of the connections is going to be used as the data source, and the other is going to be used as the data destination.

Figure 25.8 shows the Data Source screen of the wizard, with the choices presented for the Microsoft OLE DB Provider for SQL Server. Note that, as in the Designer, there is a button for setting the advanced properties of the OLE DB driver.

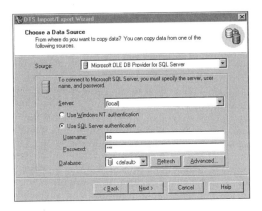

FIGURE 25.8
Choosing a data source with the DTS wizard is the same as setting up a data connection in the DTS Designer.

If a text file is chosen as the data source, the same screens that are presented in the DTS Designer for specifying text files are now presented as the next tabs in the wizard. The tab for choosing a destination is identical to the tab for choosing the source.

Transferring SQL Server Objects

The Import/Export Wizard creates two very different kinds of DTS packages. If you choose one of the first two options on the Specify Table Copy or Query screen, you will create a package that uses Transform Data tasks to accomplish its work. If you choose the third option, Copy Objects and Data Between SQL Server Databases, you will create a package that uses the Copy SQL Server Objects task.

The transfer of SQL Server objects is a little more flexible than the copying of databases, but it is not nearly as flexible as the Transform Data task. You can only transfer objects between a source and a destination that are either SQL Server 7.0 or SQL Server 2000.

When you make this selection, the Select Objects to Copy tab appears. This tab has exactly the same choices as the Copy SQL Server Objects Task Properties dialog. The three buttons on this tab, Select Objects, Options, and the expand button, bring you to the same dialogs that you would see if you were using the DTS Designer.

Chapter 13, "The Copy SQL Server Objects Task," explains the options that you have when creating this task.

> **NOTE**
>
> The Import/Export Wizard is a very useful tool when you are using it to set up data transformations, but it is not very helpful when you are copying SQL Server objects.
>
> The difference is that the Transform Data task normally works with just two tables—a source and a destination. The wizard lets you set up many Transform Data tasks at the same time and will create the destination tables if they do not exist. You can't do this nearly as quickly using the DTS Designer.
>
> The Copy SQL Server Objects task is very different. You can use this task in the DTS Designer to copy many tables at the same time. Setting up a package using this task with the DTS Designer is just as fast as using the Import/Export Wizard.

Setting Up Data Transformations

If you pick the first or second option on the Specify Table Copy or Query screen, you create a package that primarily uses the Transform Data task to move data.

Using a Query to Specify the Data to Transfer

The second option on the Specify Table Copy or Query screen lets you write an SQL statement to be used as the data source for the Transform Data task, as shown in Figure 25.9.

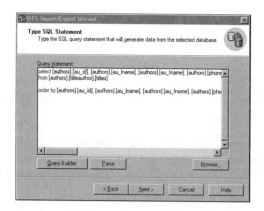

FIGURE 25.9

Note the lack of a join clause in this query generated by the wizard's Query Builder.

The Browse button provides an Open File dialog. The Parse button checks the syntax of the query. The Query Builder button directs the wizard on a path of three extra tabs that provide a simple format for creating a query.

The Select Columns tab lets you choose any field from any of the tables in the data source. The Specify Sort Order tab lets you choose fields to be sorted. The Specify Query Criteria tab lets you specify criteria to limit the rows returned. There are expand buttons for each line on this third tab, which open the Select a Value dialog. This dialog presents the actual data from the fields in the data source so that you can pick one to use as a limiting criterion in the query. Figure 25.10 shows the Specify Query Criteria tab and the Select a Value dialog.

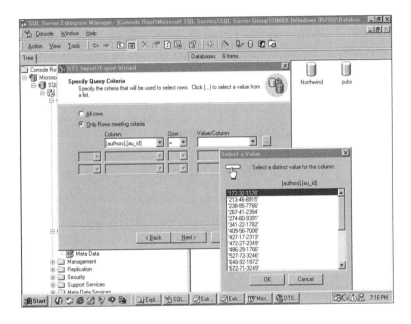

FIGURE 25.10

You can choose criteria to limit the query on the third tab of the Query Builder. Click the expand button to pick from actual source data values.

> **NOTE**
>
> The Query Builder in the DTS Wizard could be useful, but it doesn't let you specify joins except as criteria expressions on the third tab. If you include more than one table and you don't specify a join on the third tab, the query is written as a cross-join without giving any warning to the user.
>
> At first glance, this Query Builder looks like it could be useful to a person without much experience in the world of SQL. It is very easy to use—except for not providing much help with the joins.

> If you do specify joins between tables on the criteria tab, they are written with the non-ANSI standard join syntax in the WHERE clause of the SQL statement. When you're done with the Query Builder, you can edit the generated query in any way that you choose.
>
> The DTS Query Designer that's available in many different places in the DTS Designer is a far more convenient and sophisticated tool for building queries.

Copying Table(s) from the Source Database

If you pick the first of the three options on the Specify Table Copy or Query screen, the wizard presents a list of all the available tables in the data source, as shown in Figure 25.11. The capability to set up transformations for many tables at the same time is the greatest advantage that the Import/Export Wizard has over the DTS Designer.

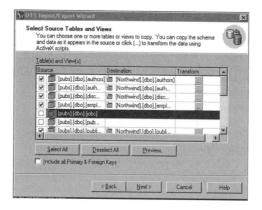

FIGURE 25.11

You can create transformations for one, many, or all of the tables in the data source.

The Destination Tables

For each table you select, the wizard automatically adds a destination table with the same name, whether or not that table actually exists. You can change the selection of the destination table by picking from a list of all the tables that exist in the data destination. You can also type a name in the destination table column for a new table that you want to be created for this transformation.

A Preview button at the bottom of the Select Source Tables and Views tab displays the View Data box, which displays up to 100 records from the data destination.

The expand button in the Transform column opens up the Column Mappings and Transformations dialog, shown in Figure 25.12.

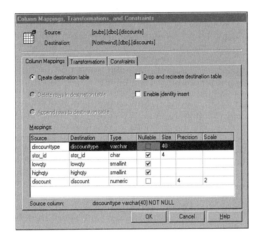

FIGURE 25.12
You can open the Column Mappings and Transformations dialog with the Expand button in the Transform column of the Select Source Tables and Views tab.

The Column Mappings and Transformations dialog has three primary choices on the Column Mappings tab:

- Create destination table.
- Delete rows in destination table.
- Append rows to destination table.

If you have chosen a destination table that does not exist, creating a destination table will be the only choice available. If you have chosen a destination table that does exist, the append rows choice will be chosen, but you can change to either of the other two.

When the option for creating a destination table is selected, the Edit SQL button is enabled. You can open the Create Table SQL Statement dialog, shown in Figure 25.13, with this button. By default, this dialog creates a destination table that is identical in structure to the source table that has been selected. You can edit the SQL statement. While editing, you can return to the automatically generated statement by selecting the Auto Generate button.

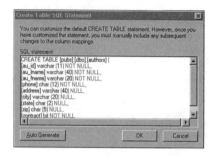

FIGURE 25.13
You use the Create Table SQL Statement dialog to write the SQL statement for creating a new table in the data destination.

NOTE

In the Data Designer, if you are setting up a transformation into a new table, that table is actually created in the data destination at the time you design it. That's not true with the wizard. No new tables are created until the package is actually run. The text that is written in the Create Table SQL Statement dialog is used in an Execute SQL task in the DTS package that the wizard creates.

When you choose the Create destination table option, you also have the choice of dropping and re-creating the destination table. When this option is selected, the wizard creates an additional Execute SQL task to drop the table. The DTS package will run successfully whether or not the table exists at the time the package is executed. An On Completion precedence constraint is set between the two Execute SQL Statements. If the table doesn't exist, the Drop Table task will fail. If the table does exist, the Drop Table task will be successful. Either way, the workflow will go on to the Create Table task. Figure 25.14 shows the DTS Designer view of a transformation where the destination table is dropped and re-created.

The option for deleting rows in the destination table sets up an Execute SQL task that deletes all the rows before the transform Data task is run.

For all three options, there is the additional possibility of selecting the Enable Identity Insert box, so that the identity_insert property is on while the transformation is being run. This property allows values to be inserted into the normally auto-generated Identity field.

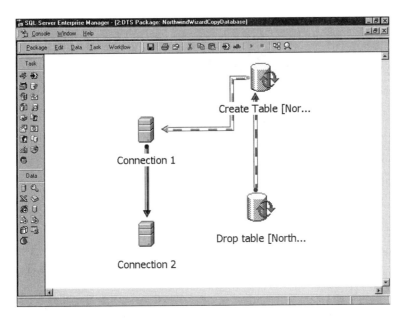

FIGURE 25.14
Two Execute SQL tasks are created to carry out the Drop Table and Create Table actions.

The Data Transformations

The bottom of the Column Mappings tab shows the actual mappings of the columns from the source to the destination. The default mapping that is prepared simply matches the first field in the source with the field in the destination, in the same way it's done in the DTS Designer. The source columns in this box can be changed so that a different column is used for a particular destination column. You can also choose to ignore a particular column in the destination. That column then does not appear in the list of fields being copied or transformed.

Figure 25.15 shows the Transformations tab of the Column Mappings and Transformations dialog.

The Transformations tab presents two of the nine built-in types of transformations—the two that were available in the DTS Designer in SQL Server 7.0:

- Copying the source columns directly to the destination columns.
- Transforming information as it is copied to the destination.

25

RAPID
DEVELOPMENT

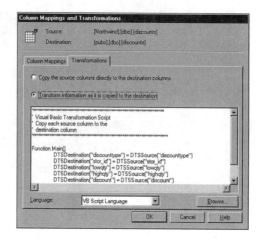

FIGURE 25.15

You can choose to copy columns or write an ActiveX Transformation Script on the Transformations tab of the Column Mappings and Transformations dialog.

When the Transform information option is selected, you are given three options:

- Writing or editing the ActiveX script used for the transformation.
- Browsing to find a file that contains an ActiveX script to use.
- Choosing a different scripting language.

A default script is generated when you first open the dialog. This script implements a simple copy of each field from the source table to the destination table, based on the mappings that have been selected on the Column Mappings tab.

If the column mappings are changed, the wizard asks if a new default script should be generated that uses the changed mappings. In the same way, if the scripting language is changed, the wizard asks if a new script should be generated using the new language. You can choose to accept the new script or leave the current script unchanged.

Executing, Scheduling, Saving, and Replicating the Package

The last step in using the Import/Export Wizard is to decide what you want to do with your new package. The Save, Schedule, and Replicate Package tab, shown in Figure 25.16, gives you all these choices.

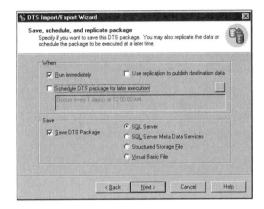

FIGURE 25.16
You can Run, Save, Schedule, and Replicate your new DTS package.

You can do four things with your new package, in various combinations:

- Run immediately. This is the only choice selected by default. No matter what else you choose to do with the package, you can still make this choice.

- Use replication to publish destination data. This choice is not available unless you also choose to run the package immediately.

- Schedule DTS Package for later execution. If you make this choice, use the expand button to bring up the Edit Recurring Job Schedule dialog. There you can schedule the package to run a single time in the future or on a regular schedule.

- Save DTS Package. This option can be chosen by itself, and it is also chosen automatically when Schedule DTS Package is chosen.

Creating a DTS Package for Replication

You choose this option if you want to use the data destination as a replication publication. This can be a convenient way to set up replication from non-SQL Server data sources. Replication normally requires a SQL Server data source. When you use DTS with this replication option, you can work around this limitation. The DTS package creates the data for the replication publication, which can then be replicated like any other publication.

The Create Publication Wizard, shown in Figure 25.17, opens automatically after the DTS Wizard is finished to allow you to set up all the choices for replication.

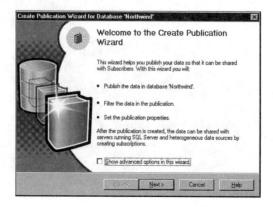

FIGURE 25.17

If you choose to create the DTS Package for replication, the Create Publication Wizard opens up when the DTS Wizard is done.

If you don't save the package, this can only be a one-time snapshot publication. If you do save it, you can set up a publication that is refreshed periodically.

Scheduling a DTS Package for Later Execution

When you choose to schedule the DTS package, the expand button is enabled. This brings you to the Edit Recurring Job Schedule dialog, shown in Figure 25.18.

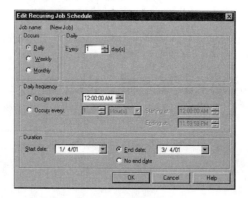

FIGURE 25.18

The wizard provides all the options for scheduling a DTS package.

If you choose to schedule the package but you don't select any particular form of scheduling, the wizard will schedule the package to be executed once a day at midnight. You can change or delete this scheduled package execution at any time in the Jobs section of the SQL Server Agent.

Saving a DTS Package

If you choose to save the DTS Package, the four package storage options are enabled: SQL Server, SQL Server Meta Data Services, Structured Storage File, and Visual Basic File.

The next tab in the wizard presents the additional choices that are needed to successfully save a DTS package. These choices are identical to the choices presented when you save a package in the DTS Designer. However, if you change your mind about which storage method you want to use, you can't change it on this tab—you have to back up to the previous tab.

Completing the Import/Export Wizard

The last screen of the DTS Wizard allows you to review the choices you have made and change any of them. When you click Finish, the transferring data box displays a progress report as your package is executed, scheduled, and/or saved. If any errors occur, you can click on the line with the error and receive a description of the error message. Figure 25.19 shows a sample error message.

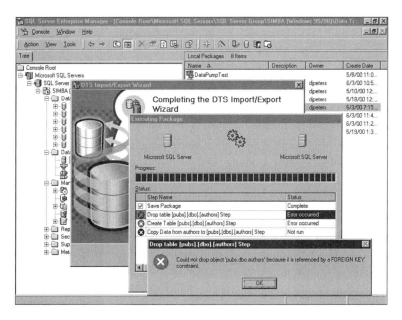

FIGURE 25.19
You can receive an error report by clicking on any errors that appear in the Transferring Data box.

Conclusion

Don't forget to use the DTS wizards. They won't give you the whole DTS programming environment, but they can make your job easier.

If you are transferring a lot of tables, you might as well start your data transformations with the wizards. You can always finish the job with the DTS Designer.

Managing Packages with Visual Basic and Stored Procedures

IN THIS CHAPTER

You can extend the flexibility of DTS by managing packages programmatically. You can manage packages with any programming language that supports COM.

This chapter focuses on managing packages with Visual Basic and with the OLE Automation system stored procedures available in SQL Server. Much of the information in this chapter is also relevant to other programming languages.

Many of the chapters in this book have examples that show how to use Visual Basic with DTS. Chapter 12, "The Execute SQL Task," and Chapter 18, "The Execute Package Task," have examples of using the OLE Automation stored procedures. Chapter 30, "Programming with the DTS Object Model," has a summary of the programming objects available in DTS. Chapters 31, "Creating a Custom Task with VB," and 32, "Creating a Custom Transformation with VC++," show how to extend DTS functionality by programming custom tasks and custom transformations.

Working with DTS Packages in Visual Basic

You have many advantages when you use Visual Basic with DTS instead of using the DTS management tools built into SQL Server 2000:

- The ability to integrate DTS functionality with the rest of your application.
- More flexibility in responding to errors generated by DTS.
- A more convenient development environment for writing programming code.

There are also some disadvantages:

- The DTS Designer and the DTS Wizard generate many DTS objects automatically. A good deal of programming is needed to re-create these structures using Visual Basic.
- The DTS Designer gives a visual representation of the programmatic flow in the data transformation. This visual representation is missing when you work with DTS in Visual Basic.

Because there are distinct advantages to working with DTS in Visual Basic and to working with the SQL Server 2000 DTS design tools, the best development strategy often uses both. Because you can save a package as Visual Basic code, you can quickly move from one environment to the other.

Installation Requirements

The earliest version of Visual Basic you can use with DTS in SQL Server 2000 is 5.0 with Service Pack 3. You also have to install the SQL Server client tools on both your development computer and all the computers that are going to be running the packages.

Saving a Package to Visual Basic

It's usually easiest to start the development of a DTS package with the DTS Wizard or the DTS Designer. When you want to work with the package's objects from Visual Basic, you can save the package to Visual Basic code. You can do this from both the DTS Wizard and the DTS Designer. The Save DTS Package dialog from the DTS Designer is shown in Figure 26.1.

FIGURE 26.1
The DTS Designer and the DTS Wizard both allow you to save a package as a Visual Basic code file.

There are several reasons why you might want to save a package to Visual Basic:

- To search for and replace variable names, DTS object names, data structure names, or server names throughout a package.
- To verify or modify a particular setting for a property in all objects of a package.
- To merge two or more packages (although you have to avoid conflicts with object names and connection ID values when you do this).
- So that you can continue development of the package in the Visual Basic development environment.
- To dynamically modify and execute the package as a part of a Visual Basic application.
- To learn about programming with the DTS object model.

There is one significant problem in saving a package to Visual Basic—you lose the package's visual display if you open it up again with the Package Designer.

The DTS Package Designer provides an excellent graphical user interface for displaying the flow of a data transformation application. You can place connection, task, and workflow icons in the places that most clearly illustrate what is happening in the data transformation.

This visual display is lost if you save a package to Visual Basic and then execute the Visual Basic code to save the package to one of the other three forms of storage. SaveToSQLServer, SaveToStorageFile, and SaveToRepository all have a parameter called pVarPersistStgOfHost, which is used to store a package's screen layout information. Unfortunately, this parameter can only be referenced internally by the DTS Designer. It is not possible to use this parameter from Visual Basic to save or re-create the package's visual display in the designer.

When a package is saved from Visual Basic using any of the DTS Save methods, the default layout is created. The wizards also use the default layout. This layout is fine for simple packages, but it's usually inadequate for more complex ones.

Figure 26.2 shows a complex package in the DTS Designer before it's saved to Visual Basic. Figure 26.3 shows the same package after it has been saved from Visual Basic and then opened again in the DTS Designer.

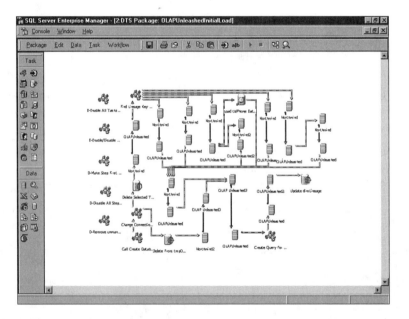

FIGURE 26.2
A complex DTS package before being saved to Visual Basic. (Sample package from Microsoft OLAP Unleashed.*)*

Managing Packages with Visual Basic and Stored Procedures

CHAPTER 26

529

26

MANAGING
PACKAGES WITH
VISUAL BASIC

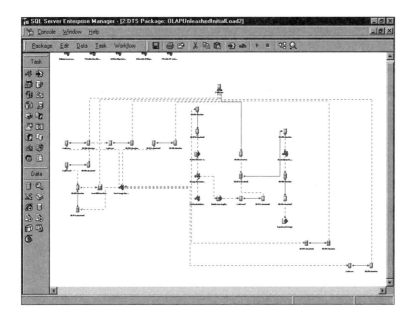

FIGURE 26.3
The same DTS package after being saved from Visual Basic with no changes.

> **NOTE**
>
> If I have a package with a complex layout and I want to make a global change of a name or a property, I often use an ActiveX Script inside the package to make the change. The loss of the package's layout makes me avoid using the Visual Basic saving option for simple changes in complex packages.

Setting Up the Visual Basic Design Environment

You can create a package in Visual Basic using any one of these project types:

- Standard EXE
- ActiveX EXE
- ActiveX Document EXE
- ActiveX DLL
- ActiveX Document DLL

Code Libraries Needed for DTS

You will need to add references to some or all of the following libraries:

- Microsoft DTSPackage Object Library (dtspkg.dll)—Required for all DTS packages.
- Microsoft DTSDataPump Scripting Object Library (dtspump.dll)—Almost always required. It contains the built-in transformations and the DTS scripting object.
- Microsoft DTS Custom Tasks Object Library (custtask.dll)—Contains the Message Queue task, the FTP task, and the Dynamic Properties task.
- DTSOLAPProcess (msmdtsp.dll)—Contains the Analysis Services Processing task.
- DTSPrediction (msmdtsm.dll)—Contains the Data Mining Prediction task.
- OMWCustomTasks 1.0 Type Library (cdwtasks.dll)—Contains the Transfer Databases task and the four associated transfer tasks.

Starting a Project with a Package Saved to Visual Basic

When you save a package to Visual Basic, a code module (*.bas) is created. Here is one of the ways you can use that code module in Visual Basic:

1. Open Visual Basic and create a new Standard EXE project.
2. Select References from the Project menu. Add the object libraries that are needed for your package.
3. Add the saved DTS code module to the project.
4. You can remove the default form from the project, if you want. It's not needed.
5. The code module contains code for both executing the package and saving it to SQL Server. When the code module is created, the line to save the package is commented out, so the package is executed but not saved.

The Structure of the Generated DTS Visual Basic Code Module

The book's CD has a simple DTS package stored in a file called Save To VB Demo Package.dts. This package has been saved to a Visual Basic code module called Save To VB Demo Package.bas. All the sample code in this section comes from this code module.

The code module that's generated when you save a package to Visual Basic has the following elements:

- Header information
- Declaration of public variables
- Main function

Managing Packages with Visual Basic and Stored Procedures

CHAPTER 26

531

26

MANAGING
PACKAGES WITH
VISUAL BASIC

- One function to create each of the tasks
- One function to create each of the transformations in the transformation tasks

Header Information

The Visual Basic code module for a DTS task starts with header information that describes the creation of the module. The header for the Save To VB Demo Package is shown in Listing 26.1.

LISTING 26.1 The Header for a DTS Visual Basic Code Module

```
'***************************************************************
'Microsoft SQL Server 2000
'Visual Basic file generated for DTS Package
'File Name: C:\Temp\Save To VB Demo Package.bas
'Package Name: Save To VB Demo Package
'Package Description: Save To VB Demo Package
'Generated Date: 8/8/2000
'Generated Time: 8:25:24 AM
'***************************************************************
```

Declaration of Public Variables

The code module declares two public variables, one for a `Package` object and the other for a `Package2` object. It's necessary to have a `Package2` object so that the extended features in SQL Server 2000 can be accessed. The `Package` object is needed to handle events in Visual Basic. Handling DTS events in Visual Basic is described in the "Executing a Package from Visual Basic" section later in this chapter.

The public variable declarations are shown in Listing 26.2.

LISTING 26.2 The Declaration of Public Variables in a DTS Visual Basic Code Module

```
Option Explicit
Public goPackageOld As New DTS.Package
Public goPackage As DTS.Package2
```

Main Function

The Main function has five sections:

- Set package properties
- Create package connections

- Create package steps
- Create package tasks
- Save or execute package

The function begins by setting the properties of the DTS package as a whole, as shown in Listing 26.3.

LISTING 26.3   Setting the Package Properties at the Beginning of the Main Function

```
Private Sub Main()

set goPackage = goPackageOld

goPackage.Name = "Save To VB Demo Package"
goPackage.Description = "Save To VB Demo Package"
goPackage.WriteCompletionStatusToNTEventLog = False
goPackage.FailOnError = False
goPackage.PackagePriorityClass = 2
goPackage.MaxConcurrentSteps = 4
goPackage.LineageOptions = 0
goPackage.UseTransaction = True
goPackage.TransactionIsolationLevel = 4096
goPackage.AutoCommitTransaction = True
goPackage.RepositoryMetadataOptions = 0
goPackage.UseOLEDBServiceComponents = True
goPackage.LogToSQLServer = False
goPackage.LogServerFlags = 0
goPackage.FailPackageOnLogFailure = False
goPackage.ExplicitGlobalVariables = False
goPackage.PackageType = 0
```

NOTE

The generated code sets many properties of DTS objects, which you don't have to explicitly set when you're creating a DTS package in Visual Basic. For example, to create, execute, and save this package, you only have to identify the Package2 object with the Package object and give the package a name:

```
Set goPackage = goPackageOld
goPackage.Name = "Save To VB Demo Package"
```

The next section has the code that creates the DTS connections, as shown in Listing 26.4.

LISTING 26.4   Code to Create the DTS Connections

```
' --------------------------------------------------------
' create package connection information
' --------------------------------------------------------

Dim oConnection as DTS.Connection2

' ------------- a new connection defined below.
'For security purposes, the password is never scripted

Set oConnection = goPackage.Connections.New("SQLOLEDB")

    oConnection.ConnectionProperties("Integrated Security") = "SSPI"
    oConnection.ConnectionProperties("Persist Security Info") = True
    oConnection.ConnectionProperties("Initial Catalog") = "pubs"
    oConnection.ConnectionProperties("Data Source") = "(local)"
    oConnection.ConnectionProperties("Application Name") = _
        "DTS Designer"
    oConnection.Name = "Pubs Connection"
    oConnection.ID = 1
    oConnection.Reusable = True
    oConnection.ConnectImmediate = False
    oConnection.DataSource = "(local)"
    oConnection.ConnectionTimeout = 60
    oConnection.Catalog = "pubs"
    oConnection.UseTrustedConnection = True
    oConnection.UseDSL = False

    'If you have a password for this connection,
    'please uncomment and add your password below.
    'oConnection.Password = "<put the password here>"

goPackage.Connections.Add oConnection
Set oConnection = Nothing
```

> **NOTE**
>
> The generated code sets several properties twice—once as objects in the ConnectionProperties collection and once as properties of the Connection2 object. You can use either method when you create connections in Visual Basic.
>
> When you create a connection, you have to specify the properties that identify the data source and the security that is needed to access that data source. You usually don't have to set the other properties—Reusable, ConnectionTimeOut, and UseDSL.
>
> One of the most important properties is ConnectionID because it is used to identify the connection when it is used with a particular text.

The next section, shown in Listing 26.5, creates the DTS steps.

LISTING 26.5   Code to Create the DTS Steps

```
'.......................................................
' create package steps information
'.......................................................

Dim oStep as DTS.Step2
Dim oPrecConstraint as DTS.PrecedenceConstraint

'------------ a new step defined below

Set oStep = goPackage.Steps.New

    oStep.Name = "DTSStep_DTSExecuteSQLTask_1"
    oStep.Description = "Update Authors"
    oStep.ExecutionStatus = 1
    oStep.TaskName = "DTSTask_DTSExecuteSQLTask_1"
    oStep.CommitSuccess = False
    oStep.RollbackFailure = False
    oStep.ScriptLanguage = "VBScript"
    oStep.AddGlobalVariables = True
    oStep.RelativePriority = 3
    oStep.CloseConnection = False
    oStep.ExecuteInMainThread = False
    oStep.IsPackageDSORowset = False
    oStep.JoinTransactionIfPresent = False
    oStep.DisableStep = False
    oStep.FailPackageOnError = False

goPackage.Steps.Add oStep
Set oStep = Nothing
```

> **NOTE**
>
> Most of the step properties can be set by default. Here's the basic code needed to create this step:
> ```
> Set oStep = goPackage.Steps.New
> oStep.Name = "DTSStep_DTSExecuteSQLTask_1"
> oStep.TaskName = "DTSTask_DTSExecuteSQLTask_1"
> goPackage.Steps.Add oStep
> Set oStep = Nothing
> ```

Managing Packages with Visual Basic and Stored Procedures

CHAPTER 26

535

26

MANAGING
PACKAGES WITH
VISUAL BASIC

The next section, shown in Listing 26.6, calls individual functions that create the tasks. These separate functions are located at the end of the code module.

LISTING 26.6   Code That Calls the Functions to Create the DTS Tasks

```
' ------------------------------------------------
' create package tasks information
' ------------------------------------------------

'call Task_Sub1 for task DTSTask_DTSExecuteSQLTask_1 (Update Authors)
Call Task_Sub1(goPackage)

' ------------------------------------------------
' Save or execute package
' ------------------------------------------------
```

The Main function concludes with code to save the package to SQL Server and execute the package. (See Listing 26.7.) The command that saves the package is commented out when the file is generated. To save the package, you have to uncomment the command and change the server name, username, and password to the appropriate values. Of course, you could also replace the `SaveToSQLServer` method with `SaveToFile` or `SaveToRepository`.

LISTING 26.7   The Last Section of the Main Function Has Code to Save and/or Execute the Package

```
'goPackage.SaveToSQLServer "(local)", "sa", ""
goPackage.Execute
goPackage.Uninitialize
'to save a package instead of executing it, comment out the _
'executing package line above and uncomment the saving package line
set goPackage = Nothing

set goPackageOld = Nothing

End Sub
```

Functions to Create the Tasks

The code module ends with individual functions that create the tasks for the package. The sample module creates one simple Execute SQL task, as shown in Listing 26.8. Much more code is needed to create any of the transformation tasks. Separate individual functions are created for each of the transformations in a transformation task.

LISTING 26.8   The Last Section of the Code Module Has the Functions That Create Each Task

```
'Task_Sub1 for task DTSTask_DTSExecuteSQLTask_1 (Update Authors)
Public Sub Task_Sub1(ByVal goPackage As Object)

Dim oTask As DTS.Task
Dim oLookup As DTS.Lookup

Dim oCustomTask1 As DTS.ExecuteSQLTask2
Set oTask = goPackage.Tasks.New("DTSExecuteSQLTask")
Set oCustomTask1 = oTask.CustomTask

    oCustomTask1.Name = "DTSTask_DTSExecuteSQLTask_1"
    oCustomTask1.Description = "Update Authors"
    oCustomTask1.SQLStatement = "Update Authors " & vbCrLf
    oCustomTask1.SQLStatement = oCustomTask1.SQLStatement & _
        "Set au_lname = 'Smith'" & vbCrLf
    oCustomTask1.SQLStatement = oCustomTask1.SQLStatement & _
        "Where au_id = '123-45-6789'"
    oCustomTask1.ConnectionID = 1
    oCustomTask1.CommandTimeout = 0
    oCustomTask1.OutputAsRecordset = False

goPackage.Tasks.Add oTask
Set oCustomTask1 = Nothing
Set oTask = Nothing

End Sub
```

> **NOTE**
>
> Most of the code used in the module is needed to correctly create this task. The two properties that could be omitted are CommandTimeout and OutputAsRecordset.

Executing a Package from Visual Basic

There are times when it is useful to execute a package from Visual Basic, even if you're not interested in saving your packages in Visual Basic code. You can load a package, handle events, and handle errors without modifying the structure of the package at all. You can also load a package and modify one or more properties before you execute it. You can create data transformation loops by executing a DTS package repeatedly.

Loading and Saving Packages

You can load a DTS package from or save it to SQL Server storage, Meta Data Services storage, or a structured storage file using the appropriate load and save methods. These methods are documented in Chapter 23, "The DTS Package and Its Properties."

You cannot load or save DTS packages dynamically using Visual Basic code file storage.

Listing 26.9 shows code that loads a package from SQL Server, changes its description, and saves it again.

LISTING 26.9 VB Code That Loads, Modifies, and Saves a Package

```
Dim pkg As New DTS.Package2
Dim sServer As String
Dim sUserID As String
Dim sPassword As String
Dim sPackageName As String

sPackageName = txtPackageName.Text
sServer = txtServer.Text
'Set security information
'If User ID is left as an empty string, Integrated Security
    'will be used
sUserID = txtUserID.Text
sPassword = txtPassword.Text

'Load the package
If sUserID = "" Then
  pkg.LoadFromSQLServer sServer, , , _
      DTSSQLStgFlag_UseTrustedConnection, , , , sPackageName
Else
  pkg.LoadFromSQLServer sServer, sUserID, sPassword, _
      DTSSQLStgFlag_Default, , , , sPackageName
End If

'Modify the package
pkg.Description = "New description for package"

'Save the package
If sUserID = "" Then
  pkg.SaveToSQLServer sServer, , , _
      DTSSQLStgFlag_UseTrustedConnection
Else
  pkg.LoadFromSQLServer sServer, sUserID, sPassword, _
```

Listing 26.9   Continued

```
      DTSSQLStgFlag_Default
End If

End Function
```

Handling Events

One of the advantages of using Visual Basic to execute a DTS package is the ability to handle events with Visual Basic code. There are five events returned from DTS, all of which are declared with the `Package` object:

- `OnStart`—Called at the beginning of each step or task.
- `OnProgress`—Provides information about the progress of a task.
- `OnFinish`—Called at the completion of each step or task.
- `OnQueryCancel`—Called to give the user an opportunity to cancel a query.
- `OnError`—Called when an error occurs.

All of the events have a parameter called `EventSource`, which normally contains the name of the step associated with the event. If you create a custom task, you can use the `EventSource` parameter for any value you choose.

You can cancel the operation of the DTS package when an `OnQueryCancel` or `OnError` event occurs. You do this by setting the `pbCancel` parameter to `TRUE`.

`OnProgress` and `OnError` have additional parameters that return more detailed information about the event that has occurred.

Here's what you have to do in order to handle DTS events in your Visual Basic project:

1. Declare a `Package` object variable using the keyword `WithEvents`. You cannot add events to a `Package2` object:

   ```
   Public WithEvents pkg70 As DTS.Package
   ```

2. If you are using SQL Server 2000 functionality, you also have to declare a `Package2` object variable and assign it to the `Package` variable. You don't have to reference the `Package` variable anywhere else in your code:

   ```
   Public pkg As New DTS.Package
   Set pkg70 = New DTS.Package
   Set pkg = pkg70
   ```

3. Write code for all five of the package events. If you don't want anything to happen for one of the events, you can just insert a comment in the error handler. You may trigger an access violation if you fail to include code for any of the events.

4. Set the `ExecuteInMainThread` property to `TRUE` for all of the steps in the package. Objects created with Visual Basic do not support multiple threads. You can do this programmatically with the following code, which should be placed after the package is loaded but before it is executed:

```
For Each stp In pkg.Steps
    stp.ExecuteInMainThread = True
Next stp
```

> **NOTE**
>
> If you save a package to a Visual Basic code module, you have to move the code into a module that defines classes, such as a form, before you can add events. Note also that you have to remove the keyword `New` from the declaration of the package variable because you can't use `New` in a variable declaration when you are using `WithEvents`.

I have written a Visual Basic application called ViewDTSEvents that allows you to look at any or all of the events generated by a DTS package. You can find the code and the compiled form of this application on the CD in these files—ViewDTSEvents.vbp, ViewDTSEvents.frm, and ViewDTSEvents.exe.

ViewDTSEvents lets you execute any DTS package stored in SQL Server storage and choose which DTS events you want to view. Each event is shown with a message box. For `OnError` and `OnQueryCancel` events, you have the opportunity to cancel the execution of the package.

Listing 26.10 shows the code from ViewDTSEvents that is used to respond to the `OnQueryCancel` event. The message box is shown if the user has selected the check box to view this event.

LISTING 26.10   Code for the `OnQueryCancel` Event from ViewDTSEvents

```
Private Sub goPackageOld_OnQueryCancel( _
        ByVal EventSource As String, pbCancel As Boolean)
    Dim msg As String
    Dim ttl As String

    ttl = "On Query Cancel"

    msg = "Event Source - " & EventSource & vbCrLf
    msg = msg & vbCrLf & vbCrLf & "Do you want to cancel?"

    If gbShowEvents Then
        Select Case MsgBox(msg, vbYesNo, ttl)
```

LISTING 26.10   Continued

```
                Case vbYes
                    pbCancel = True
                Case vbNo
                    pbCancel = False
            End Select
        End If


    End Sub
```

Handling Errors

Errors that take place during the creation or modification of DTS objects cannot be handled by the OnError event. You handle them with a normal Visual Basic error handler.

You can view errors during the execution of a DTS package in Visual Basic by using the OnError event, as described in the preceding section. You can also use the GetExecutionErrorInfo method of each of the steps to find the errors that have occurred. The ViewDTSEvents application uses this method to display a message box for each error that has taken place, using the code in Listing 26.11.

LISTING 26.11   Code to Display All the Errors That Have Occurred in a DTS Package

```
Private Sub cmdDisplayErrors_Click()

Dim stp As DTS.Step2
Dim lNumber As Long
Dim sSource As String
Dim sDescription As String
Dim sHelpFile As String
Dim lHelpContext As Long
Dim sIDofInterfaceWithError As String
Dim msg As String
Dim bError As Boolean

bError = False

For Each stp In pkg.Steps

    If stp.ExecutionStatus = DTSStepExecStat_Completed And _
            stp.ExecutionResult = DTSStepExecResult_Failure Then
```

LISTING 26.11   Continued

```
        stp.GetExecutionErrorInfo lNumber, sSource, sDescription, _
              sHelpFile, lHelpContext, sIDofInterfaceWithError

        bError = True

        msg = "Step With Error - " & stp.Name & vbCrLf
        msg = msg & "Error Code - " & CStr(lNumber) & vbCrLf
        msg = msg & "Source - " & sSource & vbCrLf
        msg = msg & "Description - " & sDescription & vbCrLf
        msg = msg & "Help File - " & sHelpFile & vbCrLf
        msg = msg & "Help Context - " & CStr(lHelpContext) & vbCrLf
        msg = msg & "ID of Interface With Error - "
        msg = msg & sIDofInterfaceWithError & vbCrLf

        MsgBox msg

    End If

Next stp

If bError = False Then
    msg = "No errors reported for any of the steps in the package."
    MsgBox msg
End If

Set stp = Nothing

End Sub
```

You can set the package's FailOnError property to TRUE if you want the package to stop its execution when the first error occurs:

```
If chkFailOnError Then
    pkg.FailOnError = True
End If
```

Dynamic Modification of Properties

You can dynamically modify the properties of a DTS package from inside that package by using the Dynamic Properties task or ActiveX Script code. But sometimes it is more convenient to modify properties of the DTS objects using Visual Basic before the package is executed. This is especially true when you are receiving some input from a user.

For example, you could have a DTS package that uses a text file as the source for a data transformation. You could load the DTS package, let the user pick the file to be loaded, set the `DataSource` property of the `Connection` object to the appropriate value, and then execute the package.

Implementing a Loop in the Data Transformation

You can create a loop inside a DTS package by modifying the step properties so that a step will execute again. This is described in Chapter 16, "Writing Scripts for an ActiveX Script Task."

You can implement a loop from Visual Basic by calling a DTS package several times. Perhaps you want to load the data from several identical files into a table. You could put all those files in a directory and create a Visual Basic application to load each file. Here's what the VB code would have to do:

1. Create or load a DTS Package.
2. Use the File System Objects from the Microsoft Scripting library to reference the directory where the files are located.
3. Set a reference to the connection that needs to be changed.
4. Execute the package for each of the files in the directory. Before each execution, change the step's `DataSource` property:

```
For Each file in folder.Files
    stp.DataSource = file.Name
    pkg.Execute
Next
```

Executing a Package from Visual Basic Using SQL Namespace

The SQL Namespace Object Library is a set of programming objects that allows you to use the Enterprise Manager's interface programmatically. You can use SQL Namespace to execute a DTS package.

When you use the `Execute` method of the `Package` object in Visual Basic, there is no visual feedback showing the progress of the package's execution. If you want a progress report or notification that the package has finished, you have to provide that information programmatically. When you use SQL Namespace to execute a package, your application uses the Executing Package dialog (see Figure 26.4) to report on the execution. The report looks the same as if you had executed the package directly in the Enterprise Manager.

Managing Packages with Visual Basic and Stored Procedures

543

CHAPTER 26

26

MANAGING
PACKAGES WITH
VISUAL BASIC

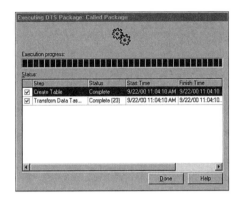

FIGURE 26.4
When you use SQL Namespace, the results of the package execution are shown in the Executing Package dialog.

SQL Namespace executes a package directly from its storage location. You do not load the package first, as you do when using the Package's Execute method. You can only execute packages stored in local SQL Server storage or in Meta Data Services storage. You can't use SQL Namespace to execute a package stored in a structured storage file.

I have written a function called fctDTSExecuteSQLNamespace that executes a DTS package using SQL Namespace. You have to specify a package name. You can also supply the name of the server where the package is stored, the username and password needed to access that server, and whether or not the package is stored in SQL Server storage. The function defaults to the local server, integrated security, and SQL Server storage. The function returns 0 if successful or the error number if an error occurs.

Listing 26.12 shows the code for the fctDTSExecuteSQLNamespace function. You can find this code on the CD in a Visual Basic project with the files DTSExecuteSQLNS.vbp, DTSExecuteSQLNS.bas, and DTSExecuteSQLNS.frm.

LISTING 26.12   A Function That Executes a Package with SQL Namespace

```
'Project must include a reference to the
'        Microsoft SQLNamespace Object Library
'This Object Library implemented in Mssql7\Binn\Sqlns.dll

Public Function fctDTSExecuteSQLNamespace( _
        sPackageName As String, _
        Optional sServer As String = "", _
        Optional sUser As String = "", _
        Optional sPassword As String = "", _
```

LISTING 26.12   Continued

```
        Optional bSQLServerStorage As Boolean = True) As Long
On Error GoTo ProcErr

Dim sqlns As New SQLNamespace
Dim sqlnsObject As SQLNamespaceObject

Dim hWnd As Long
Dim hServer As Long
Dim hDTSPackages As Long
Dim hPackages As Long
Dim hPackage As Long

Dim sConnection As String

'Create connection string
If sServer = "" Then
  sConnection = "Server=.;" 'Local server
Else
  sConnection = "Server=" & sServer & ";"
End If
If sUser = "" Then
  sConnection = sConnection & "Trusted_Connection=Yes;"
Else
  sConnection = sConnection & "UID=" & sUser & ";"
  sConnection = sConnection & "pwd=" & sPassword & ";"
End If

'Initialize the SQL Namespace, using the Server as the root node
SQLNS.Initialize "DTSExecuteSQLNamespace", _
        SQLNSRootType_Server, CStr(sConnection), hWnd

'Get a reference to the root node (the Server)
hServer = SQLNS.GetRootItem

'Get a reference to the Data Transformation Services node
hDTS = SQLNS.GetFirstChildItem( _
        hServer, SQLNSOBJECTTYPE_DTSPKGS)

'Get a reference either to the Local Packages
'    or the Meta Data Services packages node
If bSQLServerStorage = True Then
  hPackages = SQLNS.GetFirstChildItem( _
          hDTS, SQLNSOBJECTTYPE_DTS_LOCALPKGS)
Else
```

LISTING 26.12 Continued

```
hPackages = SQLNS.GetFirstChildItem( _
        hDTS, SQLNSOBJECTTYPE_DTS_REPOSPKGS)
End If

'Get a reference to the particular package
hPackage = SQLNS.GetFirstChildItem( _
        hPackages, SQLNSOBJECTTYPE_DTSPKG, sPackageName)

'Set the package to be a SQL Namespace object
Set sqlnsObject = SQLNS.GetSQLNamespaceObject(hPackage)

'Execute the package
sqlnsObject.ExecuteCommandByID _
        SQLNS_CmdID_DTS_RUN, hWnd, SQLNamespace_PreferModal

'Return with no error
fctDTSExecuteSQLNamespace = 0

ProcExit:
  Exit Function

ProcErr:
  Msgbox Err.Number & " " & Err.Description
  fctDTSExecuteSQLNamespace = Err.Number
  GoTo ProcExit

End Function
```

Working with Packages Using the OLE Automation Stored Procedures

SQL Server has a set of OLE Automation system stored procedures that allow you to work with COM objects. You can load, modify, and execute DTS packages with these stored procedures, but you cannot use them to create new tasks, connections, or steps. You also cannot respond to events in the DTS package with these stored procedures.

The OLE Automation stored procedures all have an sp_OA prefix:

- sp_OACreate
- sp_OADestroy
- sp_OAMethod

- sp_OAGetProperty
- sp_OASetProperty
- sp_OAGetErrorInfo

The scope for OLE Automation objects created with these stored procedures is a batch.

All the OLE Automation stored procedures return an integer value that indicates the success or failure of the command. Success is indicated by 0. Failure returns an integer value that includes the error that was returned by the OLE Automation server.

Using sp_OACreate and sp_OADestroy

You can use sp_OACreate to create a reference to a COM object, such as a DTS package. This stored procedure has the following parameters, which must be used by the correct position and not by name:

- Programmatic Identifier or Class Identifier—You can specify the type of object by either one of these two identifiers. The programmatic identifier is a combination of the component name and the object name separated by a period, such as "DTS.Package2". The class identifier is a character string that identifies the object. For a DTS package, the class identifier is "{10020200-EB1C-11CF-AE6E-00AA004A34D5}".
- Object Variable as an OUTPUT parameter—A local variable that you have declared to receive a reference to the object you are creating. This variable must have the integer datatype.
- Context—Optional parameter that specifies whether the execution context of the object should be in-process (1), local (4), or either (5). The default value that is used if this parameter is not supplied is either (5).

You use sp_OADestroy to release a reference to an OLE Automation object when you are no longer using it. This stored procedure has only one parameter—the object variable that is to be destroyed.

The following code creates a reference to a DTS package using a programmatic identifier, destroys the object, and re-creates the object using the class identifier:

```
DECLARE @hPkg int
DECLARE @hResult int

EXEC @hResult = sp_OACreate 'DTS.Package', @hPkg OUT
EXEC @hResult = sp_OADestroy @hPkg
EXEC @hResult = sp_OACreate
    '{10020200-EB1C-11CF-AE6E-00AA004A34D5}', @hPkg OUT
```

Using sp_OAMethod

You can call a method of an object by using the sp_OAMethod stored procedure, which has these parameters:

- The object variable.

- The name of the method.

- The return value of the method as an OUTPUT parameter. This parameter can be set to NULL if the method does not return a value.

- All the parameters that are defined for the particular method. The method's parameters can be used either by name or by position.

The following code uses the LoadFromSQLServer method to load a DTS package:

```
EXEC @hResult = sp_OAMethod @hPkg , 'LoadFromSQLServer' , NULL ,
    @ServerName = @sServerName,
    @ServerUserName = @sServerUserName,
    @ServerPassword = @sServerPassword,
    @Flags = @lFlags,
    @PackageName = @sPackageName
```

Using sp_OAGetProperty and sp_OASetProperty

There are OLE Automation procedures both for retrieving an object's property and for setting a property. You can also use the sp_OAGetProperty procedure to set a reference to an object if you already have an object to a parent object.

The sp_OAGetProperty procedure has the following parameters:

- The object variable.

- The name of the property.

- The value of the property as an output parameter.

- An optional index, which is used for indexed properties.

The sp_OASetProperty procedure has the same parameters, except that the third parameter is the new value that is to be assigned to the property.

The following code sets a new value for the Description property of the Package2 object, retrieves that new value, and prints it:

```
DECLARE @sDescription varchar(50)
EXEC @hResult = sp_OASetProperty @hPkg,
        'Description', 'New Description'
EXEC @hResult = sp_OAGetProperty @hPkg, 'Description', @sDescription
Select @sDescription
```

You can obtain a reference to the `Task` object by referencing the particular member of the `Tasks` collection as if it were a property of the `Package2` object. The `CustomTask` property of the `Task` object gives you access to all the properties of the task. Here's how you can change the `SQLStatement` property of an Execute SQL task:

```
DECLARE @hTsk int
DECLARE @hCus int
Set @hResult = sp_OAGetProperty @hPkg, 'Tasks("tskExecSQL")', @hTsk
Set @hResult = sp_OAGetProperty @hTsk, 'CustomTask', @hCus
Set @hResult = sp_OASetProperty @hCus,
        'SQLStatement', 'Select * from authors'
```

Using `sp_OAGetErrorInfo`

You can check for errors when you are using the OLE Automation stored procedures by calling `sp_OAGetErrorInfo`. Error information is reset after any of these stored procedures is used, except for `sp_OAGetErrorInfo`. If you want to know whether or not a command was successful, you have to check before the next command is issued.

The parameters for `sp_OAGetErrorInfo` are all optional. They are as follows:

- The object variable. If this parameter is specified, error information is returned specifically for this object. If `NULL` is used for this parameter, error information is returned for the batch as a whole.
- Source of the error—OUTPUT parameter.
- Description of the error—OUTPUT parameter.
- Help file for the OLE object—OUTPUT parameter.
- Help file context ID number—OUTPUT parameter.

NOTE

It's essential to retrieve error information when you're working with the OLE Automation stored procedures. No error information will be reported to you if you don't retrieve it.

Here's code that will retrieve the basic error information returned by the `Execute` method:

```
--Execute the package
EXEC @hResult = sp_OAMethod @hPkg, 'Execute', NULL
IF @hResult <> 0
BEGIN
    EXEC sp_OAGetErrorInfo NULL, @src OUT, @desc OUT
    SELECT Info = 'Execute Method', Source = @src, Description=@desc
END
```

Managing Packages with Visual Basic and Stored Procedures

CHAPTER 26

549

26

MANAGING
PACKAGES WITH
VISUAL BASIC

> **NOTE**
>
> You can also retrieve error information from the return code for any of the OLE Automation procedures. This return code has a complex hexadecimal format, which requires a special procedure for decoding. SQL Server Books Online provides a procedure for doing this in the section "OLE Automation Return Codes and Error Information."

Executing a Package with Stored Procedures

Listing 26.13 contains Transact-SQL code that loads a DTS package, executes it, and returns execution information for each step. You have to enter the package name and connection information at the top of the code. You can execute this code directly in the Query Analyzer or encapsulate it in a stored procedure. This code is on the CD in a file called ExecutePackage.sql.

LISTING 26.13   Transact-SQL Code That Executes a DTS Package and Reports on Each Step

```
--Declare variables that have to be set manually
DECLARE @sPackageName varchar(255)
DECLARE @sServerName varchar(255)
DECLARE @sServerUserName varchar(255)
DECLARE @sServerPassword varchar(255)
DECLARE @lFlags int

--Enter name of package and access information
SET @sPackageName = 'TestOA'
SET @sServerName = '(local)'
SET @sServerUserName = ''
SET @sServerPassword = ''
SET @lFlags = 256 --256 For Trusted, 0 for SQL Server Security

--Integers used as object handles
DECLARE @hPkg int
DECLARE @hSteps int
DECLARE @hStp int
DECLARE @hResult int

--Other variables
DECLARE @sMethod varchar(30)
DECLARE @sProperty varchar(30)
```

LISTING 26.13   Continued

```
DECLARE @src varchar(40)
DECLARE @desc varchar(100)
DECLARE @sStepName varchar(40)
DECLARE @sTaskName varchar(40)
DECLARE @lExecResult int
DECLARE @lExecStatus int
DECLARE @lDisableStep int
DECLARE @sExecResult varchar(20)
DECLARE @dtStartTime datetime
DECLARE @lExecutionTime int
DECLARE @dtFinishTime datetime
DECLARE @lStepCount int
DECLARE @idxStep int

SET NOCOUNT ON

--Create package object
EXEC @hResult = sp_OACreate 'DTS.Package2', @hPkg OUT
IF @hResult <> 0
BEGIN
    EXEC sp_OAGetErrorInfo NULL, @src OUT, @desc OUT
    SELECT Info = 'Create Package', Source= RTrim(@src), _
        Description=@desc
END

--Load package
SET @sMethod = 'LoadFromSQLServer'
EXEC @hResult = sp_OAMethod @hPkg , @sMethod , NULL ,
    @ServerName = @sServerName,
    @ServerUserName = @sServerUserName,
    @ServerPassword = @sServerPassword,
    @Flags = @lFlags,
    @PackageName = @sPackageName
IF @hResult <> 0
BEGIN
    EXEC sp_OAGetErrorInfo NULL, @src OUT, @desc OUT
    SELECT Info = 'Method - ' + @sMethod, Source=@src, _
        Description=@desc
END

--Execute the package
SET @sMethod = 'Execute'
EXEC @hResult = sp_OAMethod @hPkg, @sMethod, NULL
IF @hResult <> 0
```

LISTING 26.13 Continued

```
BEGIN
    EXEC sp_OAGetErrorInfo NULL, @src OUT, @desc OUT
    SELECT Info = 'Method - ' + @sMethod, Source = @src, _
        Description=@desc
END

EXEC @hResult = sp_OAGetProperty @hPkg, 'Steps', @hSteps OUT
EXEC @hResult = sp_OAGetProperty @hSteps, 'Count', @lStepCount OUT
SET @idxStep = 0

--Check each of the steps for execution information
WHILE @idxStep < @lStepCount
BEGIN

    SET @idxStep = @idxStep + 1

    SET @sProperty = 'Steps(' + Convert(varchar(10), @idxStep) + ')'
    EXEC @hResult = sp_OAGetProperty @hPkg, @sProperty, @hStp OUT

    EXEC @hResult = sp_OAGetProperty @hStp,
            'Name', @sStepName OUT
    EXEC @hResult = sp_OAGetProperty @hStp,
            'TaskName', @sTaskName OUT
    EXEC @hResult = sp_OAGetProperty @hStp,
            'ExecutionStatus', @lExecStatus OUT
    EXEC @hResult = sp_OAGetProperty @hStp,
            'DisableStep', @lDisableStep OUT
    EXEC @hResult = sp_OAGetProperty @hStp,
            'ExecutionResult', @lExecResult OUT

    IF @lExecStatus = 4 --Step completed
    BEGIN

        IF @lExecResult = 1
            Set @sExecResult = 'Failure'
        ELSE
            Set @sExecResult = 'Success'

        EXEC @hResult = sp_OAGetProperty @hStp,
                'StartTime', @dtStartTime OUT
        EXEC @hResult = sp_OAGetProperty @hStp,
                'ExecutionTime', @lExecutionTime OUT
```

LISTING 26.13   Continued

```
            EXEC @hResult = sp_OAGetProperty @hStp,
                    'FinishTime', @dtFinishTime OUT

    END
    ELSE
    BEGIN

        IF @lDisableStep <> 0
            Set @sExecResult = 'Disabled'
        ELSE
            Set @sExecResult = 'Not Executed'

        SET @dtStartTime = NULL
        SET @lExecutionTime = NULL
        SET @dtFinishTime = NULL

    END

    SELECT "Step Name" = @sStepName,
            "Task Name" = @sTaskName,
            "Result" = @sExecResult,
            "Started" = @dtStartTime,
            "Finished" = @dtFinishTime,
            "Duration" = @lExecutionTime
END

SET NOCOUNT OFF
PRINT 'Execution of Package Completed'
```

Conclusion

Visual Basic gives you more management control over DTS than you have with the DTS Designer. You can use Visual Basic to build your own interface for creating and managing DTS packages.

The OLE Automation stored procedures don't give you as much control over DTS as you have with the DTS Designer, but they do allow you to control a DTS package from Transact-SQL code. This ability can be useful when you're integrating DTS with the rest of your database applications. It can also be helpful to use the OLE Automation stored procedures in an Execute SQL task, as described in Chapter 12, "The Execute SQL Task."

For more information about using the DTS object model, see Chapter 30, "Programming with the DTS Object Model."

Handling Errors in a Package and Its Transformations

IN THIS CHAPTER

There are two kinds of errors in DTS applications:

- The errors that result from incorrect data.
- The development errors that you can work to eliminate through better programming.

This chapter describes how to deal with both kinds of errors. Several other chapters also have information about error handling:

- See Chapter 6, "The Transform Data Task," for configuring the transformation task error files.
- See Chapter 9, "The Multiphase Data Pump," for using transformation phases to respond to errors.
- See Chapter 23, "The DTS Package and Its Properties," for setting the package's error handling properties.
- See Chapter 24, "Steps and Precedence Constraints," for using Precedence Constraints to respond to errors and configure transactions.
- See Chapter 26, "Managing Packages with Visual Basic and Stored Procedures," for responding to errors when executing a package from Visual Basic.

Handling Incorrect Data

Here are some of the things that you may need to do in handling errors that result from incorrect data:

- Analyze the possibilities for incorrect data.
- Raise errors.
- Correct errors during the data transformation.
- Store error records and information about errors.
- Maintain transactional consistency.
- Inform administrators of the errors.

Analyzing the Potential Errors in the Data

The best strategy for handling data errors in a DTS package is to prevent them. Incorrect data should be fixed at the point where the errors are being made. Unfortunately, that's not always possible. You might not be able to fix the systems that are generating the errors.

If you don't expect to have many errors in your data, you could choose to terminate the package on the first error and roll back any changes. You could then fix the incorrect data and execute the DTS package again. You can terminate a package in two ways:

- Set the `Package` object's `FailOnError` property to `TRUE`.
- If you want to fail a package only if a particular task has an error, you can set the `FailPackageOnError` property to `TRUE` for the `Step` object associated with that task.

If you know that you will have specific kinds of errors in your data, you can look for them and correct the errors as a part of the data transformation.

You could choose to discard any error records. You could also store error records in a table or a data file for future analysis.

Raising Errors

Errors will be raised by the system during the processing of a package if incorrect data causes errors in the programming code. The most typical type of error is an incorrect data type, such as having a NULL value where the programming code requires a string or a numeric value.

You can also programmatically raise errors in a number of different ways:

- By setting the return value of the entry function to DTSTaskExecResult_Failure for an ActiveX Script task:

  ```
  Main = DTSTaskExecResult_Failure
  ```

- By setting the return value of the entry function to DTSTransformStat_Error for a transformation:

  ```
  Main = DTSTransformStat_Error
  ```

- With the Raise method of the Err object in VBScript code:

  ```
  Err.Raise vbObjectError + 111, "", "Missing last name.", "", 0
  ```

- With the Transact-SQL RAISERROR statement in an Execute SQL task:

  ```
  RAISERROR('Missing birth date for employee!', 11, 1)
  ```

If an error is raised in an ActiveX Script task—either by the system, by setting the return value to `DTSTaskExecResult_Failure`, or by using the `Raise` method—the `ExecutionResult` property of the associated step will be `DTSStepExecResult_Failure`.

If an error is raised in a transformation script in one of the transformation tasks, the transformation will be terminated but the task will continue until the number of errors specified by the `MaximumErrorCount` property has been exceeded. At that point, the task will be terminated and the `ExecutionResult` property of the associated step will be `DTSStepExecResult_Failure`. If errors occur in a transformation task but the maximum number of errors is not exceeded, the task will continue to completion and the step's `ExecutionResult` property will be `DTSStepExecResult_Success`.

> **NOTE**
>
> When a package is executed in the Package Designer and a transformation task has errors, the Package Execution Results message box and the Executing DTS Package dialog both report that the task has failed, even if the MaximumErrorCount is not exceeded. The precedence constraints governing the execution of other tasks will use the DTSStepExecResult_Success value of the ExecutionResult property. Steps with On Success precedence will be executed, and steps with On Failure precedence will not be executed. This situation is displayed in Figure 27.1.

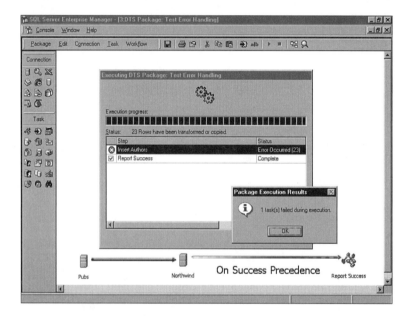

FIGURE 27.1

A transformation task that doesn't have more errors than the maximum allowed is marked as failed in the dialogs, but it's treated as a success by the precedence constraints.

You can use the RowsInError property of the transformation task to find out how many rows have failed. This property can be queried while the transformation task is being executed or after it has completed.

In an Execute SQL task, you raise an error with the RAISERROR statement. You can specify either a message or a particular error number that you have added to the sysmessages table.

If you use a severity number of 11 or higher, the ExecutionResult property of the associated step will be DTSStepExecResult_Failure:

```
RAISERROR('Missing birth date for employee!', 11, 1)
RAISERROR(50101, 11,1)
```

If you use a value of 10 or less for the severity, ExecutionResult will be DTSStepExecResult_Success:

```
RAISERROR('This error will not be noticed.', 10, 1)
```

Correcting Errors

If you know there are specific errors in your data, you can check for them in your transformation scripts. You can use a lookup to find the correct value, if you have enough information to determine it. You also can use a filler value such as "Unknown" or "Could Not Be Determined" for the incorrect field.

> **TIP**
>
> I also recommend providing a filler value when using lookups. If the lookup table doesn't contain a record, the lookup will return an Empty (unassigned) value. You can check for this Empty value and replace it with a filler such as "Unknown":
>
> ```
> sZipCode = lkpZipCode.Execute(DTSSource("City"), DTSSource("State"))
> If IsEmpty(sZipCode) Then
>     sZipCode = "Unknown"
> End If
> ```

Storing Error Records and Information

You can store error records and information in three places:

- Text files.
- Database tables.
- The DTS log.

Chapter 6 describes how to configure the text files that store error information from the three transformation tasks. One of the options is to create a Source error file that has all the fields of all the source records that have generated an error. You can use this Source error file as the source for a Transform Data task that is specifically designed to handle the error records.

You can enter error information into a database table in a number of ways:

- Generate a Source error file and bulk-copy that file into a SQL Server table.
- Use an insert Lookup query in a transformation script to insert the fields from the error record and information about the error into a table. Chapter 9 has an example that uses this strategy.
- Use one of the queries of a Data Driven Query task for inserting into an error table. Chapter 8, "The Data Driven Query Task," shows how to do this.

See Chapter 23 for a description of how to configure a DTS package to save and retrieve error information using the DTS log. See Chapter 16, "Writing Scripts for an ActiveX Script Task," to learn how to include code in your ActiveX Script task that writes error records to the log.

Maintaining Transactional Consistency

You can use a combination of package and step properties to join tasks together into a transaction. You can also create transactions that include more than one DTS package executing on more than one server.

DTS transactions are discussed in Chapter 24. Transactions that involve more than one DTS package are discussed in Chapter 18, "The Execute Package Task."

Informing Administrators of Errors

You can use precedence constraints to control the flow of the steps in your DTS package so that you can respond appropriately to errors. You could use a Send Mail task to send a message to a database administrator when a particular task fails.

You could also create a report at the end of the execution of your DTS package that includes the error status of each of the tasks, the number of records processed by each of the transformation tasks, and the number of error records for each of the transformations tasks. This report could be written with an ActiveX Script task and sent to an administrator with a Send Mail task.

See Chapter 20 for a description of the Send Mail task.

Debugging ActiveX Scripts

You can debug your ActiveX scripts using the script debugger that is included with these products:

- Windows 2000
- Windows NT 4.0 Option Pack
- Visual InterDev 6.0

You can configure the Package Designer to debug errors in scripts at runtime. Right-click Data Transformation Services in the Enterprise Manager tree and choose Properties. In the Package Properties dialog, select the Just-In-Time debugging check box, as shown in Figure 27.2.

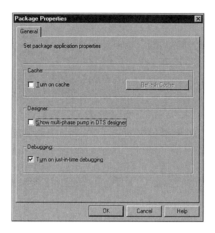

27

FIGURE 27.2
You choose just-in-time debugging in the Package Properties dialog.

NOTE

Just-in-time debugging is not a property of the DTS package, as is implied by the title of the Package Properties dialog. It is implemented as the JITDebug property of the DTS Application object. This is a Boolean property with a default value of FALSE. When selected, it is in effect for all packages executed through the Enterprise Manager on that particular server.

When just-in-time debugging is enabled, the debugger will open for any of these reasons:

- There is an error in the script code.
- An object referenced in the code raises an error.
- The code executes a Stop command, as shown in Figure 27.3.

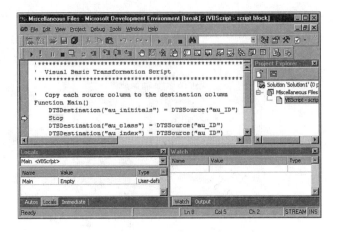

FIGURE 27.3
You can force the debugger to open by including a Stop command in your ActiveX Script.

CAUTION

Do *not* click the button that ends the execution of the script. If you do, the SQL Server Enterprise Manager will close and you will lose all unsaved changes in your packages.

The same thing will happen if you close the debugger.

You can avoid losing your changes by following the guidelines in the "Exiting the Debugger without Terminating the Enterprise Manager" section later in this chapter.

TIP

When just-in-time debugging is enabled and a Stop command is executed, you will receive the following message:

"An exception of type 'Runtime Error' was not handled. Would you like to debug the application?"

If you choose Yes, the debugger will open. If you choose No, the code will continue executing and the debugger will not be opened.

If just-in-time debugging is not enabled, the Stop command will be ignored. If you want, you can leave the Stop commands in your code in a production environment. They will not affect the execution of the scripts.

Using the Script Debugger

When the debugger opens, the line of code that is currently being executed is highlighted. You can resume the code's execution by clicking the Continue button. You can also step through the code line by line.

If the debugger has opened because of an error, or if the code reaches a line that has a runtime error, you will not be able to continue stepping through the code directly. Every time you attempt to continue, the error message will be displayed and the code execution will stay on that line.

You can change the execution to a different line of code, though. This allows you to rerun code to see what is happening before an error occurs. It also allows you to skip a line that is causing an error. Put the cursor on the next line you want to execute, and then select Set Next Statement from the Debug menu.

The script debugger has several other windows to assist you in debugging your script code:

- The Immediate window gives you the current value when you type in a variable or an expression after a question mark. You can also use the window to set any of the local variables to a different value.

- The Watch window lets you define a list of variables and expressions for which you always want the current value.

- The Locals window, shown in Figure 27.4, gives you the values of all the local variables defined in your script.

Exiting the Debugger without Terminating the Enterprise Manager

One of the problems with using the debugger is that you can terminate the Package Designer and the Enterprise Manager without going through the normal saving process. It's always good to save your package before executing it to ensure that you have saved the most current version. But it's also almost always possible to exit the debugger without terminating the Enterprise Manager.

If the debugger has been opened with the Stop command, you have two choices:

- Click the Continue button. If no error occurs, the script will terminate normally. After the script has terminated, you can close the debugger without closing the Enterprise Manager.

- Select Detach All Processes from the Debug menu. The script will continue, and you can close the debugger.

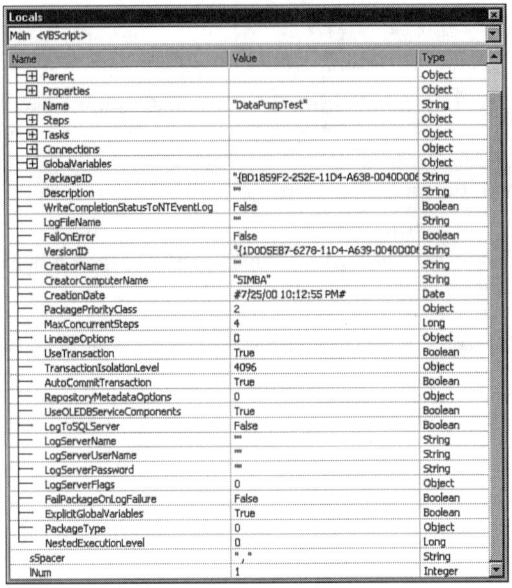

Figure 27.4

You can view the script's variables in the Locals window.

If the debugger has opened because of an error in the code or in an object, first you have to set the execution to a different line of code. Then you can select Continue or Detach All Processes. If you don't move to another line of code first, you won't be able to continue, and if you detach all processes, the debugger will just be opened again.

If you have an error in a transformation ActiveX script, it's often best to select End Function as the next line of execution. If a transformation status has not been set, the task will terminate with an error saying that an invalid status was returned. If the transformation status has already been set, you can set it to an invalid result in the immediate window. This is a convenient way to exit the task without running through the transformation script code for each of the records in the data source.

It's always safe to close the debugger if there is no script code showing and the Continue, Pause, and End buttons are disabled. The Enterprise Manager will not be terminated.

TIP

I like using message boxes when I'm writing DTS scripts. Unfortunately, sometimes I have a message box that is being executed in a loop. You can use the script debugger to get out of this loop without terminating the application. Open the debugger from the Program menu, attach the DTS script that is being executed, and choose the option to break on the next command.

Conclusion

DTS gives you many choices for handling incorrect data. You also have an excellent environment for debugging your ActiveX scripts—when you learn how to avoid exiting the debugger without saving your code.

High-Performance DTS Packages

IN THIS CHAPTER

There are many factors that affect the performance of your DTS packages, in addition to the design of the package itself:

- Server hardware—Number of processors, processor speed, amount of available memory.
- Location of data, data storage, and data access speed.
- Edition of SQL Server 2000 being used.
- SQL Server 2000 configuration.
- Amount of data.
- Different types of data stores (Oracle, Microsoft Access, SQL Server, or text files) being used for the source and destination.
- Database design—Degree of normalization, relationships between tables, use of indexes, partitioning of data.
- Simultaneous use of the databases by other users.

You have to be concerned about all these issues when you're building a high-performance DTS package. However, this chapter is going to focus specifically on DTS package design choices:

- Which task is faster?
- What effect do different properties have on performance?
- What is the effect of your package, task, and transformation design decisions on DTS performance?

If you have good enough hardware, not much data, and plenty of time available for your data transformations, you won't need this chapter. But if you receive a 1GB clickstream file at 8:00 every morning and have to update your multidimensional cubes before the 10:00 a.m. management meeting, you'll have to examine all the available performance-tuning options.

NOTE

In this chapter, we have chosen to run a few dozen tests that compare the relative performance of DTS tasks and different transformation strategies. All these tasks were run on a Windows 2000 server running the initial public (non-beta) release of SQL Server 2000. The server had dual Pentium III processors (500MHz) with 256MB of RAM. The tests were run several times, using various amounts of data (25,000 to 500,000 records).

We did not test large amounts of data. Performance issues become more complex as the amount of data increases. You have to be concerned about the limiting effect of the server's memory and excessive growth of the transaction log. It can be beneficial to replace a task that processes a large quantity of data with several tasks that share the processing.

We present our test results as the number of records inserted or updated per second. We also show the percentage difference in performance between different ways of implementing a data transformation.

The purpose of all our testing is to compare the various DTS tasks and transformation strategies. We do not intend our test results to predict the speed of your data transformations. We believe that our test results show close to the maximum possible speed for our hardware configuration because we used very narrow records. When you're using real data in a production environment, the performance will most likely be somewhat less.

> **CAUTION**
>
> Database performance results can vary greatly from one situation to another because there are so many factors involved. For this chapter, an attempt was made to run all the tests in a consistent environment.
>
> We hope our performance testing will be helpful as you consider how to optimize the performance of your DTS packages. Please remember, though, that our tests were not run in a strict testing environment. Remember also that your performance tuning must take into account the characteristics of your hardware, software, database structure, data transformation needs, and data.
>
> If you experience relative performance results that are greatly different from the test results presented here, please write us at tpeterson@sdgcomputing.com. Thank you.

DTS Transformation Goals

You need great performance from your DTS packages, but you also have to consider these other development goals:

- The rapid development of new DTS packages.
- The creation of packages that clearly document the data transformations.
- The development of packages that can be easily maintained.

The Goal of Rapid Execution

The primary goal of DTS performance tuning is to achieve the fastest possible execution of the packages. Different tasks transform the data at different speeds. The transformation tasks can be implemented in a variety of different ways, which also can dramatically affect the transformation speed. The change from a slow strategy to a fast one can result in a ten-fold or even hundred-fold increase in transformation speed.

Unfortunately, some of the strategies for increasing execution speed can be incompatible with the other development goals. High-performance packages may take longer to develop, they might not be as self-documenting as slower packages, and their code might not be as easy to maintain.

Rapid Development

The DTS Import/Export Wizard is a rapid DTS development tool. Often, the fastest way to create a DTS package is to start with the wizard and then make the necessary modifications to the Transform Data or Copy SQL Server Objects tasks that have been created. You can increase the package's performance by replacing Transform Data tasks with Bulk Insert tasks, but that will add to your time spent in package development.

Most developers find it quicker to implement data transformation logic with a script rather than in the Transform Data task's source query. However, if you can implement the logic in the source query and replace the ActiveX scripts with Copy Column transformations, often you can dramatically improve the performance of the task.

Usually you can achieve the best performance by moving transformation logic into a custom transformation built with Visual C++, but that can be the most time-consuming development strategy.

Self-Documenting Data Transformations

If you create a separate ActiveX transformation for each of your destination columns, you will have a set of scripts that clearly show how the value for each of the columns was generated. You achieve better performance, though, when you create one transformation script for all the columns together. One transformation that assigns the values to many destination columns will execute more quickly than separate transformations for each column.

Moving the transformation logic from the script into the source query can greatly improve performance, but it makes it harder to document what was done to transform each column of data.

Maintainable Code

DTS packages often need to be modified, and it can be easier to modify transformation logic in a script rather than in a source query or a custom transformation. If you are expecting future changes, you may choose to leave your logic in scripts rather than choosing one of the higher-performing options.

On the other hand, if you can capture a set of transformation logic that you need to implement in several different data transformation situations, you can save time in the long run by creating a custom transformation.

DTS Task Performance Comparison

You can make a dramatic impact on the performance of your DTS package by choosing the best-performing task. This section compares the execution speed of the DTS tasks that can be used to load data.

Loading from a Text File to a SQL Server Database

You can use a Bulk Insert task, a Transform Data task, or a Data Driven Query task to load data from a text file into SQL Server 2000.

We tested the Bulk Insert task with the default configuration selected and with the Table Lock property selected, and Table Lock gave us the best performance. We also tested the Bulk Insert statement in an Execute SQL task, using the same options. The Execute SQL task gave us the same performance as the Bulk Insert task.

A single Copy Column transformation was used for the Transform Data task. We tested the Transform Data task in three ways:

- With Fast Load enabled and the other options that gave us the best performance (Table lock selected and Fetch buffer size set to 5000).
- With Fast Load enabled and all the default options selected.
- With Fast Load disabled.

A single INSERT query called for every record was used for the Data Driven Query task.

Table 28.1 and Figure 28.1 compare the loading speed for these six options.

TABLE 28.1   Loading Text File to SQL Server

Test Description	Records Per Second	% Diff from Bulk Insert
Bulk Insert (Maximized)	49,000	0%
Transform Data (Fast Load Maximized)	17,000	65% slower
Bulk Insert (Default)	16,500	66% slower
Transform Data (Fast Load Default)	14,000	71% slower
Transform Data (Not Fast Load)	118	99.76% slower
Data Driven Query	118	99.76% slower

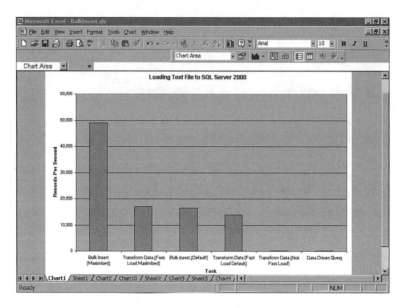

FIGURE 28.1

Records loaded per second from a text file into SQL Server for a variety of tasks.

NOTE

The benefit of using the Fast Load option is obvious in our performance testing. Fast Load inserts records into the destination in batches. You can configure the size of these batches. By default, all the records are inserted in a single batch. Without Fast Load, each record is inserted individually.

Fast Load is available only with the Transform Data task. It is not available with the other two transformation tasks, the Data Driven Query task and the Parallel Data Pump task.

You can only use Fast Load if you use the Microsoft OLE DB Provider for SQL Server for the transformation's destination connection.

The use of Fast Load interferes with the Transform Data task's handling of destination errors, which are caused by a constraint violation during an insert. You can't fail the task after a specific number of errors because the destination errors don't take place until the batch insert. You also can't write destination errors to the Destination error file.

Loading from SQL Server 2000 to SQL Server 2000

You can load data from one SQL Server 2000 database to another SQL Server 2000 database with a Transform Data task, a Data Driven Query task, a Copy SQL Server Objects task, or an Execute SQL task.

We used the same options for the Transform Data task and the Data Driven Query task as we used for the tests between a text file and SQL Server 2000, described in the previous section.

We tested the Copy SQL Server Objects task with the following options:

- Create tables not selected.
- Copy data with the append option selected.
- Use collation selected.
- Use default options selected.

We tried the Execute SQL task with an INSERT SELECT query and with a stored procedure that contained an INSERT SELECT query. We did not see a significant performance difference between the two strategies.

All the tests were run with both a cold data cache (SQL Server turned off and on immediately before testing) and a warm data cache (all the source data loaded into the cache). We did not see a significant difference in any of the tests except for the Copy SQL Server Objects task.

All the tasks showed a linear performance curve from 25,000 records through 500,000 records processed. The Copy SQL Server Objects task showed a linear performance over the testing range, but it also had an additional time period for each test. When using the warm cache, this additional time period was 6 seconds. When using the cold cache, it was 13 seconds. We subtracted this fixed period when presenting the performance results for the Copy SQL Server Objects task in the chart.

> **NOTE**
>
> This additional time period exists even when we transferred a single record. Transferring one record with the Copy SQL Server Objects task took 6 or 13 seconds, depending on whether or not there was a warm cache.
>
> We used the SQL Profiler to examine which commands DTS was using for the different tasks. The Transform Data task with Fast Load and the Copy SQL Server Objects task use the same high-performance INSERT BULK command. The difference between the two tasks is that the Copy SQL Server Objects task executes many additional commands. It performs a series of checks on the status of the source and destination databases before transferring the records. It also writes script files in the process of transferring data.

Table 28.2 and Figure 28.2 compare the loading speed from SQL Server to SQL Server with a cold cache. (The fixed period for the Copy SQL Server Objects task is not included in the chart. Actual performance for that task is worse than indicated.)

TABLE 28.2   Loading from SQL Server 2000 to SQL Server 2000

Test Description	Records Per Second	% Diff from Fast Load
Execute SQL	25,640	0%
Transform Data (Fast Load Maximized)	21,200	17% slower
Transform Data (Fast Load Default)	15,500	40% slower
Copy SQL Server Objects	3,700	85% slower
Transform Data (No Fast Load)	119	99.5% slower
Data Driven Query	117	99.5% slower

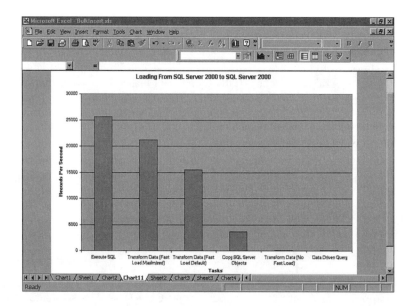

FIGURE 28.2

Records loaded per second from SQL Server 2000 into SQL Server 2000 for a variety of tasks. The Copy SQL Server Object task is shown with the fixed time period removed.

High-Performance DTS Packages

CHAPTER 28

573

28
HIGH-
PERFORMANCE
DTS PACKAGES

Performance Statistics for the Transformation Tasks

You have many options when using the transformation tasks. This section compares the relative performance of these options. Unless otherwise indicated, all the Transform Data tasks were run using Fast Load with the default options selected.

Comparing Different Transformations in the Transform Data Task

Table 28.3 and Figure 28.3 show the relative performance of several of the different string transformations. Each of the specialized transformations is compared with an ActiveX Script transformation that performs the same action.

TABLE 28.3 Relative Performance of String Transformations

Test Description	Records Per Second	% Diff from Copy Column
Copy Column	12,000	0%
Copying in ActiveX Script	5,400	55% slower
Uppercase String	12,000	0%
Uppercase in ActiveX Script	5,000	58.3% slower
Trim String	11,000	8.3% slower
Trimming in ActiveX Script	4,400	63.3% slower
DateTime String	12,000	0%
DateTime in ActiveX Script	3,300	72.5% slower

NOTE

We used different data for different sets of tests. You can see the effect of this in Tables 28.2 and 28.3. In the first test, the Transform Data task Fast Load rate was 15,500 records per second, and in the second test, it was 12,000 records per second. In the first test, comparing different tasks, we used very short strings. In the second test, comparing different transformations, we used strings that were somewhat longer. This slowed down the performance.

There are many factors that influence performance, including the characteristics of the data used.

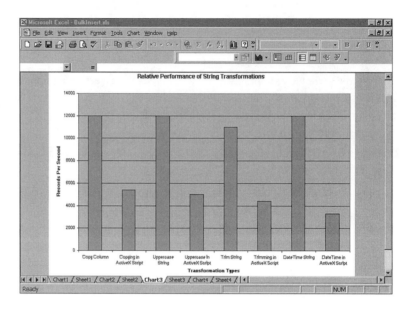

Figure 28.3

Relative performance of string transformations.

Comparing Separate and Combined Transformations

SQL Server Books Online states that you can improve performance by including all the columns in a single transformation. We could not find a significant difference when comparing 20 columns in 20 separate Copy Column transformations with 20 columns in one transformation. However, we did find a significant difference when we made the same comparison with ActiveX Script transformations. Table 28.4 and Figure 28.4 show the results of this test.

Table 28.4   Separate ActiveX Script Transformations Versus a Single ActiveX Script Transformation

Test Description Transformations	Records Per Second	% Diff from Individual
20 ActiveX Script Transformations	500	0%
One ActiveX Script Transformation	1200	140% faster

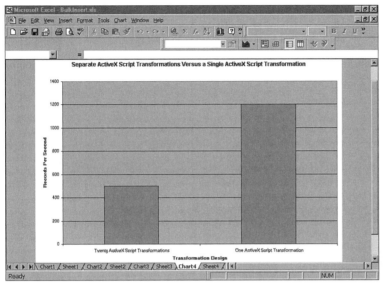

FIGURE 28.4
Separate ActiveX Script transformations versus a single ActiveX Script transformation.

Using Names or Ordinals in Script Transformation Columns

You can increase the speed of your Transform Data tasks by replacing the column names with column ordinal numbers when referencing the source column and destination column collections. SQL Server Books Online states that this improvement is not significant when fewer than 20 columns are used in the transformation, but it can be significant when many columns are used. The performance improvement using 20 source columns and 20 destination columns is shown in Table 28.5 and Figure 28.5.

TABLE 28.5 Column Names Versus Column Ordinal Numbers in Scripts in Transform Data Tasks

Test Description	Records Per Second	% Diff from Column Names
Column Names	1000	0%
Ordinal Numbers	1350	35% faster

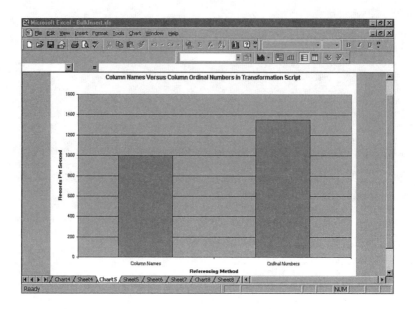

FIGURE 28.5

Column names versus column ordinal numbers in scripts in Transform Data tasks.

There are two problems with switching from column names to column ordinal numbers:

- The code is harder to read and write.
- The ordinal numbers do not consistently identify the columns. All the ordinal numbers of the columns are changed whenever you view the Source Columns tab or the Destination Columns tab of the Transformation Options dialog.

Listing 28.1 shows VBScript code for an ActiveX Script task that will dynamically modify all the ActiveX Script transformations in all the Transform Data tasks in the package, replacing the column names with the column ordinal numbers. This code is included on the CD in a package stored in the ReplaceNamesWithOrdinals.dts file. This package also has a task that switches all the ordinal numbers back to names, which can be run at the end of the package execution.

LISTING 28.1   VBScript Code That Switches Column Names to Column Ordinal Numbers for All Transform Data Tasks in a DTS Package

```
Option Explicit

Function Main()
```

LISTING 28.1   Continued

```
Dim pkg, tsk, cus, trn, col
Dim sScript, sFind, sReplace

Set pkg = DTSGlobalVariables.Parent

For Each tsk in pkg.Tasks

  Select Case tsk.CustomTaskID

    Case "DTSDataPumpTask", "DTSDataPumpTask2"

      Set cus = tsk.CustomTask

      For Each trn in cus.Transformations

        Select Case trn.TransformServerID

          Case "DTSPump.DataPumpTransformScript", _
               "DTSPump.DataPumpTransformScriptProperties2"

            sScript = trn.TransformServerProperties("Text").Value

            For Each col in trn.DestinationColumns
              sFind = "DTSDestination(""" & col.Name & """)"
              sReplace = "DTSDestination(" & CStr(col.Ordinal) & ")"
              sScript = Replace(sScript, sFind, sReplace)
            Next

            For Each col in trn.SourceColumns
              sFind = "DTSSource(""" & col.Name & """)"
              sReplace = "DTSSource(" & CStr(col.Ordinal) & ")"
              sScript = Replace(sScript, sFind, sReplace)
            Next

            trn.TransformServerProperties("Text").Value = sScript

        End Select
      Next
  End Select
Next

    Main = DTSTaskExecResult_Success
End Function
```

Fetch Buffer Size, Table Lock, and Insert Batch Size

When you use Fast Load, you can choose from several specific loading options. We found that two of the options, Table Lock and Insert Batch Size, had a definite effect on performance. We expect that some of the other Fast Load options also could have an effect on performance in specific situations.

Table 28.6 and Figure 28.6 show the effect on performance of Table Lock, Insert Batch Size, and Fetch Buffer Size, a setting that can be used whether or not Fast Load is selected. Our tests were conducted without other users in the database. The default choice, with Table Lock off, an Insert Batch Size of 0 (load all records in a single batch), and a Fetch Buffer Size of 1, is shown first. We were unable to increase the Fetch Buffer Size beyond 5000.

TABLE 28.6   The Effect of Table Lock, Insert Batch Size, and Fetch Buffer Size in the Transform Data Task

Test Description	Records Per Second	% Diff from Individual Transformations
Lock Off, Insert 0, Fetch 1	15,000	0%
Lock On, Insert 0, Fetch 1	16,000	6.7% faster
Lock Off, Insert 0, Fetch 5000	16,000	6.7% faster
Lock Off, Insert 5000, Fetch 1	13,300	11.3% slower
Lock On, Insert 100,000, Fetch 5000	21,000	40% faster
Lock On, Insert 0, Fetch 5000	22,000	46.7% faster

Moving Transformation Logic to the Source Query

Chapter 7, "Writing ActiveX Scripts for a Transform Data Task," has a series of examples that show how you can move transformation logic from an ActiveX script into a source query:

- Simple string manipulation.

```
Select au_lname + ', ' + au_fname as au_fullname
from AuthorName
```

- Assigning an unknown value:

```
select
    case
        when au_lname is null or au_lname = ''
            then 'Unknown Name'
        when au_fname is null or au_fname = ''
            then au_lname
        else
```

```
                au_lname + ', ' + au_fname
            end as au_fullname
        from AuthorName
```

- Looking up an unknown value in another table. For our test, 17% of the values were found in the lookup table. The lookup table contained a total of 23 records, so all of them could be stored in the lookup's cache at the same time:

```
select
    case
        when a.au_lname is null or a.au_lname = ''
            or a.au_fname is null or a.au_fname = ''
                then lkp.FullName
        else
                au_lname + ', ' + au_fname
        end as au_fullname
    from AuthorName a
        inner join tblAuthorNameList  lkp
            on a.au_id = lkp.au_id
```

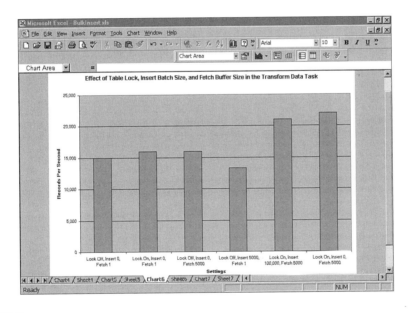

FIGURE 28.6
The effect of Table Lock, Insert Batch Size, and Fetch Buffer Size in the Transform Data task.

Table 28.7 and Figure 28.7 show the performance of these three examples, comparing between having the transformation logic in the script of an ActiveX Script transformation and having the transformation logic in the source query and using a Copy Column transformation.

TABLE 28.7   ActiveX Scripts Versus Source Queries in Transform Data Tasks

Test Description	Records Per Second	% Diff from Simple Script
Query—Simple manipulation	22,000	0%
Script—Simple manipulation	6000	72.7% slower
Query—Assigning value	21,000	4.5% slower
Script—Assigning value	4800	78.2% slower
Query—Table lookup	18,500	15.9% slower
Script—Table lookup	2700	87.7% slower

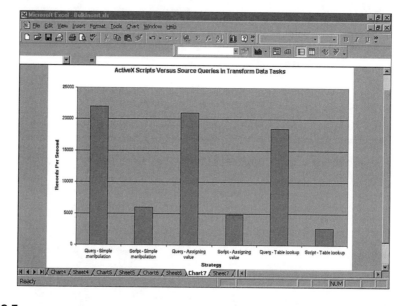

FIGURE 28.7

ActiveX Scripts versus source queries in Transform Data tasks.

> **NOTE**
>
> These tests show the performance benefits of moving transformation logic into the source query. That's especially true when a lookup is involved. In the last example in this test, the source query delivered a performance improvement by almost a factor of seven.
>
> The more complex the data transformation, the more beneficial it is to put the logic into the source query. Unfortunately, those more complex situations are where the option of writing a transformation script is the most convenient.

My development strategy is to create all but the simplest transformations with scripts and then, if I need the better performance, convert that transformation logic partially or completely into source queries.

Moving Logic into a Custom Transformation

Chapter 32, "Creating a Custom Transformation with VC++," shows how to create a custom transformation that finds the average value for a set of integer source fields. Table 28.8 and Figure 28.8 show the performance of this custom transformation compared with the performance of a transformation script and a source query with the same logic. This test was run with 10 fields being averaged together.

TABLE 28.8 Transformation Script Versus Custom Transformation Versus Source Query

Test Description	Records Per Second	% Diff from Script
Transformation Script	3333	0%
Custom Transformation	15150	354% faster
Source Query	15625	369% faster

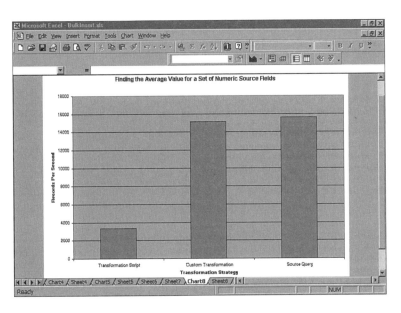

FIGURE 28.8

Transformation script versus custom transformation versus source query.

Performance of the Transform Data Task and the Data Driven Query Task

Our testing indicates that when the Transform Data task uses Fast Load, it inserts records more than 100 times faster than the Data Driven Query task. If you cannot use Fast Load, the two tasks insert records at approximately the same speed.

The reason you use the Data Driven Query task is so you can choose from between several queries as the result of a transformation. With SQL Server 2000, you can also do this with a Transform Data task by using a data modification lookup. You can reproduce the functionality of a Data Driven Query task in a Transform Data task by doing the following:

- Replacing the Insert Query with a transformation.
- Replacing the other three queries with data modification lookups.
- Changing the logic of the transformation script. When the Insert Query should be executed, return a value of DTSTransformStat_OK. When any of the other queries should be executed, return a value of DTSTransformStat_SkipInsert and include code that executes the appropriate data modification lookup.

> **NOTE**
>
> One additional advantage of using the data modification lookups is that you're not limited to four possible queries, as with the Data Driven Query task. Of course, you can also use the data modification lookups in the Data Driven Query task to give yourself the extra possibilities.

Our testing indicates that a Data Driven Query task update query is approximately 30% faster than an update performed by a lookup in a Transform Data task.

If you have a data transformation that performs an insert 10% of the time and an update 90% of the time, the data transformation should be faster with the Data Driven Query task than with the Transform Data task using Fast Load. The performance advantage of the update queries in the Data Driven Query task is greater than the performance disadvantage for the insert queries.

If you have a data transformation that performs an insert 50% of the time and update 50% of the time, the data transformation should be faster in a Transform Data task using Fast Load. The performance advantage of the Fast Load inserts in the Transform Data task should far outweigh the performance disadvantage on the updates.

Choosing a Scripting Language

You can gain a performance improvement by using a different language in your transformation scripts. Books Online states that VBScript is approximately 10% faster than JScript, and that JScript is approximately 10% faster than PerlScript.

> **NOTE**
>
> We have used VBScript exclusively in our ActiveX scripts. We have not tested the other scripting languages.

Use of Parallel Processing to Improve Performance

You can greatly improve the performance of a DTS package by maximizing the opportunities for parallel processing. This is especially true when the DTS package is executing on a server with multiple processors.

You can achieve a higher level of parallel processing by doing the following:

- Setting precedence constraints so that as many tasks as possible are allowed to execute at the same time.
- Creating additional connections to the same database. One connection cannot be used by more than one task at a time. Tasks using the same connection can't be executed in parallel.
- Setting the Step object's ExecuteInMainThread property to FALSE for all the steps. If two steps are both set to execute on the main thread, they can't be executed in parallel.
- Increasing the Package object's MaxConcurrentSteps property. By default, this property is set to 4. This is too low in situations where you have many processors available.

There are some factors that limit the use of these strategies:

- The logic of your transformation might require that some tasks be completed before others are started. If so, you can force serial execution with precedence constraints.
- If you are using transactions, you have to prevent access to a database from two different connections at the same time or the package will fail. You can avoid this problem by setting the precedence constraints so that the tasks execute serially or by only having a single connection to each database. Either way, you lose the performance benefit of parallel processing.
- There are some tasks that must be executed on the main thread or they will generate errors. This is true for any custom task that is not free-threaded (including all custom tasks built with Visual Basic), tasks that modify properties in custom tasks that are not free-threaded, and any task with a script that calls a COM object written in Visual Basic.

> **NOTE**
>
> You could divide your DTS package into several packages executed on several servers to achieve an even greater level of parallel execution. The packages can all be executed from one package with the Execute Package task described in Chapter 18.

Effect of Indexing on Performance

The indexes used on tables involved with data transformations can have a very significant impact on the performance of those transformations:

- Proper indexing on source tables can improve the speed of the transformation tasks and the Execute SQL task if those tasks are filtering the records in the data source with a WHERE clause, ordering records with an ORDER BY clause, or aggregating records with a GROUP BY clause.

- Indexes on destination tables can decrease the speed of transformations because the indexes have to be adjusted for the new records that are being entered.

The amount of performance improvement or degradation due to indexes is very dependent on the details of the particular situation. The use of indexes always involves tradeoffs:

- Is it faster to take the time to build an index that could improve performance? Is it faster to execute the source query without a proper index?

- Is it faster to drop the indexes for the data destination, import the data, and re-create the indexes? Is it faster to leave the indexes in place?

- Are all the indexes on the destination table really needed? Could some of them be eliminated so that the transformation process can be completed more quickly? Or could they be dropped and re-created after the DTS package has finished?

If you don't have any data in your destination table to begin with, normally you should drop the indexes and build them after the data transformation. If you already have data in the destination table, you should test the transformation with and without the indexes in place to see which gives you the best performance.

> **NOTE**
>
> Of course, you may need to leave indexes in place because of other users who need to access the data.

> **TIP**
>
> You can sometimes greatly improve performance by using a *covering index*. This is an index that includes all the fields used in a query, arranged in the appropriate order for that particular query. Unfortunately, because covering indexes are so large, they can significantly hurt the performance of database inserts and updates.

Considering Tools Other Than DTS Because of Performance

Sometimes you may want to consider using non-DTS tools to achieve better performance.

Using bcp for Exporting from SQL Server to Text Files

It is faster to use bcp to bulk copy data from SQL Server to a text file than to use the Transform Data task. The high-performance Bulk Insert task cannot be used for moving data from SQL Server to a text file.

Using Replication

If you want to keep two databases synchronized with each other, you should use replication instead of DTS. Replication is often easier to set up, it often has better performance, and you have more synchronization options. DTS is needed when you're changing (transforming) data. If you're just copying data between two databases on a periodic basis, consider replication.

Conclusion

DTS gives you many tools for creating high-performance transformations, but there's still a lot of work to do if you want to achieve the highest possible performance.

Integrating DTS with Meta Data Services

IN THIS CHAPTER

Meta Data Services provides a repository for storing information. You can use it in SQL Server 2000 to store information about database structures and data transformations, and you can use it with Visual Studio to share information about programming objects.

This chapter provides a brief introduction to Meta Data Services and examines how it is used with DTS to store column-level and row-level data lineage. Chapter 23, "The DTS Package and Its Properties," has information about saving and retrieving DTS packages in Meta Data Services. That chapter also discusses the use of the PackageRepository object to retrieve general information about the packages stored in Meta Data Services.

NOTE

Microsoft SQL Server 2000 Meta Data Services was called the Microsoft Repository in SQL Server 7.0. There have been many enhancements in the newer version, especially with the new Meta Data Browser and the ability to export meta data to XML.

You have two primary tools for viewing the information in Meta Data Services. You have the new Meta Data Browser. You also have the DTS Browser, which provides the same capabilities as the SQL Server 7.0 Repository Browser.

The term "repository" is still used to describe the database that physically stores the meta data (which was called "metadata" in SQL Server 7.0). SQL Server Books Online has made these changes throughout their text. You can find many instances where the older terminology is still being used in the SQL Server 2000 user interface and the DTS object model.

CAUTION

If you upgrade a server from SQL Server 7.0 to SQL Server 2000, you also have to upgrade the Meta Data Services information models. If you don't, you will receive an error and will not be allowed to save packages to Meta Data Services.

SQL Server Books Online describes how to do this upgrade at Data Transformation Services\Sharing Meta Data\DTS Information Model.

Why You Should Use Meta Data Services with DTS

Meta Data Services gives you a centralized place to store and access data transformation meta data.

Meta Data

Meta data is data *about* data. It is a description of the structures that are used to store, transform, and retrieve data. There are two kinds of meta data in an enterprise information system:

- Business meta data describes data to nontechnical users so they can understand the information they are viewing.
- Technical meta data describes data in a way that is clear and unambiguous. It is the kind of information that a computer program needs to have in order to process data correctly.

Here are some examples of business meta data:

- Descriptions of fields, tables, and databases.
- Descriptions of levels, hierarchies, dimensions, cubes, and OLAP databases.
- Descriptions of transformations and mappings.
- Descriptions of data cleansing procedures.
- The format of reports.

Here are examples of the technical meta data needed for a database:

- Names of fields, tables, and databases.
- Names of levels, hierarchies, dimensions, cubes, and OLAP databases.
- Data types, field lengths, and field nullability.
- Default values.
- Indexes, primary keys, and foreign keys.

The process of creating and running data transformations also generates technical meta data:

- Map source columns to destination columns.
- Cross-reference between database structures and their use in DTS packages.
- ActiveX Scripts used to cleanse the data.
- History of the creation and versioning of DTS packages.
- History of the execution of DTS packages.
- Data lineage of individual records.

You need this kind of information to ensure that your data is being transformed accurately. Meta Data Services gives you a place where you can store and retrieve business and technical meta data, including the full information about the transformations that have been used with the data.

29

INTEGRATING DTS WITH META DATA SERVICES

The Meta Data Services Storage Choice

You can choose to save a DTS package to SQL Server, to a structured storage file, to a Visual Basic file, or to Meta Data Services. You have to save your packages to Meta Data Services if you want to use Meta Data Services to keep track of your transformation meta data. Specifically, you need to save to Meta Data Services to do the following:

- Query Meta Data Services for information about the package design, its versions, and its execution history. This information is saved for all packages saved to Meta Data Services.

- View the column-level lineage information for the package. The column-level lineage gives you a cross-reference between your database objects and where they are used in DTS packages. You have to choose one of the scanning options for your package in order to save the column-level lineage.

- View the row-level lineage information about the package. The row-level lineage allows you to tie an individual record to a particular execution of a particular version of a DTS package. You have to configure your package to show the lineage variables, and you have to add fields to your tables to save them.

NOTE

You can keep track of transformation meta data without using Meta Data Services.

If you save a package to SQL Server, you can view all the design information and version history in the Enterprise Manager. You can also view the execution history if you enable logging for the package.

No matter where you save your packages, you can add fields to your tables to save a reference to the transformation that created the record.

You could also create the column-level lineage without using Meta Data Services, but it would require a good deal of specialized programming.

You should save packages to Meta Data Services because you want to handle the meta data in an organized and consistent way.

The DTS Browser

The SQL Server 2000 Enterprise Manager provides two ways to view the meta data of databases and DTS packages that have been stored in Meta Data Services:

- The DTS Browser is the successor to the Repository Browser in SQL Server 7.0. You can access it by highlighting the Meta Data node under the Data Transformation Services node for a particular SQL Server in the Enterprise Manager.

- The Meta Data Browser is a new tool in SQL Server 2000. You can find it in the Enterprise Manager in the Meta Data Services node for a particular SQL Server.

You can use the DTS Browser to update some of the business meta data contained in Meta Data Services, but none of the technical meta data.

The DTS Browser has three tabs, each of which has a separate tool:

- Browse—View database meta data.

- Lineage—Use the value of a lineage variable to look up package, version, and execution information.

- Package—View package meta data.

> **NOTE**
>
> It's easier to see the capabilities of the DTS Browser if some meta data has been loaded into it. Save a package to Meta Data Services and execute it a few times. Load some database meta data into Meta Data Services, as described in the following section.

The Browse Tab

The process of entering the meta data for a database into Meta Data Services is called scanning. The Browse tab (shown in Figure 29.1) provides a hierarchical view of all the databases that have been scanned into Meta Data Services.

Databases can be scanned into the repository in two ways:

- Through the scanning options of the DTS Package, described in the "Configuring DTS for Column-Level Data Lineage" section later in this chapter.

- By highlighting the Meta Data node in the Enterprise Manager console and selecting Import Metadata from the Action menu (or by right-clicking the Meta Data node and choosing Import Metadata from the Popup menu). This selection calls the Connection Properties dialog (shown in Figure 29.2), which is used to select a database to be scanned into the repository.

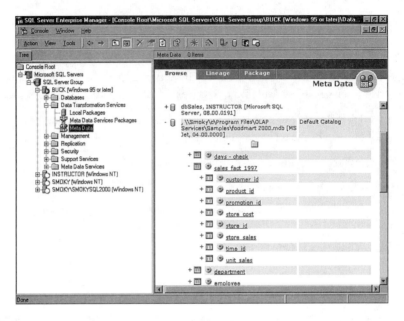

FIGURE 29.1
You can view both business and technical meta data on the Browse tab of the DTS Browser.

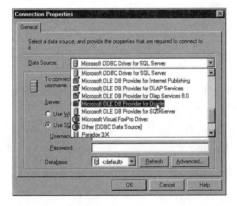

FIGURE 29.2
You can scan a database into the repository if you have an OLE DB provider for that particular data source.

The Browse tab provides a view of the following technical meta data:

- Name and version of the database system containing the database.
- Names of fields, tables, and databases.

- Data types.
- Field lengths, precision, and scale.
- Field nullability.
- Object owners.
- Column-level lineage.

When you click on the table or field hyperlink in the browser, a separate page opens that displays business meta data, as shown in Figure 29.3. The browser provides read/write access to the following business meta data:

- Descriptions of fields, tables, and databases
- Comments about fields, tables, and databases

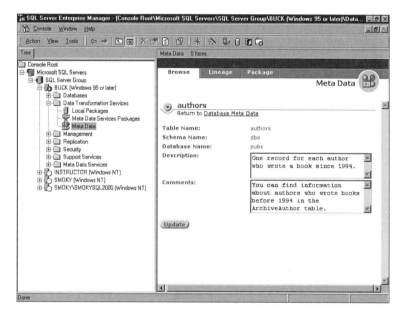

FIGURE 29.3
You can view and edit the descriptions and comments that are stored in the repository.

The Lineage Tab

The Lineage tab provides a simple tool for finding the package version and execution instance that created a particular record. The entry form for the lookup is shown in Figure 29.4. You can enter either one of the two lineage variables. The results are displayed in Figure 29.5. The configuration of a package to use lineage variables is discussed in the "Configuring DTS for Row-Level Data Lineage" section later in this chapter.

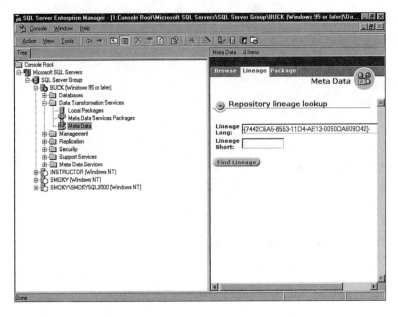

FIGURE 29.4
You can retrieve the package and execution information by entering either one of the lineage variables.

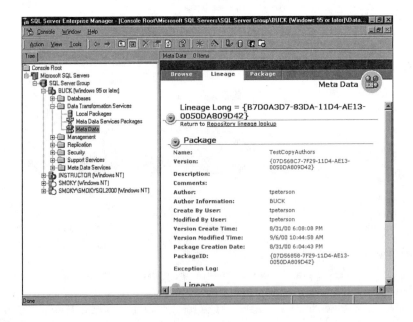

FIGURE 29.5
This is the information you receive when you look up the lineage.

The Package Tab

Information about DTS packages, package versions, and package executions is available in a
hierarchical format on the Package tab. (See Figure 29.6.) For each package, version, and execution, you have the option of viewing the package design. When you pick that option, the
DTS Package Designer opens with the selected version of the package displayed.

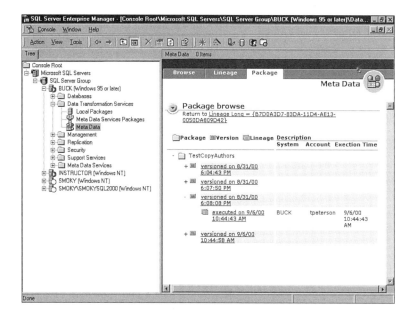

FIGURE 29.6
*The Package tab of the DTS Browser allows you to view information about all the packages that have been saved to
Meta Data Services.*

The Meta Data Browser

The Meta Data Browser is a new tool in SQL Server 2000 for accessing meta data. You can use
the Meta Data Browser in SQL Server 2000 or as a standalone snap-in for the Microsoft
Management Console.

When you use it inside SQL Server, you access the Meta Data Browser under the Meta Data
Services node in the Enterprise Manager. All the databases and packages that have been
scanned into Meta Data Services can be browsed in a tree structure, as shown in Figure 29.7.

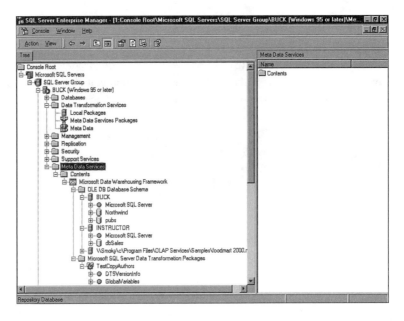

FIGURE 29.7

The Meta Data Browser allows you to browse the structure of databases and DTS packages.

Finding Information About DTS Objects and Properties

You can view the objects and properties of the DTS package in the Meta Data Browser, although some of them are hard to find. For example, here's what you have to do to view the text of an ActiveX Script:

- Find the name of the ActiveX Script task under the node for the package.
- Right-click on the Unknown node under the task and select Properties.
- Find the Body property in the Unknown Properties dialog, as shown in Figure 29.8.
- Right-click on the property, select Copy, and paste the text into Notepad.

Exporting to XML

You can use the Meta Data Browser to export data to XML. You can export a database, a table, a whole DTS package, a single task, or a single transformation. Right-click on the object you want to export and select Export To XML. You will be able to choose a path and a name for the XML file that is created. Figure 29.9 shows an ActiveX Script task that has been exported to XML. Note that the new line characters have been removed form the script.

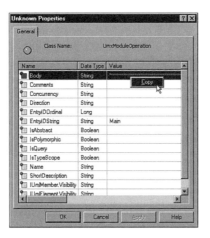

FIGURE 29.8
You can find the text of an ActiveX Script under the Body *property in the Unknown Properties dialog.*

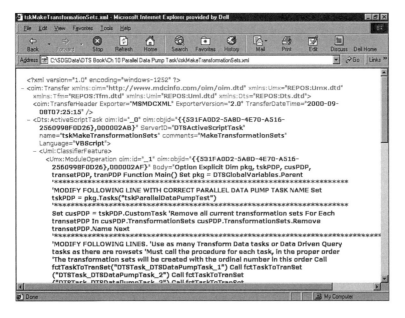

FIGURE 29.9
An ActiveX Script task that has been exported to XML.

Other Meta Data Services Tools

Meta Data Services provides a variety of other tools for storing, configuring, and accessing meta data.

The Repository Database

The *repository* is the database that is used for the physical storage of the meta data. By default, the msdb system database in SQL Server is used as the repository. The data is stored in a set of tables with prefixes that identify the various information models (Dbm for Database Model, Dtm for Data Transformation model, and so on). The information in these tables is not meant to be accessed directly. You are supposed to use the interfaces provided by Meta Data Services.

Object Models

The Microsoft Repository is organized around a set of structures called *information models*, which are templates for particular kinds of data. These information models have a hierarchical relationship, with the more specific models inheriting characteristics from their parent models.

The root model, from which all other information models are derived, is the Unified Modeling Language (UML) Model. There is an information model for COM and another one for data types. A generic model specifies the relationships between models. The information models that relate to databases and data transformations are shown in Figure 29.10.

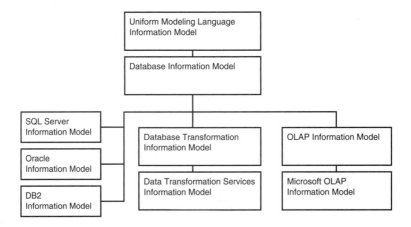

FIGURE 29.10

The Microsoft Repository has many information models that hold database information. All information models are derived from the Unified Modeling Language model.

Here are the descriptions of the models that hold database information:

- The Database Information Model is the basic model used to store database information. It is used to store the meta data about the data sources and data destinations. This model is derived from the Unified Modeling Language Information Model.

- The SQL Server Information Model, the Oracle Information Model, and the DB2 Information Model are used to store information that is specific to each database system. These models are derived from the Database Information Model.

- The Database Transformation Information Model is the basic model used to store information about data transformations. This model is also derived from the Database Information Model.

- The Data Transformation Services Information Model stores data transformation information that is specific to Microsoft's Data Transformation Services. This model is derived from the Database Transformation Information Model.

The Meta Data Services SDK

You can download the Meta Data Services Software Development Kit (SDK) from Microsoft's Web site. This SDK includes code for several sample Visual Basic programs that access and use the information stored in Meta Data Services.

> **NOTE**
>
> At the time of this writing, the most current version of the SDK was Microsoft Repository SDK Version 2.1b. Besides having code samples showing how to work with the meta data, this version of the SDK has several utilities, including a Repository Browser, an Information Model Installer, an OLE DB scanner, and an XML Import/Export tool.

DWSoft's DWGuide—A Third-Party Meta Data Tool

DWGuide from DWSoft is a tool that provides a user-friendly way to access Meta Data Services. The Enterprise Manager's Meta Data Browser is not designed for the end users of a database system. The Meta Data Services SDK gives you the tools you need to design your own application to provide meta data to your end users. DWGuide does this work for you. It allows you to customize meta data access for your end users.

Meta Data Services maintains a complex set of relationships between the components of a database or a data transformation. DWGuide allows you to hide some of the complexity of the meta data. You can create virtual relationships, connecting objects that don't have a direct link in the meta data.

When you're using DWGuide to look at the information about an individual field in a table, you can view the DTS transformation script that was used to load the data into that field. The view of the script is shown in Figure 29.11. You cannot see this kind of detail about DTS packages in the DTS Browser without opening them up in the DTS Designer. You can see this information in the Meta Data Browser, but it can be hard to find. DWGuide provides a much more direct connection between a field in a table and the transformation script that was used to generate the data for that field.

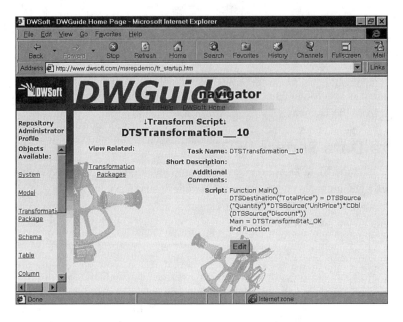

FIGURE 29.11
DWGuide allows you to see the DTS transformation script that was used for a particular field.

You can create DWGuide users that have different levels of access to view and edit the meta data. For example, you can let users edit the transformation script from within the Navigator. The Meta Data Browser in the Enterprise Manager allows a user to edit the business meta data. With DWGuide, you can let users edit both the business and technical meta data.

Configuring DTS for Column-Level Data Lineage

You enable column-level data lineage by setting the scanning options for your DTS package. Scanning a database enters its meta data into the Meta Data Services repository. Scanning a DTS package builds a cross-reference between the DTS packages, DTS transformations, and database structures.

Package Scanning Choices

Scanning is set on the Scanning Options dialog, shown in Figure 29.12. You can get to this dialog when you are saving a package by selecting the Scanning button on the Save DTS Package dialog. You can also do the following:

1. Click on the Package Designer design sheet so no DTS objects are selected.
2. Choose Properties from the Package menu.

3. Select the Advanced tab of the DTS Package Properties dialog.

4. Select the Options button in the Scanning Options section of the tab.

FIGURE 29.12
The Scanning Options dialog allows you to resolve package references to scanned catalog meta data.

Here are the choices in the Scanning Options dialog:

- A check box labeled Resolve package references to scanned catalog meta data. If you do not select this box, you will not save any of the column-level lineage for the package. The default is for this check box not to be selected.

- An option group with two choices for which catalogs should be scanned:

  Use scanned catalogs if already present in repository. This is the default choice if the scanning resolution check box has been selected.

  Scan all referenced catalogs into repository.

- An option group with two choices for specifying a scanning option:

  Scan catalog if not already present in repository. This is the default choice if the scanning resolution check box has been selected.

  Scan catalog always.

The `RepositoryMetadataOptions` Property

The DTS Object Model implements all the scanning options with a property of the `Package` object called `RepositoryMetadataOptions`. The values for this property are shown in Table 29.1. I have listed the five options in this table in the order they appear in the Scanning Options dialog (refer to Figure 29.12).

Table 29.1   The DTSRepositoryMetadata Constants

Constant	Value	Description
DTSReposMetadata_Default_	0	Does no scanner resolution. This is the default choice.
DTSReposMetadata_ UseScannedCatalogIfPresent	2	Will use any scanned objects found; nonscanned references will create local objects.
DTSReposMetadata_ RequireScannedCatalog	1	Requires that any database objects must have been scanned into repository.
DTSReposMetadata_ ScanCatalogIfNotFound	4	Package will issue a scan on all catalogs that are not found already scanned.
DTSReposMetadata_ ScanCatalogAlways	8	The package will scan all catalogs referenced, rescanning if already scanned.

Configuring DTS for Row-Level Data Lineage

Row-level lineage is the transformation history of a particular record of data. It tells you when and how a record has been transformed.

There are two lineage variables used in Meta Data Services:

- DTSLineage_Full—Unique identifier data type.
- DTSLineage_Short—Integer data type.

You can save either one or both of the lineage variables. Each one identifies a specific instance of the execution of a package. The short lineage variable has the advantage of taking less storage space (4 bytes instead of 16 bytes), but the full lineage variable gives you a higher level of uniqueness.

Lineage Variable Choices

The lineage variables are enabled in the Package Designer with two check boxes on the Advanced tab of the DTS Package Properties dialog (shown in Figure 29.13):

- Show lineage variables as source columns. If you select this option, these two lineage variables will be included as if they were source columns for every transformation in your package. By default, this option is not selected.

• Write lineage to repository. This option is available only if the other option has been selected. If you do not choose this option, the execution history of the package will not be saved in Meta Data Services. By default, this option is not selected.

FIGURE 29.13
You can set lineage options for a package by selecting none, one, or both of the Lineage check boxes.

When you select the first check box, you will see the lineage variables appear as columns in the source table on the Transformations tab of the Data Transformation Properties dialog, as shown in Figure 29.14.

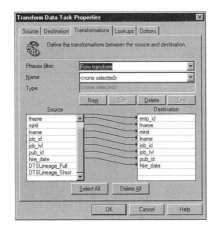

FIGURE 29.14
The lineage variables are added to the collection of source columns for every data transformation.

These lineage variables are not automatically entered into the destination records. You have to create columns to receive them and create the mappings to those columns, as with any other destination field. These mappings are shown in Figure 29.15.

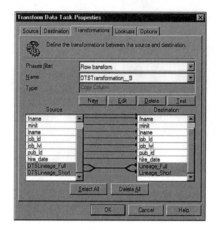

FIGURE 29.15
When one or both of the lineage variables are saved, the history of the record is preserved.

The LineageOptions Property

In the DTS Object Model, LineageOptions is a property of the Package object. This property must contain one of the values shown in Table 29.2.

TABLE 29.2   The DTSLineageOptions Constants

Constant	Value	Choose by Selecting
DTSLineage_None	0	Neither check box
DTSLineage_AddLineageVariables	1	First check box
DTSLineage_WriteToReposIfAvailable	2	Not available in interface
DTSLineage_WriteToReposRequired	3	Both check boxes

NOTE

The DTSLineage_WriteToReposIfAvailable constant is not described in detail in the product documentation. It appears to have the same behavior as DTSLineage_WriteToReposRequired.

> **NOTE**
>
> If you enable the lineage variables and then attempt to save a package to SQL Server, you will receive a warning message. If you continue saving and then execute the package, it will terminate with an error that says it could not open the Repository.

Saving the Lineage Variables

You can save the lineage variables with every record for every table in your data transformation. If the data values in a record appear to be inconsistent, you can use the lineage variables to identify the exact version and execution time of the package that created that record. If you want to examine other records created by that particular package, version, or execution, you can identify them through the lineage variables.

Instead of saving the lineage variables in every record of a data mart, you could create a lineage dimension. This dimension can provide ready access to information about the package. Some possible fields for a lineage dimension are shown in Table 29.3.

TABLE 29.3   The Fields for a Sample Lineage Dimension

Field Name	Description
LineagePK	Primary key
Lineage_Full	Long lineage variable
Lineage_Short	Short lineage variable
PackageName	Name of the DTS Package
PackageID	Package ID
VersionID	Version ID
PackageDescription	Description of the package
ExecutionStartTime	Date and time execution started
ExecutionDuration	Length of time for package execution

Accessing Lineage Information Programmatically

You can retrieve Meta Data Services package execution information through the Application object by using the PackageLineage and StepLineage objects.

> **NOTE**
>
> You access the Meta Data Services lineage information in almost the same way you access the package logging information, as described in Chapter 23.

Here is the information you can retrieve by querying the properties of a PackageLineage object:

- Name—The name of the package
- PackageID and VersionID
- LineageFullID and LineageShortID
- ExecutionDate—Date and time that the execution started
- Computer—The server the package was executed on
- Operator—The domain and username that was used for the execution of the package

Here is the information you can retrieve from the StepLineage object:

- Name—The name of the step
- StepExecutionStatus and StepExecutionResult
- StartTime, FinishTime, ExecutionTime
- ErrorCode, ErrorSource, ErrorDescription, ErrorHelpFile, and ErrorHelpContext

The code for enumerating the package lineage and the step lineage records is shown in Listing 23.1. This code is in the GetLineage.dts file. Open the package in the Package Designer and save it in Meta Data Services. Execute the package twice after saving it. The first time, no information will be returned because there is no execution information in Meta Data Services. When you execute it the second time, you will see the lineage information for the first execution.

LISTING 23.1   ActiveX Script for Displaying the Lineage Information of the Current Version of the Executing Package

```
Option Explicit

Function Main()

Dim DTSApp, PkgRepos
Dim  PkgLineages, PkgLineage
Dim StpLineages, StpLineage
```

LISTING 23.1   Continued

```
Dim pkg, sPackageVersionID
Dim prp, msg

Set pkg = DTSGlobalVariables.Parent
sPackageVersionID = pkg.VersionID

Set DTSApp = CreateObject("DTS.Application")
Set PkgRepos = DTSApp.GetPackageRepository(_
        "(local)", "msdb","","",DTSReposFlag_UseTrustedConnection)

'Enumerate all package lineage for selected package version
Set PkgLineages = PkgRepos.EnumPackageLineages(_
        sPackageVersionID, "", 0)
Set PkgLineage = PkgLineages.Next

Do Until PkgLineages.EOF

    msg = ""

    For Each prp in PkgLineage.Properties
        msg = msg & prp.Name & vbTab & prp.Value & vbCrLf
    Next

    Msgbox msg, , "Package Lineage"

    'Enumerate all step lineage for this instance of execution
    Set StpLineages = PkgRepos.EnumStepLineages(_
        PkgLineage.LineageFullID)
    Set StpLineage = StpLineages.Next

    Do Until StpLineages.EOF

        msg = ""

        For Each prp in StpLineage.Properties
            msg = msg & prp.Name & vbTab & prp.Value & vbCrLf
        Next

        Msgbox msg, , Step Lineage"

        Set StpLineage = StpLineages.Next

    Loop
```

LISTING 23.1   Continued

```
    'Get next package log record
    Set PkgLineage = PkgLineages.Next

Loop

    Main = DTSTaskExecResult_Success
End Function
```

You filter the package lineage information by using parameters with the `EnumPackageLineages` method of the `PackageRepositories` collection. The method has three parameters:

- `PackageVersionID`—You have to supply a valid `VersionID` for a package stored in Meta Data Services. You can return `PackageLineage` objects for all the times this version of the package was executed by supplying an empty string and the value 0 for the other two parameters.

- `LineageFullID`—The full lineage ID value for an instance of execution for this version. If you use this value, you will only return one `PackageLineage` object. Set this parameter to `""` if you don't want to filter on it.

- `LineageShortID`—The short lineage ID value for an instance of execution for this version. If you use this value, you will return only one `PackageLineage` object. Set this parameter to 0 if you don't want to filter on it.

You don't have any options for filtering step lineage records. You have to provide the `LineageFullID` for the execution of a package saved in Meta Data Services to return the step lineage for that execution.

Conclusion

An enterprise data transformation strategy needs an enterprise meta data strategy. You can create your own system for saving and retrieving the meta data that is important for your situation. Meta Data Services provides you with a prebuilt tool for your meta data system.

Extending the Power of DTS

PART
VI

IN THIS PART

Programming with the DTS Object Model

IN THIS CHAPTER

Programming with the DTS object model is discussed in some way in almost every chapter of this book. The purpose of this chapter is to present the DTS object model diagrams and to discuss some general issues in programming with the DTS objects, collections, and properties.

> **NOTE**
>
> As you consider various parts of the DTS object hierarchy, I encourage you to look at the objects and properties with Disconnected Edit. This tool gives you a very direct view of how DTS objects and properties are being used in a particular package.
>
> See Chapter 1, "A Quick Look at DTS," for a discussion of how to use Disconnected Edit.

Objects and Extended Objects

SQL Server 2000 has three categories of objects:

- Objects that have been left unchanged from SQL Server 7.0.
- New objects that were not available in SQL Server 7.0.
- Objects that were in SQL Server 7.0 and have now been extended in SQL Server 2000.

The objects in the third category can be referenced in two ways:

- The SQL Server 7.0 version of the object can be referenced using the same object name that was used in SQL Server 7.0.
- Appending a 2 on the end of the SQL Server 7.0 name can reference the extended version of the object implemented in SQL Server 2000.

Here are some of the objects in their SQL Server 7.0 versions and their extended versions:

- `Package` and `Package2`
- `Step` and `Step2`
- `DataPumpTask` and `DataPumpTask2`

When you use the SQL Server 7.0 version of an object, you can only use the properties and methods from SQL Server 7.0. When you use the extended objects, you can use all the properties and methods from the SQL Server 7.0 object and also the new SQL Server 2000 properties and methods.

If you execute a package in SQL Server 7.0 that uses extended objects, that package will fail. You can create a package in SQL Server 2000 that will work in SQL Server 7.0 if you use only the objects that have been unchanged and the SQL Server 7.0 versions of the extended objects.

> **NOTE**
>
> See the "Using Properties and the Properties Collection" section later in this chapter for one other potential problem with executing SQL Server 2000 packages in SQL Server 7.0.

In the object model diagrams in this chapter, the extended version of the object is referenced every time one exists. The SQL Server 7.0 versions of the objects are not shown in the diagrams. In every situation where there is an extended version of an object, you can also use the SQL Server 7.0 version.

The DTS Package Object Hierarchy

The DTS object model has two hierarchies:

- The DTS Application hierarchy, which contains information about components registered with the system and packages stored in SQL Server and Meta Data Services.
- The DTS Package hierarchy, which contains all the functional DTS elements—tasks, steps, connections, and global variables.

The DTS Application hierarchy is discussed later in this chapter. The highest levels of the DTS Package hierarchy are shown in Figure 30.1.

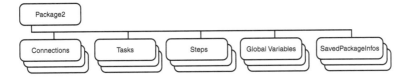

FIGURE 30.1
The highest levels of the DTS Package hierarchy.

Figure 30.2 shows the detailed hierarchy of all the objects except the Task object.

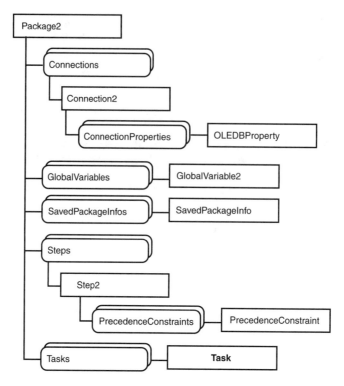

FIGURE 30.2

Details of the DTS Package hierarchy, not including the Task *object.*

NOTE

The SavedPackageInfos collection provides information about packages saved in system files. All the other objects that provide information are included under the Application hierarchy.

Figure 30.3 shows the object hierarchy for the Task object. There are two types of objects under Task—the class-specific objects for each of the different kinds of tasks, and objects that are used to implement custom tasks. The class-specific objects are discussed in Parts II, III, and IV. The objects used to implement custom tasks are

- CustomTask
- CustomTaskUI
- PersistPropertyBag

These objects are discussed in Chapter 31, "Creating a Custom Task in VB."

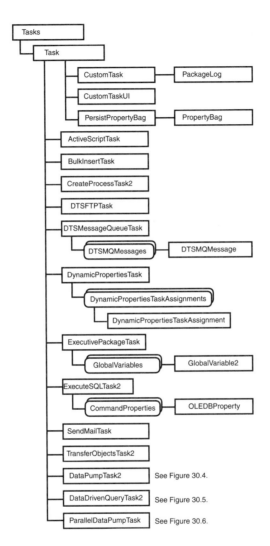

FIGURE 30.3
The Task *object portion of the Package hierarchy.*

30

PROGRAMMING
WITH THE DTS
OBJECT MODEL

The `CustomTask` property is used to gain a reference to any of the class-specific task objects. When you use the `CustomTask` property in Visual Basic, you first declare an object variable using the specific class:

```
Dim tsk As DTS.Task
Dim cusExecSQL As DTS.ExecuteSQLTask2
Set tsk = pkg.Tasks.New("DTSExecuteSQLTask")
Set cusExecSQL = tsk.CustomTask
cusExecSQL.SQLStatement = _
        "Update Employees Set Salary = Salary * 1.1"
```

The `CustomTask` interface is used when you're creating custom tasks in Visual Basic, Visual C++, or another programming interface.

The `CustomTask` object is used to define the `CustomTask` interface when that interface is used in Visual Basic programming:

```
Implements DTS.CustomTask
```

Figure 30.3 does not show the details of the three transformation tasks. Figure 30.4 displays all the details of the Transform Data task, except for the details of the transformations themselves.

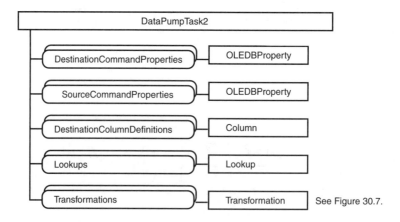

FIGURE 30.4

The Transform Data task.

The Data Driven Query hierarchy, shown in Figure 30.5, adds four additional collections.

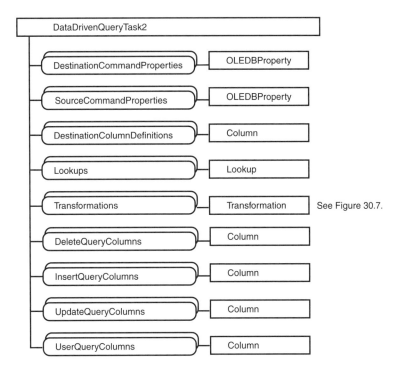

FIGURE 30.5

The Data Driven Query task.

Figure 30.6 shows the hierarchy of the Parallel Data Pump task, which is similar to the hierarchy of the Data Driven Query task. Additional levels have been added for the TransformationSets collection and the TransformationSet object.

Finally, Figure 30.7 shows the detailed structure of a Transformation object. This same structure is used in the Transform Data task, the Data Driven Query task, and the Parallel Data Pump task.

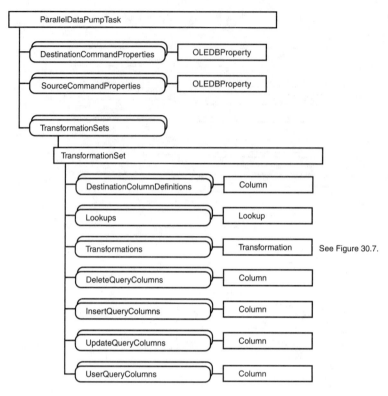

FIGURE 30.6

The Parallel Data Pump task.

NOTE

`DTSTransformScriptProperties2` is the extended object that corresponds to the SQL Server 7.0 object `DataPumpTransformScript`. This is the only extended object in the DTS object model that does not follow the convention of adding a 2 to the end of the name of the SQL Server 7.0 object. You still have to use `DataPumpTransformScript` as the `New` method parameter when creating a new transformation of this type in SQL Server 2000.

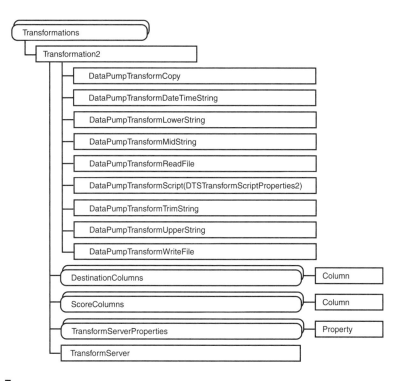

FIGURE 30.7
The hierarchy of the Transformation object.

Using Tasks and Custom Tasks

You need two object variables to work with a DTS task programmatically:

- A `Task` object that defines the properties common to all tasks.
- A class-specific `CustomTask` object that defines the unique properties for each custom task.

The `Task` object has these five properties:

- `Name`.
- `Description`.
- `Parent`—The `Tasks` collection.
- `CustomTask`—The `CustomTask` object that is paired with this `Task` object.
- `CustomTaskID`—The programmatic identifier for the type of custom task paired with this task.

All the other properties associated with a task are referenced through the `CustomTask` object, although you can also reference them as members of the `Task` object's `Properties` collection.

Referencing a Task and a Custom Task

You reference an existing task as a particular member of the package's `Tasks` collection.

You can reference a particular task by its name:

```
Set tsk = pkg.Tasks("TheNameOfTheTask")
```

If you know the position of the task in the collection, you can use the task's index. The `Tasks` collection is 1-based:

```
Set tsk = pkg.Tasks(1)
```

If you want to reference all the package's tasks, you can use a `For Next` loop:

```
For Each tsk in pkg.Tasks
    Msgbox tsk.Name
Next
```

After you have a reference to the task, you use the task's `CustomTask` property to reference the `CustomTask` object:

```
Set cus = tsk.CustomTask
```

If you are using Visual Basic, you can declare the `Task` object variable by referencing the `Task` object in the DTS library:

```
Dim tsk As DTS.Task
```

You can't do the same thing for the `CustomTask` object because, in the DTS hierarchy, it does not have the particular properties, methods, and collections that are needed for each specific custom task:

```
Dim cus As DTS.CustomTask 'This will not work!
```

You can either declare the custom task as a generic object variable or reference the class-specific object for that custom task:

```
Dim cus As Object
Dim cusExecSQL As DTS.ExecuteSQLTask2
```

Creating a New Task

You use the following steps to create a new task. These steps assume that you already have a reference to a DTS package:

1. Declare variables:

```
Dim tsk As DTS.Task
Dim cusExecSQL As DTS.ExecuteSQLTask2
```

2. Use the New method of the Tasks collection. This method requires you to specify a value for the task's CustomTaskID property, which determines the type of task you are creating:

```
Set tsk = pkg.New("DTSExecuteSQLTask")
```

3. Set a reference to the custom task variable through the CustomTask property:

```
Set cusExecSQL = tsk.CustomTask
```

4. Set the task's properties through the custom task variable. You can set the Name and the Description by referencing either the task variable or the custom task variable:

```
tsk.Name = "tskUpdateAuthors"
cusExecSQL.Description = "Update the Authors Table"
cusExecSQL.ConnectionID = 3
cusExecSQL.SQLStatement = _
        "Update Employees Set Salary = Salary * 1.1"
```

5. Add the task to the collection:

```
pkg.Tasks.Add tsk
```

> **NOTE**
>
> Instead of setting the task's properties through the custom task (step 4), you can set them by referencing the members of the Task object's Properties collection. You have to use this alternative method of referencing properties for some custom tasks, including those created in Visual Basic:
>
> ```
> tsk.Name = "tskUpdateAuthors"
> tsk.Properties("Description") = "Update the Authors Table"
> tsk.Properties("ConnectionID") = 3
> tsk.Properties("SQLStatement") = _
>         "Update Employees Set Salary = Salary * 1.1"
> ```

Object Names and Programmatic Identifiers for the Custom Tasks

When you create a new task, you need to know the programmatic identifier for the specific custom task you are creating. These programmatic identifiers are shown in the four tables in this section. These tables also show the library and object name of each custom task, which is the value that you can use when declaring an object variable for the custom task.

The different code libraries appear to have different conventions for the programmatic identifiers. The names of the programmatic identifiers are consistent within each library.

Table 30.1 shows the programmatic identifiers and names for the objects in the core DTS object library, the Microsoft DTSPackage Object Library (dtspkg.dll). The programmatic identifier is the same as the library and object name, with the dot removed. When a task is an extended object, the 2 is also removed from the name.

TABLE 30.1   Programmatic Identifiers and Names for Custom Tasks Defined in dtspkg.dll

Custom Task	Programmatic Identifier	Library.ObjectName
ActiveX Script	DTSActiveScriptTask	DTS.ActiveScriptTask
Bulk Insert	DTSBulkInsertTask	DTS.BulkInsertTask
Copy SQL Server Objects	DTSTransferObjectsTask	DTS.TransferObjectsTask2
Data Driven Query	DTSDataDrivenQueryTask	DTS.DataDrivenQueryTask2
Execute Package	DTSExecutePackageTask	DTS.ExecutePackageTask
Execute Process	DTSCreateProcessTask	DTS.CreateProcessTask2
Execute SQL	DTSExecuteSQLTask	DTS.ExecuteSQLTask2
Parallel Data Pump	DTSParallelDataPumpTask	DTS.ParallelDataPumpTask
Send Mail	DTSSendMailTask	DTS.SendMailTask
Transform Data	DTSDataPumpTask	DTS.DataPumpTask2

> **NOTE**
>
> All the objects listed as extended objects in Table 30.1 can also be declared as SQL Server 7.0 objects by removing the 2 at the end of the object name. The programmatic identifier is the same for both types of objects.

The programmatic identifiers for the tasks in the Microsoft DTS Custom Tasks Object Library (custtask.dll) look the same as those in dtspkg.dll. The library name for these tasks, DTSCustTasks, is not carried over into the programmatic identifier.

TABLE 30.2 Programmatic Identifiers and Names for Custom Tasks Defined in dtspkg.dll

Custom Task	Programmatic Identifier	Library.ObjectName
Dynamic Properties	DTSDynamicPropertiesTask	DTSCustTasks. DynamicPropertiesTask
FTP	DTSFTPTask	DTSCustTasks. DTSFTPTask
Message Queue	DTSMessageQueueTask	DTSCustTasks. DTSMessageQueueTask

You use the library name and the object name, separated by a dot, for the programmatic identifiers for the five transfer tasks in the OMWCustomTasks 1.0 Type Library (cdwtasks.dll). These programmatic identifiers are shown in Table 30.3.

TABLE 30.3 For cdwtasks.dll, the Programmatic Identifiers Are the Same as the Library.ObjectNames

Custom Task	Programmatic Identifier/Library.ObjectName
Transfer Databases	OMWCustomTasks.OMWTransferDatabases
Transfer Error Messages	OMWCustomTasks.OMWTransferErrors
Transfer Logins	OMWCustomTasks.OMWTransferLogins
Transfer Master Stored Procedures	OMWCustomTasks.OMWTransferMaster
Transfer MSDB Jobs	OMWCustomTasks.OMWTransferMSDB

Each of the two Analysis Services Processing tasks is defined in its own library, so the simple name "Task" can be used for the library's custom task. For these two tasks, the programmatic identifier is also the library name and the task name, separated by a dot.

TABLE 30.4 Programmatic Identifiers and Names for the Analysis Services Tasks

Custom Task	Programmatic Identifier/Library.ObjectName
Analysis Services Processing	DTSOlapProcess.Task
Data Mining Prediction Query	DTSPrediction.Task

30

PROGRAMMING
WITH THE DTS
OBJECT MODEL

Using Collections

Many of the collections used in DTS have similar methods and properties. There are usually two properties:

- Count—The number of items in the collection.
- Parent—A reference to the object that contains the collection.

The following methods can be used by many of the collections, including Connections, GlobalVariables, Steps, PrecedenceConstraints, Tasks, Lookups, Transformations, and TransformationSets:

- New and Add—These methods are usually used together. You create a new object with New, set required properties, and then use Add to put the object into the collection:

```
Set stp = pkg.Steps.New
stp.Name = "stpInitialize"
stp.TaskName = "tskInitialize"
pkg.Steps.Add stp
```

- Insert—This method can be used in place of Add when you want to place an object in a particular ordinal place in a collection:

```
pkg.Steps.Insert stp, 1
```

- Item—Provides a reference to one of the objects in the collection. You can specify the particular item either by its ordinal position in the collection or by the object's name:

```
Set stp = pkg.Steps.Item(1)
Set stp = pkg.Steps.Item("stpInitialize")
```

> **NOTE**
>
> Item is the default method of the collections. I haven't found any DTS collection where I have to specifically use the Item method. The following code has the same effect as the examples using Item:
>
> ```
> Set stp = pkg.Steps(1)
> Set stp = pkg.Steps("stpInitialize")
> ```

Many collections, including Steps, PrecedenceConstraints, Tasks, Transformations, and TransformationSets, also have a Remove method, which removes an item from a collection. Either the name or the ordinal position can be used to specify the object to be removed:

```
pkg.Steps.Remove 1
pkg.Steps.Remove "stpInitialize")
```

Some collections have special methods for creating a new object and adding it to the collection in a single command:

```
pkg.GlobalVariables.AddGlobalVariable "NewVar", "NewVarValue"
stpDestination.PrecedenceConstraints.AddConstraint "stpSource"
tsk.Lookups.AddLookup _
        "lkpFirstName", _
        "Select au_fname from authors where au_id = ?", _
        3, _
        100
```

Using Properties and the Properties Collection

Most DTS objects have a `Properties` collection, which can be used to reference any of that object's properties. The following two lines of code are equivalent:

```
Msgbox pkg.Description
Msgbox pkg.Properties("Description")
```

In most cases, it is easier to reference an object's properties directly. The `Properties` collection can be convenient when you want to examine all of an object's properties. It's a lot quicker to write the following code than to reference each of the `Package` object's properties by name:

```
For Each prop in pkg.Properties
    Msgbox prop.Name & " " & prop.Value
Next
```

If you reference properties through the `Properties` collection, you can reference extended properties of DTS objects even if you have created those objects to be SQL Server 7.0 objects. If you do that, you will be unable to use your SQL Server 2000 packages in SQL Server 7.0 because it will not recognize the extended properties as valid members of the `Properties` collection.

The DTS Application Object Hierarchy

You can use the DTS `Application` object for two primary purposes:

- To retrieve information about DTS objects registered with the system.
- To retrieve information about DTS packages stored in SQL Server and Meta Data Services.

30

PROGRAMMING
WITH THE DTS
OBJECT MODEL

> **NOTE**
>
> The `Application` object also has two properties that are used to set characteristics of the DTS Design environment. The `JITDebug` property determines Just-In-Time Debugging of ActiveX Scripts. The `DesignerSettings` property determines whether or not multiple phases are shown for the transformation tasks.

In Figure 30.8, these two purposes are shown as separate primary branches coming from the `Application` in the object hierarchy.

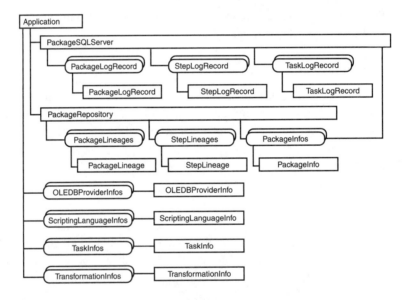

FIGURE 30.8
The DTS Application object hierarchy.

> **NOTE**
>
> The `PackageSQLServer` object and the `PackageRepository` objects have one collection (`PackageInfos`) in common.

Chapter 23, "The DTS Package and Its Properties," describes how to use the `PackageSQLServer` object to obtain information about packages stored in SQL Server. Chapter 29, "Integrating DTS with Meta Data Services," describes how to use the `PackageRepository` object to obtain information about packages stored in Meta Data Services.

The four types of system information that can be retrieved using the Application object are

- TaskInfos—All the DTS custom tasks that have been registered with the system.
- TransformationInfos—All the DTS custom transformations that have been registered with the system.
- ScriptingLanguageInfos—All the scripting languages that have been registered with the system.
- OLEDBProviderInfos—All the OLE DB providers that have been registered with the system.

You can retrieve this information with the VBScript code in Listing 30.1. This code is included on the CD in a file called DTSSystemInfo.vbs.

LISTING 30.1   VBScript Code That Writes DTS System Information to a File

```
Option Explicit

Dim app, info, prop, msg
Dim  txtstr, fso, fld, fil

Function Main()

Set fso = CreateObject("Scripting.FileSystemObject")
fso.CreateTextFile "c:\temp\DTSSystemInfo.txt"
Set fil = fso.GetFile("c:\temp\DTSSystemInfo.txt")
set txtstr= fil.OpenAsTextStream(2)

txtstr.Write "DTS System Info Report Created " & Now & vbCrLf

Set app = CreateObject("DTS.Application")

txtstr.Write vbCrLf & "Registered Tasks"  & vbCrLf & vbCrLf
For Each info in app.TaskInfos
    Call fctWriteInfo
Next

txtstr.Write vbCrLf & "Registered Transformations" & vbCrLf & vbCrLf
For Each info in app.TransformationInfos
    Call fctWriteInfo
Next

txtstr.Write vbCrLf & "Registered Scripting Languages" & _
        vbCrLf & vbCrLf
For Each info in app.ScriptingLanguageInfos
```

LISTING 30.1   Continued

```
    Call fctWriteInfo
Next

txtstr.Write vbCrLf & "Registered OLE DB Providers" & vbCrLf & vbCrLf
For Each info in app.OLEDBProviderInfos
    Call fctWriteInfo
Next
    Main = DTSTaskExecResult_Success
End Function

Function fctWriteInfo

    For Each prop in info.Properties
        txtstr.Write prop.Name & vbTab & prop.Value & vbCrLf
    Next
    txtstr.WriteLine

End Function
```

Documenting the Connections in a DTS Package

You can use your knowledge of the DTS object hierarchy to document your DTS package. One particular kind of documentation I find useful is an inventory of connections.

It's easy to see all the connection objects in the Package Designer user interface, but it's not easy to see how all those connections are being used. Listing 30.2 is an ActiveX Script for creating a text file that inventories how a package's connections are used. You can find this code on the CD in a file called ConnectionInventory.vbs and in a DTS package called ConnectionInventory.dts.

LISTING 30.2   Code That Documents the Use of a Package's Connections

```
Option Explicit
Dim txtstr, cus

Function Main()

Dim pkg, con, tsk, lkp, dpta
Dim fso, fld, fil

Set pkg = DTSGlobalVariables.Parent

Set fso = CreateObject("Scripting.FileSystemObject")
fso.CreateTextFile "c:\temp\ConnectionInfo.txt"
```

LISTING 30.2   Continued

```
Set fil = fso.GetFile("c:\temp\ConnectionInfo.txt")
set txtstr= fil.OpenAsTextStream(2)

txtstr.Write "Report Created " & Now & vbcrlf & vbcrlf
txtstr.Write "Package Name: " & pkg.Name & vbcrlf & vbcrlf

For Each con in pkg.Connections

  txtstr.Write "Connection Name: " & con.Name & vbcrlf
  txtstr.Write "Description: " & con.Description & vbcrlf
  txtstr.Write "Connection ID: " & con.ID & vbcrlf
  txtstr.Write "Provider ID: "  & con.ProviderID & vbcrlf
  txtstr.Write "DataSource: "  & con.DataSource & vbcrlf
  txtstr.Write "Catalog: "  & con.Catalog & vbcrlf & vbcrlf
  txtstr.Write "This connection is used in:" & vbcrlf & vbcrlf

   For Each tsk in pkg.Tasks

    Set cus = tsk.CustomTask

    Select Case tsk.CustomTaskID

      Case "DTSExecuteSQLTask", "DTSExecuteSQLTask2"

        If con.ID = cus.ConnectionID Then
          Call fctOutputTask ("Execute SQL Connection")
        End If

      Case "DTSDataDrivenQueryTask", "DTSDataDrivenQueryTask2"

        If con.ID = cus.SourceConnectionID Then
          Call fctOutputTask ("DDQ Source")
        End If

        If con.ID = cus.DestinationConnectionID Then
          Call fctOutputTask ("DDQ Destination")
        End If

        For Each lkp in cus.Lookups
          If con.ID = lkp.ConnectionID Then
            Call fctOutputTask ("Lookup - " & lkp.Name)
```

30

PROGRAMMING
WITH THE DTS
OBJECT MODEL

LISTING 30.2 Continued

```
        End If
      Next

Case "DTSBulkInsertTask"

  If con.ID = cus.ConnectionID Then
    Call fctOutputTask ("Bulk Insert Connection")
  End If

Case "DTSDataPumpTask", "DTSDataPumpTask2"

  If con.ID = cus.SourceConnectionID Then
    Call fctOutputTask ("Transform Data Source")
  End If

  If con.ID = cus.DestinationConnectionID Then
    Call fctOutputTask ("Transform Data Destination")
  End If

  For Each lkp in cus.Lookups
    If con.ID = lkp.ConnectionID Then
      Call fctOutputTask ( "Lookup - " & lkp.Name)
    End If
  Next

Case "DTSParallelDataPumpTask"

  If con.ID = cus.SourceConnectionID Then
    Call fctOutputTask ("Parallel Data Pump Source")
  End If

  If con.ID = cus.DestinationConnectionID Then
    Call fctOutputTask ("Parallel Data Pump Destination")
  End If

  For Each trnset in cus.TransformationSets
    For Each lkp in trnset.Lookups
      If con.ID = lkp.ConnectionID Then
        Call fctOutputTask ( "Lookup - " & lkp.Name)
      End If
```

LISTING 30.2   Continued

```
                Next
            Next

        Case "DTSDynamicPropertiesTask"

            For each dpta in cus.Assignments

                If dpta.SourceType  = 1 Then
                    If con.ID = dpta.SourceQueryConnectionID Then
                        Call fctOutputTask ("Dynamic Properties Query")
                    End If
                End if

            Next

        End Select

    Next

Next

txtstr.Close

    Main = DTSTaskExecResult_Success
End Function

Function fctOutputTask(sConnectionUse)
    txtstr.Write vbTab & "Task Name: " & cus.Name & vbcrlf
    txtstr.Write vbTab & "Description: " & cus.Description & vbcrlf
    txtstr.Write vbTab & "Use: " & sConnectionUse  & vbcrlf & vbcrlf
End Function
```

Conclusion

You can use the DTS Package object hierarchy to retrieve information, create new objects, and modify objects. You can use the DTS Application object hierarchy to retrieve system information about DTS objects and information about packages stored in SQL Server and Meta Data Services.

The next chapter explains how to create DTS custom tasks with Visual Basic.

30

PROGRAMMING
WITH THE DTS
OBJECT MODEL

Creating a Custom Task in VB

IN THIS CHAPTER

You can extend the capabilities of Data Transformation Services by creating your own custom tasks with Visual Basic, Visual C++, or another programming language that supports COM. Once you have created and registered a custom task, it will appear on the task palette in the DTS Designer and you can use it along with all the other types of tasks.

This chapter explains how to build a custom task using Visual Basic. Two sample applications are used to illustrate this process:

- File Find task—A simple custom task that checks for the existence of a file in a particular directory. This sample application is on the CD in two versions—with and without a custom user interface.

- Local Cube task—A complex custom task that automates the creation of one or more local cube files from an Analysis Services cube. A demo version of this application is on the CD.

> **NOTE**
>
> Chapter 32, "Creating a Custom Transformation with VC++," explains how to use the Active Template Library (ATL) custom transformation template that is provided with the SQL Server 2000 sample code. There are also two ATL templates provided for making custom tasks, which you can use as a starting point for building a custom task in VC++.

When You Should Create a New Custom Task

A custom task encapsulates a particular set of functionality in a way that can be reused in many packages. You can include a user interface with a custom task so that it can be adapted to different sets of data.

You should consider the following options before building a new custom task:

- If one of the existing tasks has the functionality you need, use it.

- If a set of tasks combined has the needed functionality, create a DTS template that includes all the tasks and use that template when creating a new package.

- If you need to manipulate individual rows of data, consider building a custom transformation (as described in Chapter 32) instead of a custom task.

- If you only need this functionality on a one-time basis, consider using code in an ActiveX Script task.

- If the functionality you need is already available in an external application, consider calling that application from a DTS package with an Execute Process task.

If you're comparing an external application to a custom task, you should consider the advantages of having the custom task integrated into the DTS system:

- Uniform error handling.
- The ability to set precedence based on success and failure.
- The ability to participate in transactions.

Here are some situations where a custom task could be useful:

- If you have a particular ActiveX Script task that you are using in several packages, you could convert that task into a custom task.
- You could build a custom task to automate backups in different database systems.
- You could build a custom task that would automate the reporting on the results of a DTS package execution.
- You could create a custom task to do an incremental update on a set of cubes. The Analysis Services Processing task allows you to do incremental updates on one cube or a full process on a set of cubes, but you have to create separate instances of the task for each cube incremental update.
- You could incorporate the ability to design cube aggregations into a custom task that processed cubes.

Getting Started

The first step in building a custom task is to open Visual Basic and create a new ActiveX DLL project. Give the project and the class module appropriate names. You also have to add a reference to one code library—the Microsoft DTSPackage Object Library.

NOTE

You don't need to add a reference to the Microsoft DTS Custom Task Objects Library. That's a library that contains some of the new SQL Server 2000 custom tasks. It doesn't have anything to do with creating a new custom task.

NOTE

The Find File task described in this chapter also needs a reference to Microsoft Scripting Runtime because it uses the file system objects from this library.

You can use one or more interfaces when building your custom task. The required `CustomTask` interface contains the core functionality of the custom task. The optional `CustomTaskUI` interface contains the properties and methods for building a user interface.

The LocalCubeTask project implements the `CustomTaskUI` interface. The interface for this task is shown in Figure 31.1.

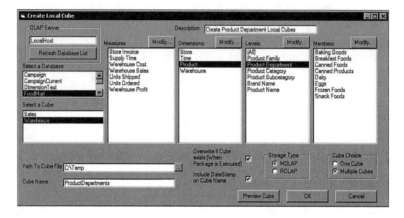

FIGURE 31.1

The user interface for the Local Cube task.

If you don't use `CustomTaskUI` DTS supplies a simple grid that displays all the custom task's properties and allows them to be changed. The default user interface, Figure 31.2, is used in the Find File task.

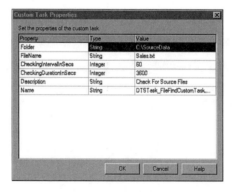

FIGURE 31.2

The default user interface for a custom task.

Implementing the Custom Task Interface

You have to implement the CustomTask interface when you are creating a custom task. You access this interface through the CustomTask object in the DTSPackage Object Library.

```
Implements DTS.CustomTask
```

> **NOTE**
>
> In C++, the Custom Task interface is defined by IDTSCustomTask, in the file dtspkg.h.

The CustomTask interface has two properties, one method, and one collection. The two properties of the CustomTask interface, Name and Description, can be referenced as properties of the Task object and the CustomTask object in the DTS object hierarchy. Any other properties you set in your code become members of the Task object's Properties collection, which are unique for each custom task.

The Name Property

The Name property must always be set because it is used to identify the objects in a DTS package. The name for each task must also be unique.

When a task icon is placed on the design sheet in the DTS Package Designer, the Package Designer assigns a value to the Name property. This value is also used in the TaskName property of the step that is associated with that task.

The Property Let code is called when a value is assigned to the Name property. The Property Get code retrieves the value.

You have two options you can use to implement the Name property. With the first option, you use a Private property declaration and a module-level variable for the name:

```
Private Property Let CustomTask_Name(ByVal sNewName As String)
    Name = sNewName
End Property

Private Property Get CustomTask_Name() As String
    CustomTask_Name = Name
End Property
```

With the second option, you use a `Public` property declaration that adds the `Name` property to the task's `Properties` collection:

```
Public Property Let Name(ByVal sNewName As String)
    Name = sNewTaskName
End Property

Public Property Get Name() As String
    Name = msTaskName
End Property
```

The first option has the following results:

- The user cannot modify the `Name` property in the properties grid or in Disconnected Edit.
- You can only refer to the `Name` property in code as a property of the `Task` or `CustomTask` object, and not as a member of the task's `Properties` collection.
- If you save the package to VB, the name will not be assigned in the VB code. If you use this VB code to execute the package, the execution will fail unless you add code to assign the name.

Here are the results for the second option:

- The `Name` property will be editable in the default Properties grid for the custom task if you do not create a user interface for the task.
- The `Name` property will be editable in Disconnected Edit.
- You can reference the `Name` property in code as a member of the task's `Properties` collection:
  ```
  Dim pkg, tsk, cus
  Set pkg = DTSGlobalVariables.Parent
  Set tsk = pkg.Tasks("NameOfOurCustomTask")
  Msgbox tsk.Properties("Name").Value
  ```
- Because the `Name` property is more exposed, it is more likely that the user will change it. If the user changes the value of the `Name` property without changing the step's `TaskName` property, the task will be separated from its corresponding step.

> **NOTE**
>
> SQL Server Books Online recommends using the first option. If the `Name` property is exposed, users might change its value and the task will become separated from the step. But if you're using the default properties grid and you don't expose the `Name` property, the name will not be saved when you're saving to VB.
>
> If you create an interface for your custom task, you can include the code that adds the `Name` property to the `Properties` collection without giving the user a place to change the name.

The Description Property

You do not have to implement the Description property of the CustomTask interface, although you do have to provide a placeholder for the property in the code. If you only provide a placeholder, your custom task will not have a label when viewed in the Package Designer.

```
Private Property Let CustomTask_Description(ByVal sDescription As String)
    'Not being used
End Property

Private Property Get CustomTask_Description() As String
    'Not being used
End Property
```

If you want to see the description and be able to modify it using the Properties grid, you have to assign the Description property, both for the CustomTask interface and as a member of the Properties collection:

```
Private Property Let CustomTask_Description(ByVal sNewDescription As String)
    msDescription = sNewDescription
End Property

Private Property Get CustomTask_Description() As String
    CustomTask_Description = msDescription
End Property

Public Property Let Description(ByVal sNewDescription As String)
    msDescription = sNewDescription
End Property

Public Property Get Description() As String
    Description = msDescription
End Property
```

The Properties Collection

You don't have to set your custom task's properties with the Properties collection of the CustomTask interface. If you set the properties to Nothing, DTS will build the Properties collection using the properties that you have created with the code in your class module:

```
Private Property Get CustomTask_Properties() As DTS.Properties
    Set CustomTask_Properties = Nothing
End Property
```

If you use this code, all `Public` variables you declare in your class module will become members of the `Properties` collection. This method of handling properties is illustrated in a file on the CD called FindFileTaskPublicVariables.cls:

```
Public Folder As String
Public FileName As String
Public CheckingIntervalInSecs As Long
Public CheckingDurationInSecs As Long
```

The preferred way to add properties to your task is to explicitly declare them as `Public` properties with the `Property Let` and `Property Get` syntax. If you do this, you don't declare the properties as `Public` variables. This method of handling properties is illustrated in a file on the CD called FindFileTaskPublicProperties.cls:

```
Private msFolder As String

Public Property Let Folder (ByVal sNewFolder As String)
    msFolder = sNewFolder
End Property

Public Property Get Folder() As String
    Folder = msFolder
End Property
```

If you want to refer to the values of the properties directly in your custom task code, you have to use the DTS `PropertiesProvider` object to explicitly assign them to the `Properties` collection:

```
Private Property Get CustomTask_Properties() As DTS.Properties
    Dim propProvider As New DTS.PropertiesProvider
    Set CustomTask_Properties = propProvider.GetPropertiesForObject(Me)
    Set propProvider = Nothing
End Property
```

The Execute Method

DTS calls the `Execute` method of the custom task when its associated step indicates that the task should be executed. All of the task's functionality is triggered by the `Execute` method. It should not be called directly by a Visual Basic application.

The `Execute` method has four parameters:

- pPackage—A reference to the parent DTS `Package2` object. You can use this object to obtain references to other objects in the DTS package. You cannot save any of these object references after `Execute` returns.

- pPackageEvents—An object used to raise events.

- pPackageLog—An object used to write to the log.
- pTaskResult—A parameter used to inform the package of the result of the task's execution. You assign one of the DTSTaskExecResult constants to this parameter:

```
If bSuccess Then
    pTaskResult = DTSTaskExecResult_Success  '0
ElseIf bRetry Then
    pTaskResult = DTSTaskExecResult_RetryStep '2
Else
    pTaskResult = DTSTaskExecResult_Failure  '1
End If
```

The use of pPackageEvents and pPackageLog is described in the section "Events, Errors, and Logs" later in this chapter.

Because you have a reference to the Package2 object through pPackage, you can dynamically modify other connections, steps, and tasks in the DTS package. You could use the AcquireConnection and ReleaseConnection methods of the Connection object to open and close connections needed for your task. You normally wouldn't want to manipulate the properties of other tasks because it would limit the use of your custom task to a package that had those particular tasks.

Listing 31.1 contains the code for the Execute method in the Find File task. Errors are raised in every situation that causes the task to fail. This causes the processing to jump to the error handler, which does three things:

- Sets the task result to DTSTaskExecResult_Failure.
- Calls a procedure to write a message to the task log.
- Raises the same error again. If an error is handled in the task's code, the calling application will not be informed of the error. If the error is raised again in the error handler, it becomes an unhandled error and the calling application can retrieve the information about it.

LISTING 31.1   The Execute Method of the CustomTask Interface from the Find File Task

```
Private Sub CustomTask_Execute( _
        ByVal pPackage As Object, _
        ByVal pPackageEvents As Object, _
        ByVal pPackageLog As Object, _
        pTaskResult As DTS.DTSTaskExecResult)
On Error GoTo ErrorHandler

Dim objPackage As DTS.Package2
Dim bFileFound As Boolean
Dim lCounter As Long
```

LISTING 31.1 Continued

```
Dim lNumberOfChecks As Long
Dim dtLastCheckCancel As Date
Dim dtLastCheckFile As Date
Dim dtStartTime As Date

Dim fso As New Scripting.FileSystemObject
Dim fil As Scripting.File
Dim fld As Scripting.Folder

'Initialize
bFileFound = False

'Checking interval must be at least 1 second.
If CheckingIntervalInSecs < 1 Then
  CheckingIntervalInSecs = 1
End If

'For Showing OnProgress Percentage
lNumberOfChecks = CheckingDurationInSecs / CheckingIntervalInSecs

'Initialize time to check duration
dtStartTime = Now

'Initialize time to check cancel
dtLastCheckCancel = DateAdd("s", -1, Now)

'Initialize time to check for file
dtLastCheckFile = DateAdd("s", -(CheckingIntervalInSecs), Now)

lCounter = 0

Do

   'See if it's time to check for cancel.
   If DateDiff("s", dtLastCheckCancel, Now) >= 1 Then
     dtLastCheckCancel = Now
     Call subCheckForCancel(pPackageEvents)
   End If

   'See if it's time to look for the file
   If DateDiff("s", dtLastCheckFile, Now) >= _
       CheckingIntervalInSecs Then

     lCounter = lCounter + 1
     dtLastCheckFile = Now
```

LISTING 31.1   Continued

```
'Check for an empty string in the Folder property
If Not Folder = "" Then

  'Check for existence of folder.
  If fso.FolderExists(Folder) Then

    Set fld = fso.GetFolder(Folder)

    'Check for an empty string in the FileName property
    If FileName = "" Then

      'When empty string, look for any file in the folder
      If fld.Files.Count > 0 Then

        bFileFound = True
        Call subWriteTaskRecord(pPackageLog, 1, "File Found.")
        Exit Do

      Else

        Call subWriteTaskRecord(pPackageLog, 1, _
          "File has not been found after " & DateDiff("s", _
          dtStartTime, Now) & " second(s).")

        Call subOnProgress(pPackageEvents, pPackageLog, _
          "FindFileCustomTask", "Checked for file " & _
          lCounter & " time(s).", lCounter * 100 / _
          lNumberOfChecks, lCounter, lCounter)

      End If

    Else

      'Now looking for a specific file.
      If fso.FileExists(Folder & "\" & FileName) = True Then

        bFileFound = True
        Call subWriteTaskRecord(pPackageLog, 1, "File Found.")
        Exit Do

      Else
```

LISTING 31.1   Continued

```
        Call subWriteTaskRecord(pPackageLog, 1, _
            "File has not been found after " & DateDiff("s", _
            dtStartTime, Now) & " second(s).")

        Call subOnProgress(pPackageEvents, pPackageLog, _
            "FindFileCustomTask", "Checked for file " & _
            lCounter & " time(s).", lCounter * 100 / _
            lNumberOfChecks, lCounter, lCounter)

      End If

    End If

  Else

    'Folder doesn't exist. Inform calling application
    'Cancel on this error only when requested to do so.
    Call subOnError(pPackageEvents, pPackageLog, _
        "FindFileCustomTask", -1, "FindFileCustomTask", _
        "Folder doesn't exist after " & DateDiff("s", _
        dtStartTime, Now) & " second(s)", "", 1, "", False)

  End If

  Else

    'Folder property was an empty string.
    Err.Raise -1, , "No folder selected."

  End If

End If

Loop Until DateDiff("s", dtStartTime, Now) >= CheckingDurationInSecs

If bFileFound = False Then
  Err.Raise -1, , "Duration expired without finding file."
End If

pTaskResult = DTSTaskExecResult_Success

ProcExit:
    Exit Sub
```

LISTING 31.1   Continued

```
ErrorHandler:
    pTaskResult = DTSTaskExecResult_Failure
    Call subWriteTaskRecord(pPackageLog, Err.Number, Err.Description)
    Err.Raise Err.Number, Err.Source, Err.Description
    GoTo ProcExit

End Sub
```

Implementing the Custom Task User Interface

If you are creating a customized user interface for your custom task, implement the CustomTaskUI interface:

```
Implements CustomTaskUI
```

This interface has seven methods, no properties, and no collections. The seven methods are as follows:

- `Initialize`—Called before `New` and `Edit`.
- `New`—Called when a new instance of this custom task is added to the package.
- `Edit`—Called when an existing instance of this custom task is opened for editing.
- `Delete`—Called when an instance of this custom task is deleted.
- `Help`—Called to display Help for the custom task.
- `GetUIInfo`—Called when the parent application is displaying a ToolTip.
- `CreateCustomToolTip`—Creates a custom ToolTip. Only used when custom ToolTips are supported.

You can use placeholders for any method that you are not using. Many of the methods have specialized purposes. They're not needed in most custom tasks.

- Custom ToolTips are not supported in the DTS Package Designer. You won't use `CreateCustomToolTip` unless you are designing your own interface to work with DTS packages.
- `GetUIInfo` is used only before a call to `CreateCustomToolTip`, to determine whether or not the custom ToolTip should be displayed.
- `Delete` is often unused. There usually isn't a particular need to do anything when an instance of the custom task is removed from a package.

The New Method

The most important methods of the CustomTaskUI interface are New and Edit.

New is called by the Package Designer when a task is first added to a package. Use New for code that does the following:

- Sets appropriate default values for custom task properties.
- Prepares the form used for the user interface so that it has the appropriate appearance for a new task.
- Shows the form. You must always show the form modally:

  ```
  frmMain.Show vbModal
  ```

  You do not have to load the form. The Package Designer loads it automatically.

- Responds to the user's choices on the form, including setting the custom task's properties.
- Unloads the form:

  ```
  Unload frmMain
  Set frmMain = Nothing
  ```

Listing 31.2 shows the New method from the Find File task with a custom user interface.

LISTING 31.2   The New Method in FindFileTaskWithUI

```
Private Sub CustomTaskUI_New(ByVal hwndParent As Long)

frmFindFile.Show vbModal

If frmFindFile.gbOK = True Then
    CheckingDurationInSecs = frmFindFile.txtCheckingDurationInSecs
    CheckingIntervalInSecs = frmFindFile.txtCheckingIntervalInSecs
    Description = frmFindFile.txtDescription
    FileName = frmFindFile.txtFileName
    Folder = frmFindFile.txtFolder
End If

Unload frmFindFile

End Sub
```

The `Edit` Method

The Package Designer calls `Edit` when a user opens the custom task's properties dialog. The code in `Edit` is very similar to the code in `New`:

- Prepare the form used for the user interface so that it has the appropriate appearance for editing. Load all the fields with the current values of the custom task's properties.
- Show the form. You must always show the form modally. You do not have to load the form. The Package Designer loads it automatically.
- Respond to the user's choices on the form, including setting the custom task's properties. If the user cancels, keep all the existing values of the properties.
- Unload the form.

The code for the `Edit` method in the Find File task is shown in Listing 31.3.

LISTING 31.3   The `Edit` Method in FindFileTaskWithUI

```
Private Sub CustomTaskUI_Edit(ByVal hwndParent As Long)
On Error GoTo ProcErr

frmFindFile.Show vbModal

If frmFindFile.gbOK = True Then
    CheckingDurationInSecs = frmFindFile.txtCheckingDurationInSecs
    CheckingIntervalInSecs = frmFindFile.txtCheckingIntervalInSecs
    Description = frmFindFile.txtDescription
    FileName = frmFindFile.txtFileName
    Folder = frmFindFile.txtFolder
End If

Unload frmFindFile

ProcExit:
    Exit Sub

ProcErr:
    subErrHandler "CustomTaskUI_Edit", Err, sInfo
    GoTo ProcExit

End Sub
```

Initialize

The `Initialize` method should be used for all the functionality that is needed for both `New` and `Edit`. Listing 31.4 shows the `Initialize` method in the Find File task.

LISTING 31.4   The `Initialize` Method in FindFileTaskWithUI

```
Private Sub CustomTaskUI_Initialize(ByVal pTask As DTS.Task)
On Error GoTo ProcErr

Dim sInfo As String

If Folder = "" Then
    Folder = "C:\Temp"
End If

'Checking interval must be at least 1 second.
If CheckingIntervalInSecs < 1 Then
    CheckingIntervalInSecs = 1
End If

'Duration for checking must be at least 1 second.
If CheckingDurationInSecs < 1 Then
    CheckingDurationInSecs = 1
End If

frmFindFile.txtCheckingDurationInSecs = CheckingDurationInSecs
frmFindFile.txtCheckingIntervalInSecs = CheckingIntervalInSecs
frmFindFile.txtDescription = Description
frmFindFile.txtFileName = FileName
frmFindFile.txtFolder = Folder

ProcExit:
    Exit Sub

ProcErr:
    subErrHandler "CustomTaskUI_Initialize", Err, sInfo
    GoTo ProcExit

End Sub
```

Help

You have three options for providing help to the users who are creating or editing an instance of your custom task:

- Provide no help. Just put a placeholder in the Help method.
- Call winhlp32.exe, specifying the appropriate help file and topic.
- Present a message box with the help information.

Listing 31.5 shows the Help method presenting a message box. The message box created by this code is shown in Figure 31.3.

LISTING 31.5   The Code for the Help Method from FindFileTaskWithUI

```
Private Sub CustomTaskUI_Help(ByVal hwndParent As Long)
'Display Help message.

Dim msg As String

msg = "Specify properties for Find File Task." & vbCrLf _
    & vbCrLf & "You must choose a folder in which to look." & _
    vbCrLf & "If you don't supply a file name, " & _
    "it will look for any file." & _
    vbCrLf & _
    "The interval and duration must be at least one second." & _
    vbCrLf & vbCrLf & _
    "The task will check for the file every (interval) seconds, " & _
    "until it is found, the duration expires, or the user cancels" & _
    " the execution."

MsgBox msg, vbInformation, "Find File Task"
End Sub
```

FIGURE 31.3

A simple Help message for a custom task.

Events, Errors, and Logs

The pPackageEvents and pPackageLog object parameters of the Execute method are used to report information while the custom task is executing. You should check the validity of both of these objects before using them. A package executed in the DTS Designer will always have pPackageEvents implemented, but pPackageLog will not be implemented unless logging has been enabled for the package. If the object has not been implemented, it will have a value of Nothing.

You can use the pPackageEvents object to raise three types of events:

- OnError—Reports an error in the custom task to the calling application, without terminating the execution. The user can cancel the task's execution in response to this event.

- OnProgress—Reports progress to the calling application.

- OnQueryCancel—Allows the user the opportunity to cancel the task's execution. Microsoft recommends calling this event every few seconds. The implementation of this event allows a user to cancel the execution of a package by clicking Cancel.

Listing 31.6 has code for procedures that implement these three events. No errors are handled in these procedures, so any errors will be propagated back to the Execute method and will be handled there.

LISTING 31.6   Code That Raises the Three Events of the pPackageEvents Object

```
Private Sub subOnProgress( _
    ByVal pPackageEvents As Object, _
    ByVal pPackageLog As Object, _
    ByVal sEventSource As String, _
    ByVal sProgressDescription As String, _
    ByVal lPercentComplete As Long, _
    ByVal lProgressCountLow As Long, _
    ByVal lProgressCountHigh As Long)

If Not pPackageEvents Is Nothing Then

    pPackageEvents.OnProgress sEventSource, sProgressDescription, _
        lPercentComplete, lProgressCountLow, lProgressCountHigh

    Call subWriteTaskRecord(pPackageLog, 1, sProgressDescription)

End If

End Sub

Private Sub subOnError( _
    ByVal pPackageEvents As Object, _
```

LISTING 31.6   Continued

```
      ByVal pPackageLog As Object, _
      sEventSource As String, _
      lErrorCode As Long, _
      sSource As String, _
      sDescription As String, _
      sHelpFile As String, _
      lHelpContext As Long, _
      sIDOfInterfaceWithError As String, _
      bCancel As Boolean)

If Not pPackageEvents Is Nothing Then

  pPackageEvents.OnError sEventSource, lErrorCode, sSource, _
      sDescription, sHelpFile, lHelpContext, _
      sIDOfInterfaceWithError, bCancel

  If bCancel = True Then
    Err.Raise lErrorCode, sSource, sDescription
  Else
    Call subWriteTaskRecord(pPackageLog, lErrorCode, sDescription)
  End If

End If

End Sub

Private Sub subCheckForCancel(ByVal pPackageEvents As Object)

Dim bCancel As Boolean

bCancel = False

If Not pPackageEvents Is Nothing Then

  pPackageEvents.OnQueryCancel Err.Source, bCancel

  If bCancel = True Then
    Err.Raise -1, , "Package Canceled by User."
  End If

End If

End Sub
```

The pPackageLog parameter is an instance of the PackageLog object. You can use either the WriteTaskRecord or the WriteStringToLog methods of the object to write records to the task log. These methods are described in Chapter 16, "Writing Scripts for an ActiveX Script Task." Listing 31.7 shows code that writes a record to the task log.

LISTING 31.7   You Can Use the pPackageLog Object to Write a Record to the Task Log

```
Private Sub subWriteTaskRecord( _
    ByVal pPackageLog As Object, _
    ErrNum As Long, _
    ErrDescription As String)

'Write to task log, if log object valid.
If Not pPackageLog Is Nothing Then
  pPackageLog.WriteTaskRecord ErrNum, ErrDescription
End If

End Sub
```

Registering a Custom Task

There are two parts to registering a custom task created in Visual Basic:

- The custom task is registered with the system when you select Make ProjectName.dll from the File menu.
- You register the custom task in the DTS Designer by selecting Register Custom Task from the Task menu. The Register Custom Task dialog is shown in Figure 31.4.

FIGURE 31.4

You can register your custom task in the Package Designer.

The Visual Basic DLL registration process creates an entry for the DLL under the \HKEY_CLASSES_ROOT\CLSID\ node in the registry. The process of registering a custom task in the Package Designer makes the following modifications to the registration of the DLL:

- The GUID for the DTS task component category is added under the Implemented Categories key. This allows DTS to recognize this DLL as a DTS task.
- A new key called DTSIconFile is added under the Class ID for the task. This key contains the full path and name for the file that contains the task's icon. By default, the Register Custom Task dialog inserts the path and name of the custom task's DLL for this value, but it can be changed to a different file.
- A new key called DTSIconIndex is added under the Class ID for the task. This key has an index that identifies the particular icon in the icon file that should be used for the task.
- A new key called DTSTaskDescription is added under the Class ID for the task. The Package Designer uses this value, together with the string " : undefined" to create the initial description for a new task.

Using a Custom Task in a DTS Package

A custom task created with Visual Basic must be executed on the main package thread in a DTS package. You can set the ExecuteInMainThread property on the Options tab of the Workflow Properties dialog. Any task that dynamically modifies the properties of your custom task must also be set to execute on the main package thread.

> **NOTE**
>
> This limitation is necessary because Visual Basic does not support multiple threads. DTS uses multiple threads so that different tasks can be executed simultaneously.

There are three possible ways to reference a custom task property of one of the built-in DTS tasks:

- As a property of the CustomTask object.
- As a member of the Properties collection of the CustomTask object.
- As a member of the Properties collection of the Task object.

You cannot reference the custom task properties directly as properties of the Task object. You can reference Name and Description through the Task object because they are assigned to the Task object in the DTS object hierarchy.

These property references are illustrated in the VBScript code in Listing 31.8.

LISTING 31.8   Valid Custom Task Property References for a Built-In Task

```
Option Explicit

Function Main()
Dim pkg, tsk, cus

Set pkg = DTSGlobalVariables.Parent
Set tsk = pkg.tasks("tskSelectAuthors") 'An Execute SQL task
Set cus = tsk.customtask

'The following are all valid property assignments.
cus.SQLStatement = "Select * From Authors"
cus.Properties("SQLStatement") = "Select * From Authors"
tsk.Properties("SQLStatement") = "Select * From Authors"

'The following is not a valid property assignment.
'It will cause an error.
tsk.SQLStatement = "Select * From Authors"

    Main = DTSTaskExecResult_Success
End Function
```

When you are using a custom task built in Visual Basic, you can only reference the custom task properties in one way—through the Properties collection of the Task object:

```
tsk.Properties("FileName") = 20010324Sales.txt
```

The other methods of referencing the custom task properties will fail. An attempt to modify the custom task properties using the Dynamic Properties task will also fail.

Listing 31.9 shows the code for an ActiveX Script task that sets all the custom task properties of the File Exists task with values from global variables. You could set the value of these global variables in the Package Designer, from a command line with DTSRun, or from another package with an Execute Package task.

LISTING 31.9   VBScript Code That Sets the Custom Task Properties of the Find File Task

```
Option Explicit

Function Main()
Dim pkg, tsk, prp

Set pkg = DTSGlobalVariables.Parent
Set tsk = pkg.tasks("tskFindFile")
```

LISTING 31.9   Continued

```
For Each prp in tsk.Properties

    If prp.Name = "Name" or prp.Name = "Description" Then
        'Don't set the generic Task object properties
    Else
        prp.Value = DTSGlobalVariables(prp.Name)
    End If

Next

Set prp = Nothing
Set tsk = Nothing
Set pkg = Nothing

    Main = DTSTaskExecResult_Success
End Function
```

You can find this code on the CD in a DTS package called FindFileSetProps.dts. You can execute this package and set all of the Find File task's custom properties by running the following
command:

```
DTSRun /S "(local)" /E /N "FindFileSetProps"
/A "FileName":"8"="TestFileName.txt"
/A "Folder":"8"="TestFolder"
/A "CheckingIntervalInSecs":"3"="5"
/A "CheckingDurationInSecs":"3"="10"
```

> **NOTE**
>
> You can't load the FindFileSetProps package if you have not registered the Find File
> task (the version without the user interface). See the previous section, "Registering a
> Custom Task."

The FindFileTask

The full code for the Find File task is on the CD in the FindFile.cls and FindFile.vbp files. The
version of this task with the user interface is contained in files called FindFileTaskWithUI.cls,

FindFileTaskWithUI.vbp, and FindFileTaskWithUI.frm. You can use either version of this custom task by doing the following:

- Opening the project in Visual Basic.
- Choosing Make *.dll from the File menu.
- Registering the custom task in the Package Designer.

The Find File task checks for the existence of a particular file in a particular directory. If the file exists, the task is completed successfully. If the file does not exist, the task waits a specified time interval and checks for the file again. After checking for the file for a particular length of time and not finding it, the task concludes with an error. At any time during its execution, the task can be cancelled.

The Find File task has these four custom task properties:

- `Folder`—The directory in which the task looks for the file.
- `FileName`—The name of the file whose existence is being checked. If this property is an empty string, the task will look for any file in the directory.
- `CheckingIntervalInSecs`—The interval of time the task waits before checking for the file again. If this value is not set, it defaults to 1 second.
- `CheckingDurationInSecs`—The duration of time during which the task checks for the file. If this value is not set, the task will only check for the file once and then report success or failure.

A task log record is written every time the task checks for a file, whether or not the check is successful.

The LocalCubeTask

A demo version of the LocalCubeTask is on the CD. You can use this task by doing the following:

- Registering the DLL with the system. You can use the following command in Start/Run, substituting the correct path for the location of the DLL:

  `regsvr32 c:\temp\LocalCubeTask.dll`

- Registering the custom task in the Package Designer.

The LocalCubeTask allows you to create local cube files from Analysis Server cubes. You can do the following:

- Connect to an Analysis Server, choose from the databases on that server, and choose from the cubes in the database.
- Create a local cube with all the elements of the Analysis Server cube, or limit the cube to a subset of the measures, dimensions, levels, or members in the source cube.
- Specify the filename and directory for the cube.
- Choose whether to append a date stamp to the front of the local cube name.
- Create a MOLAP or ROLAP local cube.
- Choose whether to overwrite an existing local cube.

NOTE

The fully functional version of LocalCubeTask also allows you to create many local cubes at the same time. For example, if you want to create a separate local cube for each product family's sales in each region, you can do so with a single instance of the LocalCubeTask.

The demo version of LocalCubeTask on the CD only allows you to create a single local cube with a single instance of the task.

Conclusion

You can build custom tasks to add new functionality to your DTS packages. Chapter 32 explains how to create custom transformations so that you can automate the process of transforming each row of data.

Creating a Custom Transformation with VC++

IN THIS CHAPTER

You can create a custom transformation that can be used in all of the DTS transformation tasks—the Transform Data task, the Data Driven Query task, and the Parallel Data Pump task. After you have created and registered your custom transformation, it will be available for selection in the Create New Transformation dialog (see Figure 32.1).

FIGURE 32.1

The AvgXform custom transformation appears in the Create New Transformation dialog.

Microsoft has not provided the interfaces that are needed to build a custom transformation in Visual Basic. They are defined only in Visual C++ header files.

Why You Should Create a Custom Transformation

There are two primary reasons to create a custom transformation:

- Improving the processing speed—Data transformation can be very time-consuming because it is often necessary to transform very large numbers of rows. Data transformation code has to be executed for each individual record. The ability to move processing code from an ActiveX script into a Visual C++ transformation can significantly reduce processing time.

- Creating an efficient development environment—Sometimes the same data transformation code is used repeatedly. If you move that code from an ActiveX script into a custom transformation, you can write and test it once and use it repeatedly.

Here are some ideas for creating custom transformations:

- Importing from or exporting to XML.
- Parsing or recombining name fields.
- Parsing, recombining, and validating address fields.
- Performing mathematical functions.

You can take any transformation with an ActiveX script and re-create it as a custom transformation. However, it won't be worth the effort unless you need the improved performance or can use the custom task repeatedly.

The Data Pump Interfaces

If you are creating a custom transformation for SQL Server 2000, you have to implement both the IDTSDataPumpTransform interface and the IDTSDataPumpTransform2 interface.

> **NOTE**
>
> In addition to these two interfaces, each custom transformation must implement the functions of the COM DLL infrastructure—DLLMain, DLLGetClassObject, DLLCanUnloadNow, DLLRegisterServer, and DLLUnregisterServer.

The IDTSDataPumpTransform interface has the following methods:

- Initialize—Stores the state of the current transform operation.
- AddVariable—Adds a variable to the transformation context. Use this method to add DTSErrorRecords, DTSGlobalVariables, and DTSLookups.
- ValidateSchema—Checks the meta data in the source and destination columns to see if they are appropriate for this transformation. This method is called before any rows are transformed.
- Execute—Called once for each row being transformed. This method is used for row-by-row data transformation. It is not used when the ProcessPhase method is used.
- OnRowComplete—Called each time Execute is called. Use this method to release variable allocations that are needed until the data is loaded into the destination.
- OnTransformComplete—Called after all the source rows have been processed so that variables can be released.

The IDTSDataPumpTransform2 interface has these methods:

- GetTransformServerInfo—Returns information about supported phases.
- PreValidateSchema—Validates schema at design time.
- SetExtendedInfo—Reserved for future use.
- ProcessPhase—Called for each phase of the transformation. For those phases that occur for every row in the data source, this method is called for each one.
- SetExecuteThreadComplete—Called when the data pump is switching execution threads.

There are four structures that contain information about the source and destination columns. This information is used in the methods of the interface to validate and process the data. The four data structures are as follows:

- DTSTransformColumnInfo—Contains a count of the columns and pointers to the DTSColumnData structures.

- DTSColumnData—Contains pointers to DBColumnInfo, DBBinding, and the data.

- DBColumnInfo—Contains information about the columns, such as name, ordinal, transformation flags, width, and data type.

- DBBinding—Contains detailed information about where the data can be found in the buffer.

Preparing the C++ Custom Transformation Development Environment

Microsoft has provided an Active Template Library (ATL) custom transformation template to assist with building a custom transformation. This template is included in a separate subdirectory with the SQL Server 2000 DTS code samples.

Here's what you have to do to install the ATL custom transformation template:

1. Install the SQL Server 2000 code samples and development tools, including headers, libraries, and debugger interface and other development tools. They are not installed with the default SQL Server 2000 installation.

2. Copy the files in the CustomTransform folder to the Visual Studio 6.0 ATL template folder. In a default installation of SQL Server, you will find this folder at the following location:

   ```
   C:\Program Files\Microsoft SQL Server\80\
   Tools\DevTools\Samples\dts\ATLTemplates\CustomTransform\
   ```

   In a default installation of Visual Studio, the destination folder will be as follows:

   ```
   C:\Program Files\Microsoft Visual Studio\Common\MSDev98\Template\ATL\
   ```

3. Double-click the DTSCuXFm.reg file to register the template. This file is also found in the CustomTransform folder.

You also have to configure the Visual C++ development environment so that it will find the required header and library files. Some of the directories may already be registered on your computer:

1. Select Options on the Visual C++ Tools menu.

2. Select the Directories tab in the Options dialog.

3. Select Executable files in the Show directories for box. Add the following directory (or the corresponding directory on your computer), as shown in Figure 32.2:

   `c:\Program Files\Microsoft SQL Server\80\Tools\Binn`

4. Select Include files in the Show directories for box. Add the following directory:

   `c:\Program Files\Microsoft SQL Server\80\Tools\DevTools\Include`

5. Select Library files in the Show directories for box. Add the following directory:

   `c:\Program Files\Microsoft SQL Server\80\Tools\DevTools\Lib`

6. Select Source files in the Show directories for box. Add the following directory:

   `c:\Program Files\Microsoft SQL Server\80\Tools\DevTools\Include`

32

CREATING A
CUSTOM
TRANSFORMATION

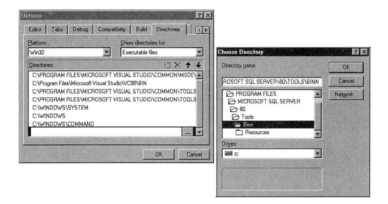

FIGURE 32.2
You have to configure C++ so that it will find the SQL Server files.

You only have to add the required header and configuration files once on your development computer.

You also have to add the definition of one preprocessor symbol. This symbol has to be added each time you create a custom transformation project:

1. Open your custom transformation project.
2. Select Settings on the Project menu.
3. Select the C/C++ tab on the Project Settings dialog.
4. Add a comma and the following preprocessor symbol into the Preprocessor definitions box:

   `_ATL_NO_UUIDOF`

Creating a Custom Transformation

This section explains how to create a custom transformation called AvgXform. This custom transformation finds the average of the values from the source columns and puts that value in the destination column. The transformation has one property, which allows you to set the number of significant digits to the right of the decimal in the destination column.

The AvgXform custom transformation has the following requirements:

- There must be one or more source columns.
- The source columns must be two-byte or four-byte integers.
- There must be exactly one destination column.
- The destination column must be a two-byte integer, a four-byte integer, a four-byte real, or an eight-byte float.

The AvgXform transformation can only be used once in each Transform Data task. If it is used more than once, it will write incorrect data to the data destination for all except one of the transformations.

You can find the source files for the AvgXform sample custom transformation on the CD. You can copy these files into a directory and open the workspace file, Average.dsw, in Visual C++. You will then be able to look at the files in the project and build the custom transformation. The compiled transformation is called Average.dll. The rest of this chapter explains how to use Visual C++ to create the custom transformation.

> **NOTE**
>
> Our testing indicates that the AvgXform custom transformation provides performance that is about five times faster than an ActiveX Script task that does the same calculation. Chapter 28, "High-Performance DTS Packages," has a chart that compares the performance of the AvgXform custom transformation with that of other transformation strategies.

Starting the Project

Follow these steps to start the new custom transformation project:

1. Select New on the File menu.
2. Select the Projects tab in the New dialog.
3. Select the ATL Com AppWizard, enter Average as the project name, and enter a directory in which to save the project.

4. When you click OK, the ATL COM AppWizard will appear. Select Dynamic Link Library and click Finish.

5. Select New ATL Object on the Insert menu.

6. On the first screen of the ATL Object Wizard, select DTS Custom Objects in the Category box and DTS Transformation in the Objects box.

7. In the ATL Object Wizard Properties dialog, type AvgXform in the Short Name box. All the other name boxes will be filled in automatically.

8. On the Attributes tab of the ATL Object Wizard Properties dialog, select the following options:

   Threading Model—Both

   Interface—Dual

   Aggregation—No

9. For the check boxes on the Attributes tab, select Support IsupportErrorInfo.

10. Add the _ATL_NO_UUIDOF preprocessor symbol, as described earlier in this chapter.

32

CREATING A
CUSTOM
TRANSFORMATION

NOTE

You can continue building the AvgXform transformation by following the instructions in the rest of this chapter. You can also replace three of the files in the project—AvgXform.cpp, AvgXform.h, and Average.idl—with the sample files on the CD and build the DLL.

Adding a Property to the Custom Transformation

You can add a property with the following steps:

1. Select the ClassView tab in the Workspace window.

2. Right-click on the custom transformation's interface (IAvgXform).

3. Select Add Property. The Add Property to Interface dialog is shown in Figure 32.3.

AvgXform requires one custom property, Decimals, which allows the user to specify the number of digits saved to the right of the decimal point. Enter the following information for this property in the Add Property dialog:

- Property type—int
- Property name—Decimals
- No parameters
- Select Get Function, Put Function, and the PropPut option

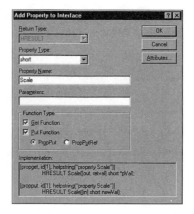

FIGURE 32.3

You can add a new property to your custom transformation with the Add Property to Interface dialog.

When you click OK, the shells for the property's Get and Put functions will be added to the code in the AvgXform.cpp file. You have to add the content to those functions. The Get and Put functions for `Decimals` are shown in Listing 32.1.

LISTING 32.1   The Get and Put Function Definitions for the `Decimals` Property

```
STDMETHODIMP CAvgXform::get_Decimals(
        /* [retval][out] */ int __RPC_FAR *pRetVal){
    //START ADDED CODE - Decimal Property---------------------
  if (!pRetVal)
    return E_POINTER;
  *pRetVal = m_iDecimals;
  //END ADDED CODE----------------------------------------------
  return NOERROR;
}

STDMETHODIMP CAvgXform::put_Decimals(
        /* [in] */ int NewValue)
{
    //START ADDED CODE - Decimal Property---------------------

  // Number of decimals must be between 0 and 16.
  if (NewValue >= 16) {
    m_iDecimals = 16;
    return NOERROR;
  }

  if (NewValue < 0) {
    m_iDecimals = 0; (
```

LISTING 32.1   Continued

```
    return NOERROR;
  }

  if ((NewValue < 16) && (NewValue >= 0)) {
    m_iDecimals = NewValue;
  }

  //END ADDED CODE----------------------------------------------

  return NOERROR;
}(
```

This code uses the m_iDecimals variable, which you have to declare and initialize in the AvgXform.h header file:

```
private:
    //-----Variable Declarations for Properties---------
    int    m_iDecimals;
    //-------------------------------------------------
public:
    CAvgXform()
    {
        //------Initialize variables for Properties--------|
        m_iDecimals = 0;
        //-----------------------------------------------|
    }(
```

Adding Code for the `PreValidateSchema` Method

The code for the `PreValidateSchema` method checks that the number and data type of the source and destination columns are appropriate for this transformation. The data types of the source columns are checked in a loop so that each one can be checked individually.

The code for the method is shown in Listing 32.2. The code for this and all the other methods is found in the AvgXform.cpp file. An integer variable called datatype is used in this method and some of the other methods to keep track of the datatypes of the columns used in the transformations. Add the declaration of this variable at the top of the AvgXform.cpp file after the include statements:

```
short datatype;
```

LISTING 32.2   The Code for the Custom Transformation's PreValidateSchema Method

```
STDMETHODIMP CAvgXform::PreValidateSchema(THIS_
     // May be NULL if not required by Transform Server
     DP_IN LPCDTSTransformColumnMetadata pSrcMetadata,
     // May be NULL if not required by Transform Server
     DP_IN LPCDTSTransformColumnMetadata pDestMetadata,
     // Input Flags for Transformation validation and execution
     DP_IN DTSTransformFlags eTransformFlags,
     // Phase(s) for which this Transform is to be called.
     DP_IN DTSTransformPhaseEnum ePhases
   )
{
  //START ADDED CODE - Pre-validate schema--------------------

  //Validate the count of source and destination columns.
  if (pDestMetadata->cColumns != 1) {
    return DTSAvgXform_Error_WRONG_NUM_DEST_COLS;
  }

  //Get the source data and the destination type.
  const DBCOLUMNINFO* pDestDBColumnInfo =
       &(pDestMetadata->rgDBColumnInfo[0]);
  WORD wDestType = (pDestDBColumnInfo->wType & (~DBTYPE_BYREF));

  //Validate that the destination column is in our range of types.
  switch (wDestType) {
  case DBTYPE_I2:
    //Destination column type is 2-byte integer.
    datatype = DBTYPE_I2;
    break;
  case DBTYPE_I4:
    //Destination column type is 4-byte integer.
    datatype = DBTYPE_I4;
    break;
  case DBTYPE_R4:
    //Destination column type is 4-byte real.
    datatype = DBTYPE_R4;
    break;
  case DBTYPE_R8:
    //Destination column type is 8-byte real.
    datatype = DBTYPE_R8;
```

LISTING 32.2   Continued

```
  break;
default:
  return DTSAvgXform_Error_NOT_CORRECT_TYPE;
  break;
}

//Validate that the source column(s) are in our range of types.
for (UINT i = 0; i < pSrcMetadata->cColumns; i++)
{
  const DBCOLUMNINFO* pSrcDBColumnInfo =
      &(pSrcMetadata->rgDBColumnInfo[i]);
  WORD wSourceType = (pSrcDBColumnInfo->wType & (~DBTYPE_BYREF));

  switch (wSourceType) {
  case DBTYPE_I2:
    //Source column type is 2-byte integer.
    break;
  case DBTYPE_I4:
    //Source column type is 4-byte integer.
    break;
    default:
    return DTSAvgXform_Error_NOT_CORRECT_TYPE;
    break;
  }
}
//END ADDED CODE----------------------------------------------

  return NOERROR;
}
```

Adding Code for the `ValidateSchema` Method

Microsoft recommends that the same checks that were done in the PreValidateSchema method should also be done in the ValidateSchema method. The PreValidateSchema method is used at the time the user is designing the DTS package, whereas the ValidateSchema method is run when the package is executed.

Listing 32.3 contains the code used in the `ValidateSchema` method. It is very similar to the code used in the `PreValidateSchema` method, but some of the data structures that are used are different. Note these in particular:

- `pDestMetadata` is replaced with `pDestColumnInfo`. In `PreValidateSchema`, you get the source data with the following:

```
const DBCOLUMNINFO* pDestDBColumnInfo =
       &(pDestMetadata->rgDBColumnInfo[0]);
```

In `ValidateSchema`, you retrieve the source data with the following:

```
const DBCOLUMNINFO* pDestDBColumnInfo =
       (pDestColumnInfo->rgColumnData[0].pDBColumnInfo);
```

- `pSrcMetadata` is replaced with `pSrcColumnInfo`.

LISTING 32.3   The Code for the Custom Transformation's `ValidateSchema` Method

```
STDMETHODIMP CAvgXform::ValidateSchema(THIS_
        // Transform server state data.
    DP_IN LPBYTE pvTransformServerData,
        // Source columns and rowdata
    DP_INOUT LPCDTSTransformColumnInfo pSrcColumnInfo,
        // Dest columns and rowdata
    DP_INOUT LPCDTSTransformColumnInfo pDestColumnInfo,
        // Pointer to the data conversion interface
    DP_IN IDTSDataConvert *pIDTSDataConvert,
        // Input Flags for Transformation validation and execution
    DP_IN DTSTransformFlags eTransformFlags
    )
{
//START ADDED CODE - Validate schema -------------------------

//Validate the count of source and destination columns.
if (pDestColumnInfo->cColumns != 1) {
  return DTSAvgXform_Error_WRONG_NUM_DEST_COLS;
}

//Get the source data and the destination type.
const DBCOLUMNINFO* pDestDBColumnInfo =
    (pDestColumnInfo->rgColumnData[0].pDBColumnInfo);
WORD wDestType = (pDestDBColumnInfo->wType & (~DBTYPE_BYREF));

//Validate that the destination column is in our range of types.
switch (wDestType) {
case DBTYPE_I2:
  //Destination column type is 2-byte integer.
```

LISTING 32.3   Continued

```
    datatype = DBTYPE_I2;
    break;
  case DBTYPE_I4:
    //Destination column type is 4-byte integer.
    datatype = DBTYPE_I4;
    break;
  case DBTYPE_R4:
    //Destination column type is 4-byte real.
    datatype = DBTYPE_R4;
    break;
  case DBTYPE_R8:
    //Destination column type is 8-byte real.
    datatype = DBTYPE_R8;
    break;
  default:
    return DTSAvgXform_Error_NOT_CORRECT_TYPE;
    break;
  }

  //Validate that the source column(s) are in our range of types.
  for (UINT i = 0; i < pSrcColumnInfo->cColumns; i++)
  {
    const DBCOLUMNINFO*  pSrcDBColumnInfo =
        pSrcColumnInfo->rgColumnData[i].pDBColumnInfo;
    WORD wSourceType = (pSrcDBColumnInfo->wType & (~DBTYPE_BYREF));

    switch (wSourceType) {
    case DBTYPE_I2:
      //Source column type is 2-byte integer.
      break;
    case DBTYPE_I4:
      //Source column type is 4-byte integer.
      break;
        default:
      return DTSAvgXform_Error_NOT_CORRECT_TYPE;
      break;
    }
  }
  //END ADDED CODE----------------------------------------------

  return NOERROR;
}
```

Adding Code for the `ProcessPhase` Method

The `ProcessPhase` method is the place where you put the code that does the work of your transformation. This method is called for each phase of the transformation that has been implemented.

> **NOTE**
>
> For the `IDTSDataPumpTransform` interface in SQL Server 7.0, the work of the custom transformation was accomplished in the `Execute` method. `ProcessPhase` replaces the `Execute` function in the `IDTSDataPumpTransform2` interface so that the processing of multiple phases can be accomplished.

The first thing that `ProcessPhase` does is check which phase has been called. If you have implemented multiple phases, you will call the individual procedures for each phase at this point. Only the Transform phase is implemented in AvgXform. If other phases are called from the Data Pump, the code will ignore them.

The code for the `ProcessPhase` method is shown in Listing 32.4.

LISTING 32.4   The Code for the Custom Transformation's `ProcessPhase` Method

```
STDMETHODIMP CAvgXform::ProcessPhase(THIS_
    // Transform server state data.
    DP_IN LPBYTE pvTransformServerData,
    // Source columns and rowdata
    DP_IN LPCDTSTransformColumnInfo pSrcColumnInfo,
    // Dest columns and rowdata
    DP_INOUT LPDTSTransformColumnInfo pDestColumnInfo,
    // Pointer to the data conversion interface
    DP_IN IDTSDataConvert *pIDTSDataConvert,
    // Pointer to phase info structure
    DP_IN LPCDTSTransformPhaseInfo pPhaseInfo,
    // Result of transform
    DP_OUT LPDTSTransformStatus pTransformStatus
  )
{

  //START ADDED CODE - Process Phase ----------------------------

  // Only do something for the Transform phase.
  if (pPhaseInfo &&
    !(pPhaseInfo->eCurrentPhase & DTSTransformPhase_Transform) ) {
```

LISTING 32.4   Continued

```
    return NOERROR;
}

// Get destination binding and data structures
DTSColumnData* pDTSDestColumnData =
    &(pDestColumnInfo->rgColumnData[0]);
const DBBINDING* pDBDestBinding =
    pDTSDestColumnData->pDBBinding;

// Set the destination length to maximum length.  Initialize to 0.
ULONG ulDestMaxLen = pDBDestBinding->cbMaxLen;
LPBYTE pDestData =
    (pDTSDestColumnData->pvData + pDBDestBinding->obValue);

//Pointers to destination length and status buffers
ULONG* pulLength = (ULONG *)
    (pDTSDestColumnData->pvData + pDBDestBinding->obLength);
ULONG* pulStatus = (ULONG *)
    (pDTSDestColumnData->pvData + pDBDestBinding->obStatus);

// Variables for the average calculation
double sum = 0;
double* pSum = &sum;
//double* pAverage = &sum;

//----Variables for the possible---------------|
//----destination field data types-------------|
double dAverage = 0;
double* pdAverage = &dAverage;

float fAverage = 0;
float* pfAverage = &fAverage;

long laverage = 0;
long* plAverage = &laverage;

short saverage = 0;
short* psAverage = &saverage;
//---------------------------------------------|

// Get length of destination field
ULONG ulMaxDataLen = ulDestMaxLen;

for (UINT i = 0; i < pSrcColumnInfo->cColumns; i++)
{
```

LISTING 32.4   Continued

```
// Get source binding and data structures
DTSColumnData* pDTSSourceColumnData =
            &(pSrcColumnInfo->rgColumnData[i]);
const DBBINDING* pDBSourceBinding =
            pDTSSourceColumnData->pDBBinding;

// Get source type and status
ULONG wSourceType = (pDBSourceBinding->wType);
ULONG ulSourceStatus = *(ULONG *)
    (pDTSSourceColumnData->pvData + pDBSourceBinding->obStatus);
ULONG ulSourceLength = *(ULONG *)
    (pDTSSourceColumnData->pvData + pDBSourceBinding->obLength);
LPBYTE pSourceData;

// Get pointer to source data
if (wSourceType & DBTYPE_BYREF) {
    pSourceData = *(LPBYTE *)(pDTSSourceColumnData->pvData +
                pDBSourceBinding->obValue);
}
else {
  pSourceData =
      pDTSSourceColumnData->pvData + pDBSourceBinding->obValue;
}


if (ulSourceStatus != DBSTATUS_S_ISNULL) {

  wSourceType &= ~DBTYPE_BYREF;
  long lTemp = 0;
  long* pTemp = &lTemp;
  memcpy(pTemp, pSourceData, ulSourceLength);
  *pSum += (double)*pTemp;
}

else {
  *pulStatus = DBSTATUS_S_ISNULL;
}
}

*pSum = *pSum / pSrcColumnInfo->cColumns;

int j;
for (j = 0; j < m_iDecimals; j++) {
```

LISTING 32.4   Continued

```
   *pSum = *pSum * 10;
}

long cint = (long) *pSum;

*pulLength = ulMaxDataLen;

switch (datatype) {
case DBTYPE_I2:

  //Destination column type is 2-byte integer.
  *psAverage = (short) cint;

  for (j = 0; j < m_iDecimals; j++) {
    *psAverage = *psAverage / 10;
  }
  memcpy(pDestData, psAverage, *pulLength);
  break;

case DBTYPE_I4:

  //Destination column type is 4-byte integer.
  *plAverage = (long) cint;

  for (j = 0; j < m_iDecimals; j++) {
    *plAverage = *plAverage / 10;
  }
  memcpy(pDestData, plAverage, *pulLength);
  break;

case DBTYPE_R4:

  //Destination column type is 4-byte real.
  *pfAverage = (float) cint;

  for (j = 0; j < m_iDecimals; j++) {
    *pfAverage = *pfAverage / 10;
  }
  memcpy(pDestData, pfAverage, *pulLength);
  break;

case DBTYPE_R8:
```

LISTING 32.4 Continued

```
//Destination column type is 8-byte real.
*pdAverage = (double) cint;

for (j = 0; j < m_iDecimals; j++) {
  *pdAverage = *pdAverage / 10;
}
memcpy(pDestData, pdAverage, *pulLength);
break;

default:

  *pdAverage = (double) cint;

  for (j = 0; j < m_iDecimals; j++) {
    *pdAverage = *pdAverage / 10;
  }
  memcpy(pDestData, pdAverage, *pulLength);
  break;
}

*pulStatus = DBSTATUS_S_OK;
//END ADDED CODE---------------------------------------------

return NOERROR;
}
```

Adding the Project's Error Definitions

If you want to return specific error codes for conditions that occur in your custom transformation, add them in the *.idl file following this line:

```
import "ocidl.idl";
```

The code that defines the errors for the AvgXform task is shown in Listing 32.5.

LISTING 32.5   The Error Definitions for the Custom Task

```
//-----------Error codes for the Average Transform--------------------
    typedef [helpstring(
        "Error codes generated by the average transform")]
        enum DTSAvgTransformError {
        DTSAvgXform_Error_WRONG_NUM_DEST_COLS       =   0x80041001,
        DTSAvgXform_Error_NOT_CORRECT_TYPE          =   0x80041002
    } DTSAvgXformError, *LPDTSAvgXformError;
//--------------------------------------------------------------------
```

Registering the Custom Transformation

The ATL COM wizard creates the code to register the custom transformation during the build process. You can register the transformation on other computers by using the `regsvr32` command-line utility:

```
regsvr32 <Path>\Average.dll
```

Unlike the registration of custom tasks, there are no special registry entries that need to be created for a custom transformation.

Conclusion

DTS provides many excellent built-in tools. One of the best characteristics of DTS, though, is its extensibility. You can build new tools within the DTS environment to handle new data transformation situations more effectively.

Build a custom transformation when you need the best possible performance, or when you are using a particular ActiveX transformation script repeatedly.

32

CREATING A
CUSTOM
TRANSFORMATION

~

INDEX

A

C

cache, DTS packages, 56

calculating values, 37

Called Package, 385, 386

calling
functions, 535
wizards, 504-507

capturing rowsets, 299-300

case sensitivity, 197-198

Catalog property, 108

categories, objects, 612

CCLine property, 407

cdw command-line utility, 505

changing Server property, 368

chaos, 483

Check Constraints property, 281-282

CheckingDurationIn Secs property, 656

CheckingIntervalInSecs property, 656

child packages, 378-383

child rowsets, 249

cleansing data, 89, 91

clearing objects, 317-320

clickstream data, 39-40, 60

CloseConnection property, 496

closing connections, 122-123, 480

clustering data, 67

code
events, 42
libraries, 530
pages, 284-285
wizards, 506-507
writing phases, 228
  Batch Complete, 228
  On Batch Complete, 240-241
  On Insert Failure/Success, 228, 239-240
  On Transform Failure, 228
  Post Source Data, 228, 241-242
  Pre Source, 228
  Pump Complete, 228, 242
  Row Transform, 228

collation, 314

collections
Add method, 624
Count property, 624
CustomTask interface, 639-640
Insert method, 624
Item method, 624
methods, 625
New method, 624
Package2 object, 445
Parallel Data Pump task, 252
Parent property, 466, 624

Properties, 625
referencing, 350
transformations, 146-147

columns, 159
creating, 167-169
destination, 139-141, 143
identity, 283
lineage, 600-601
mappings, 519-520
names, 575-577
ordinal numbers, 575-577
prediction queries, 419
properties, 159-160
referencing, 183
rowsets, 249
scripts, 187
source, 139-141, 143
Transform Data task, 138

COM objects
accessing, 27
creating, 243
references, 546

command-line utilities
cdw, 505
DTSQiz, 505
DTSRun, 53, 427
osql, 427
wizards, 505-506

CommandProperties property, 294

commands, 21-22

CommandTimeout property, 294

Commit On option, 482